ANNUAL EDITIONS

Urban Society

Fifteenth Edition

EDITOR

Myron A. Levine
Wright State University

Myron Levine is a Professor of Urban Affairs and Geography at Wright State University in Dayton, Ohio. He is the author of *Urban Politics: Power in Metropolitan America.* His writings on urban policy in the United States and Europe have appeared in the *Journal of Urban Affairs,* the *Journal of the American Planning Association,* and the *Urban Affairs Review.* He has been a Fulbright Professor in Germany, Latvia, the Netherlands, and the Slovak Republic, as well as a NEH Fellow in France.

Connect
Learn
Succeed™

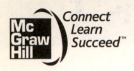

ANNUAL EDITIONS: URBAN SOCIETY, FIFTEENTH EDITION

1 2 3 4 5 6 7 8 9 0 QDB/QDB 1 0 9 8 7 6 5 4 3 2 1

ISBN 978-0-07-805098-5
MHID 0-07-805098-7
ISSN 0735-2425 (print)
ISSN 2158-4087 (online)

Managing Editor: *Larry Loeppke*
Developmental Editor: *Debra A. Henricks*
Senior Permissions Coordinator: *Shirley Lanners*
Senior Marketing Communications Specialist: *Mary Klein*
Senior Project Manager: *Joyce Watters*
Design Coordinator: *Margarite Reynolds*
Buyer: *Susan K. Culbertson*
Media Project Manager: *Sridevi Palani*
Cover Designer: *Kristine Jubeck*

Compositor: Laserwords Private Limited
Cover Images: © Lars Niki (inset); Stockbyte/Getty Images (background)

Editors/Academic Advisory Board

Members of the Academic Advisory Board are instrumental in the final selection of articles for each edition of ANNUAL EDITIONS. Their review of articles for content, level, and appropriateness provides critical direction to the editors and staff. We think that you will find their careful consideration well reflected in this volume.

ANNUAL EDITIONS: Urban Society
15th Edition

EDITOR

Myron A. Levine
Wright State University

ACADEMIC ADVISORY BOARD MEMBERS

Preface

Cities are vibrant entities, the centers of ideas and production. Cities are more than mere economic centers; they are also places where people share experiences and ideas; cities are centers of innovation.

Throughout history, cities have been the hubs of commerce, administration, industry, communication, education, and arts and culture. Even in Medieval Europe, Paris, London, Florence, and other cities were the sites of great universities, places where "science" was kept alive and where the exploration of ideas led to new modes of administration and production and, eventually, to the revolutionary ideas that restructured society. At a later point in time, cities provided the concentrations of labor and capital necessary for an Industrial Revolution based on mass production. In today's post-industrial era, where advances in telecommunications have seemingly freed people and industries from the need to be located in close proximity to one another, cities continue to serve as places for the vital interchange of ideas and sharing of knowledge, places where face-to-face discussion and the agglomeration of different support activities facilitates high-paced technological innovation.

Even in a suburban age, a nation's economic growth and prosperity continues to be dependent on its cities or, more properly, its city-regions (a city and its surrounding suburbs). Because of the many functions that they service, cities are resilient. Cities offer advantages of "agglomeration"—the concentration of related activities—that are not easily reproduced in suburbs. The United States needs New York City and the concentration of banking and financial activities located in Wall Street and Lower Manhattan—as well as the corporate headquarters, communications, and creative industries situated elsewhere in the city. Consequently, the terrorist attacks of 9/11 resulted in only a temporary falloff in New York City's economic vitality. In the years that followed, the city rebounded and reinforced its position as a vital global center.

Yet, not all cities occupy such a central position in the global system. Not all cities enjoy equivalent growth and continued prosperity. Cities like Detroit, Cleveland, and Buffalo, for instance, have suffered much more extensive losses of industry and population, without being able to find an new niche for themselves in a global age. The leaders of such cities have had to cope with "shrinking" and greening strategies, attempts to find viable paths to cope with long-term decline. New Orleans, a city that plays a relatively peripheral role in the global economy,

has only partially rebounded after the devastation of Hurricane Katrina. The city suffered extensive poverty and numerous economic and social problems before Katrina hit. The storm's destruction magnified the city's problems, especially as the flooding effectively demolished a number of low-lying low-income areas. Extensive intergovernmental aid assisted local recovery efforts as New Orleans residents rebuilt their city. New Orleans, too, came back, but with a population that had shrunk in size. Many buildings stand empty, awaiting demolition, and entire neighborhoods essentially lie fallow.

Since the 1950s, the story of a great many U.S. cities is one of long-term decline, with automation and deindustrialization leading to a loss of jobs and the suburban exodus resulting in a loss of population to the suburbs. In the Northeast and Midwest, big cities, and sometimes even entire metropolitan areas, declined as population and economic activity shifted not only to the suburbs but to the Sunbelt, that is, to communities in the South and the Southwest. As a whole, Sunbelt communities fared better than did rapidly declining Frostbelt cities. Yet, rapid growth brought numerous problems to Sunbelt cities, which also had large pockets of poverty. As the housing foreclosure and abandonment crisis has recently revealed, cities in the Sunbelt, too, suffer severe economic and social problems. In both the Frostbelt and the Sunbelt, cities face new competition from abroad as advances in transportation and telecommunications have enabled firms to outsource jobs to low-wage sites located overseas. Voter-imposed anti-tax initiatives and cutbacks in federal and state aid have further impaired the ability of cities across the nation to deliver essential municipal services. The urban crisis in the United States is not confined to a single region; it is a national crisis.

Yet, there is also good news for cities. Major cities no longer teeter on the brink of bankruptcy, as New York and Cleveland did in the 1970s. The downtowns of many big cities, largely overlooked and forgotten only three decades ago, have experienced a revival as tourist and entertainment destinations and as the locus of high-rise office and residential condominium construction. Once-declining core neighborhoods have also exhibited a rebirth as a result of gentrification, as the well-paid workers of the new global economy have discovered the excitement and convenience of living in areas close to the job and cultural activities of a city's downtown. In poor people's neighborhoods, citizen activism has also changed, with the more rancorous protest style of the 1960s giving way to a search for building and maintaining cooperative partnerships focused on such tasks and constructing and managing affordable housing and providing residents with health care, job training, and other important community services.

The occasional visitor to the U.S. city is likely to be impressed with the apparent "comeback" of cities, as visible in thriving downtowns and the active cafes and street life of neighborhoods undergoing gentrification. But these impressions should not serve to hide the larger truth: not all is well with cities. The revival of a city's downtown and a few newly fashionable neighborhoods does nothing to guarantee the improvement of life in neighborhoods that suffer from extensive abandonment, where organized theft rings stripping abandoned housing of their copper plumbing, bathroom facilities, bricks, and anything else of value. Such abandoned housing becomes the locus of drug dealing, gang activity, and arson that drains the life from a community.

Cities today are marked by an exaggerated dualism; well-off residents live quite comfortably, but the most distressed areas continue to decline and the homeless live in cardboard boxes or in unsatisfactory single-room-occupancy (SRO) hotels. The racial imbalance of public school classrooms has actually gotten worse in recent years, with signs pointing to a resegregation of urban schools. Problems of ghettoization, urban education, and crime are so complex that they appear, to a great degree, to be unsolvable. Even the most intensive efforts appear to yield only incremental results. Many older suburbs, too, are exhibiting economic and social ills that are usually associated with declining central cities.

The first decade of the twenty-first century has shown the degree to which cities and suburbs are highly vulnerable to economic downturns that impose additional costs of service provision while reducing municipal revenues. Decreases in federal aid over the years also served to make localities more vulnerable to economic cycles. The Obama administration launched a new program of spatial-base aid to help communities form the partnerships essential to their rebirth. Cities welcomed the Obama policy as an expression of interest in the revival of cities, a policy area largely overlooked by a number of previous Washington administrations. But the amounts of money the Obama administration offered could not match the scope of the housing foreclosure and other problems faced by core communities. More conservative critics argued that the Obama initiative was largely worthless, a waste of taxpayer money, as that the government could not undo the accumulated toll taken by years of neglect; nor, they argued, can government reverse the choices of businesses and residents to leave cities and distressed neighborhoods.

This book is devoted to the importance of cities. The poor and the immigrants recognize the significance of cities, continuing to migrate to cities in search of opportunity and refuge. That is just one of the beauties of cities. It is in cities—and increasingly in suburbs as well—that the United States will either live up to its ideals, or the American dream will be shown to be largely an illusion.

The 15th *Annual Editions: Urban Society* edition continues to examine the continuing evolution of cities, paying close attention to how cities are attempting to adjust to a new global economy. Special attention is given to questions of race, ethnicity, and equity in the urban arena. Gunnar Myrdal once called the problem of race the "American dilemma." If race is the American dilemma, it is particularly the dilemma of the contemporary city and suburb. The pictures of poor people, largely African-American, stranded in the New Orleans Superdome in the midst of Hurricane Katrina, and the story of how African-American evacuees were turned back by armed police from seeking refuge in suburban Gretna, are reminders of the continuing importance of race in urban affairs. Just what are the prospects for integrating public schools? Will urban school reform offer real opportunities to children left behind in underperforming public schools?

The 15th edition continues to give attention to urban development—and its sustainability—around the word, not just in the United States. The volume includes articles on global processes as well as on patterns of growth and development in Mexico, Brazil, India, Japan, and Europe. Indeed, the material on globalization and World Cities is now so extensive that the book can even be used as a supplemental text in a course focused on a comparative examination of cities around the globe. Still, much of the book remains focused on United Sates cities, an appropriate balance given the fact that the book will likely be used in a variety of classes that give their primary attention to an examination of urban development and problems in the United States. The world is rapidly shrinking as a result of advances in transportation and telecommunications. The student of urban studies in the United States needs to understand just where the U.S. experience is typical and where it is exceptional. The student of urban studies needs to formulate opinions as to just what reforms and solutions tried in other countries can—and cannot—be transferred to the United States.

This book advocates no single ideological point of view. It reviews both government-based and market-oriented approaches to solving urban ills. It recognizes the critical importance of establishing effective public-private partnerships in such areas as economic development, education, law enforcement, and affordable housing production. Where space allows, articles are paired: one article may point to the virtues inherent in gentrification, the New Urbanism, or in municipal policies aimed at attracting the "creative class" to a city; another article may then point to the weaknesses and disadvantages inherent in such a process or strategy. The book provides much material for debate. It is up to the reader to decide which policies work and what path of action should be chosen.

Two new learning features have been added to this edition to aid students in their study and expand critical thinking about each article topic. Located at the beginning of each unit, *Learning Outcomes* outline the key concepts that students should focus on as they are reading the material. *Critical Thinking* questions, located at the end of each article, allow students to test their understanding of the key concepts. A *Topic Guide* assists students in finding other articles on a given subject within this edition, while a list of recommended *Internet References* guides them to the best sources of additional information on a topic.

At the back of the book, you will find a card to mail to the publisher. Your comments will help to improve the next edition of *Urban Society*. Your advice will help determine which articles are kept, and which are swept aside, when the time comes to publish the book's 16th edition. I also ask for your assistance in helping to identify new articles for possible inclusion in future volumes, insightful articles that will help make *Annual Editions: Urban Society* a lively and informative classroom resource.

Myron A. Levine
Editor

Contents

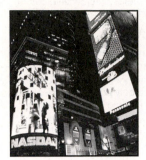

UNIT 1
Urban Growth, Decline, and Renaissance

The concepts in bold italics are developed in the article. For further expansion, please refer to the Topic Guide.

UNIT 2
Gentrification, Globalization and the City

The concepts in bold italics are developed in the article. For further expansion, please refer to the Topic Guide.

UNIT 3
Competitive Pressures and Economic Development

The concepts in bold italics are developed in the article. For further expansion, please refer to the Topic Guide.

UNIT 4
Citizen Participation

UNIT 5
School Choice and School Reform

The concepts in bold italics are developed in the article. For further expansion, please refer to the Topic Guide.

The concepts in bold italics are developed in the article. For further expansion, please refer to the Topic Guide.

UNIT 6
Policing and Crime

UNIT 7
A Suburban Nation: Suburban Growth, Diversity, and the Possibilities of "New Urbanism" and "New Regionalism"

The concepts in bold italics are developed in the article. For further expansion, please refer to the Topic Guide.

The concepts in bold italics are developed in the article. For further expansion, please refer to the Topic Guide.

UNIT 8
Toward Sustainable Cities and Suburbs?

UNIT 9
The Future of Cities and Suburbs:
The United States and the World

The concepts in bold italics are developed in the article. For further expansion, please refer to the Topic Guide.

The concepts in bold italics are developed in the article. For further expansion, please refer to the Topic Guide.

The concepts in bold italics are developed in the article. For further expansion, please refer to the Topic Guide.

Topic Guide

This topic guide suggests how the selections in this book relate to the subjects covered in your course. You may want to use the topics listed on these pages to search the Web more easily.

On the following pages a number of websites have been gathered specifically for this book. They are arranged to reflect the units of this Annual Editions reader. You can link to these sites by going to www.mhhe.com/cls.

All the articles that relate to each topic are listed below the bold-faced term.

Comparative urban policy
9. Outsourcing: Beyond Bangalore
40. New German Community Models Car-Free Living
43. Japan's Cities Amid Globalization
44. Reinventing Rio: The Dazzling but Tarnished Brazilian City Gets a Makeover As It Prepares for the 2014 World Cup and 2016 Olympic Games
45. Demolishing Delhi: World Class City in the Making
48. Femicide in Ciudad Juárez: What Can Planners Do?
49. Are Europe's Cities Better?

Crime and policing
28. Broken Windows
29. How an Idea Drew People Back to Urban Life
30. 200 Cops to be Reassigned from Community Policing

Economic development
1. Why Cities Matter
2. Eds, Meds and Urban Revival
3. Can They Save Youngstown?
4. Return to Center
7. Movers and Shakers: How Immigrants Are Reviving Neighborhoods Given up for Dead
8. Swoons over Miami
9. Outsourcing: Beyond Bangalore
10. The Rise of the Creative Class
11. Too Much Froth
13. Throwaway Stadium
14. Skybox Skeptics
15. "A Lot of Hooey": Heywood Sanders on Convention Center Economics
16. Eminent Domain Revisited
29. How an Idea Drew People Back to Urban Life
43. Japan's Cities Amid Globalization
44. Reinventing Rio: The Dazzling but Tarnished Brazilian City Gets a Makeover As It Prepares for the 2014 World Cup and 2016 Olympic Games
45. Demolishing Delhi: World Class City in the Making

Environment, "Green" policy, and sustainability
34. Principles of New Urbanism
39. Firebugs: Build It in California's Foothills, and It Will Burn
40. New German Community Models Car-Free Living
41. Traffic: Why It's Getting Worse, What Government Can Do
42. Is Congestion Pricing Ready for Prime Time?

Future of cities and suburbs
2. Eds, Meds and Urban Revival
3. Can They Save Youngstown?
10. The Rise of the Creative Class
41. Traffic: Why It's Getting Worse, What Government Can Do
42. Is Congestion Pricing Ready for Prime Time?
43. Japan's Cities Amid Globalization
44. Reinventing Rio: The Dazzling but Tarnished Brazilian City Gets a Makeover As It Prepares for the 2014 World Cup and 2016 Olympic Games
45. Demolishing Delhi: World Class City in the Making
49. Are Europe's Cities Better?

Gentrification
10. The Rise of the Creative Class
11. Too Much Froth
12. Studies: Gentrification a Boost for Everyone

Globalization
7. Movers and Shakers: How Immigrants Are Reviving Neighborhoods Given up for Dead
8. Swoons over Miami
9. Outsourcing: Beyond Bangalore
10. The Rise of the Creative Class
43. Japan's Cities Amid Globalization
44. Reinventing Rio: The Dazzling but Tarnished Brazilian City Gets a Makeover As It Prepares for the 2014 World Cup and 2016 Olympic Games
45. Demolishing Delhi: World Class City in the Making

History: Evolution of cities and suburbs
1. Why Cities Matter
31. The Six Suburban Eras of the United States
33. Affluent, but Needy (First Suburbs)

Hurricane Katrina
6. Bridge Blockade after Katrina Remains Divisive Issue

Housing
5. Predatory Lending: Redlining in Reverse
19. New Life in Newark
36. HOPE VI and the New Urbanism: Eliminating Low-Income Housing to Make Mixed-Income Communities
45. Demolishing Delhi: World Class City in the Making
46. No Excuses Slum Upgrading
47. Urban Legends: Why Suburbs, Not Cities, Are the Answer

Immigration
7. Movers and Shakers: How Immigrants Are Reviving Neighborhoods Given up for Dead

National and state urban policy
2. Eds, Meds and Urban Revival
3. Can They Save Youngstown?
4. Return to Center
5. Predatory Lending: Redlining in Reverse
16. Eminent Domain Revisited
36. HOPE VI and the New Urbanism: Eliminating Low-Income Housing to Make Mixed-Income Communities
41. Traffic: Why It's Getting Worse, What Government Can Do
49. Are Europe's Cities Better?

Neighborhoods, community development, and citizen participation
5. Predatory Lending: Redlining in Reverse
10. The Rise of the Creative Class
11. Too Much Froth
12. Studies: Gentrification a Boost for Everyone
17. Jane Jacobs' Radical Legacy
18. Neighbor Power: Building Community the Seattle Way

Internet References

The following Internet sites have been selected to support the articles found in this reader. These sites were available at the time of publication. However, because websites often change their structure and content, the information listed may no longer be available. We invite you to visit www.mhhe.com/cls for easy access to these sites.

Annual Editions: Urban Society 15/e

General Sources

Yahoo Social Science/Urban Studies
http://dir.yahoo.com/social_science/urban_studies

Yahoo provides links to sources on urban growth, urban ecology, sprawl, sprawl and urban theory and theorists.

UNIT 1: Urban Growth, Decline, and Renaissance

Coney Island History Site
www.westland.net/coneyisland

This website presents the fascinating story of the changing face of Coney Island, the beach and boardwalk mecca that provided recreation for millions of New York City immigrants who sought relief from the city's summer heat. Initially a resort for the city's elite, Coney Island's beach and amusement parks soon provided a recreational outlet for the immigrants from Europe who lived in the city's overcrowded tenement districts. Today, a changing Coney Island serves a "new immigration."

First Suburbs, The Brookings Institution
www.brookings.edu/topics/first-suburbs.aspx?page=2

Many of the nation's inner-ring suburban communities, once centers of easy living and prosperity, are showing new weaknesses, with infrastructure, housing, and social problems that have more in common with the central cities than with rapidly growing exurbs and edge cities. The Brookings Institution presents solid documentation and policy recommendations for a nation that, over the years, will have to cope with the problems of older, more mature suburbs.

Katrina Reading Room, The Brookings Institution—Quality material that reviews the rebuilding of New Orleans and the Gulf region in the years following the devastation of the storm and the flooding.
www.brookings.edu/metro/katrina-reading-room.aspx

The Brookings Institution presents a variety of studies which reviews the results of various policy instruments as they have been used to aid the rebuilding of New Orleans.

Kirwan Institute, The Ohio State University
http://kirwaninstitute.org

In its own words, the Kirwan Institute seeks to "deepen our understanding of the causes and solutions to racial and ethnic disparities and hierarchies." The Institute details racial imbalances in urban development, housing, and schools; it explores fair housing and regional equity solutions.

National Fair Housing Alliance
www.nationalfairhousing.org

This bipartisan group is dedicated to ending discrimination in housing. It promotes "fair housing" and seeks to combat the continuing existence of racial steering and discrimination in housing markets.

Public Policy Institute of California
www.ppic.org/main/policyareas.asp

The PPIC is a nonpartisan institute that presents research on a wide variety of policy issues in California, including how global forces and various state and national policies affect the Los Angeles region and communities throughout California. PPIC's focus includes economic development, education, immigration, the impact of state and national fiscal and budgetary decisions, and the alternative financial tools for providing the infrastructure to support the state's future growth.

UNIT 2: Gentrification, Globalization and the City

Creative Class
http://creativeclass.com

This website reflects the writings and ideas of economist Richard Florida who seeks to identify the various means by which cities can attract and support the "creative class." The site maintains a Media Showcase that includes various television and radio interviews with Dr. Florida.

Gentrification Web
http://members.lycos.co.uk/gentrification

This website, designed by Tom Slater, provides a bibliography and various articles on the impacts of gentrification. Highly critical of market-led gentrification, the site provides links to works that rebut the claim that gentrification brings substantial benefits to the residents of poorer communities.

Gotham Gazette
www.gothamgazette.com/city

Gotham Gazette is a daily publication that reviews politics and urban development in New York City. Among the Gazette's interests are: the city's post-9/11 rebuilding efforts, projects aimed at downtown and community revitalization, the continuing controversy over the construction of new sports stadiums and arenas, and the impact of immigration on the city.

Great Cities Institute, at the University of Illinois-Chicago
www.uic.edu/cuppa/gci/index.shtml

The GCI explores the changes that post-industrialism and globalization have brought to Chicago and other major cities in the national and world economy. Be sure to look at the series of GCI Working Papers that GCI sometimes makes available online.

National Immigration Forum
www.immigrationforum.org

This advocacy group welcomes continued immigration as congruent with the best of America's traditions and values. The Forum argues that immigrants contribute to the national and local economies as well as to the vibrant life of local communities. The Forum seeks to rebut many of what it sees as the specious arguments that exaggerate the negative impacts of immigration.

Internet References

Urban Institute

www.urban.org

Simply one of the premier organizations when it comes to the scholarly study of urban issues and public policy, the Urban Institute presents in-depth intensive analyses of immigration, housing revitalization, welfare reform, education performance innovations, and local public finance and tax policy.

UNIT 3: Competitive Pressures and Economic Development

Field of Schemes

www.fieldofschemes.com

This companion website to the book *Field of Schemes: How the Great Stadium Swindle Turns Public Money into Private Profit* by Neil deMause and Joanna Cagan, presents links to a great many articles that cast a critical eye on the vast public subsidies given to new sports stadiums and convention centers.

UNIT 4: Citizen Participation

Governance Institute: Citizen Participation

http://andromeda.rutgers.edu/~egovinst/website/citizenspg.htm

Discusses the various opportunities that changes in e-technology will bring to the realm of citizen participation, including new opportunities for citizen engagement in local government.

National Civic Review

www.ncl.org/publications/ncr

For more than a century, the National Civic League has been an important voice in the urban reform movement in the U.S. Its journal, the *National Civic Review,* offers numerous examples of urban reform efforts, including innovations designed to enhance citizen participation in local affairs and new efforts to promote intergovernmental cooperation in the metropolis. A number of the journal's articles are available online, free of charge. Other articles can be obtained via subscription or through your university library.

Shelterforce

www.shelterforce.org

This journal is devoted to the development of a more equitable city. It presents articles on neighborhood organizing efforts, affordable housing, and community and local economic development.

UNIT 5: School Choice and School Reform

Brookings Institution: School Choice; School Vouchers; Charter Schools; Urban and Inner-city Schools

www.brookings.edu/topics/school-choice.aspx
www.brookings.edu/topics/school-vouchers.aspx
www.brookings.edu/topics/charter-schools.aspx
www.brookings.edu/topics/urban-and-innercity-schools.aspx

This Washington "think tank" presents research reports and the transcripts of scholarly forums that review the evidence regarding choice programs and other reform measures undertaken and an effort to improve inner-city education.

Center for Education Reform

www.edreform.com

This advocacy group urges that governments expand school choice.

Civil Rights Project, UCLA

www.civilrightsproject.ucla.edu

Initially founded at Harvard University in 1996, the CRP monitors the nation's policies and progress on civil rights, with a special focus on the racial integration of schools.

Center for School Reform at the Heartland Institute

www.heartland.org/schoolreform-news.org/index.html

This "think tank" highlights a number of reports and news articles as part of its commitment to promoting individual freedom and free-market policy solutions, including choice in education.

National Center on School Choice, Vanderbilt University

www.vanderbilt.edu/schoolchoice/research-home.html

The Center presents studies on the impacts of a variety of school choice programs, including vouchers, charter schools, and magnet schools.

School Choice, Wisconsin

www.schoolchoiceinfo.org

A collection of news articles and more scholarly studies that analyze the impact of school choice programs, with a special focus on the Milwaukee school voucher program and Milwaukee's use of charter schools.

Thomas B. Fordham Institute

www.fordhaminstitute.org/template/index.cfm

A think-tank committed to the advancement of school choice and other educational reform measures.

UNIT 6: Policing and Crime

Prof. Wesley G. Skogan Home Page: Community Policing; Crime and Disorder

www.skogan.org

Professor Skogan is one of the nation's foremost experts on the subject of community policing. His website offer an extensive listing of book chapters, articles, and research reports. Be sure to look at the site's links to studies of the broken-windows approach to order maintenance as well as Skogan's and his team's numerous studies of community policing in Chicago and Britain.

The Urban Institute, Policing and Crime Prevention

www.urban.org/center/jpc/projects/Policing-and-Crime-Prevention.cfm

A Washington-based "think tank" that explores a variety of urban policy initiatives, including the effectiveness of various approaches to reducing crime in the city and in public housing.

UNIT 7: A Suburban Nation: Suburban Growth, Diversity, and the Possibilities of a "New Urbanism" and a "New Regionalism"

The Brookings Institution: First Suburbs

www.brookings.edu/topics/first-suburbs.aspx

This Washington-based "think tank" presents numerous research reports and newspaper articles as it examines the current state of America's older suburbs and the policies that can prevent their decline.

Congress for a New Urbanism

www.cnu.org

CNU is one of the strongest voices for New Urbanism. Its numerous publications and reports, including the *Charter for a New Urbanism,* detail the principles of the New Urbanism movement and various efforts to create move livable and sustainable inner-city communities and suburbs.

First Suburbs Coalition

www.marc.org/firstsuburbs

How should the nation deal with the jobs, housing, and infrastructure problems of America's aging suburbs, communities that enjoyed rapid growth following World War II, but many which are suffering decline today? The focus of this site is on efforts in Missouri and Kansas. Be sure to look at the links to similar efforts undertaken in other Midwest states, including Michigan and Ohio.

Internet References

National Geographic Magazine, Urban Sprawl
http://ngm.nationalgeographic.com/ngm/data2001/07/01/html/
ft_20010701.3.html

Useful and quite readable material on sprawled development and its impacts.

Newurbanism.org
www.newurbanism.org

This is another excellent site that presents more reports, ideas, and illustrative examples from the New Urbanism movement as it seeks to build livable and sustainable communities by reducing sprawl and promoting both walkable communities and the use of mass transit.

Sierra Club, Stopping Sprawl
www.sierraclub.org/sprawl

The Sierra Club is the long-serving advocate for preserving the natural environment of the U.S.

Smart Communities Network: Urban Growth Boundaries
www.smartcommunities.ncat.org/landuse/urban.shtml

This site provides links to various resources on urban growth boundaries in metropolitan (Portland) Oregon, and in other U.S. and foreign cities.

Sprawl Watch Clearinghouse
www.sprawlwatch.orgl

A wealth of articles on sprawl, it impact, and on various policies for containing future sprawled development.

UNIT 8: Toward Sustainable Cities and Suburbs?

The Brookings Institution: Transportation
www.brookings.edu/topics/transportation.aspx

The Brookings Institution presents a discussion of numerous alternative transportation policies for Urban America.

Green Cities
http://greencities.com

Explores green construction practices and various measures that can be taken to make urban development more compatible with environmental values.

Our Green Cities, featuring Dr. Kent Portney, Tufts University
http://ourgreencities.com/
www.brookings.edu/topics/transportation.aspx

Dr. Portney is one of the leading experts on sustainable cities, attempting to discover policies that advance all three legs of the sustainable development triangle.

Resources For the Future: Transportation and Urban Land
www.rff.org/Focus_Areas/Pages/Transportation_and_Urban_Land.aspx

RFF looks at alternative ways at reducing the strain that urban growth places on resources. It probes alternative policies to reduce the social costs of driving, including the development of cleaner cars, and incentives to promote the use of mass transit. RFF also advocates water conservation and smart growth.

Sierra Club
www.sierraclub.org/sprawl

Founded in 1892, the Sierra Club is America's oldest environmental organization. As part of its agenda of environmental protection, the Sierra Club seeks alternatives to continued sprawled development. Particularly noteworthy are the organization's reports on *Building Better.*

Smart Growth America
http://smartgrowthamerica.org

This advocacy group seeks to curb sprawled development in order to promote historic preservation, the protection of farmland and green spaces, and the development of "healthy" cities and suburbs.

Sprawl & Growth
www.plannersweb.com/articles/sprawl-articles.html

Various articles from *Planning Commissioners Journal* present competing views on urban sprawl and the desirability of smart-growth policies.

Sustainable Cities
http://sustainable cities.net

The name of this organization says it all. Can policies be adopted to make urban growth and development more compatible with environmental values?

UNIT 9: The Future of Cities and Suburbs: The United States and the World

Planetizen
www.planetizen.com

Tons of discussion of various urban planning issues, including transportation, and the environment.

Planum
www.planum.net

The e-zine of the European Journal of Planning, this online forum presents a large number of articles on various aspects of European urban planning, including the impact of immigration and the European city of the future.

Squatter City
http://squattercity.blogspot.com

Robert Neuwirth is the author of *Shadow Cities: A Billion Squatters, A New Urban World,* in which he recounted his experiences living in the slums and *favelas* of India, Brazil, and Kenya. In this blog, he continues the discussion of the various housing problems that poor people face in LDCs and the government policies that too often exacerbate those problems.

United Nations Human Settlements Programme
www.unhabitat.org

UN-Habitat seeks to promote shelter for all, with a particular focus on providing alternatives to the slum/squatter communities in lesser developed countries. Particularly noteworthy are the UN-Habitat reports on such topics as *Cities in a Globalizing World* and *The Challenge of Slums.*

U.S. Department of Housing and Urban Development
www.hud.gov

This national government department devoted to urban affairs presents a broad series of reports on government policies toward cities, including housing (notably reports on efforts to combat homelessness and the government's HOPE VI efforts to tear down and replace high-rise public housing), and local community and economic development. During the Obama administration, HUD has also given new emphasis to inter-departmental action at neighborhood stabilization, efforts to build partnerships that will help stem the decline of distressed communities, especially communities hard-hit by housing foreclosures and abandonment. Also noteworthy is the Department's efforts at "fair housing." Be sure to hit on the site's "Library" link in order to access a wide variety of reports and analyses.

UNIT 1

Urban Growth, Decline, and Renaissance

Unit Selections

1. **Why Cities Matter,** Edward L. Glaeser
2. **Eds, Meds and Urban Revival,** Rob Gurwitt
3. **Can They Save Youngstown?,** Brentin Mock
4. **Return to Center,** Christopher D. Ringwald
5. **Predatory Lending: Redlining in Reverse,** Gregory D. Squires
6. **Bridge Blockade after Katrina Remains Divisive Issue,** Chris Kirkham and Paul Purpura

Learning Outcomes

After reading this unit, you should be able to:

- Describe the functions of cities, that is, why cities exist and the purposes that cities serve.

- Identify the various factors that have led to the economic and population decline of many central cities.

- Explain why numerous central cities have begun to focus their efforts on the medical and educational sectors and no longer concentrate solely on efforts to recruit more traditional manufacturing plants.

- Give examples of how the policies of the 50 states affect local communities.

- Suggest possible strategies by which state governments can assist the health of local communities.

- Detail the goals and major provisions of the Community Reinvestment Act (CRA).

- Explain the policy of deregulation and indentify its advocates.

- Identify the predatory lending practices of more unscrupulous private home-finance lenders.

- Compare the competing positions of those who blame the CRA for the rash of home foreclosures and boarded-up properties in inner-city neighborhoods and those who seek to absolve the CRA of blame.

- Assess the extent to which "race" continues to be a factor that shapes urban and suburban development and the extent to which the United States has moved beyond the racial prejudices that shaped cities and suburbs during an earlier age.

- Evaluate the extent to which private choice and a free-market has determined patterns of urban growth, decline, and racial segregation—versus the extent to which urban patterns and problems are the result of government policies and the manipulations of private actors that prevented the workings of a truly free and unbiased market.

Student Website

www.mhhe.com/cls

Internet References

Coney Island History Site
www.westland.net/coneyisland

First Suburbs, The Brookings Institution
www.brookings.edu/topics/first-suburbs.aspx?page=2

Katrina Reading Room, The Brookings Institution
www.brookings.edu/metro/katrina-reading-room.aspx

Kirwan Institute, The Ohio State University
http://kirwaninstitute.org

National Fair Housing Alliance
www.nationalfairhousing.org

Public Policy Institute of California
www.ppic.org/main/policyareas.asp

Cities serve important functions. Cities are the centers where close interaction allows the exchange of ideas that serve to advance the country's economic, intellectual, and cultural growth (Article 1 "Why Cities Matter").

Yet, despite their importance, cities in the United States, especially the older industrial centers of the Northeast and the Midwest, have suffered a long-term loss of both population and economic activity. Urban decline, however, is not confined solely to central cities. Older, once exclusive **first suburbs,** too, are suffering housing vacancies, closed stores in local shopping strips, a loss of jobs, and a weakened tax base as both businesses and population move further out to more distant and newer facilities on the suburban rim. Hard-hit, poverty-stricken **disaster suburbs,** such as East Cleveland (Ohio), East St. Louis (Illinois), and Compton (outside of Los Angeles), in many ways have more in common with problem-torn inner cities than with the prosperous, middle-class residential or **dormitory suburbs.**

Today, the United States and other advanced industrial and post-industrial countries, are no longer experiencing a simple **urbanization,** where population from the countryside moves to the city in search of jobs and economic opportunity. Of course, such internal migration still continues, and the arrival of immigrants from overseas accounts for much of the population growth reported by a number of U.S. cities over the past decade. As Americans prospered and new innovations in transportation and telecommunications technology permitted, middle-class Americans began to leave the cities for the "good life" of the suburbs. Over the past half century, **urbanization** has been more than counterbalanced by the stronger wave of **counterurbanization** or **suburbanization.** Manufacturing, retail, and entertainment activity soon followed exodus to suburbia. The impact on central cities and core urban neighborhoods was devastating. Today, central cities and older suburbs are frequently marred by closed stores and vacant housing. In many metropolitan areas, central cities are no longer the real center of daily life. Instead, economic activity has drifted to suburban shopping malls and to suburban **edge cities** with their concentrations of office towers, shopping gallerias, and cinema multiplexes and other entertainment places.

Deindustrialization, too, has undermined the economic base of many former manufacturing centers, forcing many to adapt by finding a new niche to play in a post-industrial society (Article 2 "Eds, Meds and Urban Revival"). Some central cities and older suburbs have enjoyed a renaissance and have become new centers of banking, finance, corporate headquarters, and tourism in a post-industrial age. Their turnaround is best exemplified by New York City, which teetered on the edge of municipal bankruptcy in the 1970s, but today is the site of so much economic activity that even the 9/11 attacks posed only a temporary disruption to the city's economic resurgence. Once-bypassed inner-city neighborhoods in the United States, Britain, Germany, and Australia (to name only a few countries) are experiencing substantial **gentrification** as "yuppies," and upscale professionals have bought houses and rented apartments in neighborhoods

© TongRo Image Stock/Alamy

close to the entertainment and job opportunities of thriving downtowns. Yet, the picture is not equally bright for all cities.

Not all cities are experiencing an urban renaissance. Detroit, Youngstown, and a number of cities are still coping with the problems of long-term decline, and have turned to **shrinking strategies** and attempts at **greening the city** that has much more housing stock than its diminished population requires (Article 3 "Can They Save Youngstown?").

Why have some cities, suburbs, and neighborhoods experienced continued growth and prosperity while others have suffered? What determines the growth and decline of urban communities?

Of course, natural forces and the working of free choice and a free market help determine where residents and businesses choose to locate. People with the money to do so can leave the congestion and crime of the inner city, seeking the more pleasant family-oriented environments of the suburbs and the **Sunbelt,** the newer, growing communities of the South and Southwest. Poorer persons and newly-arrived immigrants have little choice but to occupy the units the up-movers have left behind. Advances in transportation and communications technology help determine how far a person—and a business—can move from the city center. The invention of the electric streetcar opened up rural areas on the city's rim to **suburbanization.** The automobile opened up a great many more areas, leading to the **sprawl** of urban settlements over a much larger metropolitan area. The development of trucks enabled manufacturing and warehousing to seek sites in the suburbs. Manufacturers found cheap, suburban land suitable for land-intensive assembly lines. Advances in telecommunications and computerization freed office firms of the need to be close to one another in the central city. Older buildings in the central city lacked the floor plans and the wiring and digital infrastructure to compete successfully with new suburban office complexes. Not often discussed, air conditioning was a technological advance that effectively opened up communities in the Sunbelt to new development, leading to the decline of cities and suburbs in the Northeast and Midwest.

To recognize the "natural" causes and the depth of the urban problems does *not* to imply that government can do absolutely nothing to help distressed cities and troubled neighborhoods. Urban growth and decline are *not* dictated solely by natural factors and the workings of a free market. Government actions—public policy—too has had important urban impacts, contributing to the growth of some communities while, too often, inadvertently contributing to the problems experienced by others. Government highway programs, sewer and hospital construction subsidies, and tax programs that favor homeowners all helped to fuel suburban growth and urban sprawl and the concomitant problem of central-city decline. Programs such as the tax breaks for home owners and the home-buying assistance provided by the Federal Housing Administration and Veterans Administration have had noble purposes; they helped make America a nation of home owners. But the program also exerted a negative impact on a great many cities, as the tax incentives and home insurance and other subsidies helped to fuel the population exodus from the cities to the suburbs and eventually to the Sunbelt as well. The impact of these programs on urban growth and decline is so great that they can be said to constitute a **hidden urban policy,** or more accurately, a hidden anti-urban policy.

If past government programs inadvertently exacerbated urban problems, present-day government programs can also be structured to help undo some of the damage. State actions can be particularly helpful—or harmful—to cities. A state's decision to choose central-city as opposed to suburban sites for governmental offices, for instance, can contribute to the economic revitalization of core-city communities (Article 4, "Return to Center").

Urban development has never really been purely the result of a free market and free choices. Racial discrimination has often prevented a truly free market from operating. For a long time, **restrictive covenants** were written into property contracts, barring the sale or rental of a house to an African-American, Asian, Latino, or Jew, whoever was the unpopular minority in a city. The Supreme Court in 1948 finally voided the enforcement of restrictive covenants, after the racial border lines of many city neighborhoods had already been established. **Racial steering** also prevented African-Americans and other minorities from buying into white communities even when families had the income to do so; real estate agents helped to maintain segregation by showing whites and minorities houses in different parts of the metropolis. The **Fair Housing Act** made the practice illegal, although more subtle forms of racial steering continue as they are hard to detect and discrimination is difficult to prove in court.

For a long time, banks and insurance instances refused to finance housing and businesses in large portions of the inner city, refusing to extend loans and insurance even to good families with a strong job history and a sound record of financial decision making. In a process known as **redlining,** banks and other credit institutions refused to make or approve of loans in an entire section of a community, in some cases even drawing a red line on a map around a No-Go area of the city, cutting off money for new investment or upgrading, a **disinvestment** practice that guaranteed a community's speedy decline. Even the Federal Housing Administration for many years practiced both redlining and racial steering, refusing to insure loans for the renovation of inner-city properties and refusing to approve loans to racial minorities who sought to move into white neighborhoods.

The **Community Reinvestment Act (CRA)** put an end to redlining and sought to promote **greenlining,** banks lending money to communities throughout their service area, including to persons in poorer neighborhoods. Conservatives were hostile to what they saw as the government's interference with sound business practices. In the early 2000s, conservative critics blamed the CRA and similar government programs for the crisis in the sub-prime housing market and the rash of foreclosures that jeopardized the nation's economy. The CRA did lead banks to advance some home loans in the city that were indeed unwise. Yet, it appears that such a broad-scale attack on the CRA is largely driven by ideology and is not merited by the facts. The CRA had been in existence for three decades before the credit crisis arose, even during periods of dynamic national economic expansion. Also, the vast majority of bad loans did not involve properties that received loans subject to CRA regulations! In fact, it was just the opposite. Instead many of the loan foreclosures involved expensive homes and condominiums, including upscale housing communities built in prosperous areas of the Sunbelt, that were *not* subject to CRA regulations. Republican-era **deregulation policies** had allowed a large number of smaller credit institutions to enter the housing field, businesses that were allowed to offer housing lands and were not subject to CRA review. As Gregory Squires (Article 5, "Predatory Lending: Redlining in Reverse") describes, deregulation has actually served to diminish the reach of CRA regulations in poorer urban neighborhoods. Deregulation enabled unscrupulous private lenders new leeway to make loans to people who were in no position to repay them. Squires details the many abuses of **predatory lenders** who made quick profits with unethical practices that took advantage of poor and working-class home buyers and eventually led to the wave of home foreclosures

Fortunately, the laws have changed, and the most blatant practices of racial discrimination have diminished over the years. Yet, the influence of race persists, and cities and metropolitan areas remain racially divided, some more so than others. A particularly dramatic reminder **of the continuing influence of race** was provided when a group of poor, Black residents of New Orleans attempted to escape the devastation of Hurricane Katrina only to meet armed officers from suburban Gretna who blocked the bridge and their escape to safety (Article 6, "Bridge Blockade after Katrina Remains Divisive Issue").

Why Cities Matter

EDWARD GLAESER

Cities often form for obvious and ordinary reasons. An island in the Seine was a good place for Romans and Franks to defend themselves against Huns and Vikings. The tip of Manhattan is a splendid natural port, with access to a deep river that cuts more than three-hundred miles into the American hinterland. But the magic of urban density means that agglomerations of people come together for simple reasons and often achieve amazing things. Most of mankind's cultural, economic, political, and social accomplishments have occurred in cities.

Dominic Pacyga's *Chicago* is a biography of a great and comparatively young city. It provides a comprehensive overview of Chicago's meteoric growth in the nineteenth century and its survival in the leaner years of the late twentieth century. Along the way, Pacyga reminds us of the remarkable things that can result when human beings interact with each other in dense, urban areas.

William Cronon's *Nature's Metropolis,* which appeared in 1991, is the reigning interpretation of Chicago's early growth. The city's natural advantages—its waterways and its proximity to lumber and wheat and livestock—turned a dusty outpost on the American frontier into a metropolis of millions in a few short decades. Pacyga notes that "[t]he city developed into a vast marketplace for lumber, grain, livestock, and produce even as it became a distribution point for eastern goods such as stoves, clothing, and hardware."

In the twentieth century, we became used to accidental urban giants, such as Las Vegas and Los Angeles. Such places are self-reinforcing groups of people who value being near each other (and sunshine), but they could have been located anywhere nearby. No geographical feature determined the placement of Los Angeles. In the nineteenth century, by contrast, when transportation costs were high and natural resources were critical, urban locations in America were practically fixed by geography.

Every one of the twenty largest cities in the United States in 1900 was on a waterway—from the oldest places that perched on the eastern seaboard's natural harbors to the youngest city, Minneapolis, located on the northernmost navigable point of the Mississippi. Pacyga remarks that Chicago's "canal proved to be crucial for the future of the city": it made Chicago the linchpin of a vast watery arc that stretched from New York to New Orleans. As much as cavalrymen and cowboys, city slickers tamed the west by creating the transport network that brought the products of the prairie to the customers of the east.

But Chicago did not grow from a city of 4,500 people in 1840 to a city of 3.4 million ninety years later merely as a center of water-borne, or rail-borne, commerce. The city's vast size reflects its abundance of industrial entrepreneurs. Some, such as Cyrus McCormick and his mechanical reapers, made their inventions in the east and moved to Chicago to be close to agricultural customers. As Pacyga writes, "McCormick moved west because he felt that the natural market for the new machines would be on the prairie." Others, such as George Pullman, produced their ideas in Chicago: "In the winter of 1857–58, he entered into a partnership with two brothers, Benjamin and Norman Field, to construct and operate sleeping cars on two Illinois railroad lines." By connecting people, cities help the spread of ideas, which in turn lead to new inventions, like Pullman's "Palace" cars, thus making inter-continental transportation far more pleasant.

Perhaps the most remarkable of Chicago's collaborative inventions was the skyscraper itself, which did so much to change the shape of cities throughout the world. There is a lively discussion among architectural historians about who deserves the credit for inventing the skyscraper, roughly defined as a building that stands tall thanks to a load-bearing steel skeleton. The Chicago engineer and architect William Le Baron Jenney is often described as the "Father of the Skycraper," but there is plenty of room to debate that title. Jenney's claim is based on Chicago's Home Insurance Building, which does have metal-framing, but only on two sides. Burnham and Root's earlier Montauk building also had some iron-reinforced walls; such iron-frames were hardly unknown in industrial structures. The case gets even murkier because Burnham had once worked for Jenney, and for his fire-proofing contractor, the remarkable Peter B. Wight, a former disciple of John Ruskin who "proposed a fireproof iron-frame-supported column as early as 1874."

The quest for the skyscraper's paternity often misses the far more important truth: the real father of the skyscraper was Chicago itself. In the wake of the Great Fire of 1871, the city attracted a remarkable collection of architectural and engineering talent that was needed to rebuild a city. After all, even with the buildings gone, Chicago's future remained assured thanks to its enormous geographical advantages. Those minds then learned from each other and borrowed each others' ideas and collectively remade architecture. Ayn Rand's Frank Lloyd Wright, fictionalized as Howard Roark in *The Fountainhead,* is a particularly misleading portrait of an architect. Wright was no Gary Cooper-esque loner who sprang alone into the world as if from the head of Zeus. Wright was part of a chain of Chicago architects, and his ideas built on those of his mentor, Louis Sullivan, who had worked with Jenney himself. They were all part of the great web of creative interchange created by the city that emerged from Chicago's canal and stockyards.

Pacyga is interested in ordinary people, too. In 1900, Chicago attracted a gigantic inflow of immigrants, particularly Germans and Scandinavians. The city offered, after all, some of the highest wages on the planet. In later decades, Chicago provided a way out for many African-Americans, including the writer Richard Wright, fleeing the Jim Crow south. Cities such as this one have always had a comparative advantage in assimilating migrants, who have usually done well in Chicago and helped to give the city its character. When I was a graduate student in Chicago in the late 1980s, the blackboards still had bilingual signs in English and Polish.

Through the 1920s, Chicago was run by native born Americans, such as Big Bill Thompson. A colorful character who once staged a debate with live rats, he was one of the city's many powerful Republicans who "relied on their white Amercianborn base and on African-American votes." After all, Lincoln himself had first been nominated by the Republican Party in the Chicago Wigwam. The Republican Party's commitment to prohibition gave it a natural appeal to Chicago's bootlegging entrepreneurs, notably Al Capone, who had much to lose from the legalization of liquor.

But Anton Cermak, a Czech immigrant and a determined "wet," bested Thompson and turned Chicago into a permanently Democratic city. As Pacyga tells it, "On April 7, 1931, Cermak beat Thompson by 191,916 votes, and the West Side Czech who Thompson had referred to as a 'Bozo' and a 'Bohunk' won all but five wards as Chicago placed the Democrats in power and set the stage for the 1932 presidential election." Cermak and his successors forged a durable Democratic machine that maintained its power through patronage and neighborhood outreach. (Cermak himself died in 1933 taking a bullet that was meant for F.D.R. Pacyga repeats the much-disputed tale that Cermak told the President, "I'm glad it was me instead of you." Others think that Cermak just uttered an expletive.)

In the 1950s, Cermak's machine was inherited by Chicago's first Mayor Daley. Father and son, the two Daleys have led Chicago for forty-two of the last fifty-five years. The durability

of their dominance is a puzzle that Pacyga could have done more to explain. In many large cities, such as New York, the New Deal and the expansion of relatively uncorrupt Federal patronage broke the back of older machines. In Chicago, the Daleys proved remarkably adept at surviving through changing times, much like the city itself. Indeed, one not insignificant reason for their success is that Chicago has managed to thrive despite the declining importance of the natural advantages that once determined the city's growth.

Post-war urban America was hit by changing transportation technologies that enabled families to move to the suburbs and the Sun Belt. All but two of America's ten largest cities in 1950 are less populated now than they were at the time. (The exceptions are New York and Los Angeles.) Chicago is about 23 percent smaller today than it was in that year, but this decline is quite modest compared to the more than 50 percent population drops seen in erstwhile urban giants like Cleveland, Detroit, and St. Louis.

Chicago's continued survival is a reflection of sensible leadership and—even more importantly—smart people who learn from one another in skyscrapers and scattered neighborhoods. The death of distance may have made Chicago's factories far less important, but globalization and new technologies have also increased the returns on being smart. Cities enable people to become smart by learning from other smart people. Like millions of others, I myself have done plenty of learning in the Windy City.

Pacyga's book is a fine introduction to Chicago's history, though it tries to do so much that it lacks the unified narrative and overarching theme that made *Nature's Metropolis* truly great. Pacyga's *Chicago* is closer in spirit to *Gotham,* Edwin Burrows and Mike Wallace's wonderful history of New York up to 1898. If Pacyga does not quite reach their lofty heights, he has still produced a very fine volume that should grace the bookshelves of every Chicago buff and every urbanist.

Critical Thinking

1. Why do cities exist? What are the important functions that cities serve?

2. What factors made Chicago so important; explaining its growth from a prairie town into a major city?

EDWARD GLAESER is the *Glimp Professor of Economics* at Harvard. He directs the Taubman Center for State and Local Government and the Rappaport Institute for Greater Boston.

Eds, Meds and Urban Revival

In many cities, a big university is becoming the economic engine that a big corporation used to be.

ROB GURWITT

Look out from an upper-floor window of the old Sears building on the edge of downtown Birmingham, Alabama, and you can begin to appreciate the sweep of the city's history.

Close by, just beyond the vacant lot across the street, run the train lines whose arrival in the 1870s gave birth and shape to the city. Away to the south on Red Mountain, his upraised arm like an admonition on the horizon, stands a giant statue of Vulcan, the Roman god of the forge—a bittersweet reminder of the iron and steel works that fed Birmingham's industrial might for close to a century, until U.S. Steel left town in the early 1980s. But it's what lies in the middle that really matters now. Sprawling across 82 city blocks between the tracks and the mountain is the University of Alabama at Birmingham, known to all hereabouts as UAB. It is the largest employer in the city—indeed, in the entire state of Alabama. It has grown at such a prodigious clip in recent decades that locals joke that its initials stand for "the University that Ate Birmingham."

Most of them say this fondly, for the plain truth is that without UAB, Birmingham would have collapsed when U.S. Steel walked away. The university's steady growth, its reach and national prominence as a medical school, hospital system and health sciences complex, its researchers' ability to bring in hundreds of millions of dollars every year in grants and contracts, its 17,000 students and 19,000 employees, its impact on the city's restaurants, arts and entertainment—all of this makes it, in the words of former Mayor Richard Arrington, "our economic life's blood."

It's not that the university is the only economic game in the Birmingham area. Honda and Mercedes now have automotive plants nearby, the insurance and financial sectors remain strong, and one of the country's top 10 banks—Regions—has its headquarters here. Yet for all this, there is a growing conviction in Birmingham that if the city's future dynamism lies anywhere, it is with the researchers, doctors, engineers, faculty members and sheer intellectual heft of UAB. Accustomed to thinking of Birmingham as the undisputed kingpin of Alabama's economy, the city's corporate leaders have watched with dismay in recent years as development momentum has shifted to Mobile, where

the port is bustling, the German steel giant ThyssenKrupp is building a $3.7 billion plant, and the U.S. Air Force's new aerial refueling tanker will be manufactured; and to Huntsville, where a new genetics research institute and companies drawn by NASA's presence have created an air of high-tech vitality. Birmingham used to have four major bank headquarters; Regions' is the only one left. BellSouth, one of the city's most prominent corporate players, has been taken over by AT&T. Other companies have left for New York, Tennessee and Texas.

"With the consolidation of the banking industry, the consolidation of the utility industry, how long will we be like we are?" asks Charles McCrary, the president and CEO of Alabama Power and a boardroom pacesetter both locally and statewide. "UAB is the only sustainable economic development engine we have in Birmingham." The pressing question for both Birmingham and UAB, he has come to believe, is whether they can sort out what to do with it.

Bell Towers for Smokestacks

Plenty of states, cities, academic institutions and medical centers are grappling with a similar challenge. In an era when technological know-how and innovation have become prime economic drivers, "eds and meds" have become indispensable anchors of urban growth. "In many respects," a report by CEOs for Cities and the Initiative for a Competitive Inner City commented a few years ago, "the bell towers of academic institutions have replaced smokestacks as the drivers of the American urban economy."

Yet until relatively recently, most universities and the cities surrounding them went about their business without taking full stock of what each meant to the other. Many local and state government leaders, notes Temple University political scientist Carolyn Adams, "don't see these institutions as having an economic development function much beyond employment and land development." For their part, hospitals and academic institutions aren't accustomed to thinking of themselves as de facto economic bigwigs or pondering the responsibilities that go along with that status; for many, the prevailing attitude toward the communities that host them has essentially been, "You should just thank your lucky stars we're here."

And to a degree, of course, they're right. A 1999 Brookings Institution report by University of Pennsylvania historian Ira Harkavy and Harmon Zuckerman—now the chief planner for Douglas County, Nevada—found that in the 20 largest U.S. cities, "eds and meds" accounted for 35 percent of the workforce employed by the top 10 private employers; in many cities, a university or medical system was the largest private employer, and in four of them—Washington D.C., Philadelphia, San Diego and Baltimore—medical systems and universities generated more than half the jobs among the 10 largest private employers. While no similar study has been done since then, Harkavy, now director of Penn's Netter Center for Community Partnerships, believes all this has only been magnified over the past decade. "There's been a general increase in the size of these institutions," he notes, "especially on the medical side."

Moreover, "eds and meds" have two attributes much appreciated by local political leaders: They have money to spend, and they stay put. As New Haven, Rochester, Philadelphia, Baltimore and other struggling cities all found to their good fortune during the depths of the urban crisis, universities and large medical centers don't get bought out or relocated by their owners. And as their resources have swelled—last year, 76 universities around the country had endowments exceeding $1 billion—institutions such as Harvard, Columbia, Penn, Johns Hopkins and Case Western Reserve have become ambitious and powerful land developers. Sometimes they feel an expand-or-die imperative; sometimes they simply want to improve life in nearby neighborhoods and have grown tired of waiting for financially pressed local governments to jump-start the process.

Yet as Birmingham's example suggests, universities and medical centers are more than just steadfast employers and major land developers. They are "the generators of development across the city," says Harkavy, coming to shape local economies through the research and activities they sponsor. Universities and research institutions undergird what Carolyn Adams calls "networks of knowledge and entrepreneurship that create new products and processes." In other words, they convene faculty, students, researchers, investors, entrepreneurs and others who can share ideas and dream up new ventures—the old Sears building in Birmingham, for instance, is now the Innovation Depot, an incubator designed in part to take the fruits of UAB's research and spin them into businesses. Coupled with the stable incomes they provide, the cosmopolitan tastes they house and the cultural vibrancy they stimulate, it's no surprise that universities have come to anchor many cities' prospects for growth.

What is just beginning to happen is a mutual coming to terms. Local political and civic leaders are starting to think strategically about how to use academic institutions to spur further economic and community development, while university administrators are getting accustomed to the higher expectations thrust on them by their size, resources and place in the changing economic firmament. Some places are further along on this path than others: Pittsburgh, for instance, where the Allegheny Conference on Community Development and the state's Ben Franklin Partnership began in the 1980s to harness innovative thinking at local universities to the cause of economic development; or Philadelphia, where the University of Pennsylvania has a staggering array of initiatives aimed at improving the city's general well-being; or Atlanta, where the Georgia Research Alliance brings government officials, business leaders and university administrators together to attract world-class researchers and labs to the state and then to help them spin ventures off into the marketplace.

Most communities, however, are more like Birmingham: aware of the possibilities and the need to take advantage of them, but not yet organized to get there. "Our growth and development have been so extraordinarily fast," says Dr. Max Michael, dean of UAB's School of Public Health, "that only within the last few years have folks within the community and at UAB lifted up their heads and said, 'Oh my God, here's this big thing in the city,' and begun figuring out a role and responsibilities for the university. A lot of urban universities are in this position: Now we're here, what do we do?"

Unlikely Colossus

That UAB should be in such a position at all would seem remarkable to those who saw it in its early days. It began in the 1930s as a small extension school of the University of Alabama's main Tuscaloosa campus, then in the mid-1940s added a hospital, dental school and medical college on three blocks of Birmingham's south side, surrounded by a neighborhood of small houses, a few stores and restaurants, a quickie car wash and a miniature golf course.

University administrators now work where Birmingham's kids played putt-putt, and the rest of the neighborhood—along with several others in every direction—is long gone as well. UAB has mushroomed from a medical school and hospital offering extension programs for commuting students to a major university with schools of business, education, engineering, arts and humanities, sciences and mathematics—but most important, a gigantic health complex with a $400 million-a-year research enterprise known internationally for its work on cancer, bioengineering, diabetes, heart disease and social and behavioral medicine. And it continues to grow. The university as a whole adds about 225,000 square feet of space each year, says Sheila Chaffin, its planning director. "That's about as much as we did in the entire City University of New York system when I was there," she adds. "It's very aggressive."

UAB helped Birmingham meet the two biggest challenges of its modern life: overcoming the legacy of the fire hoses, police dogs and church bombing with which the more extreme members of white Birmingham responded to the civil rights movement in the 1960s; and reshaping its economy after the departure of U.S. Steel. The first came in mostly quiet ways, through civic leaders who'd grown up elsewhere and come to Birmingham because of the university, and more parochially through the recruiting of black physicians and faculty members, a university-approved move to desegregate the county medical society, the admission of black students and later, when Arrington was mayor, a push to use minority-owned firms to work on campus expansion. When U.S. Steel left, UAB's expansion and the sheer number of white-collar jobs it generated were crucial to keeping the city afloat.

These days, more people work at UAB than in downtown Birmingham. The hospital system alone is a $1.5 billion-a-year enterprise. "Our research expenditures by themselves probably contribute a couple of hundred million dollars to Birmingham in terms of payroll," says Richard Marchase, the university's vice president for research and economic development. "We expect a [researcher] we bring in will hire eight to 10 people and have half a million dollars in payroll, and we see that avenue as among the most important ways we contribute to the city." The university has started to work with the city's economic development team to lure a major pharmaceutical manufacturer to Birmingham. "They wouldn't even look at us were it not for UAB," says Griffin Lassiter, who does business recruitment for the city.

And the new Innovation Depot, located midway between downtown and UAB, pairs the university with a former county- and city-supported incubator; spinoffs from UAB research—on everything from cancer-preventive drugs to toxin detection to cell modeling and molecular screening—form a significant part of its clientele. The university, says Innovation Depot's CEO, Susan Matlock, "is the way to our future as a city."

Yet for all this, it doesn't take many conversations with leaders from both UAB and the city to get the sense that the two still have a ways to go if they're to become true collaborators. "There's no way Birmingham would be the relatively thriving city it is today without the presence of UAB," says Mark Kelly, a local writer who specializes in the city's business and political history. "The flip side is, the UAB attitude has often been, 'You wouldn't be here without us, so we do our civic part by being the largest employer in the state,' and there really has not been a strong connection in terms of planning or strategic thinking between the city and UAB. UAB is almost a city unto itself."

Saving the Neighborhood

This is hardly a complaint unique to Birmingham; there probably isn't a university community in the country where you can't hear some version of it. Still, Harkavy believes, the picture has begun to change in recent years. "Higher education and medical institutions have begun to understand their role better," he says. "There's much more pressure on higher-ed institutions to illustrate their role in the local environment."

One of the most compelling illustrations is taking place in Baltimore, where Johns Hopkins is far and away the largest private employer. In an effort that joins the university, the city and the mega-developer Forest City Enterprises, the John Hopkins medical system is building an immense new life sciences park aimed at spinning off business opportunities from its research, and is placing the park in the deeply struggling East Baltimore neighborhood the school inhabits. In conjunction with the Annie E. Casey Foundation and the city, it has created a public-private enterprise, East Baltimore Development Inc., whose job is to oversee an ambitious effort to rehabilitate the neighborhood by building new housing for its residents, helping them

with family and health counseling, creating a new elementary and middle school, and perhaps most important, crafting work-force development programs to place East Baltimore residents in the construction, health care and bioscience jobs generated by the project. "The plan acknowledges that Hopkins is a great strength in that community," says Deputy Mayor Andrew Frank, "and Hopkins, in its own enlightened self-interest, felt it was important to work with the community and the city to revitalize the neighborhoods around the huge investment in their campus. So we're looking for a transformation of the community that still connects it to its roots."

UAB's president, Carol Garrison, insists that her university, too, has "a plan and partnership with the larger community in terms of how we all move forward together. I'm fond of saying that as goes the city, so goes UAB, and as goes UAB, so goes the city." She points to the close ties between the university's school of education and teachers in area public schools, research on such issues as homelessness and drug addiction being carried on by the UAB faculty, summer programs for high school students, the school of public health's collaboration with storefront churches on health education, and the huge amounts of outside funding UAB brings into Birmingham through its research. "I would say we're doing considerable things in the community," she says.

But there is a perception both within and outside the university that it could be doing more—not so much in terms of discrete efforts, but as the most powerful institution in Birmingham. "From a public health point of view, it's one thing for the medical center to say we provide a kajillion dollars in uncompensated care," says School of Public Health Dean Max Michael. "It's another to say we have rampant poverty, high homicide rates, breathtaking levels of illiteracy and other problems of urban blight that we ought to have a role in addressing. We have any number of faculty who interact with community groups and have developed great trust; the challenge now is how do you coalesce that and make it a longitudinal culture of partnership?"

What makes this a particular challenge is that the priorities of the university, the city and the state all move in different directions, making intensive collaboration difficult to build. "In terms of how do we need to keep this institution alive and growing," says Bob Corley, who chairs UAB's Global and Community Leadership Program, "we're not looking to the city in particular to help that occur. We're looking to the federal government. We're looking to the state government. We're looking to the families and our students who support us through their tuition. Nearly all of them are somewhere outside the city of Birmingham. So the ways in which we can assist the future development and economic development of Birmingham—it's a consideration, but not at the center of what makes us exist. We're not Alabama Power. We don't rely on or require that continuing kind of growth in the economy to make us go."

Similarly, there's a growing chorus within Birmingham arguing that the city—both its public and private leaders—and the state have failed to recognize just how crucial an economic engine UAB has become. "UAB speaks a different language than the state speaks, it speaks a different language than the city speaks, and in all candor, there's not the strongest relationship between the city's business community and UAB," says Jim Hayes, who directs the corporate-financed Economic Development Partnership of Alabama. "I don't know that there's fault at that—I think it's a matter of putting your head down and doing your business every day and not spending your time with the other. But if we ever let UAB lose its momentum, there's not enough money in the state of Alabama to get it back."

Which is why Hayes, Alabama Power's Charles McCrary and others have begun to argue that the way the Alabama legislature funds UAB—which now gets less than a quarter of its money from the state budget—needs to change. In essence, the university draws its state money from the same pool of funds as elementary and secondary schools, which means that every year it is competing with the powerful Alabama Education Association for legislators' attention, even as neighboring Georgia, with its well-funded research alliance, tries to poach UAB's leading researchers. "Right now, UAB lives from budget cycle to budget cycle," says Hayes. "But that's not a strategy. A dollar here and a dollar there equals two dollars. But if you build a system like Georgia's, a dollar here and a dollar there equals five dollars. That's where we've got to go, but it's a leadership issue. State leaders have to recognize that we have to build a system that fosters this kind of growth. And we as a community—and this is part UAB's fault and part the private community's fault—could be much better advocates for UAB to help facilitate a change."

McCrary insists that's starting to happen, although slowly. There's more informal communication between the business community and UAB's leadership—President Garrison, for instance, just spent a year as head of the regional chamber of commerce—and collaboration on Innovation Depot and several pharmaceutical ventures also has strengthened ties. "For so long, it was just, 'They're over there, we're over here,'" says McCrary. "But now we're saying, 'We need you,' and whenever you tell someone you need them, they say, 'Gee, yeah, you do need me, and I need you.'"

Critical Thinking

1. How is the economy of big cities like Birmingham and Philadelphia quite different today than a half century ago?

2. Why have cities turned their attention to "Eds and Meds?" How does the growth of Eds and Meds represent a shift in city economic development strategies, from the "smokestack" chasing of old to more contemporary "smart cities" policies?

3. Are all cities capable of attracting Eds and Meds?

Can They Save Youngstown?

Brentin Mock

One frequently asked question in Youngstown is: Who's responsible for cutting my neighbor's grass?

It's hard to imagine hearing this often in any city, but there it is on the "Frequently Asked Questions" page of Youngstown's official website, *cityofyoungstownoh.org.* The page provides the obvious answer: the owner. Concerning what to do if the owner refuses to landscape, Youngstown bluntly instructs: "Call the Police!"

The city council recently raised this "infraction" to a misdemeanor 3—a classification shared by prostitution in Ohio. Youngstown absolutely won't tolerate grass growth. Actually, the city hasn't welcomed growth in general since the '50s, when it began hemorrhaging residents at an average population decline of 16 percent annually, from over 170,000 to 73,817 today. Youngstown is a shrinking city, a municipality of arrested or regressive development, both in financial and demographic terms. Most cities in this predicament hunker down, then spend big on casinos, sports stadiums, convention centers, hotels and nightclubs to attract new residents. The success rate for this model is unpromising, however, especially for smaller cities that will never compete with large metropolises.

Youngstown's plan is to embrace stunted growth. The "shrinking city model," as it's called, reasons that a city suffering post-industrial blues and losing residents by the thousands won't suddenly charm people back by way of huge commercial bells and blockbuster whistles. Instead, the shrunk city demolishes blocks, converting its abandoned buildings and houses into open space for neighborhood enterprises and to nurture greenery. The method is fashionably known in Europe as "unbuilding the city," finding purposes for the "terrain vague"—unused land and property—other than habitation, profit or attraction.

So far, only Eastern Europe has successfully enacted these "smart decline" plans, reducing dozens of cities where deindustrialization had taken hold in the aftermath of World War II. In Germany, cities such as Halle and Leipzig have effectively worked their shrinkage into sustainability in the years following the dismantling of the Berlin Wall. Old mills, factories and abandoned homes were put to creative use by the few residents left behind.

It's a bit like telling a bald guy to shelve the Rogaine and the fancy toupees, and work instead with the little bit of hair he has. Youngstown is by no means the only U.S. city that's balding. Virtually any city in Ohio, Pennsylvania and West Virginia that relied on steel production in the 20th century now struggles with the loss of its assets and former status. Unlike many of these cities, Youngstown is owning its population deficit. Through its "Youngstown 2010" plan, led by Mayor Jay Williams, the city plans to remain competitive by investing in 127 small neighborhoods throughout the region.

Virtually any city in Ohio, Pennsylvania and West Virginia that relied on steel production in the 20th century now struggles with the loss of its assets and former status.

But how exactly does a city sustain itself while shrinking? By 2030, a population of 73,000 will become 54,000, which will eventually become 20,000—and then what? Size may not matter, but density does, especially to solidify a tax base that can support schools and media. Is Youngstown sealing its fate by shrinking out of existence?

A Plan Hatched by Town And Gown

The name, "Youngstown 2010," shouldn't be confused with projected development goals, since none exist (at least none to be met by 2010). The year refers instead to census markers. "We don't know how long this process will take," says Phil Kidd, the city's downtown events director and founder of Defend Youngstown, a self-described "movement dedicated to the advancement of the city of Youngstown" with a popular local Web site. "The implementation stage does not have a timeline. In 2010, we'll stop and ask what's working and what's not working."

William D'Avignon, the city's deputy director of planning, adds, "We're not saying everything we want to carry out will be completed by 2010, but we're going to plan for anything that's achievable by 2010."

The idea of shrinking first occurred to Youngstown after closing out the 20th century with three consecutive decades of decline. On Sept. 19, 1977, "Black Monday," the Sheet and Tube steel company closed doors on its mills, triggering the eventual closure of the rest of Youngstown's steel industry. As population withered so did the housing stock, from over 50,000 units built before 1950 to just over 37,000 today. White flight reduced that demographic from two-thirds of the city in 1980 to less than half today; the black population rose from one-third in 1980 to 45 percent today. And if the 4,213 Hispanic and Latino-American population seems minute, bear in mind that that number is 200 percent higher than in 1990.

In the infant years of the new millennium, the city realized it urgently needed a new vision. Jay Williams was working as the city's director of community development in 2001 when the planning department sought out the expertise of Youngstown State University (YSU), the leading employer for the city and Williams's alma mater. YSU had plans in mind for its own growth, but ended up nurturing a rehabilitative partnership with the city. Williams, along with D'Avignon and Anthony Kobak, the current chief city planner, teamed with YSU academics piqued by the research of new urbanists such as Stephen Graham and Ann Markusen. Youngstown came to recognize itself, in the words of Markusen's theoretical work, not as a "sticky" place—an urban center that continuously draws people (Los Angeles, Atlanta, New York City)—but as "slippery"—one where it's easy for, say, a YSU student to slip into the city, and then slip out due to lack of jobs or housing.

"Our right-sizing plan came out of talks we were having internally acknowledging that although our population wouldn't be going back to the hundreds of thousands, but that smaller didn't mean inferior," says Mayor Williams. "The question we asked was, because we were once so much larger how can we take the remnants of what made us large and build upon that?"

The planning team began to consider a counterintuitive approach to development: rather than grow the city, it should clean and "green" up the unoccupied real estate. They conceived and presented a basic "right-sizing" formula to the Youngstown public, who fleshed out the plan with their ideas and expectations. Or, depending on whom you ask, the planners consulted the public first and then drew up a blueprint for Youngstown 2010.

No matter its genesis, the eventual plan reflected three years of public surveys and town hall meetings aimed at understanding the city's needs. "Overwhelmingly, people said they wanted the city shrunken, and they were for cleaning up the blighted situations that were causing different variations of decay, crime and abandonment," Kidd says. Thousands of citizens were consulted, and hundreds of students and professionals logged the process. The plan went into high gear after Williams was elected mayor in 2005. At 34, he was the youngest mayor Youngstown ever elected, and also the first African American—two identity aspects that resonated with college students and the emerging black majority.

The Antidote to Racism

"He's kind of like the Barack Obama of Youngstown," says Rev. Michael Harrison, pastor of Union Baptist Church in the Northside. "I was pretty skeptical of the 2010 plan in the beginning, only because I did not fully understand it. Once the mayor explained it to a group of us pastors, whom he brought together, and showed us exactly how we all could benefit, I bought it hook, line and sinker."

Like Obama, Williams comes across as a figure whose blackness alone is the presumed antidote to racism. As Kobak says, "A lot of people use Jay Williams's getting elected as mayor as a symbolic gesture of moving on, given our history of racial tension."

African-American steelworkers in Youngstown and Western Pennsylvania have historically struggled with discrimination at least as far back as the late 1910s, when white labor unions went on strike against the steel companies. African Americans who were bussed in at that time were seen as scabs, although from their perspective, they were just taking advantage of previously unavailable opportunities.

Hostility toward African-American steelworkers has remained entrenched ever since. They have worked the least desirable and most dangerous jobs for the least amount of pay and lowest chance for promotion. Not until 1974, when the U.S. Department of Labor enforced a federal consent decree on companies practicing racial discrimination, did working conditions for African Americans begin to improve. But Black Monday arrived three years later, rendering the law moot by leaving scores of black men unemployed. Notoriously racist banks refused African Americans home loans, which left neighborhoods segregated all the way through the 20th century.

Ironically, Williams came from the banking industry before he began working for the city. "I started off as a young loan officer and making sure people weren't signing up with fly-by-night loan predators," says Mayor Williams. "I also spent time going out to neighborhood churches and community organizations to do outreach emphasizing the importance of working with local financial institutions and preparing themselves from a credit standpoint. I told the banks they have an obligation to lend on fair terms. But ultimately we were out there in the community educating the people as well. To this day, I still have people who will walk up to me with tears in their eyes talking about when they got their first home loan."

The Youngstown 2010 plan lists improving residents' quality of life as one of its "major vision principles" (its goals), a component aim of which is to "begin dealing with difficult issues such as public safety and racism." The two often go discomfortingly hand-in-hand. To tackle crime, as one of his first acts, Mayor Williams increased the budget for demolitions of abandoned buildings, understood to be havens for criminals. Race is trickier, however, especially when it's inextricably linked to labor and class. Kobak says the city has produced three television shows based on town hall meetings that address issues of race. But eliminating racism won't be as easy as identifying buildings to tear down—longstanding ideas about race and class can't simply be demolished and erased.

It's acknowledged across the board that when cities shrink, the neighborhoods that end up most expendable are typically low-income and often predominantly African- or Latino-American communities. Kobak says these issues need not be seen as black-and-white—"People make them such."

"What we're trying to do is bring people from all walks of life toward a common cause," says Kobak. "We want to remove all the racial issues and bring the city to the forefront by suggesting that these are neighborhood issues, not black-and-white issues." So far, the consensus approach seems to have worked. Rev. Harrison, who's black, says African Americans have been granted "equal opportunity and access" in the new plan, while Kidd says race hasn't been a "major issue."

Cities Shrink, But Problems Grow

Inevitably, unforeseen problems will impinge on Youngstown's plan. For example, another labor conflict—this one not racially loaded—played out as recently as 2004, when the staff of the daily newspaper *Vindicator* went on strike for improved wages. One thing Youngstown possibly overlooked is that as the city shrinks, so does the circulation, subscription, advertising and revenue base for local media. City hall may not have been concerned with drawing people from other cities for growth, but the *Vindicator* was. With a depleted staff, but a mandate to continue publishing, the independent, family-owned *Vindicator* began recruiting journalists from as far away as New Orleans—while the strike was still in effect.

Another problem with shrinking is that fewer competing investors increases the chance for one or a small few to buy up more than a fair share of property—as is the case with downtown Youngstown, where Louis A. Frangos, the single largest property owner, occasionally poses a problem for those trying to preserve the city.

Among the many bank and realty office buildings he owns is the Stambaugh building, a 13-story structure of 531 windows, some of which had been crashing to the sidewalk. Frangos initially proposed getting rid of the building, calling it a "lost cause." The building, however, has historic preservation status. When Frangos suggested replacing the broken windows with unsightly plywood, the city's elite balked: a letter signed by 17 "prominent players" asked the mayor to have Frangos take better care of his buildings. The letter referred to his properties as "a real-life Monopoly game that is occurring in our downtown."

"By no means do we think we have it all figured out," says Kidd. "We all want to clean and green our city so that at some point we can be positioned for growth again, but right now we just have to clean up the house."

Small Town Business

At the same time that the city prepares to shrink, the mayor and his planners are eyeballing potential growth through regional partnerships, including the neighboring municipalities of Austintown, Boardman, Camfield, Campbell and Struthers. Youngstown wants to establish a joint economic development district (JEDD) plan encompassing the Mahoning River Corridor. In the proposed arrangement, the suburban townships will depend on Youngstown's water supply, and residents who work in the city will pay an income tax directed to business expansion efforts.

Youngstown expects the JEDD to produce some 3,750 jobs and $439 million in revenue over the next 20 years. The only problem is that suburbanites aren't interested in financing Youngstown's growth with their own income and water taxes. Some municipalities have retained lawyers specifically trained in JEDD policies to protect themselves from the plan.

For now, though, the principal growth efforts are community empowerment groups. Six neighborhoods, including Wick Park, which Kidd calls home, have been targeted for investment. In concert with the city and YSU, community organizations from each will establish their own development goals, to be executed by volunteer residents and reinforced by the city. Successfully implemented plans will serve as templates for other neighborhoods, as well as for future city-community governance. "A lot of people in this city are used to taking orders through a chain of command," says Kidd. "In this instance, it's a 50-50 partnership between the communities and the city."

The downtown central business district is also being revived. Under the Youngstown Business Incubator program, start-up knowledge- and technology-based companies are nestled under one roof and assisted by federal grants. The one major requirement for inclusion is that the start-ups exchange notes so that they can build as a cluster. One company from this program, Turning Technologies, has already taken off, voted the top software company in the country last year by *Ir. Magazine*.

After two failed attempts, Youngstown also finally won the National Planning Excellence Award for Public Outreach last year, awarded by the American Planning Association. The lesson, apparently, is that sometimes you have to shrink.

Critical Thinking

1. What factors led to the long-term decline of cities like Youngstown?

2. How does Youngstown's "shrinking cities" model represent a bold attempt to re-imagine the city and to reposition itself for a better future?

3. What, if anything, can be done to reverse the decline of former industrial cities? What specific policies or actions do you suggest?

Return to Center

**States that moved offices and jobs out to
the suburbs are moving them back downtown.**

CHRISTOPHER D. RINGWALD

Last spring, New York's Department of Environmental Conservation moved back where it started out: downtown Albany. After 30 years in a headquarters just off Interstate 87, in the suburb of Colonie, the agency and its 1,900 employees packed up and relocated to 625 Broadway, a few blocks from the state capitol.

Not every employee is happy—most had grown accustomed to off-ramp freeway access, massive parking lots and other accoutrements of a suburban location. On the other hand, there are compensations. "I like having sidewalks to walk on," says Franz Litz, a DEC attorney, standing outside his new 14-story office building after strolling back from lunch at a nearby restaurant. "I can walk to some meetings," says one of his colleagues. "Before, I used to have to drive to all of them."

Whether they approve of it or not, however, the return to downtown Albany is a change that thousands of New York State employees will need to get used to. The DEC is only one of the agencies involved. The state's Dormitory Authority, which finances and constructs major public facilities, has moved to a five-story glass-and-granite box at 515 Broadway, down the street from DEC. The state Comptroller's office is consolidating its workforce a few blocks away. In the past five years, more than 4,500 state employees have relocated into the city's center.

None of this is a coincidence. New York's General Services Commissioner, Kenneth Ringler, puts it succinctly. "The governor," he says, "has a downtown policy."

This is not the first time that major efforts have been launched to rescue downtown Albany. During the 1960s and 1970s, Governor Nelson Rockefeller—with the strong support of Democratic Mayor Erastus Corning II—cleared 80 acres in the center of the city and built the Empire State Plaza, nine giant buildings arrayed on a marble mall with vast reflecting pools. Grandiose, windswept and impersonal, the project has always generated more critics than admirers. Still, it did serve the purpose of concentrating thousands of state workers in the vicinity of the capitol.

But as the workforce ballooned in the 1980s, little effort was made to accommodate the new growth in the center of the city. Many agencies located in the suburbs. By the early 1990s, downtown Albany was again forlorn, Empire State Plaza notwithstanding. The new governor, George Pataki, decided it was time to try again.

That in itself might seem a little surprising. Pataki did not come into office with a reputation as an urbanist—all of his prior experience had been in Peekskill, a small village in northern Westchester County, where he was mayor and served as a state legislator. But Peekskill underwent its own miniature revival in the 1990s as artists from New York were enticed by cheap studio space and old houses.

This hometown experience had its effect on Pataki. In 1998, he proposed and the legislature approved a $240 million "Albany plan," built around returning the central city to its former role as the nerve center of state government. "By moving state facilities into downtown areas and neighborhoods," Pataki said, "we can revitalize the cities that are so important to the state, and particularly the city of Albany. We are committed to Albany being not just the capital, but being a revitalized capital."

The Pataki administration is trying not to repeat the mistakes of the previous era. "It is important how we locate in downtowns," Ringler says, "and not just that we do so." Instead of bulldozing vast sections of town to build a massive complex, the state has built at modest scale at various locations within the existing downtown grid. The buildings line up along the sidewalk; the new architecture blends reasonably well with historic appearances.

No state government is currently attempting anything as ambitious as New York's, but a surprising number of them have a similar idea. In New Jersey, where much of the state workforce moved to leased suburban space during the 1980s, the departments of Human Services and Education have both moved back to downtown Trenton. Former Governor Christine Todd Whitman halted construction of a Revenue Division building in suburban Hamilton Township "because it was going to move jobs out of the city," according to Robert Runciano, the state's former director of Property Management and Construction.

Two years ago, Kentucky was ready to build a new office for its Transportation Cabinet. Many state legislators favored moving it out of the capital area in central Frankfort. The business community wanted to keep it there. Business won. Construction started last month on the new Transportation center, a five-story, $113 million downtown building that will house several hundred workers. "The construction of it has spurred a lot of other developments, new water and sewer lines and also private development," says Don Speer, commissioner of the state Department of Administration. Meanwhile, a nearby public-private project, the Sullivan Square Office Building, has consolidated state workers from scattered spots and attracted a graphics firm with 50 employees.

Alabama's capital, Montgomery, lost so many state offices to the suburbs that, as one visitor put it, the city presented the image "of these gleaming alabaster government buildings up on a hill and down below it was a desperate scene" of urban decay. It was the state pension fund for civil servants and teachers that turned the tide by building six prime office buildings, one of them 26 stories, to lease to state agencies along Commerce Street, in the heart of downtown, and on Dexter Avenue, which leads up to the capitol. "It stabilized a deteriorating and dying central business district," says Tommy Tyson, the city's director of planning. The influx of money and workers has generated new restaurants and led to the opening of two hotels.

The phenomenon exists in even the smallest state capitals. In Montpelier, Vermont (population 8,000), rented state offices on the outskirts are being moved to retrofitted state-owned buildings downtown. And a $10 million state office project is on the drawing board. "The policy is to invest in downtowns whenever renovating or building state office space," says Thomas Torti, Vermont's Building and General Services commissioner. "If you're coming to see the tax people, drop something off at motor vehicles and then check on personnel, those are all near each other now." The new facilities in Montpelier aim to stimulate other development through multi-use buildings with room for retail and commerce. A new state parking complex is slated to include offices and housing.

In New York's case, the Albany plan is more complicated than just a one-way return to the city. It is actually a game of musical buildings. While some agencies head back downtown, others are being shuffled around to take advantage of the space being vacated. The Transportation Department will occupy the offices that the Department of Environmental Protection has given up. The Depression-era Alfred E. Smith building, an ornate downtown landmark badly in need of renovation, is being fixed up to house workers coming in from the 350-acre Harriman campus, built in the 1960s on the outskirts of the city. The state has yet to decide whether the 16 Harriman buildings will be sold to private developers. By preliminary estimates, the plan could save at least $86 million in renovation costs and recoup millions more from sales.

Albany is not the only city in the area benefiting from the urban commitment. Across the Hudson, in tiny, blue-collar Rensselaer, the state's Office of Children and Family Services consolidated its workers, previously spread across various sites, into a renovated felt factory. Ten miles upriver in Troy, the state restored two historic structures and a defunct mall and moved

in more than 1,000 workers from the Health, Labor and Law departments. About 20 miles west, Schenectady, already home to the headquarters of the state lottery, is gaining 450 Department of Transportation workers and a new office building. In distant Buffalo, an old windshield wiper factory was remodeled to create 60,000 square feet of space for the New York State Office of Temporary Disability Assistance and other tenants. "The local mayors are ecstatic," says Ringler, the General Services administrator.

Not everyone is on board. Critics trace the Troy moves to log-rolling, saying that these came at the behest of Joseph Bruno, the Senate majority leader who represents Troy. Others challenge the deal between Pataki and Jerry Jennings, the Democratic mayor of Albany, that led to the ongoing $11 million reconstruction of Pearl Street, the city's downtown backbone.

And there are those who complain that the Albany Plan relies too heavily on the buildings themselves, rather than on the less tangible investments needed for urban recovery. "State workers are downtown, and that's more people downtown," says Paul Bray, a local planning and environmental attorney and founder of a monthly civic forum, the Albany Roundtable. "But building a city is a much more nuanced, complex thing than moving offices."

Bray wants the state to provide incentives for its employees to live downtown, as well as work there, so that the city's core no longer will empty out after the work day. Critics also say the money spent on construction of bulky parking garages for each new building—a feature demanded by public employee unions—could have been used for improved bus lines or other alternatives to the automobile. "Cities make poor suburbs," Bray says. "You really need to concentrate on mass transit more than parking garages."

In truth, no one can guarantee that the return of state government to any downtown will generate a local economic revival. The sidewalks of downtown Troy, a treasure-trove of 19th-century buildings, are busier since the civil servants began arriving in 1995. But Mayor Mark Pattison warns his counterparts in New York and elsewhere not to expect new government offices to work miracles. "They are not causing the economic boom that people thought they might," Pattison told a local newspaper reporter earlier this year. "The myth of the state worker is that they don't work hard. In fact, they have just a half-hour for lunch, and when they're done working, they go back home to the family and kids just like we all do. They bring a little bit of additional business but not quite the amount we expected."

Meanwhile, at the Stagecoach coffee and sandwich shop in downtown Albany, just across the park from the new Environmental Conservation building, a longtime employee concedes it is taking a while for the relocated workers to reorient themselves to city life. "It's been good for business, but not as great as we expected," she said last fall. "They complain because there's no mall to go to, they don't have enough shops to go to. A lot of them get an hour for lunch, and they don't know what to do with themselves."

But some of the restaurant's employees have been working longer hours since the Environmental Conservation building opened.

And a couple of blocks away, the owners of Lodge's, a small department store dating back to the 1800s, are renovating four long-empty storefronts for interested retail and commercial tenants.

Whatever the economic impact turns out to be, long-suffering downtown Albany seems convinced that the plan will have been worth the effort, and the cost—if only for reasons of simple logic. "It's the capital," says Chungchin Chen, executive director of the Capital District Regional Planning Commission. "The agencies are supposed to be there—instead of dispersed in the suburbs."

Critical Thinking

1. What actions have New York State, Kentucky, and Alabama taken in an effort to help reverse urban decline?

2. Go on the "web" (or find a good urban politics textbook) and look up "Dillon's Rule." What exactly is the constitutional position of cities, as Justice Dillon articulated in Dillon's Rule? Explain why, under Dillon's Rule, the actions of the states are so critical to the health of cities.

From *Governing,* April 2002, pp. 34–36. Copyright © 2002 by *Congressional Quarterly,* Inc. Reprinted by permission.

Predatory Lending: Redlining in Reverse

GREGORY D. SQUIRES

The proverbial American dream of owning a home has become an all-too-real nightmare for a growing number of families. Take the case of Florence McKnight, an 84-year-old Rochester widow who, while heavily sedated in a hospital bed, signed a $50,000 loan secured by her home for only $10,000 in new windows and other home repairs. The terms of the loan called for $72,000 in payments over 15 years, after which she would still owe a $40,000 one-time payment. Her home is now in foreclosure.

Unfortunately, this is not an isolated incident. Predatory lending has emerged as the most salient public policy issue in financial services today. If progress has been made to increase access to capital for racial minorities, low-income families and economically distressed communities, that progress has always come with great struggle. And it appears there are few, if any, permanent victories. The emergence of predatory lending practices demonstrates that the struggle against redlining has not been won, but has simply taken some new turns.

After decades of redlining practices that starved many urban communities for credit and denied loans to racial minorities, today a growing number of financial institutions are flooding these same markets with exploitative loan products that drain residents of their wealth. Such "reverse redlining" may be as problematic for minority families and older urban neighborhoods as has been the withdrawal of conventional financial services. Instead of contributing to homeownership and community development, predatory lending practices strip the equity homeowners have struggled to build and deplete the wealth of those communities for the enrichment of distant financial services firms.

There are no precise quantitative estimates of the extent of predatory lending. But the growth of subprime lending (higher cost loans to borrowers with blemishes on their credit records) in recent years, coupled with growing law enforcement activity in this area, clearly indicates a surge in a range of exploitative practices. Not all subprime loans are predatory, but virtually all predatory loans are subprime. Some subprime loans certainly benefit high-risk borrowers who would not qualify for conventional, prime loans. Predatory loans, however, charge higher rates and fees than warranted by the risk, trapping homeowners in unaffordable debt and often costing them their homes and life savings. Examples of predatory practices include:

- Balloon payments that require borrowers to pay off the entire balance of a loan by making a substantial payment after a period of time during which they have been making regular monthly payments;
- Required single premium credit life insurance, where the borrower must pay the entire annual premium at the beginning of the policy period rather than in monthly or quarterly payments. (With this cost folded into the loan, the total costs, including interest payments, are higher throughout the life of the loan);
- Homeowners insurance where the lender requires the borrower to pay for a policy selected by the lender;
- High pre-payment penalties that trap borrowers in the loans;
- Fees for services that may or may not actually be provided;
- Loans based on the value of the property with no regard for the borrower's ability to make payments;
- Loan flipping, whereby lenders use deceptive and high-pressure tactics resulting in the frequent refinancing of loans with additional fees added each time;
- Negatively amortized loans and loans for more than the value of the home, which result in the borrower owing more money at the end of the loan period than when they started making payments.

Here are some numbers to illustrate the extent of the problem: The Joint Center for Housing Studies at Harvard University reported that mortgage companies specializing in subprime loans increased their share of home purchase mortgage loans from 1 to 13 percent between 1993 and 2000. Economists at the Office of Federal Housing Enterprise Oversight found that subprime loans are concentrated in neighborhoods with high unemployment rates and declining housing values. Almost 20 percent of refinance loans to borrowers earning less than 60 percent of area median income in 2002 were made by subprime lenders, compared to just over 7 percent for borrowers earning 120 percent of median income or higher, according to research by the Association of Community Organizations for Reform Now (ACORN). The Center for Community Change reported that African Americans are three times as likely as whites to finance their homes with subprime loans; this is true even between upper-income blacks and whites. The Joint Center for Housing Studies has also revealed that race continues to be a factor in the distribution of subprime loans after other individual and neighborhood factors are taken into consideration.

One cost of the sudden increase in subprime lending has been an increase in foreclosure rates. According to the Joint Center for Housing Studies, borrowers with subprime loans are eight times more likely to default than those with prime conventional loans. Yet, it has been estimated that between 30 and 50 percent of those receiving subprime loans would, in fact, qualify for prime loans.

Ironically, some of the steps taken to increase access to credit for traditionally underserved communities have inadvertently created incentives for predatory lending. The Community Reinvestment Act of 1977, which banned redlining by federally chartered banks and savings institutions, provided incentives for lenders to serve minority and low-income areas. So did the Fair Housing Act of 1968, which prohibited racial discrimination in home financing. FHA insurance and securitization of loans (lenders sell loans to the secondary mortgage market, which packages them into securities to sell to investors) reduce the risk to lenders and increase the capital available for mortgage lending. In addition, the federal government established affordable housing goals for the two major secondary mortgage market actors, Fannie Mae and Freddie Mac. Fifty percent of the mortgages they buy must be for low- and moderate-income households.

All these actions have increased access to capital, but sometimes by predatory lenders. Wall Street has become a major player by securitizing subprime loans. The involvement of investment banks in subprime lending grew from $18.5 billion in 1997 to $56 billion in 2000.

With passage of the Financial Services Modernization Act of 1999, the consolidation of financial services providers received the blessing of the federal government. Between 1970 and 1997 the number of banks in the U.S. dropped from just under 20,000 to 9,100, primarily as a result of mergers among healthy institutions. The 1999 Act removed many post Depression-era laws that had provided for greater separation of the worlds of banking, insurance and securities. Subsequent to this "reform," it became far easier for financial service providers to enter each of these lines of business. One result is that commercial banks and savings institutions, which used to make the vast majority of mortgage loans, now make about a third of them. Mortgage banking affiliates of depository institutions, independent mortgage banks, insurance companies and other institutions that are not regulated by the federal government, including predatory lenders, have become a far bigger part of this market.

A critical implication of deregulation is the declining influence of the Community Reinvestment Act. In conjunction with the Fair Housing Act and other fair lending initiatives, the CRA is credited with generating more than $1 trillion in new investment for low- and moderate-income neighborhoods and for increasing the share of loans going to economically distressed and minority markets. Concentration and consolidation among financial institutions that had taken place for years—trends that were exacerbated by the 1999 Act—reduced the impact of CRA by making it easier for many financial institutions that are not covered by the 1977 law to enter the mortgage market. The share of mortgage loans subject to intensive review under the CRA dropped from 36.1 percent to 29.5 percent between 1993 and 2000. And the share of loans going to low-income and minority markets declined in 2001 after steadily increasing throughout the 1990s.

But these are not the last words in this debate. In many ways, community-based organizations, fair housing groups and elected officials are responding to these developments and the predatory practices that have proliferated.

Reactions to Predatory Lending

Public officials, prodded by aggressive community organizing, have proposed many regulatory and legislative changes. As of the beginning of 2004, at least 25 states and 11 localities, along with the District of Columbia, had passed laws addressing predatory lending. These proposals call for limits on fees, prepayment penalties and balloon payments; restrictions on practices that lead to loan flipping; and prohibitions against loans that do not take into consideration borrowers' ability to repay. They provide for additional disclosures to consumers of the risks of high cost loans and of their right to credit counseling and other consumer protections.

In 2000, the Office of the Comptroller of the Currency reached a $300 million settlement with Providian National Bank in California to compensate consumers hurt by its unfair and deceptive lending practices. Later that year, Household International reached a $484 million agreement with a group of state attorneys general in which it agreed to many changes in its consumer loan practices. Household agreed to cap its fees and points, to provide more disclosure of loan terms and to provide for an independent monitor to assure compliance with the agreement. Household also negotiated a $72 million agreement with ACORN for interest rate reductions, waivers of unpaid late charges, loan principal reductions and other initiatives to help families avoid foreclosure.

In response to information provided and pressure exerted by consumer groups, the Federal Trade Commission (FTC) took enforcement action against 19 lenders and brokers for predatory practices in 2002 and negotiated the largest consumer protection settlement in FTC history with Citigroup. The company agreed to pay $215 million to resolve charges against its subsidiary, The Associates, for various deceptive and abusive practices. The suit was aimed primarily at unnecessary credit insurance products The Associates packed into many of its subprime loans.

A number of nonprofits have developed programs to help victims of predatory lending to refinance loans on more equitable terms that serve the financial interests of the borrowers. Many lenders, often in partnership with community-based groups, have launched educational and counseling programs to steer consumers away from predatory loans.

But progress cannot be assumed. Three federal financial regulatory agencies (Comptroller of the Currency, National Credit

Union Administration, and Office of Thrift Supervision) have issued opinions that federal laws preempt some state predatory lending laws for lenders they regulate. In communities where anti-predatory lending laws have been proposed, lobbyists for financial institutions have introduced state level bills to preempt or nullify local ordinances or to weaken consumer protections. Legislation has also been introduced in Congress to preempt state efforts to combat predatory lending. Preliminary research on the North Carolina anti-predatory lending law—the first statewide ban—suggested that such restrictions reduced the supply and increased the cost of credit to low-income borrowers. Subsequent research, however, found that the law had the intended impact; there was a reduction in predatory loans but no change in access to or cost of credit for high-risk borrowers. Debate continues over the impact of such legislative initiatives. And the fight against redlining, in its traditional or "reverse" forms, remains an ongoing struggle.

The Road Ahead

The tools that have been used to combat redlining emerged in conflict. The Fair Housing Act was the product of a long civil rights movement and probably would not have been passed until several years later if not for the assassination of Martin Luther King Jr. that year. Passage of the CRA followed years of demonstrations at bank offices, the homes of bank presidents and elsewhere. And recent fights against predatory lending reflect the maturation of several national coalitions of community advocacy and fair housing groups that include ACORN, the National Community Reinvestment Coalition, the National

Training and Information Center, the National Fair Housing Alliance and others. As Frederick Douglass famously stated in 1857:

"If there is no struggle, there is no progress . . . Power concedes nothing without a demand. It never did, and it never will."

Homeownership remains the American dream, though for all too many it is a dream deferred. As Florence McKnight and many others have learned, it can truly become a family's worst nightmare. The unanswered question remains: for how long will the dream be denied?

Critical Thinking

1. What exactly is predatory lending? Give three or four clear examples of predatory lending practices.

2. Why was the Community Investment Act (CRA) passed in 1978? What are its major provisions?

3. What is deregulation? Who pushed for deregulation? How did deregulation reshape the banking and home mortgage industry?

4. Was it the regulations of the CRA or the policies of deregulation that led to the wave of bad loans and the flood of housing foreclosures that plagued communities in the United States during the early 2000s?

GREGORY D. SQUIRES chairs the Sociology Department at George Washington University and is editor of the book, *Why the Poor Pay More: How to Stop Predatory Lending.*

Bridge Blockade after Katrina Remains Divisive Issue

CHRIS KIRKHAM AND PAUL PURPURA

Two years later, anger creeps up in Kim Cantwell Sr. when he thinks about the Jefferson Parish deputy who aimed an assault rifle at his 22-year-old son's face, barring the family with five children in tow, some as young as 8 months old, from walking across the Crescent City Connection to their Algiers Point home in the days after Hurricane Katrina.

"I wonder to this day what was he thinking about?" Cantwell asked recently. "Did he even care? You bet I'm pissed. I bury it every day, but you bet I'm still pissed."

Three miles away in Gretna, Police Chief Arthur Lawson, one of three law enforcement leaders who sanctioned the blockade, makes no excuses for his actions.

"I don't second-guess this decision. I know I made it for the right reasons," said Lawson, referring to law enforcement's desire to prevent the looting and crime in New Orleans from spreading across the river. "I go to sleep every night with a clear conscience."

The two men have never met, but they represent opposite ends of one of the most controversial chapters of Katrina's aftermath: the decision to close the bridge to people, mostly African-Americans, trying to flee the chaos and flooding that engulfed New Orleans.

Not only did the blockade spawn state and federal investigations and five lawsuits targeting Gretna, its police force, Lawson, Jefferson Parish Sheriff Harry Lee and other law enforcement agencies, the episode vaulted the New Orleans area's historical struggle with race and class onto an international stage.

It seared images and stirred racial tensions as tales of white shotgun-toting cops and attack dogs keeping desperate African-Americans from entering the suburban West Bank community began circulating in the hectic days after the storm. But interviews with dozens of those involved, including Gretna officials speaking for the first time, paint a more nuanced picture of the blockade.

On one side are those who say Lawson, who is white, and other suburban police authorities placed more value on property than human life.

On the other are many Gretna residents, black and white, who firmly support law enforcement's decisions.

While they stand by their actions, leaders of the enclave of 17,000 residents—12 percent of whom are African-American, according to the 2000 census—say they welcomed many families flooded out of New Orleans since the storm. They are confident the court of law will correct judgments made about their city in the court of public opinion.

"Am I going to be stuck with the 'racist' legacy of what happened on the bridge?" asked Gretna Mayor Ronnie Harris, who is white. "Maybe so. Do I think it's fair? It's not. There's another chapter to be told, hopefully."

Evacuees Stream In

Versions of the story differ widely. Evacuees say they were turned back at gunpoint by unreasonable officers. West Bank officials talk about monumental miscommunication and strained resources.

In the eyes of Gretna police officials, the Jefferson Parish Sheriff's Office and other West Bank leaders, Gretna went into lockdown immediately after the storm. Armed officers and junk vehicles blocked major entrances into the city.

No one was allowed in without proof of residence, and those who remained in the city were urged to leave if they could.

But beginning Aug. 31, two days after the storm, a stream of evacuees started appearing at Gretna's city limits. Some had walked across the bridge to the Terry Parkway exit; some were brought in by Regional Transit Authority bus drivers desperately trying to ferry people out of the floodwaters.

Gretna officials said storm victims came to Terry Parkway because New Orleans police officers were blocking the exit ramps to General de Gaulle Drive, the first exit on the West Bank end of the bridge which is within the city limits of New Orleans. NOPD spokesman Sgt. Joe Narcisse said officers never blocked the ramps.

As hundreds and eventually thousands of evacuees collected beneath the West Bank Expressway across from Oakwood Center that day, Gretna officials said they had little food or water to offer.

So police and city workers broke into a Jefferson Parish bus barn and hotwired two buses later that afternoon. Another police officer owned a school bus. For more than 12 hours they brought the evacuees across the Huey P. Long Bridge to dry land on the east bank at Causeway Boulevard and Interstate 10 in Metairie, where a makeshift evacuation hub had been established.

Lawson and Harris estimate they evacuated close to 6,000 people, with the help of some Jefferson Parish sheriff's deputies. But the crowds continued to grow under the elevated expressway at Whitney Avenue on the West Bank, they said.

"It was getting to the point where we just couldn't physically continue to run the buses 24 hours a day evacuating people," Lawson said. "The more people we would move, the more were coming."

Waiting for Buses

On Aug. 31, Harris said he reached the governor's office and arranged a hasty, 2 A.M. meeting with the governor's husband, Raymond "Coach" Blanco, and Sam Jones, an aide to the governor. Lawson, Harris, Jefferson Parish Councilman Chris Roberts and other Gretna police officials were present.

At that time, West Bank officials said they were promised that hundreds of buses were coming to evacuate the Superdome and the Ernest N. Morial Convention Center.

In a recent interview, Jones said his recollection of the meeting was vague, but he believed buses naturally would have come up at some point.

"There were buses going in from the beginning, but it was a trickle," said Jones, now special assistant to the governor. "We were operating in the environment of a Mad Max movie. You were scrapping for every drop of gasoline, every set of wheels you could get. You sent them where you heard the screaming."

With the knowledge that buses were arriving, Lawson said he met soon after with the sheriff, who gave the thumbs up to the decision. On the morning of Sept. 1, Lawson and Sheriff's Office Deputy Chief Craig Taffaro met with the Crescent City Connection police and decided to block the bridge to pedestrians. Vehicles were allowed to cross.

Gretna police took the West Bank-bound lanes, the Sheriff's Office the east bank-bound lanes and the bridge police took the commuter lanes.

Around the same time, looters set fire to Oakwood mall.

"Whatever spin anyone puts on it, we do know in our hearts that it was the right thing to do," Taffaro said. "It made no sense to leave one deplorable area to come to another."

Meanwhile, close to 8,000 mostly white evacuees from St. Bernard Parish were being brought to Algiers from the Chalmette ferry landing via boats and barges. Buses were sent to Algiers to evacuate those storm victims, Jones said.

Gretna officials said they knew of that operation but discouraged state officials from directing the evacuees into their city for the same reasons they closed the bridge: They didn't have the resources to provide for them.

Eventually the buses came. But they went to New Orleans, not Gretna, West Bank law enforcement officials said.

Blocked from Their Home

The Cantwells, who are white, rode out the storm at a Canal Street hotel, and their car was trapped in a nearby parking garage. The hotel met their needs, but food and fuel for the generator ran low. They had to make a move, and after hearing a radio report of people walking across the bridge, they decided to go to their Delaronde Street home in Algiers Point, where they could get a car to leave the area.

They set out Sept. 1, 2005, about noon with their children among them. The youngest was 8 months old.

Carrying gear and pushing two baby strollers as they walked up the Camp Street off-ramp from the Pontchartrain Expressway, they encountered some New Orleans police officers and National Guardsmen, who offered them food and water. None told them they could not cross the bridge, Cantwell said.

Others were walking across the bridge to the West Bank too, he said. They snapped pictures of themselves, relieved and smiling because they were going to their home, Cantwell said.

They got no farther than the toll plaza, where the bridge meets the ground in Algiers. There, the Jefferson Parish deputy immediately called out through his car's loudspeaker, "You're not walking into this parish," Cantwell said, puzzled because they never planned to walk into Jefferson.

His son, Kim Cantwell Jr., then 22, tried to show the deputy his driver's license, with their Delaronde Street address. They pointed toward Algiers. It was for naught.

"Instead of talking to us, he pulled an M-16 and pointed it at my son's face," Cantwell said.

Turned back and escorted to the east bank by the deputy and a Crescent City Connection police officer, the Cantwells later trudged through waist-high water, holding the younger children and their gear above the waterline, as they walked to the Superdome, where they spent a harrowing night.

After standing in line for more than 13 hours, they boarded a bus the next evening that took them to Fort Worth, Texas.

Mixed Signals

When the blockade was brought to the public's attention, accusations began to fly about shotguns being fired over evacuees' heads and callous police officers turning away families and people in wheelchairs.

Lawson admits that one of his officers, who is black, fired a warning shot over his shoulder when a crowd started to threaten to throw him off the bridge.

Larry Bradshaw and Lorrie Beth Slonsky, two San Francisco paramedics in the city for a convention, said they were told to cross the bridge by New Orleans police stationed near Harrah's New Orleans Casino. They are white.

"I always think unless there's a compelling reason not to help somebody, that you help somebody in need," Bradshaw said recently. "It's part of the whole American frontier character, and it seemed like Gretna violated that."

The New Orleans Police Department has denied it ever officially directed evacuees over the bridge. However, Mayor Ray Nagin, in an "SOS" statement that was quoted by CNN, said to the thousands of people gathered at the Convention Center that "we are now allowing people to march. They will be marching up to the Crescent City Connection to the (West Bank-bound) expressway to find relief."

In a recent interview, Nagin said the statement was meant to heighten awareness of the problems at the Convention Center, not to encourage people to cross the bridge into Gretna. Even two years later, he referred to police on the bridge using "attack dogs and machine guns," rumors at the time that law enforcement officials vehemently deny.

"All the neighboring parishes—Plaquemines, St. Bernard— were bringing their people here. We were kind of the dropping-off point for all these places," Nagin said. "So for another neighboring parish to say 'no' was pretty unnerving."

Lawson said he has had no communication with New Orleans officials or the mayor's office since the storm. Harris, the Gretna mayor, had a brief conversation with Nagin about the bridge incident in January 2006 at a Louisiana Conference of Mayors meeting, after several unsuccessful attempts. He explained his reasoning to Nagin, who didn't accuse him or Lawson of racism. They haven't spoken since, Harris said.

Support and Scorn

In the weeks after Hurricane Katrina tore through stained-glass windows and flooded parts of his Gretna church, the Rev. Orin Grant's cell phone was abuzz with questions from congregants and longtime friends.

There were the usual concerns: How was his family? When would worship services begin? Then there were the news updates: "The power is back on in Gretna" . . . "Oh, and did you hear about the people on the bridge?"

Though he was in a Houston hotel, details of the bridge blockade flowed in. From the outset, Grant, who is black, quickly threw his support behind law enforcement.

"If I thought this was a negative racial incident, I would have spoken up," said Grant, pastor of St. Paul's Baptist Church in the city's largely African-American McDonoghville neighborhood. "I don't take sides; I take a stand."

Grant's opinion is not unusual among residents.

In the weeks and months after the storm, hundreds of yard signs supporting Lawson and city workers sprang up across town. The Gretna and Jefferson Parish councils passed resolutions supporting the decision, and Lawson was presented with an award for his services by the Jefferson Parish Martin Luther King Jr. Task Force this year.

"Arthur Lawson is our employee, we are his boss," said Joe Roppolo, a white businessman whose Gretna Sign Works printed up about 600 of the support signs. "No matter what the rest of the world thinks, he did what his constituents wanted him to do. So we should take the heat if anyone does."

Some resentment still lingers.

Percy Jupiter Jr., who is black, watched the evacuees stream over the bridge from the Fischer public housing development in Algiers.

"It looked like the New York marathon, except these people were running for their lives," said Jupiter, who now lives in Gretna. "The bottom line is that Gretna and Jefferson Parish thinks everyone across the river is a hoodlum. Gretna did not want them over here."

Others say the issue has largely faded as more pressing issues have come to the forefront. Rhonda Royal and her family saw the blockade, heard the warning shots and decided to turn around rather than approach the police on the bridge. Her home in eastern New Orleans was flooded, but she's since moved to Gretna.

"Some people might bring it up, but most are just trying to get on and rebuild what they've got," said Royal, who is black.

The Rev. Jesse Pate, pastor of Harvest Ripe Church in Gretna, still comes down on both sides of the debate two years later, but he understands the outrage that persists.

"You can look at it and say, 'It would have been chaotic, people would have looted houses.' It was just one of those crazy moments in time, that anything would have been acceptable," said Pate, who is black. "But during that time, (law enforcement) valued property over the lives of those people. And that's where the tragedy is."

Public Report Elusive

With five lawsuits and a criminal investigation in Orleans Parish looming, Gretna has largely borne the brunt of the fallout from the bridge incident.

"Our community has taken it on the chin at a national level," Harris said. "When civil order was breaking down, we did something about it. Yet when we take a common sense approach when buses are coming, we get our heads knocked in a PR battle."

State Attorney General Charles Foti completed an investigation and turned over his findings to both the Orleans Parish district attorney's office and the U.S. attorney's office in New Orleans a year ago.

Foti's office will not release the findings to the public. New Orleans District Attorney Eddie Jordan also declined to make the report public. In August 2006, Jordan's then-spokeswoman told The Times-Picayune that prosecutors were preparing to present the matter to a grand jury. The district attorney's current spokesman said last week nothing has been presented.

The American Civil Liberties Union and The Times-Picayune also have been spurned in their attempts to get the report released to the public.

"Because the investigation is still pending, my office is unable to provide you with information at this time," Jordan wrote Aug. 15 in rejecting the newspaper's request under the state's public records law.

The U.S. Justice Department, the FBI and the U.S. attorney's office in New Orleans also received Foti's report and monitored the case. The agencies have not found evidence sufficient to move forward with any criminal charges, U.S. Attorney Jim Letten said.

"It's not an active investigation at this time," Letten said.

But attorneys in five civil lawsuits are pressing ahead their query.

Of the lawsuits, filed on behalf of both black and white plaintiffs, one is pending in Orleans Parish Civil District Court. The other four are in U.S. District Court in New Orleans, all allotted to Judge Mary Ann Vial Lemmon, an appointee of President Clinton.

As chairman of the Local and Municipal Affairs Committee, state Sen. Cleo Fields, D-Baton Rouge, monitored the progress Foti's office made in its investigation of the blockade, presiding over a November 2005 hearing at which the attorney general testified on his query.

A month later, Fields' Baton Rouge law firm filed a lawsuit in federal court on behalf of a couple, followed by a second one filed on Aug. 29, 2006, which seeks class-action status.

The federal court cases allege that police violated an array of constitutional rights, including freedom to assemble, freedom from excessive search and seizure and the right to travel.

Most of the cases are still in early stages, although one is scheduled for trial in January.

But one substantive ruling could have reverberations in the other three federal cases.

On March 30, in a victory for Gretna and the Jefferson Parish Sheriff's Office, Lemmon dismissed in one case the claim that the police violated the right to travel—a claim made in other lawsuits.

She ruled that while people have "a fundamental right" to cross state lines, the U.S. Supreme Court has not ruled on the question of intrastate travel, or that within a state.

Gretna's attorney, Franz Zibilich, said at the time the ruling "gutted" the lawsuit. Fields, representing the plaintiffs in that case, said the intrastate travel argument was "a very small portion of the lawsuits."

The ruling also is expected to affect other cases, said attorney Dane Ciolino, a Loyola University law professor who is not involved in the litigation.

"The basis for the dismissal of the intrastate travel argument should also apply to all cases, given that in all cases the plaintiffs were traveling from one point in Louisiana to another," Ciolino said in an e-mail.

Despite Lemmon's ruling, attorney Julian Baudier of New Orleans has kept the right-to-travel argument alive in representing an Algiers family that was turned back by Gretna police and now is suing them.

"My argument was, how do you know where my people were going?" Baudier said, adding that his clients' interstate travel right could have been violated because they considered fleeing to Texas. They ended up in Baton Rouge, he said.

Of the four cases in federal court, two were brought by Algiers families trying to return to their homes from downtown New Orleans.

"If it brings a little more humanity to a future catastrophe, that wouldn't hurt my feelings," Cantwell said of his lawsuit. "If I don't get a nickel out of this, maybe that cop, he'll think a little better."

Other than a general description—"a middle-aged guy with salt and pepper hair and a mustache"—they still do not know the deputy's name.

Despite his anger, Cantwell said he has tried to move on with his life.

"What happened happened," he said. "You can't relive bad parts of your life every day. That's like quicksand. It's going to suck you down."

Critical Thinking

1. What exactly happened at the bridge connecting New Orleans to Gretna?

2. Is urban growth and decline purely the result of a free market and free choice? Are all people in the metropolis free to move to wherever they want, depending on their income and buying power? What do you think the incident at Gretna bridge reveals?

UNIT 2

Gentrification, Globalization and the City

Unit Selections

Learning Outcomes

After reading this unit, you should be able to:

- Explain how immigration actually has been a quite positive factor in the contributing to the economic health of many neighborhoods and cities.

- Formulate what you think is "wise" immigration policy as opposed to an unwise immigration policy, as judged in terms of the impacts that immigration has on the population and economic stability of cities.

- Identify the various aspects of globalization.

- Distinguish between a "global city" and cities that have fewer of the characteristics associated with global cities; explain why not every city is able to adapt to a changing economy by becoming a successful global city.

- Explain how intercity and global competition affects local economies and serves to constrain the policy choices of city leaders.

- Evaluate Richard Florida's "creative class" theory as to what are the critical factors that make an economically healthy city.

- Evaluate how gentrification is changing numerous inner-city neighborhoods, pointing both to the benefits and to the costs of gentrification.

- Formulate possible policies by which a city can reduce some of the more harmful impacts of gentrification.

Student Website

www.mhhe.com/cls

Internet References

Creative Class
http://creativeclass.com
Gentrification Web
http://members.lycos.co.uk/gentrification
Gotham Gazette
www.gothamgazette.com/city
Great Cities Institute, at the University of Illinois-Chicago
http://uic.edu/cuppa/gci/index.shtml
National Immigration Forum
www.immigrationforum.org
Urban Institute
www.urban.org

Cities exist on a global stage. Continuing advances in transportation, computerization, and telecommunications have served to diminish the importance of a city's borders. In a **global age,** cities are influenced by events, decisions, and forces from beyond local borders, even from overseas.

Extensive new immigration is helping to change the face of U.S. cities. Today, the **new immigration** comes to the U.S. from parts of the world—East Asia, South Asia, Africa, and Latin America (especially from Mexico) quite different from the earlier age of immigration that came from Europe. Critics argue that the new arrivals compete with other poor residents for low-wage jobs. The critics further point to the burdens that the immigrants place on state and local authorities, adding to the costs of schooling, policing, and public welfare services. Yet, the defenders of immigration counter that immigrants contribute to the local economy, paying taxes and assuming physically demanding jobs that other Americans refuse to take. Immigration has added to the vitality of inner-city areas neighborhoods that would have suffered extensive housing abandonment and advanced social decay were it not for the presence of the new arrivals. In New York, Los Angeles, Chicago, Dallas, Miami, and San Francisco, **immigrant entrepreneurs** have contributed to the local economy, bringing new life to communities that were once considered beyond hope (Article 7, "Movers & Shakers: How Immigrants Are Reviving Neighborhoods Given up for Dead").

Immigration is one aspect of the **globalization** process. The most successful global cities are centers of international corporate headquarters, banks, and financial firms, with the financial and administrative decisions made in these locations having an impact on investment in cities around the world. New York, London, and Tokyo have such a dense concentration of international firms that the three are generally recognize as occupying the top tier of the **global cities hierarchy.** Other cities exhibit various degrees of globalization, including a diversity of people, ideas, and cultures that add to a city's vibrancy (Article 8, "Swoons over Miami").

Globalization has also heightened intercity **competition,** which has increasingly become international in scope. National and local leaders feel that they are in competition with one another for multinational businesses that can choose to locate their headquarters and production facilities in any one of the number of cities around the globe. With advances in digital communications and transportation, U.S. cities face increasing competition from cities like Bangalore, the center of the computer and information technology in India. Increasingly, corporation firms that are located in the United States are able to **outsource** data-processing and other back office and support jobs to low-wage sites overseas. However, Bangalore, Hyderabad, and other cities in India are finding that they, too, are facing new competition from cities in Russia, Eastern Europe, and China (Article 9, "Outsourcing: Beyond Bangalore"). While the competitive pressures facing American cities are increasingly intense, many firms also face problems in shifting production and support services overseas. Not every firm finds it easy to leave U.S. cities for the promise of cost savings elsewhere.

© Hisham F. Ibrahim/Getty Images

Lowering costs and taxes are not the only strategies that a city can use to attract businesses. Economist Richard Florida argues that corporate headquarters, financial business, and technology-oriented firms will be especially attracted to those cities that can provide the talented, educated, and innovative work force critical to a business' success. According to Professor Florida, cities cannot rely solely on offering tax breaks and other subsidies to businesses; as such concessions are easily matched by competitor cities. Instead, in books such as *The Rise of the Creative Class* and *Who's Your City?,* Professor Florida argues that cities will be successful in attracting top-end businesses if they first succeed in attracting the **creative class**—the young, talented, and entrepreneurial professionals that world class firms desire (Article 10, "The Rise of the Creative Class").

Should a city dedicate itself to supporting those amenities (neighborhoods with sidewalk cafes) and lifestyle activities (building paths for biking and opening up a city's rivers to canoeing) desired by members of the creative class? Do such investments represent the best possible use of city resources? Not all Urbanists agree. Some argue that an investment in "cool cities" may have only a minimal payoff. A city, instead, should focus its investments on improved trash collection, public safety and public schools, the provision of **basic public services** that serve to make cities attractive to working- and middle-class families as well as corporate leaders (Article 11, "Too Much Froth"). Other critics worry that by facilitating neighborhood upgrading and *gentrification,* city actions may set in motion a rise in land values that ultimately wind up "pushing out" the urban poor.

Gentrification or the resettlement and upgrading of once-declining inner-city neighborhoods occurs when young professionals place new value on city living, on being close to the jobs and night life of the city. The arrival of new home buyers, the rehabilitation of older homes, the tearing-down and replacement of older structures, and the conversion of apartments to condominiums, however, often lead to the **displacement** of lower-income (often racial minority) residents who are pushed out of their neighborhoods undergoing change. Neighborhoods are upgraded, and the city is made more attractive to business. But the result is also a heightening of **urban dualism,** where the affluent live good lives but share the city with poor people living on the margins, who gain little from the new prosperity. Even traditional centers of African-American life, like New York's Harlem, are undergoing change, as both black and white upscale homeowners seek to buy into city neighborhoods with solid housing structures, historical character, and ethnic diversity.

Some studies, however, point to the benefits that neighborhood upgrading can bring the poor who now have a better choice of stores, who live in safer neighborhoods that receive a higher level of public services, and who now have new channels or paths to employment (Article 12, "Studies: Gentrification a Boost for Everyone").

Critics, however, respond that such an assessment overstates the benefits that neighborhood upgrading brings to poorer residents, especially families who must cope with the burden of paying higher rents in an area that is suddenly attractive. Gentrification does little to improve the lives of the poor who must move out of a neighborhood that is being transformed. Gentrification also often does little to improve a neighborhood's public schools, as gentrifiers often choose to send their children to private schools or simply decide to move to the suburbs when their children reach school age.

Globalization and gentrification point to the continuing evolution of the city. But these processes also raise important questions: Just whom do cities serve? Who has a right to the city?

Movers & Shakers

How Immigrants Are Reviving Neighborhoods Given up for Dead

JOEL KOTKIN

For decades the industrial area just east of downtown Los Angeles was an economic wreck, a 15-square-block area inhabited largely by pre–World War II derelict buildings. Yet now the area comes to life every morning, full of talk of toys in various South China dialects, in Vietnamese, in Korean, in Farsi, in Spanish, and in the myriad other commercial languages of the central city.

The district now known as Toytown represents a remarkable turnaround of the kind of archaic industrial area that has fallen into disuse all across the country. A combination of largely immigrant entrepreneurship and the fostering of a specialized commercial district has created a bustling marketplace that employs over 4,000 people, boasts revenues estimated at roughly $500 million a year, and controls the distribution of roughly 60 percent of the $12 billion in toys sold to American retailers.

"In December we have about the worst traffic problem in downtown," proudly asserts Charlie Woo, a 47-year-old immigrant who arrived in 1968 from Hong Kong and is widely considered the district's founding father. During the holiday season, thousands of retail customers, mostly Latino, come down to the district seeking cut-rate toys, dolls, and action figures, including dubious knockoffs of better-known brands. For much of the rest of the year, the district sustains itself as a global wholesale center for customers from Latin America and Mexico, which represent nearly half the area's shipments, as well as buyers from throughout the United States.

Few in L.A.'s business world, City Hall, or the Community Redevelopment Agency paid much attention when Woo started his family's first toy wholesaling business in 1979. "When Toytown started, the CRA didn't even know about it," recalls Don Spivack, now the agency's deputy administrator. "It happened on its own. It was a dead warehouse district."

How dead? Dave Zoraster, an appraiser at CB Richard Ellis, estimates that in the mid-1970s land values in the area—then known only as Central City East—stood at $2.75 a square foot, a fraction of the over $100 a square foot the same property commands today. Vacancy rates, now in the single digits, then hovered at around 50 percent. For the most part, Spivack recalls, development officials saw the district as a convenient place to cluster the low-income, largely transient population a safe distance from the city's new sparkling high-rises nearby.

To Charlie Woo, then working on a Ph.D. in physics at UCLA, the low land costs in the area presented an enormous opportunity. Purchasing his first building for a mere $140,000, Woo saw the downtown location as a cheap central locale for wholesaling and distributing the billions of dollars in toys unpacked at the massive twin ports of Long Beach and Los Angeles, the nation's dominant hub for U.S.–Asia trade and the world's third-largest container port. Woo's *guanxi,* or connections, helped him establish close relationships with scores of toy manufacturers in Asia, where the vast majority of the nation's toys are produced. The large volume of toys he imported then allowed him to take a 20 percent margin, compared with the 40 to 50 percent margins sought by the traditional small toy wholesalers. Today Woo and his family own 10 buildings, with roughly 70 tenants, in the area; their distribution company, Megatoys, has annual sales in excess of $30 million.

Toytown's success also has contributed to a broader growth in toy-related activity in Southern California. The region—home to Mattel, the world's largest toy maker—has spawned hundreds of smaller toy-making firms, design firms, and distribution firms, some originally located in Toytown but now residing in sleek modern industrial parks just outside the central core. Other spin-offs, including a new toy design department at the Otis College of Art and Design in West Los Angeles and the Toy Association of Southern California, have worked to secure the region's role as a major industry hub.

Woo envisions Toytown as a retail center. But whatever its future, the district's continuing success stands as testament to the ability of immigrant entrepreneurs and specialized industrial districts to turn even the most destitute urban neighborhoods around. Woo notes: "The future of Toytown will be as a gathering point for anyone interested in toys. Designers and buyers will come to see what's selling, what the customer wants. The industry will grow all over, but this place will remain ground zero."

For much of the 19th and early 20th centuries, immigrants filled and often dominated American cities. With the curtailment of immigration in the 1920s, this flow was dramatically reduced, and urban areas began to suffer demographic stagnation, and in some places rapid decline. Only after 1965, when immigration laws were reformed, did newcomers return in large numbers, once again transforming many of the nation's cities.

This was critical, because despite the movement of young professionals and others into the urban core, native-born Americans continued, on balance, to flee the cities in the 1990s. Only two of the nation's 10 largest metropolitan areas, Houston and Dallas, gained domestic migrants in the decade. As over 2.5 million native-born Americans fled the nation's densest cities, over 2.3 million immigrants came in.

The impacts were greatest in five major cities: New York, Los Angeles, San Francisco, Miami, and Chicago. These cities received more than half of the estimated 20 million legal and 3 million to 5 million illegal immigrants who arrived over the past quarter century. Without these immigrants, probably all these cities would have suffered the sort of serious depopulation that has afflicted such cities as St. Louis, Baltimore, and Detroit, which until recently have attracted relatively few foreigners.

In this two-way population flow, America's major cities and their close suburbs have become ever more demographically distinct from the rest of the country. In 1930, one out of four residents of the top four "gateway" cities came from abroad, twice the national average; by the 1990s, one in three was foreign-born, five times the norm. Fully half of all new Hispanic residents in the country between 1990 and 1996 resided in the 10 largest cities. Asians are even more concentrated, with roughly two in five residing in just three areas: Los Angeles, New York, and San Francisco.

In places such as Southern California, immigration has transformed the economic landscape. Between 1992 and 1999, the number of Latino businesses in Los Angeles County more than doubled. Some of these businesses have grown in areas that previously had been considered fallow, such as Compton and South-Central Los Angeles. In these long-established "ghettos," both incomes and population have been on the rise largely because of Latino immigration, after decades of decline.

A similar immigrant-driven phenomenon has sparked recoveries in some of the nation's most distressed neighborhoods, from Washington, D.C., to Houston. Along Pitkin Avenue in Brooklyn's Brownsville section, Caribbean and African immigrants, who have a rate of self-employment 20 to 50 percent higher than that of native-born blacks, have propelled a modest but sustained economic expansion.

"Immigrants are hungrier and more optimistic," says Harvard's William Apgar. "Their presence is the difference between New York and Detroit."

The recovery of such once forlorn places stems largely from the culture of these new immigrants. Certainly Brooklyn's infrastructure and location remain the same as in its long decades of decline. Along with entrepreneurship, the newcomers from places such as the Caribbean have brought with them a strong family ethic, a system of mutual financial assistance called *susus,* and a more positive orientation to their new place. "Immigrants are hungrier and more optimistic," notes William Apgar of Harvard's Joint Center for Housing Studies. "Their upward mobility is a form of energy. Their presence is the difference between New York and Detroit."

It is possible that newcomers to America might even be able to revive those cities that have not yet fully felt the transformative power of immigration. A possible harbinger can be seen on the South Side of St. Louis, a city largely left out of the post-1970s immigrant wave. Once a thriving white working-class community, the area, like much of the rest of the city, had suffered massive depopulation and economic stagnation.

This began to change, however, in the late 1990s, with the movement into the area of an estimated 10,000 Bosnian refugees, along with other newcomers, including Somalis, Vietnamese, and Mexicans. Southern Commercial Bank loan officer Steve Hrdlicka, himself a native of the district, recalls: "Eight years ago, when we opened this branch, we sat on our hands most of the time. We used to sleep quite a lot. Then this place became a rallying place for Bosnians. They would come in and ask for a loan for furniture. Then it was a car. Then it was a house, for themselves, their cousins."

In 1998, largely because of the Bosnians, Hrdlicka's branch, located in a South St. Louis neighborhood called Bevo, opened more new accounts than any of the 108-year-old Southern Commercial's other six branches. Over the last two years of the 1990s, the newcomers, who have developed a reputation for hard work and thrift, helped push the number of accounts at the branch up nearly 80 percent, while deposits have nearly doubled to $40 million.

"Bosnians," says one immigrant, "don't care if they start by buying the smallest, ugliest house. At least they feel they have something."

A translator at the Bevo branch, 25-year-old Jasna Mruckovski, has even cashed in on the Bosnians' homebuying tendencies. Moonlighting as a real estate salesperson, she has helped sell 33 homes in the area over the past year, all but one to Bosnian buyers. In many cases, she notes, these homes were bought with wages pooled from several family members, including children. Mruckovski, a refugee from Banjo Luka who arrived in St. Louis in 1994, observes: "St. Louis is seen as a cheap place to live. People come from California, Chicago, and Florida, where it's more expensive. Bosnians don't care if they start by buying the smallest, ugliest house. At least they feel they have something. This feeling is what turns a place like this around."

Immigration also helps cities retain their preeminence in another traditional urban economic bastion: cross-cultural trade. Virtually all the great cities since antiquity derived much of their sustenance through the intense contact between differing peoples in various sorts of markets. As world economies have developed through the ages, exchanges between races and cultures have been critical to establishing the geographic importance of particular places. Historian Fernand Braudel suggests, "A world economy always has an urban center of gravity, a city, as the logistic heart of its activity. News, merchandise, capital, credit, people, instructions, correspondence all flow into and out of the city. Its powerful merchants lay down the law, sometimes becoming extraordinarily wealthy."

Repeatedly throughout history, it has been outsiders—immigrants—who have driven cross-cultural exchange. "Throughout the history of economics," observes social theorist Georg Simmel, "the stranger appears as the trader, or the trader as stranger." In ancient Greece, for example, it was *metics,* largely foreigners, who drove the marketplace economy disdained by most well-born Greeks. In Alexandria, Rome, Venice, and Amsterdam—as well as the Islamic Middle East—this pattern repeated itself, with "the stranger" serving the critical role as intermediary.

As in Renaissance Venice, the increasing ethnic diversity of America's cities plays a critical role in their domination of international trade.

As in Renaissance Venice and early modern Amsterdam or London, the increasing ethnic diversity of America's cities plays a critical role in their domination of international trade. Over the past 30 years, cities such as New York, Los Angeles, Houston, Chicago, and Miami have become ever more multiethnic, with many of the newcomers hailing from growing trade regions such as East Asia, the Caribbean, and Latin America. The large immigrant clusters in these cities help forge critical global economic ties, held together not only by commercial bonds but by the equally critical bonds of cultural exchange and kinship networks.

These newcomers have redefined some former backwaters into global trading centers. Miami's large Latino population—including 650,000 Cubans, 75,000 Nicaraguans, and 65,000 Colombians—has helped turn the one-time sun-and-fun capital into the dominant center for American trade and travel to South America and the Caribbean. Modesto Maidique, president of Florida International University, who is himself a Cuban émigré, observes: "If you take away international trade and cultural ties from Miami, we go back to being just a seasonal tourist destination. It's the imports, the exports, and the service trade that have catapulted us into the first rank of cities in the world."

Like the *souk* districts of the Middle East, diversified cities provide an ideal place for the creation of unique, globally oriented markets. These *souks,* which are fully operational to this day, are home mostly to small, specialized merchants. In most cases, the districts consisted of tiny unlighted shops raised two or three feet from street level. Stores are often grouped together by trade, allowing the consumer the widest selection and choice.

The emergence of the Western *souk* is perhaps most evident in Los Angeles, home to Toytown. Within a short distance of that bustling district are scores of other specialized districts—the downtown Fashion Mart, the Flower district, and the jewelry, food, and produce districts are crowded with shoppers, hustlers, and buyers of every possible description. These districts' vitality contrasts with the longstanding weakness of downtown L.A.'s office market, which has been losing companies and tenants to other parts of the city.

Similar trade-oriented districts have arisen in other cities, such as along Canal Street in New York, in the "Asia Trade District" along Dallas's Harry Hines Boulevard, and along the Harwin Corridor in the area outside the 610 Loop in Houston. Once a forlorn strip of office and warehouse buildings, the Harwin area has been transformed into a car-accessed *souk* for off-price goods for much of East Texas, featuring cut-rate furniture, novelties, luggage, car parts, and electronic goods.

These shops, owned largely by Chinese, Korean, and Indian merchants, have grown from roughly 40 a decade ago to more than 800, sparking a boom in a once-depressed real estate market. Over the decade, the value of commercial properties in the district has more than tripled, and vacancies have dropped from nearly 50 percent to single digits. "It's kind of an Asian frontier sprawl around here," comments David Wu, a prominent local store owner.

Indeed, few American cities have been more transformed by trade and immigration than Houston. With the collapse of energy prices in the early 1980s, the once booming Texas metropolis appeared to be on the road to economic oblivion. Yet the city has rebounded, in large part because of the very demographic and trade patterns seen in the other Sun Belt capitals. "The energy industry totally dominated Houston by the 1970s—after all, oil has been at the core of our economy since 1901," explains University of Houston economist Barton Smith. "Every boom leads people to forget other parts of the economy. After the bust, people saw the importance of the ports and trade."

Since 1986, tonnage through the 25-mile-long Port of Houston has grown by one-third, helping the city recover the jobs lost during the "oil bust" of the early 1980s. Today, Smith estimates, trade accounts for roughly 10 percent of regional employment and has played a critical role in the region's 1990s recovery: By 1999 a city once renowned for its plethora of "see-through" buildings ranked second in the nation in total office space absorption and third in rent increases.

Immigrants were the critical factor in this turnaround. Between 1985 and 1990, Houston, a traditional magnet for domestic migrants, suffered a net loss of over 140,000 native-born residents. But the immigrants kept coming—nearly 200,000 over the past decade, putting the Texas town among America's seven most popular immigrant destinations.

Among those coming to Houston during the 1970s boom was a Taiwan-born engineer named Don Wang, who in 1987 founded his own immigrant-oriented financial institution, Metrobank. Amid the hard times and demographic shifts, Wang and his clients—largely Asian, Latin, and African immigrants—saw an enormous opportunity to pick up real estate, buy homes, and start businesses. Minority-owned enterprises now account for nearly 30 percent of Houston's business community.

Says Wang: "In the 1980s everyone was giving up on Houston. But we stayed. It was cheap to start a business here and easy to find good labor. We considered this the best place to do business in the country, even if no one on the outside knows it. . . . When the oil crisis came, everything dropped, but it actually was our chance to become a new city again."

Increasingly, the focus of immigrants—and their enterprise—extends beyond the traditional *souk* economy to a broader part of the metropolitan geography. Most dramatic has been the movement to the older rings of suburbs, which are rapidly replacing the inner city as the predominant melting pots of American society. This trend can be seen across the nation, from the Chinese- and Latino-dominated suburbs east of Los Angeles to the new immigrant communities emerging in southern metropolitan areas such as Houston, Dallas, and Atlanta. This move marks a sharp contrast to the immediate postwar era, when these suburbs, like their high-tech workforces, remained highly segregated.

The demographic shift in the near suburbs started in the 1970s, when African-Americans began moving to them in large numbers. In the ensuing two decades, middle-class minorities and upwardly mobile recent immigrants have shown a marked tendency to replace whites in the suburbs, particularly in the inner ring, increasing their numbers far more rapidly than their Anglo counterparts. Today nearly 51 percent of Asians, 43 percent of Latinos, and 32 percent of African Americans live in the suburbs.

This development is particularly notable in those regions where immigration has been heaviest. Among the most heavily Asian counties in the nation are such places as Queens County in New York, Santa Clara and San Mateo counties in Northern California, and Orange County, south of Los Angeles. Queens and Fort Bend County, in suburban Houston, rank among the 10 most ethnically diverse counties in the nation.

Today these areas have become as ethnically distinctive as the traditional inner cities themselves, if not more so. Some, like Coral Gables, outside of Miami, have become both ethnic and global business centers. Coral Gables is home to the Latin American division headquarters of over 50 multinationals.

Other places, such as the San Gabriel Valley east of Los Angeles, have accommodated two distinct waves of ethnic settlement, Latino and Asian. Cities such as Monterey Park, Alhambra, and San Gabriel have become increasingly Asian in character; areas such as Whittier and La Puente have been transformed by Latino migration. Yet in both cases, the movement is predominantly by middle-class homeowners. "For us this isn't a dream, this is reality," notes Frank Corona, who moved to the area from East Los Angeles. "This is a quiet, nice, family-oriented community."

The melting pot has spilled into the suburbs. About 51 percent of Asians, 43 percent of Latinos, and 32 percent of African Americans live in the suburbs.

The reason the melting pot has spilled into the suburbs lies in the changing needs of immigrants. In contrast to the early 20th century, when proximity to inner-city services and infrastructure was critical, many of today's newcomers to a more dispersed, auto-oriented society find they need to stop only briefly, if at all, in the inner cities. Their immediate destination after arrival is as likely to be Fort Lee as Manhattan, the San Gabriel Valley as Chinatown or the East L.A. barrios. Notes Cal State Northridge demographer James Allen: "The immigrants often don't bother with the inner city anymore. Most Iranians don't ever go to the center city, and few Chinese ever touch Chinatown at all. Many of them want to get away from poor people as soon as possible."

As proof, Allen points to changes in his own community, the San Fernando Valley, which for a generation was seen as the epitome of the modern suburb. In the 1960s, the valley was roughly 90 percent white; three decades later it was already 44 percent minority, with Latinos representing nearly one-third the total population. By 1997, according to county estimates, Latinos were roughly 41 percent of the valley population, while Asians were another 9 percent.

Similarly dramatic changes have taken place outside of California. Twenty years ago, Queens County was New York's largest middle-class and working-class white bastion, the fictional locale of the small homeowner Archie Bunker. Today it is not Manhattan, the legendary immigrant center, but Queens that is easily the most diverse borough in New York, with thriving Asian, Latino, and middle-class African-American neighborhoods. Over 40 percent of the borough's businesses are now minority-owned, almost twice as high as the percentage in Manhattan.

This alteration in the suburban fabric is particularly marked in the American South, which largely lacks the infrastructure of established ethnic inner-city districts. Regions such as Atlanta experienced some of the most rapid growth in immigration in the last two decades of the millennium; between 1970 and 1990, for example, Georgia's immigrant population grew by 525 percent. By 1996, over 11.5 million Asians lived in the South. Yet since most Southern cities lacked the preexisting structure of an ethnic Asian or Latino community to embrace the newcomers, most new immigrants chose to cluster not in the central city but in the near suburbs.

"Well, we still have one fried-chicken place left somewhere around here," jokes Houston architect Chao-Chiung Lee over dim sum in one of the city's heavily Asian suburbs. "It's a kind of the last outpost of the native culture lost amid the new Chinatown."

Yet if the successes of immigrants represent the success of the melting pot, the demographic shift also presents some potential challenges. In addition to a swelling number of entrepreneurs and scientists, there has been a rapid expansion of a less-educated population. For example, Latinos, the fastest-growing group in Silicon Valley, account for 23 percent of that region's population but barely 7 percent of its high-tech work force. Part of the problem lies with education: Only 56 percent of Latinos graduate from high school, and less than one in five takes the classes necessary to get into college.

Indeed, as the economy becomes increasingly information-based, there are growing concerns among industry and political leaders that many of the new immigrants and, more important, their children may be unprepared for the kind of jobs that are opening up in the future. Immigrants may be willing to serve as bed changers, gardeners, and service workers for the digital elites, but there remains a serious question as to whether their children will accept long-term employment in such generally low-paid and low-status niches.

George Borjas, a leading critic of U.S. immigration policy and professor of public policy at Harvard's John F. Kennedy School of Government, suggests that recent immigration laws have tilted the pool of newcomers away from skilled workers toward those less skilled, seriously depleting the quality of the labor pool and perhaps threatening the social stability of the immigration centers. "The national economy is demanding more skilled workers," Borjas says, "and I don't see how bringing more unskilled workers is consistent with this trend. . . . When you have a very large group of unskilled workers, and children of unskilled workers, you risk the danger of creating a social underclass in the next [21st] century."

In the coming decades, this disconnect between the labor force and the economy in some areas could lead to an exodus of middle-class people and businesses to less troubled places, as happened previously in inner cities. Across the country, many aging suburbs, such as Upper Darby near Philadelphia and Harvey outside Chicago, are well on the way to becoming highly diverse suburban slums as businesses move farther out into the geographic periphery. Others—in regions including Boston, New Orleans, Cleveland, St. Louis, Dallas, and Indianapolis—now struggle to retain their attractiveness.

If unchecked, a broader ghettoization looms as a distinct possibility, particularly in some of the older areas filled with smaller houses and more mundane apartment buildings. These areas could become—as have some suburbs of Paris—dysfunctional, balkanized losers in the new digital geography. "It's a different place now. We can go either way," says Robert Scott, a former L.A. planning commissioner and leader of the San Fernando Valley's drive to secede from Los Angeles.

No longer "lily white" enclaves, suburbs must draw their strength, as the great cities before them did, from their increasingly diverse populations.

Scott grew up in the once all-white, now predominantly Latino community of Van Nuys. "The valley can become a storehouse of poverty and disenchantment," he says, "or it can become a series of neighborhoods with a sense of uniqueness and an investment in its future." As Scott suggests, for these new melting pots, the best course may be not so much to try clinging to their demographic past as to find a way to seize the advantages of their more diverse roles, both economically and demographically. No longer "lily white" enclaves, such communities increasingly must draw their strength, as the great cities before them did, from the energies, skills, and cultural offerings of their increasingly diverse populations.

Critical Thinking

1. How does the story of Charlie Woo and Toytown illustrate the often overlooked contributions that immigration makes to a city and its neighborhoods?

2. Which are the top five "gateway cities" in the United States? How did immigration to these cities help to prevent their descent into the spiral of deep decline apparent in cities like Detroit and St. Louis?

3. Why are immigrants today increasingly found in suburbia, as contrasted to the immigration of the early 20th century?

JOEL KOTKIN (jkotkin@pacbell.net) is a senior fellow with the Pepperdine University Institute for Public Policy and a research fellow of the Reason Public Policy Institute. Excerpted from the book *The New Geography: How the Digital Revolution Is Reshaping the American Landscape* by Joel Kotkin. Copyright © 2000 by Joel Kotkin. Reprinted by arrangement with Random House Trade Publishing, a division of Random House Inc.

From *Reason Magazine*, December 2000, pp. 40–46. Excerpted from *The New Geography: How the Digital Revolution Is Reshaping the American Landscape* (Random House 2000). Copyright © 2000 by Joel Kotkin. Reprinted by permission of the author.

Swoons over Miami

A conversation with author Saskia Sassen, who coined the term "global city." As she tells **Foreign Policy:** Don't focus only on London and New York. The rest of the world should want to be the next Miami.

CHRISTINA LARSON

In the 1970s and 80s, back when crime peaked in Manhattan and downtowns across the United States and talent and money were draining out to the suburbs, a young sociologist named Saskia Sassen had a hunch the emerging conventional wisdom about the death of the city was wrong.

Then a researcher in New York City, conversant in five languages, she spent her time trolling the small shops and businesses around Wall Street. Even as the city's local economy was struggling, she recognized the emergence of new ties to the world beyond New York—small, specialized financial and marketing firms with global links, immigrant communities with ties back home, museum curators drawing upon international networks. Sassen predicted that the Big Apple was not dead, but about to spring back to life, with more international clout than ever.

In 1991, when Sassen published her first book, *The Global City,* which popularized the term, many onlookers were skeptical. After all, the United States was then mired in recession, and urban planners weren't yet talking about how to reinvent downtown or attract a "**creative class.**" Many thought that opportunities would flourish outside cities, and telecommuting might soon make the morning commute obsolete. But in the two decades since, history has proven Sassen right. Today, cities are increasingly important, both as places where people desire to live and as global nodes of commerce, culture, and ideas.

On the occasion of the publication of **Foreign Policy**'s 2010 **Global Cities Index,** we caught up with Sassen to ask her to pick the next round of urban winners and losers for the 21st century. The most extraordinary success? The rise of Miami. Missed opportunity? Beirut.

Foreign Policy: What distinguishes a **global city**?

Saskia Sassen: A global city makes new norms. And two requirements for that happening are complexity and diversity. Quite often, in countries around the world, it's the most global city, especially New York, where new national and international norms are made.

FP: Is a global city always a megacity, and vice versa?

SS: I'm so glad you asked. Most global cities are really not megacities. Some are, but the question of size is a tricky one. Size is important for a global city because you need enormous diversity in very specialized sectors, a whole range of them. Some of the leading global cities are very large, like Tokyo or Shanghai. On the other hand, you have cities that are simply very large, like Mumbai or Sao Paulo. I don't think Lagos is a global city; it's just a huge city. You have a lot of very large cities that are not necessarily global cities.

FP: Can any city become a global city?

SS: No, I don't think that any city can.

FP: So what's the magic recipe?

SS: Many of today's global cities are old-world cities that reinvented themselves. Like London or Istanbul, they already had enormous complexity and diversity. On the other hand, there are old-world cities, like Venice, that are definitely not global cities today.

And then there's Miami. Never an old-world city, today Miami is certainly a global city—why? It's quite surprising. Where did its diversity and complexity come from? Let's go back to the history. Before the 1990s, Miami was sort of a dreadful little spot, frankly. There was lots of domestic tourism; it was cheap; it was rundown; it was seen as dominated by the Cubans. But several important things happened. One was the infrastructure of international trade that the Cubans in Miami developed. There was also real estate development, often spurred by wealthy individuals from South America.

All this coincided with the opening of Latin America. In the 1990s and early 2000s, firms from all over the world—the Taiwanese, Italians, Korean, French, all over—set up regional headquarters in Miami. In the 1990s, there was also deregulation, so Miami becomes the banking center for Central America. Then the art circuit, the designers' circuit, and other things began to come into the city. Large international corporations began to locate branches there, forging a strong bridge with Europe that doesn't run through New York. That mix of cultures—in such a concentrated space, and covering so many different sectors—created remarkable diversity and complexity. Of course, the Miami case is rather exceptional.

FP: So what's the future Miami of Africa?

SS: You have probably two cities that people could think of as complex places in sub-Saharan Africa. One is Nairobi, Kenya, where some of the architecture still reflects British colonial history. The other one is Johannesburg, South Africa. In recent years, I would say Jo'burg is more dynamic, but Nairobi has lost ground.

FP: And the Miamis of Asia?

SS: In China, there are fast-growing cities like Shenzhen, which is also a port and a place where things come together. But Chinese cities are too controlled to be equivalent to Miami.

Two similar cases might be Singapore and Dubai. Both have constructed themselves arduously, with a lot of resources and government-driven projects, mind you. The market alone could not have done it in either Singapore or Dubai. In a sense, the whole city is a government-driven project—they have constructed themselves as global cities, and very significant ones.

Elsewhere? Quito, Ecuador; Bogotá, Colombia; Caracas, Venezuela—these are all cities with deep colonial histories; they were important nodes, part of a colonial empire, so there was a strong international connection already. They are cities to watch.

But Miami, a little outpost that suddenly explodes—that is still very rare. Dubai and Singapore are the only great similar examples.

FP: How do you explain them?

SS: Well, I think Dubai and Singapore are government-driven projects. It took a lot of hard work. In a way Singapore is surprising. Culturally it's not cosmopolitan; on the other hand, there was the obligation to learn several languages. Everybody had to study English.

FP: Are there any cities that missed, or are missing, their chance to be global cities?

SS: Beirut, if it had not had a civil war that destroyed it. Beirut had once been the global financial center and banking and commercial center for that whole region. The networks of the Lebanese are truly global and enormously sophisticated; they're everywhere. That keeps sustaining Beirut a bit, but really can't transform it. And I think that void in the region is partially what allowed Dubai to become a major trading center, and then a financial center and global city.

Dubai, you know, has it all supposedly—including skiing now, which is ridiculous, so that you can function there. Still, it's difficult to invest in real estate for the long term there. So many people who actually work in Mumbai prefer to live in Dubai. The flights that go from Dubai to Mumbai are HUGE! And the planes are full of business people! And I've flown that. The first class is fantastic, and it's not that long between flights because there is a lot of traffic between those two cities now.

FP: Is old Europe then old news?

SS: Well, I think Copenhagen, in a way, is becoming the Dubai of Europe. I love that image. I just get so amused by these things. It used to be that London was the platform for Europe. The Japanese firms, the Dutch, German, Spanish, Italian, even the French firms—if they wanted to operate in Europe, they located in London.

But today, you don't need that single platform. So Copenhagen and Zurich are two cities that have become very attractive for all kinds of reasons to firms, whether European firms or firms from the rest of the world. And so they locate in Copenhagen, which is a very reasonable city: much cheaper, well organized, and it ranks as one of the top cities in terms of reliability, investors' protections, good on everything. And Zurich, I don't know if you have been to Zurich, but if you can live in Zurich, why live anywhere else in Europe? It's absolutely so stunning.

FP: Where did you grow up?

SS: Well I grew up, first of all, in five languages. And I lived in the Netherlands, Argentina, Italy, and then I studied in France, I came to the United States, and I went back to France, and so that kind of a life. I speak like a native from Buenos Aires, you know, a particular city.

FP: Can you speculate on what FP's Global Cities rankings might look like in 15 years?

SS: I think that many of today's top global cities are here to stay. Of course there'll be some shift in their relative influence. And trends like the ascendance of Dubai or of Copenhagen over the last few years. Or Singapore—15 years ago Singapore was radically different. Maybe it looked the same, but it was a different type of global city—it was not a global city, really.

Istanbul is going to be enormously significant. I mean, who are the top investors in Istanbul today? They are from both the West and the East. The East includes Kazakhstan, China, Russia, Bulgaria; it's just extraordinary.

The other thing that is happening is of course China. In the future, I think that China and Chinese cities will be even more significant.

FP: Will China's emerging megacities be global cities? By 2030, McKinsey and Co. projects there will be 221 cities in China with populations of more than 1 million.

SS: Not global cities in the same way—they will be *Chinese* global cities. What I mean is that Beijing will never be a global city *of* the world, but it will be a global city *in* the world. The distinction is that *of* the world means that you have to really become a bit de-nationalized, more ethnically and linguistically diverse. Beijing is still quite homogeneous. Same thing with Tokyo. Tokyo never became a global city *of* the world. It's not. But *in* the world, it's very powerful. In China, only Hong Kong is *of* the world, because it has been evolving global connections there for a hundred years.

FP: So there's no mainland Chinese Miami?

SS: Please tell me if you discover it.

Critical Thinking

1. What is globalization? Can you identify the various processes or aspects of globalization and how they affect cities?

2. What makes a Global City different from any other big or medium-sized city?

CHRISTINA LARSON is a contributing editor at *Foreign Policy* and a fellow at the New America Foundation.

Saskia Sassen is Robert S. Lynd professor of sociology at Columbia University and Centennial visiting professor at the London School of Economics. She is the author, most recently, of *Territory, Authority, Rights: From Medieval to Global Assemblages,* among other works.

Reprinted in entirety by McGraw-Hill with permission from *Foreign Policy,* August 27, 2010. www.foreignpolicy.com. © 2010 Washingtonpost.Newsweek Interactive, LLC.

Outsourcing: Beyond Bangalore

Companies are increasingly sending IT work to hubs outside India. They're saving money but facing a whole new raft of challenges.

Rachael King

After 10 months of working with software developers in Bangalore, India, Bill Wood was ready to call it quits. The local engineers would start a project, get a few months' experience, and then bolt for greener pastures, says the U.S.-based executive. Attrition rose to such a high level that year that Wood's company had to replace its entire staff, some positions more than once. "It did not work well at all," recalls Wood, vice-president of engineering at Ping Identity, a maker of Internet security software for corporations. Frustrated, Wood began searching for a partner outside India. He scoured 15 companies in 8 different countries, including Russia, Mexico, Argentina, and Vietnam.

That path is being trod by a lot of executives, eager for new sources of low-cost, high-tech talent outside India. Many are fed up with the outsourcing hub of Bangalore, where salaries for info tech staff are growing at 12% to 14% a year, turnover is increasing, and an influx of workers is straining city resources. Even Indian outsourcing pioneers Tata Consultancy Services, Wipro Technologies (WIT), and Infosys Technologies (INFY), which have helped foreign companies shift software development and other IT operations to Bangalore, are starting to expand into smaller Indian cities, as well as China (see BusinessWeek.com, 11/14/06, "Patience is a Virtue in China, India IT Learns"). "Overall, in terms of productivity and quality of life, beyond Bangalore is better," says Wipro Chief Information Officer Laxman Badiga. "Bangalore is getting more crowded, and the real infrastructure is getting stretched."

So companies are setting their sights on a slew of emerging hot spots for IT outsourcing. Need a multilingual workforce adept at developing security systems and testing software? *Buna ziua,* Bucharest. Want low-cost Linux developers? *Bienvenidos a* Buenos Aires, where many companies adopted open-source software after the devaluation of the peso in 2002 made licenses from abroad prohibitively expensive. Other cities on the list include Moscow and St. Petersburg in Russia and Prague in the Czech Republic, according to consulting firm neoIT. Other hot spots include Mexico City, São Paulo, and Santiago in Latin America; and within Asia, Dalian, China, and Ho Chi Minh City, Vietnam.

The Search for Lower Costs

Make no mistake: India remains an IT outsourcing powerhouse, with $17.7 billion in software and IT services exports in 2005, compared with $3.6 billion for China and $1 billion for Russia, according to trade organizations in each country. And India's outsourcing industry is still growing at a faster pace than that of Russia and other wannabe Bangalores.

Yet many companies can't resist the lure of cheaper labor. "Ninety percent of all outsourcing deals in the market today have been structured around cost improvement only," says Linda Cohen, vice-president of sourcing research at consulting firm Gartner (IT). By the third year of an outsourcing deal, after all the costs have been squeezed out, companies get antsy to find a new locale with an even lower overhead.

But moving IT operations into developing countries like Vietnam or China can also pose big risks, such as insurmountable language and cultural differences, geopolitical instability, and the risk of stolen intellectual property. "You keep following the money, but how often are you going to move people around?" asks Cohen. Even the routine day-to-day management of an offshore team can require significant project management expertise. "If you don't have experience and don't do it well, it can negate savings," says Barry Rubenstein, program manager of application outsourcing and offshore services at IDC.

Mix of Outsourcing Locations

Plenty of providers are ready to help clients overcome those obstacles. Companies including Accenture (ACN), EDS (EDS), IBM Global Services (IBM), and Genpact are building global networks, comprised of operations in a variety of cities, aimed at giving customers a mix of worker skills and labor costs. "We tailor where you want your people, based on the premium you want to pay," says Charlie Feld, executive vice-president of portfolio development at EDS.

Continental Airlines (CAL), for instance, uses an EDS center in India for development of some software that runs on mainframes, but the airline handles some finance work through an EDS office in Brazil. Accenture uses its global network of facilities in a similar fashion. "Today we are about 35% in high-cost locations, such as the U.S. and Britain; 20% in medium-cost locations like Spain, Ireland, and Canada; and about 45% in low-cost locations like the Philippines, India, China, and Eastern Europe," says Jimmy Harris, global managing director of infrastructure outsourcing at Accenture.

When Bob Gett, CEO of Boston systems integration firm Optaros, decided to hire an overseas outfit to handle development of some applications or programs designed to perform specific tasks, he scouted out six or seven countries in Eastern Europe. He finally settled on Akela, an outsourcing company in Bucharest, Romania. Gett found Romania attractive because of its good education system, multilingual population, and abundance of technical talent.

Benefiting from Geography

The move reduces costs by 60% to 75%, Gett figures, letting Optaros offer competitive pricing to customers. "We're going to where the most cost-effective talent is in the world, but it has to be feasible," he says. "It can't be where there are economic, time zone, or language barriers." In fact, Gett needs his application developers to interact directly with customers in the U.S. and Western Europe, so he appreciates that Akela workers speak English and French and are closer to the Optaros Geneva office than workers in India would be.

Companies such as Genpact, Accenture, Wipro, and Infosys are hoping Romania's expected admission to the European Union will make it even more appealing for companies from Western Europe to do business there.

Dalian, a seaport in northeast China, is also turning out to be an ideal center for outsourcing, in large part because of its geography and history. Located in the northeast corner of China, Dalian is close to both Korea and Japan and was, in the first half of the 20th century, occupied by Japan. So there's still a labor pool of Japanese speakers (see BusinessWeek.com, 3/28/05, "China: Golf, Sushi—and Cheap Engineers").

Intellectual Property Issues

Dalian's labor costs are lower than in Japan, so it's become a center for application development for Japanese companies. U.S. firms outsource some technology work there as well. General Electric (GE) and Nissan (NSANF) outsource work to Genpact's operations in Dalian. Genpact was the first outsourcing firm to locate in the city in June, 2000. Accenture and IBM Global Services have since moved in.

There are certainly challenges for companies that wish to outsource to China, including the potential theft of intellectual property. To combat this, Infosys Technologies has disabled USB drives on PCs to limit the ability of workers to take data out of the office. "We've taken extraordinary efforts to protect the intellectual property of our clients," says Stephen Pratt, CEO Infosys Consulting, a subsidiary of Infosys Technologies, which has operations in Shanghai.

For U.S. companies that need to collaborate closely with offshore workers, South America is an attractive option because

the time zones are similar and the infrastructure is strong (see BusinessWeek.com, 1/30/06, "Can Latin America Challenge India?").

Infrastructure Counts

Brazil boasts a mature software and IT industry, and the nation's providers such as Politec, Stefanini IT, and ActMinds are keen to do more offshore business. Stefanini, which has served clients such as Whirlpool (WHR) and Johnson & Johnson (JNJ), derives about 20% of its revenue from international operations, but the company would like to expand that to 50% by 2008.

Total Brazilian software and IT services revenue is $17.16 billion, while revenue from offshore software development is a much smaller $205.3 million, according to Brazil IT, an association of Brazilian IT services providers. "If we can get a client interested enough that they will go to Brazil, they will do business with us," says Eric Olsson, principal consultant with Politec, which has done work for clients such as insurer MetLife (MET), software colossus Microsoft (MSFT), and SAIC (SAI), a provider of a host of scientific and engineering services. Companies are drawn to Brazil's modern infrastructure, with airports and highways that are first world, says Olsson, whose company is the largest IT services provider in Brazil.

Good roads and the developers who drive on them don't come cheap, though. A software engineer in Brazil costs $20 to $35 per hour. That's lower than in the U.S. but pricier than in India.

Threat to U.S. Workers

And while a technically skilled global labor force is a boon to companies, the picture isn't so rosy for U.S. workers. Instead of competing with just India, now U.S. IT workers will need to go up against workers all over the world. In 2005, about 24% of North American companies used offshore providers to meet some of their software needs, according to Forrester Research (FORR). Over the next five years, spending on offshore IT services is set to increase at a compound annual growth rate of 18%, according to IDC.

The effect in the U.S. is that starting salaries in the engineering field—when adjusted for inflation—have stayed constant or decreased in the past five years or so, says Vivek Wadhwa, executive in residence at Duke University. "It doesn't make much sense to get into programming anymore," says Wadhwa, who worries that a lack of talent in certain industries, such as telecom, along with the outsourcing of research and development will erode U.S. competitiveness (see BusinessWeek.com, 11/7/06, "The Real Problem with Outsourcing"). But U.S. companies say that hiring programmers in India, who might make a fifth of what programmers do in the U.S., allows the companies to survive in a globally competitive economy.

After traveling the world, Ping Identity's Wood finally settled on Luxoft, an outsourcing provider based in Moscow that has served high-profile clients such as Boeing (BA), Citigroup's (C) Citibank, and Dell (DELL). While programmers are typically 20% more expensive in Moscow than in Bangalore, Wood found that there wasn't much difference in the hourly rate for the kind of work that he needed. "Indian companies are cheap until you ask for people with experience, and we wanted workers with eight years or more of experience," he says.

Russia's high-end software developers are drawing plenty of offshore business to Moscow and St. Petersburg, which together account for about 60% of the country's software development exports. Those exports have grown from $352 million in 2002 to nearly $1 billion in 2005, according to RUSSOFT, an association of software development firms from Russia, Belarus, and Ukraine (see BusinessWeek.com, 1/30/06, "From Russia with Technology?"). Providers EPAM and Luxoft are starting to gain some international recognition as well, both making Brown & Wilson's Top 50 Best Managed Global Outsourcing Vendors for the first time in 2006.

For Wood, the biggest benefit of working with Luxoft is a cultural one. "One of the reasons we're in Russia is that we found a common value set. Their work ethic is strong, and these people are very outspoken," says Wood. He says engineers in Moscow have no trouble proposing a different course of action when necessary. He says he found workers in Bangalore to be reticent. And since Russian developers stick around longer—turnover is now in the low teens—Wood has plenty of time to take those opinions to heart.

Critical Thinking

1. How does the digitalization of information create a world that, to use the words of Thomas Friedman, is "flat?" How has Bangalore come to symbolize all that a "flat world" represents?

2. As seen in the growth of Bangalore, how does a "flat world" affect the economic prospects of U.S. cities?

3. Are there limits to a "flat world" and global competition? Why don't all industries essentially leave the United States and shift more of their production overseas?

RACHAEL KING is a writer for *BusinessWeek.com* in San Francisco.

The Rise of the Creative Class

Why cities without gays and rock bands are losing the economic development race.

RICHARD FLORIDA

As I walked across the campus of Pittsburgh's Carnegie Mellon University one delightful spring day, I came upon a table filled with young people chatting and enjoying the spectacular weather. Several had identical blue t-shirts with "Trilogy@CMU" written across them—Trilogy being an Austin, Texas-based software company with a reputation for recruiting our top students. I walked over to the table. "Are you guys here to recruit?" I asked. "No, absolutely not," they replied adamantly. "We're not recruiters. We're just hangin' out, playing a little Frisbee with our friends." How interesting, I thought. They've come to campus on a workday, all the way from Austin, just to hang out with some new friends.

I noticed one member of the group sitting slouched over on the grass, dressed in a tank top. This young man had spiked multi-colored hair, full-body tattoos, and multiple piercings in his ears. An obvious slacker, I thought, probably in a band. "So what is your story?" I asked. "Hey man, I just signed on with these guys." In fact, as I would later learn, he was a gifted student who had inked the highest-paying deal of any graduating student in the history of his department, right at that table on the grass, with the recruiters who do not "recruit."

What a change from my own college days, just a little more than 20 years ago, when students would put on their dressiest clothes and carefully hide any counterculture tendencies to prove that they could fit in with the company. Today, apparently, it's the company trying to fit in with the students. In fact, Trilogy had wined and dined him over margarita parties in Pittsburgh and flown him to Austin for private parties in hip nightspots and aboard company boats. When I called the people who had recruited him to ask why, they answered, "That's easy. We wanted him because he's a rock star."

While I was interested in the change in corporate recruiting strategy, something even bigger struck me. Here

was another example of a talented young person leaving Pittsburgh. Clearly, my adopted hometown has a huge number of assets. Carnegie Mellon is one of the world's leading centers for research in information technology. The University of Pittsburgh, right down the street from our campus, has a world-class medical center. Pittsburgh attracts hundreds of millions of dollars per year in university research funding and is the sixth-largest center for college and university students on a per capita basis in the country. Moreover, this is hardly a cultural backwater. The city is home to three major sports franchises, renowned museums and cultural venues, a spectacular network of urban parks, fantastic industrial-age architecture, and great urban neighborhoods with an abundance of charming yet affordable housing. It is a friendly city, defined by strong communities and a strong sense of pride. In the 1986 Rand McNally survey, Pittsburgh was ranked "America's Most Livable City," and has continued to score high on such lists ever since.

Yet Pittsburgh's economy continues to putter along in a middling flat-line pattern. Both the core city and the surrounding metropolitan area lost population in the 2000 census. And those bright young university people keep leaving. Most of Carnegie Mellon's prominent alumni of recent years—like Vinod Khosla, perhaps the best known of Silicon Valley's venture capitalists, and Rick Rashid, head of research and development at Microsoft—went elsewhere to make their marks. Pitt's vaunted medical center, where Jonas Salk created his polio vaccine and the world's premier organ-transplant program was started, has inspired only a handful of entrepreneurs to build biotech companies in Pittsburgh.

Over the years, I have seen the community try just about everything possible to remake itself so as to attract and retain talented young people, and I was personally involved in many of these efforts. Pittsburgh has launched a multitude

The Creativity Index

The key to economic growth lies not just in the ability to attract the creative class, but to translate that underlying advantage into creative economic outcomes in the form of new ideas, new high-tech businesses and regional growth. To better gauge these capabilities, I developed a new measure called the Creativity Index (column 1). The Creativity Index is a mix of four equally weighted factors: the creative class share of the workforce (column 2 shows the percentage; column 3 ranks cities accordingly); high-tech industry, using the Milken Institute's widely accepted Tech Pole Index, which I refer to as the High-Tech Index (column 4); innovation, measured as patents per capita (column 5); and diversity, measured by the Gay Index, a reasonable proxy for an area's openness to different kinds of people and ideas (column 6). This composite indicator is a better measure of a region's underlying creative capabilities than the simple measure of the creative class, because it reflects the joint effects of its concentration and of innovative economic outcomes. The Creativity Index is thus my baseline indicator of a region's overall standing in the creative economy and I offer it as a barometer of a region's longer run economic potential. The following tables present my creativity index ranking for the top 10 and bottom 10 metropolitan areas, grouped into three size categories (large, medium-sized and small cities/regions).

—Richard Florida

of programs to diversify the region's economy away from heavy industry into high technology. It has rebuilt its downtown virtually from scratch, invested in a new airport, and developed a massive new sports complex for the Pirates and the Steelers. But nothing, it seemed, could stem the tide of people and new companies leaving the region.

I asked the young man with the spiked hair why he was going to a smaller city in the middle of Texas, a place with a small airport and no professional sports teams, without a major symphony, ballet, opera, or art museum comparable to Pittsburgh's. The company is excellent, he told me. There are also terrific people and the work is challenging. But the clincher, he said, is that, "It's in Austin!" There are lots of young people, he went on to explain, and a tremendous amount to do: a thriving music scene, ethnic and cultural diversity, fabulous outdoor recreation, and great nightlife. Though he had several good job offers from Pittsburgh high-tech firms and knew the city well, he said he felt the city lacked the lifestyle options, cultural diversity, and tolerant attitude that would make it attractive to him. As he summed it up: "How would I fit in here?"

This young man and his lifestyle proclivities represent a profound new force in the economy and life of America. He is a member of what I call the creative class: a fast-growing, highly educated, and well-paid segment of the workforce on whose efforts corporate profits and economic growth increasingly depend. Members of the creative class do a wide variety of work in a wide variety of industries—from technology to entertainment, journalism to finance, high-end manufacturing to the arts. They do not consciously think of themselves as a class. Yet they share a common ethos that values creativity, individuality, difference, and merit.

More and more businesses understand that ethos and are making the adaptations necessary to attract and retain creative class employees—everything from relaxed dress codes, flexible schedules, and new work rules in the office to hiring recruiters who throw Frisbees. Most civic leaders, however, have failed to understand that what is true for corporations is also true for cities and regions: Places that succeed in attracting and retaining creative class people prosper; those that fail don't.

Stuck in old paradigms of economic development, cities like Buffalo, New Orleans, and Louisville struggled in the 1980s and 1990s to become the next "Silicon Somewhere" by building generic high-tech office parks or subsidizing professional sports teams. Yet they lost members of the creative class, and their economic dynamism, to places like Austin, Boston, Washington, D.C. and Seattle—places more tolerant, diverse, and open to creativity. Because of this migration of the creative class, a new social and economic geography is emerging in America, one that does not correspond to old categories like East Coast versus West Coast or Sunbelt versus Frostbelt. Rather, it is more like the class divisions that have increasingly separated Americans by income and neighborhood, extended into the realm of city and region.

The Creative Secretary

The distinguishing characteristic of the creative class is that its members engage in work whose function is to "create meaningful new forms." The super-creative core of this new class includes scientists and engineers, university professors, poets and novelists, artists, entertainers, actors, designers, and architects, as well as the "thought leadership" of modern society: nonfiction writers, editors, cultural figures, think-tank researchers, analysts, and other opinion-makers. Members of this super-creative core produce new forms or designs that are readily transferable and broadly useful—such as designing a product that can be widely made, sold and used; coming up with a theorem or strategy that can be applied in many cases; or composing music that can be performed again and again.

Beyond this core group, the creative class also includes "creative professionals" who work in a wide range of knowledge-intensive industries such as high-tech sectors, financial services, the legal and healthcare professions,

Table 1   Large Cities Creativity Rankings

Rankings of 49 metro areas reporting populations over 1 million in the 2000 Census

The Top Ten Cities	Creativity Index	% Creative Workers	Creative Rank	High-Tech Rank	Innovation Rank	Diversity Rank
1. San Francisco	1057	34.8%	5	1	2	1
2. Austin	1028	36.4%	4	11	3	16
3. San Diego	1015	32.1%	15	12	7	3
3. Boston	1015	38.0%	3	2	6	22
5. Seattle	1008	32.7%	9	3	12	8
6. Raleigh–Durham–Chapel Hill	996	38.2%	2	14	4	28
7. Houston	980	32.5%	10	16	16	10
8. Washington–Baltimore	964	38.4%	1	5	30	12
9. New York	962	32.3%	12	13	24	14
10. Dallas	960	30.2%	23	6	17	9
10. Minneapolis	960	33.9%	7	21	5	29

The Bottom Ten Cities	Creativity Index	% Creative Workers	Creative Rank	High-Tech Rank	Innovation Rank	Diversity Rank
49. Memphis	530	24.8%	47	48	42	41
48. Norfolk–Virginia Beach, VA	555	28.4%	36	35	49	47
47. Las Vegas	561	18.5%	49	42	47	5
46. Buffalo	609	28.9%	33	40	27	49
45. Louisville	622	26.5%	46	46	39	36
44. Grand Rapids, MI	639	24.3%	48	43	23	38
43. Oklahoma City	668	29.4%	29	41	43	39
42. New Orleans	668	27.5%	42	45	48	13
41. Greensboro–Winston-Salem	697	27.3%	44	33	35	35
40. Providence, RI	698	27.6%	41	44	34	33

and business management. These people engage in creative problem-solving, drawing on complex bodies of knowledge to solve specific problems. Doing so typically requires a high degree of formal education and thus a high level of human capital. People who do this kind of work may sometimes come up with methods or products that turn out to be widely useful, but it's not part of the basic job description. What they are required to do regularly is think on their own. They apply or combine standard approaches in unique ways to fit the situation, exercise a great deal of judgment, perhaps try something radically new from time to time.

Much the same is true of the growing number of technicians and others who apply complex bodies of knowledge to working with physical materials. In fields such as medicine and scientific research, technicians are taking on increased responsibility to interpret their work and make decisions, blurring the old distinction between white-collar work (done by decisionmakers) and blue-collar work (done by those who follow orders). They acquire their own arcane bodies of knowledge and develop their own unique ways of doing the job. Another example is the secretary in today's pared-down offices. In

many cases this person not only takes on a host of tasks once performed by a large secretarial staff, but becomes a true office manager—channeling flows of information, devising and setting up new systems, often making key decisions on the fly. These people contribute more than intelligence or computer skills. They add creative value. Everywhere we look, creativity is increasingly valued. Firms and organizations value it for the results that it can produce and individuals value it as a route to self-expression and job satisfaction. Bottom line: As creativity becomes more valued, the creative class grows.

The creative class now includes some 38.3 million Americans, roughly 30 percent of the entire U.S. workforce—up from just 10 percent at the turn of the 20th century and less than 20 percent as recently as 1980. The creative class has considerable economic power. In 1999, the average salary for a member of the creative class was nearly $50,000 ($48,752), compared to roughly $28,000 for a working-class member and $22,000 for a service-class worker.

Not surprisingly, regions that have large numbers of creative class members are also some of the most affluent and growing.

The New Geography of Class

Different classes of people have long sorted themselves into neighborhoods within a city or region. But now we find a large-scale re-sorting of people among cities and regions nationwide, with some regions becoming centers of the creative class while others are composed of larger shares of working-class or service-class people. To some extent this has always been true. For instance, there have always been artistic and cultural communities like Greenwich Village, college towns like Madison and Boulder, and manufacturing centers like Pittsburgh and Detroit. The news is that such sorting is becoming even more widespread and pronounced.

In the leading centers of this new class geography, the creative class makes up more than 35 percent of the workforce. This is already the case in the greater Washington, D.C. region, the Raleigh-Durham area, Boston, and Austin—all areas undergoing tremendous economic growth. Despite their considerable advantages, large regions have not cornered the market as creative class locations. In fact, a number of smaller regions have some of the highest creative-class concentrations in the nation—notably college towns like East Lansing, Mich. and Madison, Wisc. (See Table 3, "Small-size Cities Creativity Rankings")

At the other end of the spectrum are regions that are being bypassed by the creative class. Among large regions, Las Vegas, Grand Rapids and Memphis harbor the smallest concentrations of the creative class. Members of this class have nearly abandoned a wide range of smaller regions in the outskirts of the South and Midwest. In small metropolitan areas like Victoria, Texas and Jackson, Tenn., the creative class comprises less than 15 percent of the workforce. The leading centers for the working class among large regions are Greensboro, N.C. and Memphis, Tenn., where the working class makes up more than 30 percent of the workforce. Several smaller regions in the South and Midwest are veritable working class enclaves with 40 to 50 percent or more of their workforce in the traditional industrial occupations.

These places have some of the most minuscule concentrations of the creative class in the nation. They are symptomatic of a general lack of overlap between the major creative-class centers and those of the working class. Of the 26 large cities where the working class comprises more than one-quarter of the population, only one, Houston, ranks among the top 10 destinations for the creative class.

Chicago, a bastion of working-class people that still ranks among the top 20 large creative centers, is interesting because it shows how the creative class and the traditional working class can coexist. But Chicago has an advantage in that it is a big city, with more than a million members of the creative class. The University of Chicago sociologist Terry Clark likes to say Chicago developed an innovative political and cultural solution to this issue. Under the second Mayor Daley, the city integrated the members of the creative class into the city's culture and politics by treating them essentially as just another "ethnic group" that needed sufficient space to express its identity.

Las Vegas has the highest concentration of the service class among large cities, 58 percent, while West Palm Beach, Orlando, and Miami also have around half. These regions rank near the bottom of the list for the creative class. The service class makes up more than half the workforce in nearly 50 small and medium-size regions across the country. Few of them boast any significant concentrations of the creative class, save vacationers, and offer little prospect for upward mobility. They include resort towns like Honolulu and Cape Cod. But they also include places like Shreveport, Lou. and Pittsfield, Mass. For these places that are not tourist destinations, the economic and social future is troubling to contemplate.

Plug-and-Play Communities

Why do some places become destinations for the creative while others don't? Economists speak of the importance of industries having "low entry barriers," so that new firms can easily enter and keep the industry vital. Similarly, I think it's important for a place to have low entry barriers for people—that is, to be a place where newcomers are accepted quickly into all sorts of social and economic arrangements. All else being equal, they are likely to attract greater numbers of talented and creative people—the sort of people who power innovation and growth. Places that thrive in today's world tend to be plug-and-play communities where anyone can fit in quickly. These are places where people can find opportunity, build support structures, be themselves, and not get stuck in any one identity. The plug-and-play community is one that somebody can move into and put together a life—or at least a facsimile of a life—in a week.

The plug-and-play community is one that somebody can move into and put together a life—or at least a facsimile of a life—in a week.

Creative centers also tend to be places with thick labor markets that can fulfill the employment needs of members of the creative class, who, by and large, are not looking

Table 2 Medium-Size Cities Creativity Rankings

Rankings of 32 metro areas reporting populations 500,000 to 1 million in the 2000 Census

The Top Ten Cities	Creativity Index	% Creative Workers	Creative Rank	High-Tech Rank	Innovation Rank	Diversity Rank
1. Albuquerque, NM	965	32.2%	2	1	7	1
2. Albany, NY	932	33.7%	1	12	2	4
3. Tuscon, AZ	853	28.4%	17	2	6	5
4. Allentown–Bethlehem, PA	801	28.7%	16	13	3	14
5. Dayton, OH	766	30.1%	8	8	5	24
6. Colorado Springs, CO	756	29.9%	10	5	1	30
7. Harrisburg, PA	751	29.8%	11	6	13	20
8. Little Rock, AR	740	30.8%	4	10	21	11
9. Birmingham, AL	722	30.7%	6	7	26	10
10. Tulsa, OK	721	28.7%	15	9	15	18

The Bottom Ten Cities	Creativity Index	% Creative Workers	Creative Rank	High-Tech Rank	Innovation Rank	Diversity Rank
32. Youngstown, OH	253	23.8%	32	32	24	32
31. Scranton–Wilkes-Barre, PA	400	24.7%	28	23	23	31
30. McAllen, TX	451	27.8%	18	31	32	9
29. Stockton–Lodi, CA	459	24.1%	30	29	28	7
28. El Paso, TX	464	27.0%	23	27	31	17
27. Fresno, CA	516	25.1%	27	24	30	2
26. Bakersfield, CA	531	27.8%	18	22	27	19
25. Fort Wayne, IN	569	25.4%	26	17	8	26
24. Springfield, MA	577	29.7%	13	30	20	22
23. Honolulu, HI	580	27.2%	21	14	29	6

just for "a job" but for places that offer many employment opportunities.

Cities and regions that attract lots of creative talent are also those with greater diversity and higher levels of quality of place. That's because location choices of the creative class are based to a large degree on their lifestyle interests, and these go well beyond the standard "quality-of-life" amenities that most experts think are important.

The list of the country's high-tech hot spots looks an awful lot like the list of the places with highest concentrations of gay people.

For instance, in 1998, I met Gary Gates, then a doctoral student at Carnegie Mellon. While I had been studying the location choices of high-tech industries and talented people, Gates had been exploring the location patterns of gay people. My list of the country's high-tech hot spots looked an awful lot like his list of the places with highest concentrations of gay people. When we compared these two lists with more statistical rigor, his Gay Index turned out to correlate very strongly to my own measures of high-tech growth. Other measures I came up with, like the Bohemian Index—a measure of artists, writers, and performers—produced similar results.

Talented people seek an environment open to differences. Many highly creative people, regardless of ethnic background or sexual orientation, grew up feeling like outsiders, different in some way from most of their schoolmates. When they are sizing up a new company and community, acceptance of diversity and of gays in particular is a sign that reads "non-standard people welcome here."

The creative class people I study use the word "diversity" a lot, but not to press any political hot buttons. Diversity is simply something they value in all its manifestations. This is spoken of so often, and so matter-of-factly, that I take it to be a fundamental marker of creative class values. Creative-minded people enjoy a mix of influences. They want to hear different kinds of music and try different kinds of food. They want to meet and socialize with people unlike themselves, trade views and spar over issues.

As with employers, visible diversity serves as a signal that a community embraces the open meritocratic values of the creative age. The people I talked to also desired nightlife with a wide mix of options. The most highly

Table 3 Small-Size Cities Creativity Rankings

Rankings of 63 metro areas reporting populations 250,000 to 500,000 in the 2000 Census

The Top Ten Cities	Creativity Index	% Creative Workers	Creative Rank	High-Tech Rank	Innovation Rank	Diversity Rank
1. Madison, WI	925	32.8%	6	16	4	9
2. Des Moines, IA	862	32.1%	8	2	16	20
3. Santa Barbara, CA	856	28.3%	19	8	8	7
4. Melbourne, FL	855	35.5%	1	6	9	32
5. Boise City, ID	854	35.2%	3	1	1	46
6. Huntsville, AL	799	35.3%	2	5	18	40
7. Lansing–East Lansing, MI	739	34.3%	4	27	29	18
8. Binghamton, NY	731	30.8%	12	7	3	60
9. Lexington, KY	717	27.0%	28	24	10	12
10. New London, CT–Norwich, RI	715	28.1%	23	11	13	33

The Bottom Ten Cities	Creativity Index	% Creative Workers	Creative Rank	High-Tech Rank	Innovation Rank	Diversity Rank
63. Shreveport, LA	233	22.1%	55	32	59	57
62. Ocala, FL	263	16.4%	63	61	52	24
61. Visalia, CA	289	22.9%	52	63	60	11
60. Killeen, TX	302	24.6%	47	47	51	53
59. Fayetteville, NC	309	29.0%	16	62	62	49
58. York, PA	360	22.3%	54	54	26	52
57. Fayetteville, AR	366	21.1%	57	57	42	17
56. Beaumont, TX	372	27.8%	25	37	56	55
55. Lakeland–Winter Haven, FL	385	20.9%	59	56	53	5
54. Hickory, NC	393	19.4%	61	48	32	30

valued options were experiential ones—interesting music venues, neighborhood art galleries, performance spaces, and theaters. A vibrant, varied nightlife was viewed by many as another signal that a city "gets it," even by those who infrequently partake in nightlife. More than anything, the creative class craves real experiences in the real world.

They favor active, participatory recreation over passive, institutionalized forms. They prefer indigenous street-level culture—a teeming blend of cafes, sidewalk musicians, and small galleries and bistros, where it is hard to draw the line between performers and spectators. They crave stimulation, not escape. They want to pack their time full of dense, high-quality, multidimensional experiences. Seldom has one of my subjects expressed a desire to get away from it all. They want to get into it all, and do it with eyes wide open.

Creative class people value active outdoor recreation very highly. They are drawn to places and communities where many outdoor activities are prevalent—both because they enjoy these activities and because their presence is seen as a signal that the place is amenable to the broader creative lifestyle. The creative-class people in my studies are into a variety of active sports, from traditional ones like bicycling, jogging, and kayaking to newer, more extreme ones, like trail running and snowboarding.

Places are also valued for authenticity and uniqueness. Authenticity comes from several aspects of a community—historic buildings, established neighborhoods, a unique music scene, or specific cultural attributes. It comes from the mix—from urban grit alongside renovated buildings, from the commingling of young and old, long-time neighborhood characters and yuppies, fashion models and "bag ladies." An authentic place also offers unique and original experiences. Thus a place full of chain stores, chain restaurants, and nightclubs is not authentic. You could have the same experience anywhere.

Today, it seems, leading creative centers provide a solid mix of high-tech industry, plentiful outdoor amenities, and an older urban center whose rebirth has been fueled in part by a combination of creativity and innovative technology, as well as lifestyle amenities. These include places like the greater Boston area, which has the Route 128 suburban complex, Harvard and MIT, and several charming inner-city Boston neighborhoods. Seattle has suburban Bellevue and Redmond (where Microsoft is located), beautiful mountains and country, and a series of revitalized urban neighborhoods. The San Francisco Bay area has everything from posh inner-city neighborhoods to ultra-hip districts like SoMa (South of Market) and lifestyle enclaves like Marin County as well as the Silicon Valley. Even Austin includes traditional high-tech developments to the north, lifestyle centers for cycling and outdoor activities, and a revitalizing university/downtown community centered on vibrant Sixth Street, the warehouse district and the music scene—a critical element of a thriving creative center.

Institutional Sclerosis

Even as places like Austin and Seattle are thriving, much of the country is failing to adapt to the demands of the creative age. It is not that struggling cities like Pittsburgh do not want to grow or encourage high-tech industries. In most cases, their leaders are doing everything they think they can to spur innovation and high-tech growth. But most of the time, they are either unwilling or unable to do the things required to create an environment or habitat attractive to the creative class. They pay lip service to the need to "attract talent," but continue to pour resources into recruiting call centers, underwriting big-box retailers, subsidizing downtown malls, and squandering precious taxpayer dollars on extravagant stadium complexes. Or they try to create facsimiles of neighborhoods or retail districts, replacing the old and authentic with the new and generic—and in doing so drive the creative class away.

It is a telling commentary on our age that at a time when political will seems difficult to muster for virtually anything, city after city can generate the political capital to underwrite hundreds of millions of dollars of investments in professional sports stadiums. And you know what? They don't matter to the creative class. Not once during any of my focus groups and interviews did the members of the creative class mention professional sports as playing a role of any sort in their choice of where to live and work. What makes most cities unable to even imagine devoting those kinds of resources or political will to do the things that people say really matter to them?

The answer is simple. These cities are trapped by their past. Despite the lip service they might pay, they are unwilling or unable to do what it takes to attract the creative class. The late economist Mancur Olson long ago noted that the decline of nations and regions is a product of an organizational and cultural hardening of the arteries he called "institutional sclerosis." Places that grow up and prosper in one era, Olson argued, find it difficult and often times impossible to adopt new organizational and cultural patterns, regardless of how beneficial they might be. Consequently, innovation and growth shift to new places, which can adapt to and harness these shifts for their benefit. This phenomenon, he contends, is how England got trapped and how the U.S. became the world's great economic power. It also accounts for the shift in economic activity from the old industrial cities to newer cities in the South and West, according to Olson.

Olson's analysis presciently identifies why so many cities across the nation remain trapped in the culture and attitudes of the bygone organizational age, unable or unwilling to adapt to current trends. Cities like Detroit, Cleveland, and my current hometown of Pittsburgh were at the forefront of the organizational age. The cultural and attitudinal norms of that age became so powerfully ingrained in these places that they did not allow the new norms and attitudes associated with the creative age to grow up, diffuse and become generally accepted. This process, in turn, stamped out much of the creative impulse, causing talented and creative people to seek out new places where they could more readily plug in and make a go of it.

Most experts and scholars have not even begun to think in terms of a creative community. Instead, they tend to try to emulate the Silicon Valley model which author Joel Kotkin has dubbed the "nerdistan." But the nerdistan is a limited economic development model, which misunderstands the role played by creativity in generating innovation and economic growth. Nerdistans are bland, uninteresting places with acre upon acre of identical office complexes, row after row of asphalt parking lots, freeways clogged with cars, cookie-cutter housing developments, and strip-malls sprawling in every direction. Many of these places have fallen victim to the very kinds of problems they were supposed to avoid. The comfort and security of places like Silicon Valley have gradually given way to sprawl, pollution, and paralyzing traffic jams. As one technology executive told *The Wall Street Journal,* "I really didn't want to live in San Jose. Every time I went up there, the concrete jungle got me down." His company eventually settled on a more urban Southern California location in downtown Pasadena close to the CalTech campus.

Kotkin finds that the lack of lifestyle amenities is causing significant problems in attracting top creative people to places like the North Carolina Research Triangle. He quotes a major real estate developer as saying, "Ask anyone where downtown is and nobody can tell you. There's not much of a sense of place here. . . . The people I am selling space to are screaming about cultural issues." The Research Triangle lacks the hip urban lifestyle found in places like San Francisco, Seattle, New York, and Chicago, laments a University of North Carolina researcher: "In Raleigh-Durham, we can always visit the hog farms."

The Kids Are All Right

How do you build a truly creative community—one that can survive and prosper in this emerging age? The key can no longer be found in the usual strategies. Recruiting more companies won't do it; neither will trying to become the next Silicon Valley. While it certainly remains important to have a solid business climate, having an effective people climate is even more essential. By this I mean a general strategy aimed at attracting and retaining people—especially, but not limited to, creative people. This entails remaining open to diversity and actively working to cultivate it, and investing in the lifestyle amenities that people really want and use often, as opposed to using financial incentives to attract companies, build professional sports stadiums, or develop retail complexes.

The benefits of this kind of strategy are obvious. Whereas companies—or sports teams, for that matter—that get financial incentives can pull up and leave at virtually a moment's notice, investments in amenities like urban parks, for example, last for generations. Other amenities—like bike lanes or off-road trails for running, cycling, rollerblading, or just walking your dog—benefit a wide swath of the population.

There is no one-size-fits-all model for a successful people climate. The members of the creative class are diverse across the dimensions of age, ethnicity and race, marital status, and sexual preference. An effective people climate needs to emphasize openness and diversity, and to help reinforce low barriers to entry. Thus, it cannot be restrictive or monolithic.

Openness to immigration is particularly important for smaller cities and regions, while the ability to attract so-called bohemians is key for larger cities and regions. For cities and regions to attract these groups, they need to develop the kinds of people climates that appeal to them and meet their needs.

Yet if you ask most community leaders what kinds of people they'd most want to attract, they'd likely say successful married couples in their 30s and 40s—people with good middle-to-upper-income jobs and stable family lives. I certainly think it is important for cities and communities to be good for children and families. But less than a quarter of all American households consist of traditional nuclear families, and focusing solely on their needs has been a losing strategy, one that neglects a critical engine of economic growth: young people.

Young workers have typically been thought of as transients who contribute little to a city's bottom line. But in the creative age, they matter for two reasons. First, they are workhorses. They are able to work longer and harder, and are more prone to take risks, precisely because they are young and childless. In rapidly changing industries, it's often the most recent graduates who have the most up-to-date skills. Second, people are staying single longer. The average age of marriage for both men and women has risen some five years over the past generation. College-educated people postpone marriage longer than the national averages. Among this group, one of the fastest growing categories is the never-been-married. To prosper in the creative age, regions have to offer a people climate that satisfies this group's social interests and lifestyle needs, as well as address those of other groups.

Furthermore, a climate oriented to young people is also attractive to the creative class more broadly. Creative-class people do not lose their lifestyle preferences as they age. They don't stop bicycling or running, for instance, just because they have children. When they put their children in child seats or jogging strollers, amenities like traffic-free bike paths become more important than ever. They also continue to value diversity and tolerance. The middle-aged and older people I speak with may no longer hang around in nightspots until 4 A.M., but they enjoy stimulating, dynamic places with high levels of cultural interplay. And if they have children, that's the kind of environment in which they want them to grow up.

My adopted hometown of Pittsburgh has been slow to realize this. City leaders continue to promote Pittsburgh as a place that is good for families, seemingly unaware of the demographic changes that have made young people, singles, new immigrants, and gays critical to the emerging social fabric. People in focus groups I have conducted feel that Pittsburgh is not open to minority groups, new immigrants, or gays. Young women feel there are substantial barriers to their advancement. Talented members of racial and ethnic minorities, as well as professional women, express their desire to leave the city at a rate far greater than their white male counterparts. So do creative people from all walks of life.

Is there hope for Pittsburgh? Of course there is. First, although the region's economy is not dynamic, neither is it the basket case it could easily have become. Twenty years ago there were no significant venture capital firms in the area; now there are many, and thriving high-tech firms continue to form and make their mark. There are signs of life in the social and cultural milieu as well. The region's immigrant population has begun to tick upward, fed by students and professors at the universities and employees in the medical and technology sectors. Major suburbs to the east of the city now have Hindu temples and a growing Indian-American population. The area's gay community, while not large, has become more active and visible. Pittsburgh's increasing status in the gay world is reflected in the fact that it is the "location" for Showtime's "Queer as Folk" series.

Many of Pittsburgh's creative class have proven to be relentless cultural builders. The Andy Warhol Museum and the Mattress Factory, a museum/workspace devoted to large-scale installation art, have achieved worldwide recognition. Street-level culture has a growing foothold in Pittsburgh, too, as main street corridors in several older working-class districts have been transformed. Political leaders are in some cases open to new models of development. Pittsburgh mayor Tom Murphy has been an ardent promoter of biking and foot trails, among other things. The city's absolutely first-rate architecture and urban design community has become much more vocal about the need to preserve historic buildings, invest in neighborhoods, and institute tough design standards. It would be very hard today (dare I say nearly impossible) to knock down historic buildings and dismember vibrant urban neighborhoods as was done in the past. As these new groups and efforts reach critical mass, the norms and attitudes that have long prevailed in the city are being challenged.

For what it's worth, I'll put my money—and a lot of my effort—into Pittsburgh's making it. If Pittsburgh, with all of its assets and its emerging human creativity, somehow can't make it in the creative age, I fear the future does not bode well for other older industrial communities and established cities, and the lamentable new class segregation among cities will continue to worsen.

Critical Thinking

1. Who are the "creative class"?
2. What should a city do if it wishes to attract the creative class and creative industries?

RICHARD FLORIDA is a professor of regional economic development at Carnegie Mellon University and a columnist for *Information Week*. This article was adapted from his forthcoming book, *The Rise of the Creative Class: and How It's Transforming Work, Leisure, Community and Everyday Life* (Basic Books).

Too Much Froth

The latte quotient is a bad strategy for building middle-class cities.

JOEL KOTKIN AND FRED SIEGEL

Like smokers seeking a cure from their deadly habits, city politicians and economic development officials have a long history of grasping at fads to solve their persistent problems and rebuild middle class cities. In the 1960s and 1970s, the fad was for downtown malls. In the 1980s, it was convention centers and sports stadiums. But none of the fads came close to living up to their lofty billings.

Today, a new fad is bewitching urbanists and pols alike. Known as the "creativity craze," it promotes the notion that "young creatives" can drive an urban revival. It is a belated extension of the New Economy boom of the late 1990s. As with the idea of a New Economy, there is some merit to the focus on creativity. But as we learned from the dot-com bust that followed the boom, even the best ideas can be oversold.

Long before the current craze, Robert D. Atkinson of the Progressive Policy Institute wrote, "The ticket to faster and broader income growth is innovation." And one of the keys to innovation, he noted in describing his Metropolitan New Economy Indexes, is the ability to attract talented and innovative people. But he also emphasized the importance of school reform, infrastructure investments, work force development partnerships, public safety, and reinventing—and digitizing—city government. All these critical factors have been widely ignored by those who've discovered the magic bullet of "creative" urban development.

The new mantra advocates an urban strategy that focuses on being "hip" and "cool" rather than straightforward and practical. It is eagerly promoted by the Brookings Institution, by some urban development types, and by city pols from both parties in places like Cincinnati, Denver, Tampa, and San Diego. It seeks to displace the Progressive Policy Institute's New Economy Indexes with what might be called a "Latte Index"—the density of Starbucks—as a measure of urban success. Cities that will win the new competition, it's asserted, will be those that pour their resources into the arts and other cultural institutions that attract young, "with-it" people who constitute, for them, the contemporary version of the anointed. Call them latte cities.

But, like all the old bromides that were supposed to save America's cities, this one is almost certain to disappoint. Based partly on the ideas in Carnegie Mellon professor Richard Florida's book, *Rise of the Creative Class,* the notion of hip *uber alles* reminds one of the confectionary world of earlier gurus such as Charles Reich, author of *The Greening of America,* and John Naisbitt, author of *Megatrends.* Both promised a largely painless path to a brave new world, but both now are largely forgotten.

It's not surprising that after 50 years of almost uninterrupted middle class and job flight to the suburbs—even with the partial urban revival of the 1990s—urban officials might be tempted to clutch at straws. The appeal of such fads is plain to see. They seem to offer a way around the intractable problems of schools that fail to improve, despite continuous infusions of money; contentious zoning and regulatory policies that drive out business; and politically hyperactive public-sector unions and hectoring interest groups that make investment in cities something most entrepreneurs studiously avoid.

The "creative solution" pointedly avoids such hurdles, suggesting that the key to urban resurgence lies in attracting the diverse, the tolerant, and the gay. Having such a population is well and good, but unlikely by itself to produce a revival, let alone a diversified economy. Those most outspoken about such a culture- and lifestyle-based urban revival have all the heady passion of a religious movement; indeed, they've organized themselves into something called the Creative Class. One hundred of them—they called themselves the "Creative 100"—met in Memphis last spring to lay out their principles in a document called the Memphis Manifesto. Their mission, it reads, is to "remove barriers to creativity, such as mediocrity, intolerance, disconnectedness, sprawl, poverty, bad schools, exclusivity, and social and environmental degradation." The 1934 Soviet constitution couldn't have said it better.

This is an urban strategy for a frictionless universe. There is no mention of government or politics or interest groups. There's no recognition of the problems produced by outmoded regulations, runaway public spending, or high taxes. Instead we get the following froth: "Cultivate and reward creativity. Everyone is part of the value chain of creativity. Creativity can happen at any time, anywhere, and it's happening in your community right now."

Why do supposedly serious people embrace such ideas? After decades of decline and often fruitless political combat, mayors, city councils, and urban development officials seem ready to embrace any notion that holds out hope without offending the entrenched constituencies that resist real reform.

"The economic development people will buy anything that makes it seem easy," suggests Leslie Parks, former chairwoman of the California Economic Development Corp. "They see a schtick that requires few hard choices, and they bought it."

Parks traces much of the current enthusiasm for the "creative" strategy to the late 1990s dot-com boom. In this period, there was a palpable economic surge in certain cities—San Francisco; Portland, Ore.; Seattle; Austin, Texas; New York—that also attracted bright, "creative" young people, and, incidentally, many gays. These are the cities that Florida and his acolytes have held up as models for other towns.

Yet virtually all these places have been hemorrhaging jobs and people since the boom busted. San Francisco, according to economist David Friedman, has actually lost employment at a rate comparable to that of the Great Depression. Roughly 4 percent of the population has simply left town, often to go to more affordable, if boring, places, such as Sacramento. San Francisco is increasingly a city without a real private-sector economy. It's home to those on the government or nonprofit payroll and the idle rich—"a cross between Carmel and Calcutta," in the painful phrase of California state librarian Kevin Starr, a San Francisco native.

As for the others, they are no bargain either. Seattle has also lost jobs at a far faster rate than the rest of the country and has its own litany of social problems, including a sizable homeless population; the loss of its signature corporation, Boeing; and growing racial tensions.

Although Portland is often hailed as a new urban paradise, it is in a region suffering very high unemployment. "They made a cool place, but the economy sucks," notes Parks, who conducted a major study for the Oregon city. "They forgot all the things that matter, like economic diversification and affordability."

New York City has also suffered heavy job losses. Gotham's population outflows, which slowed in the late 1990s, have accelerated, including in Manhattan, the city's cool core. In contrast, New York's relatively unhip suburbs, particularly those in New Jersey, quietly weathered the Bush recession in fairly fine fettle.

Today, economic growth is shifting to less fashionable but more livable locales such as San Bernardino and Riverside Counties, Calif.; Rockland County, N.Y.; Des Moines, Iowa; Bismarck, N.D.; and Sioux Falls, S.D.

In many cases, this shift also encompasses technology-oriented and professional service firms, whose ranks ostensibly dominate the so-called "creative class." This trend actually predates the 2000 crash, but it has since accelerated. Since the 1990s, the growth in financial and other business services has taken place not in New York, San Francisco, or Seattle, but in lower-cost places like Phoenix; Charlotte, N.C.; Minneapolis; and Des Moines.

Perhaps more important, the outflow from decidedly un-hip places like the Midwest has slowed, and even reversed. Employers report that workers are seeking more affordable housing, and, in many cases, less family-hostile environments.

To be sure, such cities are not without their share of Starbucks outlets, and they have put great stress on quality-of-life issues—like recreation and green space—that appeal to families and relocating firms. But the watchword is livability, not coolness. "It's gotten very easy to get workers to relocate here," notes Randy Schilling, founder and CEO of Quilogy, a St. Louis-area technology company. "You get a guy here from Chicago, New York, and San Francisco, and even if he gets a pay cut, he and his family lives better."

There is, fortunately, an alternative to a hollow urban politics that relies mainly on the hip and the cool. Such a politics lies not in trendy ideas that will be forgotten a decade from now, but in commonsense policies that stress basic services like police and firefighters, innovative public schools that are not beholden to teachers' unions, breaking down of barriers to new housing construction, and policies that lead local businesses to expand within the urban area. It's a politics that, to paraphrase the great urbanist Jane Jacobs, seeks not to "lure" a middle class with bars, bells, and whistles, but instead aims to create one at the grassroots level.

That's the kind of "creativity" that cities, and Democrats, really need to embrace.

Critical Thinking

1. How can cities be criticized for the various strategies they use to attract the creative class and major global corporations?

JOEL KOTKIN is a senior fellow at the Davenport Institute for Public Policy at Pepperdine University. He is writing a history of cities for Modern Library. **FRED SIEGEL** is a professor at The Cooper Union and culture editor of *Blueprint*.

Studies: Gentrification a Boost for Everyone

Everyone knows gentrification uproots the urban poor with higher rents, higher taxes and $4 lattes. It's the lament of community organizers, the theme of the 2004 film *Barbershop 2* and the guilty assumption of the yuppies moving in.

RICK HAMPSON

But everyone may be wrong, according to Lance Freeman, an assistant professor of urban planning at Columbia University.

In an article last month in *Urban Affairs Review*, Freeman reports the results of his national study of gentrification—the movement of upscale (mostly white) settlers into rundown (mostly minority) neighborhoods.

His conclusion: Gentrification drives comparatively few low-income residents from their homes. Although some are forced to move by rising costs, there isn't much more displacement in gentrifying neighborhoods than in non-gentrifying ones.

In a separate study of New York City published last year, Freeman and a colleague concluded that living in a gentrifying neighborhood there actually made it less likely a poor resident would move—a finding similar to that of a 2001 study of Boston by Duke University economist Jacob Vigdor.

Freeman and Vigdor say that although higher costs sometimes force poor residents to leave gentrifying neighborhoods, other changes—more jobs, safer streets, better trash pickup—encourage them to stay. But to others, gentrification remains a dirty word.

"All you have to do is talk to people around here," says James Lewis, a tenant organizer in Harlem, New York's most famous black neighborhood. "Everybody with money is moving into Harlem, and the people who are here are being displaced."

Even residents who have survived gentrification tend to believe it forces people out.

Maria Marquez, 37, has slept on the sofa for 12 years to give her mother and son the two bedrooms in their apartment in Chicago's gentrifying Logan Square area. But eventually, she says, "we're gonna get kicked out. It's a matter of time."

Kathe Newman, assistant professor of public policy at Rutgers University, argues that Freeman's research in New York understates the extent of displacement. But she says he has raised a good question: How, in the face of relentlessly higher living costs, do so many poor people stay put?

A Hot-Button Issue

Gentrification has spawned emotional disputes in cities around the nation:

- In northwest Fort Lauderdale, where streets are named for the district's prominent old African-American families, three of four new home buyers are white, according to a survey by the *Sun-Sentinel*. City Commissioner Carlton Moore told the newspaper his largely black constituency fears displacement, even though he says it won't happen.

- In the predominantly Latino working class barrio of East Austin, the new Pedernales Lofts condominiums have raised adjacent land values more than 50% since 2003. Last fall, someone hung signs from power lines outside the lofts saying, "Stop gentrifying the East Side" and "Will U give jobs to longtime residents of this neighborhood?"

- In Charlotte, a City Council committee voted in December to remove language from a city planning department report that downplayed gentrification's threat to neighborhoods. Development could uproot some people, councilman John Tabor told the *Charlotte Observer* "If there are people in these neighborhoods who have to move because they can't afford their taxes, that's who I want to help," he said.

- In Boston's North End, the destruction of the noisy Central Artery elevated highway promises to attract younger, more affluent new residents and dilute the traditional Italian immigrant culture.

In the two decades after World War II, government urban renewal schemes tore down whole neighborhoods and scattered residents.

Gentrification, which appeared in the 1970s, was something else. Motivated by high gasoline prices, suburban sprawl and a new taste for old architecture, some middle class whites began moving into neighborhoods that had gone out of fashion a generation or two earlier.

Here's how it works: A dilapidated and depopulated but essentially attractive neighborhood—solid housing stock, well laid-out streets, proximity to the city center—is discovered by artists, graduate students and other bohemians.

Block by block, the neighborhood changes. The newcomers fix up old buildings. Galleries and cafes open, and mom 'n' pop groceries close. City services improve. Finally, the bohemians are joined by lawyers, stockbrokers and dentists. Property values rise, followed by property taxes and rents.

To some urban planners, gentrification is a solution to racial segregation, a shrinking tax base and other problems. To others, it *is* a problem: Poor blacks and Hispanics, who've held on through hard times and sometimes started the neighborhood's comeback, are ousted by their own success.

Jose Sanchez, an urban planning expert at Long Island University in Brooklyn, says some changing neighborhoods stabilize with a mixture of people. But he says the poor—and the bohemian pioneers—can also be "washed out" by scheming landlords or government policies such as rezoning and urban renewal.

The Poor Stay Put

Freeman and Vigdor say gentrification has gotten a bad rap. When they studied New York City and Boston, respectively, they found that poor and less educated residents of gentrifying neighborhoods actually moved less often than people in other neighborhoods—20% less in New York.

For his national study published this year, Freeman found only a slight connection between gentrification and displacement. A poor resident's chances of being forced to move out of a gentrifying neighborhood are only 0.5% greater than in a non-gentrifying one.

So how do some neighborhoods change so dramatically? Freeman says it's mostly the result of what he calls "succession": Poor people in gentrifying neighborhoods who move from their homes—for whatever reason—usually are replaced by people who have more income and education.

Freeman and Vigdor say skeptics who view gentrification merely as "hood snatching" should remember three things:

- Many older neighborhoods have high turnover, whether they gentrify or not. Vigdor says that over five years, about half of all urban residents move.
- Such neighborhoods often have so much vacant or abandoned housing that there's no need to drive anyone out to accommodate people who want to move in. A quarter of the housing in one section of Boston's South End was vacant in 1970; the population had dropped by more than 50% over 20 years. Today, the population has increased more than 50%, and the vacancy rate is less than 2%.
- Rising housing costs in gentrifying districts may ensure that poor residents who do move leave the neighborhood, rather than settle elsewhere in it. Since

their places usually are taken by more affluent, better educated people, the neighborhood's character and demographics change.

Vigdor argues that hatred of gentrification is largely irrational: "We were angry when the middle class moved out of the city," he says. "Now we're angry when they move back."

He asks whether Detroit, which in 50 years has lost half its population and most of its middle class, would not have been better off with gentrification than it has been without it.

A Housing Shortage

Gentrification is a symptom of a bigger problem: Metro areas don't create enough housing, Vigdor says. When prices in the suburbs get high enough, home buyers start looking at "undervalued" urban housing. If it's close to downtown and has some period charm, so much the better.

But critics insist gentrification does real harm to real people. Lewis, the Harlem organizer, says he can't get statements from people who were forced out because he doesn't know where they went.

A surprising number of poor people, however, manage to hold on. Some explanations:

- **Homeownership.** Homeowners face rising property taxes, but unlike renters they also stand to gain from rising values. Idida Perez, 46, complains that taxes and escrow payments on her two-family house near Logan Square in Chicago have jumped $300 a month over the past few years. But the house, which she and her husband bought for $200,000 in 1990, is now worth $400,000.
- **Rent control.** Samuel Ragland, 82, pays $115 a month for his one-room rent-controlled apartment on fast-gentrifying West 120th Street in Harlem. His building is being converted into condos, but under New York law, his landlord can't move him out unless he's given a comparable apartment at a comparable rent in the same area.
- **Government subsidies.** Carole Singleton, 52, had to retire from her job as a hospital administrator after she got cancer. But she's been able to stay in Harlem because she pays only $300 of the $971 rent for her apartment; a federal housing subsidy covers the rest.
- **Doubling (or tripling) up.** After the rent on Ofelia Sanchez's one-bedroom apartment in the Logan Square area went from $500 to $600, she and her two kids moved into a three-bedroom with Sanchez's mother and her sister's family. The apartment houses 10 people. Sanchez and her son share a bed, and her daughter sleeps on the floor. But Sanchez won't move; she works as a tutor at the local elementary school, and her mother babysits while she takes classes at Chicago State University. "This is home," she says of the neighborhood where she's lived for 26 of her 27 years. "I don't know anyone anywhere else."

- **Landlord-tenant understandings.** In return for $595 monthly rent for a two-bedroom apartment, tenant Maria Marquez rakes the leaves and shovels the front walk. She lays floor tile, repairs holes in the porch and changes light fixtures. It enables her, her son and her mother to stay in an area of Chicago where two-bedrooms rent for $1,000.

- **More income devoted to rent.** Poor New York households in gentrifying neighborhoods spent 61% of their income on housing, compared with 52% for the poor in non-gentrifying ones, Freeman found. Klare Allen, who is in her mid-40s, has been able to keep her three-bedroom apartment in Roxbury, a black neighborhood close to downtown Boston. But she has to pay $1,400 a month—75% of her monthly income.

- **Prayer.** Alma Feliciano, 46, of Boston asked God for an affordable apartment that would allow her and her four children to stay in Roxbury and continue to attend her church, Holy Tabernacle. Her prayers were granted—a unit in a federally subsidized complex. Otherwise, she says, she would have had to leave the city.

One reason poor families make such heroic efforts to stay is because the quality of life is improving—partly thanks to gentrification.

In the Logan Square area, Marquez says, an influx of higher-income newcomers has coincided with what seems like more aggressive policing.

"The gang bangers are not around as much, and you don't see the prostitutes on the corners like you used to," she says.

Idida Perez hates the rising prices but admits, "There are a lot more small cafes owned by people from the neighborhood, and I am a big coffee drinker." And new businesses mean new jobs: Someone has to pour those lattes.

Critical Thinking

1. Why do cities pursue gentrification?
2. What criticisms are often made of gentrification?
3. Are there benefits that gentrification can bring to poorer residents of an inner-city neighborhood that is undergoing upgrading?
4. How do critics attack the more positive assessment of gentrification presented in this article?

UNIT 3

Competitive Pressures and Economic Development

Unit Selections

Learning Outcomes

After reading this unit, you should be able to:

- Understand why, for many cities, economists do not consider subsidies to sports stadiums and arenas to be a good investment for a city.

- Understand why city and state officials continue to give extensive subsidies for the development of sports stadiums and arenas despite evidence that casts doubts as to their cost-effectiveness.

- Propose a "good" deal for a city when it comes to subsidizing the construction of sports stadiums and arenas and how such a "good" deal differs from a "bad" deal for the city.

- Identify the members of a city's "growth coalition" and the actions that members of the growth coalition take in their effort to gain public and political support for the construction of new sports arenas and convention centers.

- Defend a city's use of eminent domain powers to "take" private property for local economic development.

- Criticize a city's use of eminent domain powers to "take" private property for local economic development.

- Appraise the action of the states in defining local eminent domain powers in the wake of the U.S. Supreme Court's *Kelo* decision.

Student Website

www.mhhe.com/cls

Internet Reference

Field of Schemes
www.fieldofschemes.com

As Paul Peterson observed in his influential book *City Limits,* a city must attract and keep business in order to keep the local economy and tax base in good shape. But businesses often have a fairly wide choice of communities in which to locate their headquarters and production facilities. As a result, localities—and city-regions—wind up **competing with one another** to attract desirable businesses.

Cities in the United States often offer a major employer extensive tax breaks and other subsidies in an effort to influence a business' siting decisions. Cities also pay for the infrastructure improvements that make a place attractive to business—strengthened roadways that can support heavy trucks; the installation of new sewer lines; updated telecommunications wiring and fiber optics networks; and sophisticated satellite uplinks and teleports. The revenues lost through tax concessions and the various subsidies given businesses represent a diversion of funds that can no longer be used for other important public services. The question is: Just when is it wise for a city to offer such concessions to business? When are such concessions unnecessary and a waste of taxpayer money?

Members of the local **growth coalition**—downtown business owners, real estate interests, organized labor, and other groups who gain profits or jobs from a city's continued growth—often push for new development projects that require extensive financing by local government. The leaders of the growth coalition argue that such investment is essential for the future competitiveness or prosperity of the community. How, they ask, can a city attract visitors and retain its reputation for being a major-league community if it lacks a modern convention center, a casino, or state-of-the-art sports arenas and stadiums. The growth coalition argues that a city that fails to act will see business and economic activity drift to other cities. In most cities, politicians endorse proposed publicly-funded stadiums from fear of being blamed if the local sports franchise decides to leave town.

Yet, the members of the growth coalition often understate the costs and overstate the benefits that the city receives from new development projects, such as the building of a new stadium or convention centers. When voters have to pick up the tab for costly failure, the result is a new public skepticism. Charles Mahtesian (Article 13, "Throwaway Stadium") points to the numerous instances where cities have subsidized new sports facilities only to find that the facilities are often soon deemed to be antiquated by team owners who then demand that city taxpayers pick up the cost of building new and even more grand facilities, with skyboxes and the sale of seat licenses that add to the owners' profits. Stadiums seldom deliver the municipal revenues and the full public benefits that their growth coalition backers promised (Article 14, "Skybox Skeptics"). In Seattle, Miami, and Minneapolis, citizens and public officials have both become increasingly reluctant to fund the construction of the new stadiums and arenas. Nonetheless, as evident in the Minnesota decision to help finance the construction of Target Field to replace the baseball Twins' old Metrodome home, even reluctant localities eventually cede to much of the demands of team owners, from fear of seeing the team move elsewhere.

© Ingram Publishing

Heywood Sanders (Article 15, "A Lot of Hooey": Heywood Sanders on Convention Center Economics) questions whether investment in a new convention center really makes sense in most cities. In city after city, the growth coalition has hired expert financial consultants who deliver elaborate presentations loaded with graphs and statistics that attempt to document the extensive economic benefits that a new convention center will bring to a community and how the cost to taxpayers will be quite manageable. These studies often show that a convention center will be self-sustaining, that the shows and conventions will yield so much new revenue for the city that the new facility essentially pays for itself. Yet, Sanders points to the suspect nature and methodology of such analyses, especially when the national consulting firms often present the same analysis with much of the same exact language, in the quite optimistic reports they deliver to city after city. Such reports, apparently, are not really based on careful analysis. As Sanders points out, convention centers have too many idle days—days during which the halls and meeting rooms lie vacant—to deliver the extensive revenues and economic gains that the growth coalition predicted. There are just too few good-paying conventions to justify the building of expensive facilities in so many cities. Only a small handful of cities will find that their convention centers will run "in the black." In most cities, instead of paying for themselves, the operation of convention centers requires a never-ending stream of subsidies from taxpayers.

One of the most explosive contemporary controversies in the field of local economic development revolves around the use of **eminent domain** powers, the ability of the government to take private land for **public use,** paying fair compensation to the owners (Article 16, "Eminent Domain Revisited"). Many Americans concerned with the protection of individual property rights are unaware that the power of eminent domain is actually mentioned in the United States Constitution. The **Fifth Amendment** permits "private property [to] be taken for public use," with the requirement that the government pay the owners "just compensation."

But what constitutes "public use"? Most Americans have no objection when the government takes a private parcel of land, compensating the owner, in order to complete such public facilities as a road, bridge, prison, airport, or a university campus. But can a local government seize the property of one person in order to give it to a new private owner who intends to build a new upscale housing project or shopping center, projects that may bring businesses, jobs, and increased tax revenues back to a troubled community?

New London, Connecticut, used its eminent domain powers to assemble the land for a local economic development project that included new offices, residences, shopping malls, and a resort hotel. A number of local property owners objected, and the controversy worked its way up to the U.S. Supreme Court. In its **Kelo decision,** the Court ruled on behalf of the local government, that New London had the right to take private property for economic development. For a city suffering continued economic woes, projects aimed at local economic development and the creation of jobs constitute a sufficient public purpose to justify the exercise of eminent domain powers.

The Court's decision, however, did not end the controversy. Cities are the creations of the state; technically speaking, cities are mere administrative subunits of state government. Each state decides just what powers its local governments possess. Most states, under their constitutions, retain the authority to withdraw or modify the powers granted local governments. As the public outcry over the use of eminent domain mounted (especially as right-wing talk-radio focused on the issue, even exaggerating the likelihood that governments would seize churches and their property), state after state has placed additional restrictions limiting the use of eminent domain powers by local governments.

Do the new laws serve to protect individual property rights, thwarting new projects that often wind up doing little more than enriching powerful developers? Do the new restrictions help protect the urban poor and minorities who often find that they are the victims of displacement as the city takes property core neighborhoods at the behuest of powerful institutions undergoing expansion? Or do the new state restrictions represent an unwise intrusion of local authority that places one more obstacle in the path of distressed communities as they desperately seek to initiate actions that will commence a city's economic rebound?

Throwaway Stadium

The fancy new arena you build today may be a white elephant before you know it.

CHARLES MAHTESIAN

When the dazzling new Staples Center arena opened in Los Angeles last October, basketball and hockey fans marveled at the $400 million building's amenities. The design, more Architectural Digest than Sports Illustrated, features massive glass atriums, terrazzo floors, a state-of-the-art scoreboard, restaurants, retail stores and a swank private club. Some hailed it as the most spectacular arena ever built. And yet, on opening night, the Los Angeles Times greeted the occasion with this yawning headline: "When Will It Become Obsolete?"

It's a fair question to ask. Staples Center represents the cutting-edge for the time being, but if the nation's stadium- and arena-building boom continues, even gaudy Staples may find itself reaching obsolescence not too far in the future. In that case, it will join a growing herd of white elephants that now clutters the urban and suburban landscape.

The remarkable thing about America's discarded sports facilities is that, for the most part, they are not ancient or dilapidated. Most of them were built within the past 30 years. They have become casualties of the throwaway stadium syndrome that is afflicting professional sports all over the country.

A few miles outside the nation's capital, in Landover, Maryland, the USAirways Arena sits empty. Considered a state-of-the-art building when it opened in 1973, it has been stripped of its professional basketball and hockey teams. Once the Wizards and Capitals departed for a newly constructed facility in downtown Washington, D.C., the arena was reduced to scrambling for the occasional horse show, concert or rally to fill a few of its 19,000 seats.

Dozens of cities are currently stuck with empty, obsolete or underutilized arenas. According to Fitch ICBA, a bond rating agency, 41 major league sports teams are playing in facilities built since 1990. Another 49 are either seeking new facilities or have them under construction. Approximately $6 billion is projected to be spent on new ones that will open over the next several years. You don't have to be a municipal finance expert or even a sports fan to figure out that for almost every new major league palace that opens, another one loses its reason for existence.

Some of the lifeless arenas and stadiums—or at least the properties—do eventually find a productive role to play. Baltimore recently approved a proposal from a nonprofit, church-based group that would turn the site of Memorial Stadium, abandoned home of the Orioles, into a YMCA and housing for low- and moderate-income senior citizens. More often, though, the ultimate fate is simply conversion to asphalt. The site of what used to be Atlanta's Fulton County Stadium is now a parking lot for Turner Field. In Denver, some of the 28 acres occupied by the soon-to-be-razed McNichols Arena will provide parking for a new football stadium.

Like USAirways Arena, some facilities survive by accepting second-banana status, hosting tractor pulls, school graduations and minor league sports. In some instances, that model works well. Philadelphia's Spectrum, the city's premier arena for nearly three decades, now serves to complement the First Union Center, its newer rival, as part of the First Union Complex. The two stadiums engage in joint marketing campaigns, share staffs and are positioned for different event markets. The hockey Flyers and basketball 76ers take advantage of the 126 luxury suites in the new building, while the Spectrum hosts more modestly priced minor league hockey and soccer games, as well as events too small to occasion the newer building.

But arenas in most cities don't have that sort of option. And since many of them are either publicly owned, publicly financed or otherwise integral to a community's development and planning scheme, an ever-increasing number of localities are being forced to come to grips with the harsh economic realities of the throwaway era.

Five years from now, says Bill Dorsey of the Association of Luxury Suite Directors, "just about everyone will have a new field. These things have been romanticized by writers, but these are just buildings. They're a business and they have a price."

The dawn of the throwaway era can be traced back to 1988, when both the Miami Arena and the Palace of Auburn Hills, in Michigan, opened their doors. Both buildings looked glitzy and modern, but the glitz concealed a fundamental difference. The Miami Arena, although built at a cost of $52 million, had 16 luxury suites for well-heeled and free-spending clientele. The Palace boasted 180 suites. Within a matter of months, the fate of both arenas was sealed. The Palace was going to be a success; the Miami Arena was not.

Within a few years, the NBA Miami Heat were looking to flee to a new home more hospitable to the heavy wallets. This year, they got it: the brand-new $185 million AmericanAirlines Arena, with six $500,000-a-year "star boxes," 20 suites, 54 lounges and 304 courtside luxury seats. The cheapest premium package sells for $10,000 a year. The Miami Arena, meanwhile, lost not only the Heat but also the National Hockey League Panthers, who received their own new facility in neighboring Broward County.

Today, the 11-year-old, 20,000 seat Miami Arena is used for minor league hockey and a few other not-ready-for-prime-time events. The Detroit Pistons, meanwhile, remain happily ensconced in their Auburn Hills home. "Premium seating is the financial underpinning of the modern arena," says Dorsey. "It is largely responsible for this. Once that started happening, other teams had to do it in order to compete."

Pro sports haven't been so kind to all the suburban arenas. Back in the 1970s and '80s, the trend was for teams to follow the out-migration from the central cities. Now, the trend has been reversed—teams are moving back downtown. Unlike shuttered downtown facilities, the suburban arenas have limited options for reuse.

When an arena is located downtown, it sometimes can be used to complement a convention center trade. That doesn't work for places such as the USAirways Arena, 15 miles beyond the city limits. The suburban white elephant arenas aren't much use for office space, either, so frequently the only choice is to go for commercial development—provided someone can be found who is interested in the property.

As quite a few communities have learned, those customers aren't easy to find. In 1996, when the NFL Detroit

Built and Abandoned

Name/Location	Opened	Lost Major Franchise	Current Status
Atlanta-Fulton County Stadium	1965	1996	Demolished
USAirways Arena, Landover, Md.	1973	1997	Occasional events
Cobo Arena, Detroit	1965	1997	Occasional events
McNichols Arena, Denver	1975	1999	Set for demolition in 2000
Memorial Stadium, Baltimore	1950	1997	Set for demolition in 2000
Miami Arena	1988	1999	Occasional events
Philadelphia Spectrum	1967	1996	Occasional events
St. Louis Arena	1929	1994	Demolished

Source: GOVERNING research.

Lions announced their move out of the Silverdome in suburban Pontiac, and back to the big city, Pontiac officials hastily convened a task force on the field's 50-yard line to explore alternative uses for the domed stadium. They disbanded just as quickly.

The one consolation for Pontiac has been the Lions' lease on the city-owned Silverdome, which runs until 2004. Since the team plans to break ground on the new stadium sometime this year, they will likely have to pay Pontiac to escape. Meanwhile, Pontiac officials continue to mull over options for future use of the land. The Silverdome is located at the intersection of two major freeways along the I-75 corridor, so an industrial park is one possibility; there is also talk of an Indian gambling casino, with visions of new gold in property-tax payments and thousands of new jobs for local residents. But those dreams are still a long way from fulfillment, or even ground-breaking.

No matter what Pontiac decides, it is unlikely to replicate the solution found by Ohio's rural Richfield Township. Built in the middle of farmland halfway between Akron and Cleveland, the Richfield Coliseum became home in the 1970s to the NBA Cleveland Cavaliers. The Cavaliers' owner gambled that commercial development would surely follow the franchise. He was wrong. The Coliseum bathed in red ink for years, and when the city of Cleveland came calling with a sweetheart arena deal to move the Cavaliers back downtown in 1994, the team jumped at the offer. The owners of the Coliseum, a building whose heating costs alone ran as high as $250,000 per month, decided it made more sense to keep the place dark than to operate it.

Meanwhile, the owners entertained a variety of proposals that included turning the arena into a televangelist's headquarters, a private jail, a movie-production facility, a retirement village, an Olympic training center, or an outlet shopping mall. In the end, though, the Coliseum found a use that no one predicted. In January of last year, the 327-acre property was purchased by the Trust for Public Land, which then transferred it to the National Park Service to become part of the Cuyahoga Valley National Recreation Area. "It doesn't have unique attributes as such, but it does have some wetlands," says Christopher Knopf of the Trust for Public Land. "It was really a preventative action to keep traffic from going through the national park."

For environmentalists and many local residents, the deal represented a major victory in a battle over development that had been going on since the early 1970s. But not everyone was thrilled. When the owners mothballed the Coliseum, local schools took a hard hit from the loss of tax revenues. Now, there will be no chance to recoup those losses, or for any further development at the site.

"The county probably should have stepped up to the plate, bought the facility and the 250 acres and land banked it for long-term economic development," says Summit County Councilman John Bolek, whose district includes the Coliseum site. "It does look nice now, but was it really in our best interests to add 250 acres to the eight or nine thousand acres already in the park?"

Critical Thinking

1. What does the author mean by referring to US Airways Arena (outside of Washington DC) and the Pontiac Silverdome (just north of Detroit) as "white elephants"?

2. Should a city help to subsidize the building of a new stadium or sports arena?

Skybox Skeptics

It's getting harder and harder for baseball teams to wangle public money for new stadiums.

JOSH GOODMAN

Many traveling salesmen have met the fate David Samson encountered in Portland, Oregon, a few months ago. When the Florida businessman ventured to town to hawk his goods, he was greeted with a curt "No, thank you" and a metaphorical slam of the door. Salesmen get used to that. What makes Samson unusual, however, is that his product wasn't a line of clothing or some useless gizmo. It was a product one would expect to generate a good deal of excitement: a major league baseball team.

Samson, president of the Florida Marlins, went to Portland to discuss relocation of the two-time World Series champions. If the goal of his trip was either to pressure Florida legislators to chip in money toward a new stadium or to find a new home that would, he failed spectacularly. Tom Potter, Portland's mayor, not only reasserted his opposition to public financing of a stadium but insisted he spoke for most of his constituents. Asked whether most Portlanders "couldn't care less about a baseball team," he replied, "That's my very strong sense."

Although Potter's bluntness is unusual, his perspective is not unique. Local and state governments are putting up increasing resistance to the idea of paying for new baseball stadiums. The Minnesota Twins have spent a decade trying to win public funds for a new ballpark but have been rebuffed by the legislature every time, most recently last year. The Marlins began seeking new suitors after the Florida legislature refused to contribute state money to build the team a new home. And the District of Columbia's City Council has already demanded, and won, multiple renegotiations of the deal that brought the Washington Nationals to town last year.

Public funding for stadiums has not exactly dried up. Since 2000, the average new major league baseball stadium has been built with 54 percent public funds, compared with 55 percent for new professional football stadiums. But the trend clearly seems to be moving in the other direction. The one ballpark completed in the past two years, in St. Louis, was built almost entirely with private money.

Communities are playing hardball with the national pastime largely as a result of two developments. First, elected officials have begun to accept academic research showing that the economic benefits of subsidizing stadiums doesn't justify the costs. Second, threats by team owners to leave town are losing their potency because it is widely known that there are very few attractive markets for them to move to. Against this backdrop, baseball's supporters may have to turn to a different argument: that the sport is worth subsidizing simply because it is integral to a community's quality of life.

Negative Numbers

Until recently, baseball teams didn't worry much about strategy when they sought public money for stadiums. They talked about economic development, and assumed (correctly) that few would question them. This was especially true when teams sought subsidies from new territory they were hoping to enter. To begin with, owners argued, the construction of a stadium would be a plentiful source of jobs. Then, once it became operational, hundreds of thousands of fans would pour in, patronizing restaurants, bars and retailers in the area before and after games. As a result, a new stadium could serve as the linchpin to the revival of an entire community.

Business groups and other stadium backers still make this argument, but they are facing increasing skepticism. In the past decade, economist after economist has lambasted the idea that governments are making a prudent choice when they invest in stadiums. Their central point has been that most people have relatively fixed entertainment budgets. That means a dollar spent on baseball is a dollar not spent elsewhere in the local economy. Many academics are also skeptical that stadiums can revitalize neighborhoods. When a new stadium goes up in any city, says Villanova University's Rick Eckstein, "you can see for yourself, even if you're a lay person, that there's not much going on there except on game days."

Many elected officials who oppose subsidizing stadiums make ample use of the economic data. John Marty, a Minnesota state senator, argues that the issue should not be whether the subsidy produces some tangible benefit but whether the benefit is equal to the cost. "If I give you $150 million, it's going to stimulate the economy, I guarantee it." Marty says. "But $150 million doesn't come out of thin air."

The shift in sentiment has hit baseball harder than it has hit other sports. Despite pro football's popularity, few teams ever argued seriously that an NFL stadium could spur an economic revitalization. With only eight regular-season home games per year, there simply weren't enough game days to boost area businesses. Major League Baseball, with a home schedule in each stadium of 81 games per year, did make this argument. So baseball had more to lose if the economic reasoning came into question—and that is what is occurring now.

The result is that longstanding stadium foes—critics on the right who see public financing as an impetus for higher taxes and critics on the left who view it as welfare for billionaires—have more influence than they did in the past. The recent spats in Florida, Minnesota and D.C. have shown that political opposition, in conjunction with budgetary pressures, can turn the tide against public financing. "Local governments have enormous needs and those needs are increasing each year and they're becoming more complicated and more expensive," says Ian Yorty, Miami-Dade County's tax collector and negotiator of the Marlins stadium deal that the legislature failed to ratify last year. "If you don't have a direct mandate from the voters, it's hard to find enough money to throw at a sports stadium."

No Place to Go

Baseball owners have one other serious credibility problem, especially when it comes to cities with existing franchises: They frequently talk about moving out of town, but they almost never do. The Montreal Expos, who became the Washington Nationals last year, are the only team to change cities in the past three decades. In the Expos' case, it took years of miserable attendance before the team finally left.

Football teams switch cities far more frequently, and the reason isn't difficult to understand. Filling a stadium eight times a year is a test even small cities can meet if given the chance. Green Bay, Wisconsin, with a population of 101,000, sells out Lambeau Field for every Packers game. It could never support a baseball team, nor would any baseball owner ever consider locating there. That is true of other cities several times the size of Green Bay. In fact, some observers doubt whether any locale that doesn't already have a major league baseball team—Portland, San Antonio, Las Vegas and Norfolk, Virginia, are mentioned most frequently as possible destinations—could support a franchise. "Market size is important to baseball in a way that it isn't to any other sport," says Neil deMause, an author who is critical of public financing of stadiums. "The NFL can put teams anywhere they want."

The lack of attractive destinations hasn't stopped owners from threatening relocation, but it has made the threats much less effective in recent years. The Twins have been rumored to be heading out of town for much of John Marty's 20-year tenure in the Minnesota Senate, and at one point Major League Baseball publicly contemplated folding the franchise. "They kept hyping it so much," says Marty. "They were going to contract the team, they were going to move the team, they were going to sell the team, but after three or four times people realize it's bogus."

Supporters of public funding for a new Twins stadium continue to warn that the team might actually leave in the absence of a new ballpark, noting that the Expos, did, in the end, move to Washington. But the widespread perception that Twins threats have been idle has encouraged lawmakers to take a stance against public funding. Last year, the legislature failed to give approval to a plan for a new stadium, even though the public costs would have been borne exclusively by Hennepin County, which approved the funding package. A court ruled last month that the Twins are not bound to stay in their current stadium, the Metrodome, beyond this season, a decision that may put pressure on lawmakers to make a final decision.

In Florida, the threat of a Marlins departure also backfired. After team officials met with Las Vegas representatives to discuss a possible move there, Florida Senate President Tom Lee, rather than seeking additional state money to keep the team in town, accused the Marlins of "blackmail," declaring that "I don't negotiate with terrorists." Later in the year, the team reached a deal with Miami-Dade County officials that was predicated on the legislature kicking in $60 million in state money. Legislators balked at that sum and the measure stalled.

More Like a Museum

If baseball teams can no longer make a persuasive claim that they are engines of economic development, or pressure communities by threatening to leave town, what might they use as a strategy for obtaining public money?

Mike Opat, a commissioner in Hennepin County, Minnesota, thinks he has the answer. Opat, a sponsor of the Twins funding proposal that the legislature rejected, makes an analogy between stadiums and cultural amenities such as museums and theaters: No one argues for a new museum on the grounds that it will create jobs or revitalize a neighborhood. But people enjoy museums, vibrant communities have them, and citizens come to expect them.

Opat acknowledges that, from an economist's perspective, publicly financed stadiums aren't always worth the price, but wishes there was more focus on the qualitative benefits of a new ballpark. "I can't put a dollar value on the number of seniors or young people who follow the team," he says. "There are just a host of intangibles."

The question going forward is whether this "quality of life" argument will be enough to sustain support for public financing—whether the situations in Florida and Minnesota are aberrations or a sign of more resistance to come. Baseball is only a quality of life issue as long as people care about the games. In this regard, there are some disturbing omens. World Series audience ratings have dropped dramatically over the past two decades, which seems to suggest that Potter's assessment of fan interest is true in many places beyond Portland. But, if baseball has been anything over the course of its history, it has been resilient. That trait may be more necessary than ever in an era in which public financing will not be easily won.

Critical Thinking

1. What are the "negative numbers" that cast doubt on the assertion that constructing a new stadium is usually a good investment for a city?

2. In Minnesota, state and local government decision makers for a number of years resisted using taxpayer money to build a new stadium for the Twins. Eventually, however (in a decision that was made after the article was written), state and local officials relented and agreed to help build a new ballpark, although without the expensive retractable roof that the team owners wanted. Why do you think that Minnesota officials changed their minds and eventually decided to support construction of a new ballpark?

3. Can you think of ways to finance a new stadium that would be fairer than levying taxes on all voters in order to pay off the money a city borrows to help finance a new stadium?

From *Governing*, March 2006, pp. 40–43. Copyright © 2006 by Congressional Quarterly, Inc. Reprinted by permission.

"A Lot of Hooey"

Heywood Sanders on Convention Center Economics

NEIL DEMAUSE

Heywood Sanders of the University of Texas-San Antonio is undoubtedly the best-known (and best informed) independent critic of publicly financed convention centers, a multi-billion-dollar business that is starting to rival sports stadiums in its ubiquity and cost to taxpayers. In late July 2004, Neil deMause spoke with Sanders about the convention-center game for fieldofschemes.com; an edited transcript follows.

It seems that from an economic development standpoint, convention centers should be a better deal than other development, because it's all fresh blood, right?

That's what always intrigued me about it. The argument is that, compared to a stadium or arena that would simply be moving around existing dollars, the logic of the convention center is that it's bringing in people from out of town. So it's effectively importing new dollars. Compared to other big economic investments, that should be a big plus.

That's the theory, at least. And to the extent that it does that in practice, it should be a boon to the community. It just doesn't happen.

Have there been a lot of studies of economic impact of convention centers?

There are comparable to the stadium side, which you've seen and talked about in Field of Schemes, and which Public Dollars, Private Stadiums talks about. Almost every center and/ or expansion comes with a consultant feasibility study that says so many new people will come, and those people will stay multiple days in local hotels, and will spend hundreds of dollars every one of those days, and will yield ultimately hundreds of thousands in new direct spending multiplied by some inappropriate multiplier, generating massive economic impact numbers. I have an office and a house filled with such studies.

I've tried to look at it in the terms that the impact studies have, and that is: If you build it, do they come, in what volume, for how long? And how has that evolved over time? Because we're looking at a situation that is subject to a whole series of larger cyclical and systemic market changes over time. When

[New York's] Javits [Convention Center] was first proposed in the early '80s and ultimately built, the situation changed as the national economy expanded and evolved during the '90s, and today its situation is remarkably different.

Among other things, we've seen a massive increase in the last ten or 15 years in the availability of convention center exhibit space. In the period since Javits opened, there are new centers in Washington, in Boston—which just opened in June—in Philadelphia. There is a new center that will open up in 2005 in downtown Hartford. There is a center that opened after Javits in Providence. The state of New York has Buffalo sitting on a host of studies for a new convention center, Albany doing likewise, with the state legislature having just approved the creation of a convention center authority in Albany. We have folks in Syracuse looking at the development of a new headquarters hotel to serve their convention center, and the possibility of an expansion of their center. We have Pittsburgh just having opened their center about a year and a half ago. And that's just in the region!

This amounts to about a 50% increase in space—and lots more space coming on line. Another half million square feet in Chicago, another half million in New Orleans.

So while the logic of the convention center is that it's bringing people from out of town, you have to flip that logic on its head. Because to some extent the stadium's market is guaranteed: Local as it is, some number of people will go to a game—even to a Jets game. But in a market where dozens and dozens of cities are building new or expanded convention centers, the likelihood of any one city, including New York, substantially gaining market share . . .

Is there any evidence, either in terms of broad studies or specific anecdotal evidence, of how different centers have done when they expanded?

Sure. They either don't gain business or they lose it.

Let me give a tiny bit of background. The newest fillip of this is the contention by the standard industry consultants that a large headquarters hotel is essential to the convention center business. That is, in fact, part of the argument with the Javits.

In an article Government Finance Review published in June, I looked into how many of those hotels these days are publicly owned. What I call "hotel socialism" is alive and well and spreading, and cities around the country are literally getting into the hotel business in situations where private capital can't or won't take on the risk.

The idea being that a hotel is necessary in order to book the convention space?

That's right. So this article looks at four of these cases, to see how that actually works: Once you have the hotel, what happens, both to the hotel and to the convention center? In perhaps the most intriguing case, the city of St. Louis largely bankrolled, in part using a $98 million federal empowerment zone bond, with some private equity investment, a new 1081-room Marriott Renaissance Hotel. It opened in 2003. It was supposed to do 62% occupancy; it has done under 50%. It has run in the red since it opened. It has only made its payments on that $98 million bond by going into credit reserves. Moody's downgraded the bond in September from the bottom investment grade to a speculative grade. They have subsequently put it on their watch list, because it looks like it's going even further under, and the thing is burning money. *[Editor's note: Moody's further downgraded the bonds last month, adding: "Unless the local convention business improves significantly, we expect continued credit deterioration absent third-party financial support of the hotel."]*

It was built with the argument that St. Louis had, circa '98 or '99, 33 major convention events a year. The CDB director argued that with the hotel, they'd get 50. A spokesman for the hotel developer argued that they'd get 56. So what did they do last year? *Twenty-four.*

We are simply looking at a market that, by all accounts, is enormously overbuilt. Cities around the country are discounting convention center rates, and in a number of cases, literally giving away the space for free.

That was the other thing I was going to ask you about. Obviously it's not just a question of how many conventions you hold, but whether or not they pay full rate.

Well, increasingly nobody pays full rate. I'm finishing up a piece for Brookings looking at precisely this phenomenon, and tracing the recent performance of 15 or 20 major centers around the country. What folks have not much noticed buried in the Price Waterhouse Coopers feasibility study is that Javits has seen a significant decrease in its business, from about 1.4 million annual attendance to 1 million.

I'm sure that they would argue that that's because it's too small to book the larger conventions.

They'll never get larger conventions. Even the convention centers that have expanded—Las Vegas, for example, expanded its public convention center, adding a million square feet to a million-square-foot center. So with double the space, as of January 2002, what happened to the attendance at the Las Vegas Convention Center in 2002? It went down. And what happened in 2003? It went down again.

So this is the question everyone always asks me about stadiums, but: If it's such a terrible deal, why is everyone rushing to do this?

Because this has nothing to do with the ostensible public argument or economic discourse about job creation and importing spending, and everything to do with the politics of land development. A fact that is, in the case of Javits, all the more obvious, for the enormous impact on adjacent private development that Javits has had in the years since it's been opened—and that is to say, essentially, nothing. You can't get a hotel room nearby. You can barely get anything to eat nearby. If all of these people are coming, with all of this money to spend, why have they not generated much new private development?

The answer in the case of Javits is they're really not coming, and they're really not spending. In fact, the Javits center is notable because it has about the lowest yield of hotel room nights to attendance of any center in the country. The argument typically goes that all of the attendees are coming from some distant place, staying lots of nights at hotel rooms, and leaving lots of cash behind. But a great many of the events that happen at convention centers, particularly in the case of Javits, are trade show events, not professional meetings, in which you come in, do a turn or two around the exhibit at the center, and leave. In that case, particularly given Manhattan's hotel rates, it's easy to get into Javits, spend a day or two, and go.

At the same time, many of the events at Javits attract folks who are already in the metropolitan area. Those folks might invest in subway fare, or take a PATH train across the Hudson. But what they're not doing is spending lots of money staying over.

So do you have a sense of why this has such political support?

These things have enormous political support in lots of places. If you go online and rummage a little bit, you're going to get some numbers on how the new Boston center is doing. They were supposed to do over 300,000 attendees this year; they'll actually do something on the order of 50,000. Four events this year. They now have about 50 booked through 2010, of which half are events that were already in Boston.

That's important to understand: If you have a bigger center, you give George Little and Reed Exhibitions and the other folks in the business more space to sell. It's great for them. But you don't necessarily draw more people. The assumption, which I take apart in some detail in the piece I'm doing for Brookings, that the business is constantly expanding so you need to keep up, is a lot of hooey. It stopped expanding a while ago, and it's not clear there's anything to keep up with.

So how do the consultants justify projecting huge growth?

It depends on which consultant, and which city, and what they're arguing. I just had a conversation with one of my former students who's now a news reporter here in San Antonio, which is talking about substantial public funding for a 1000-room headquarters hotel. And the consultant turned in a report on how San Antonio lacks a major headquarters hotel. Now, there's a 1001-room Marriott directly across the street. And they termed that not a "headquarters hotel" but a "primary hotel." It turns out, however, that in two previous studies, one in Denver, one in Fort Worth, by the same consulting firm, in a table constructed in exactly the same way, that hotel is listed as a: headquarters hotel!

Have you seen anywhere that a city has put money into a convention center, and it's actually been money well spent?

There are two places that have historically done well in expanding their convention business: that's Las Vegas and Orlando. And historically, they have managed to grow their business with great regularity. New Orleans for a long time in the 1990s seemed to be successful. Anaheim and San Diego may, but because of a lack of available information that I've been able to get my hands on, it's not entirely clear.

But there's something in common certainly about the first two of them, and to some extent, about the other three, that's worth noting.

You also did say that Las Vegas just doubled their space, though—

And there I would argue that in fact the historical performance clearly is no real guide to the current market environment.

So would you say that we've really tapped out the need for convention center space? Is there any need for anybody to build anything, or is there enough room for everybody to rattle around at this point?

Let me put it this way. If we're talking about large centers seeing attendance declines on the order of 40 or 50% or more, the question becomes: Even if the economy has turned around, even if people do start traveling more regularly, even if the convention and trade show business has not seen substantial erosion by the changes in various economic sectors, changes in the popular desire to travel, changes in technology and communication, it's going to take a while of double-digit growth to get those cities back to where they were four or five years ago. And once they're back there, assuming they get there, there are two other things. First, between now and then, we know there's more space coming on the market. That's in the works—the bonds have been sold, that steelwork is up.

Secondly, even if you get back to where you were, you still have to compete with everybody else who has space. And again, centers are engaged in a price war. The internet brings every day news of a center that's offering its space for free. If a place like Dallas is offering rebates on hotel rooms, where does that leave the most expensive destination in the continental U.S.?

Critical Thinking

1. City after city has built or modernized convention centers, yet few cities find that such centers are profitable. Why is it that convention centers are so seldom self-sustainable—that so few actually make money?
2. Who are the members of a city's "growth coalition"? Why do the members of a growth coalition support continued investment in new convention centers?
3. What role do consultant studies play in justifying the construction of new convention centers? Why do convention centers, after they are built, seldom generate the economic impact that the expert studies predicted would occur?

Eminent Domain Revisited

MARK BERKEY-GERARD

Joy Chatel fears she will lose the house that has been her life for decades.

The four-story brick building on Duffield Street in Brooklyn serves as her home, a classroom where she home schools her seven grandchildren, and a business where she operates a hair salon.

Under the city's plan to rezone and develop downtown Brooklyn, approximately 130 residences and 100 businesses, including Chatel's, would be condemned. The city says the plan to replace them is a key element in a larger strategy to retain jobs that are leaving for New Jersey and elsewhere—and that it will ultimately benefit the residents of Brooklyn and the entire city.

Chatel argues there is more at stake than her private property. She and several other building owners in the area say that their houses are historic treasures where slaves found sanctuary as part of the "underground railroad," a claim the city disputes.

"Oral history is all we have to prove there was an underground railroad," she told the Daily News. "It's not like they have a neon sign outside."

In New York City, the government's power to take over private property—eminent domain—is a factor in so many pending development projects that the one involving Joy Chatel's home is actually among the least-known current battles.

In Prospect Heights, Brooklyn, the real estate developer Forest City Ratner Companies has a proposal to take over private homes and businesses and replace them with the Atlantic Yards project, a basketball arena, thousands of condos, and 16 towers.

In upper Manhattan, Columbia University is considering eminent domain as an option in its efforts to expand its campus.

And in Willets Point, Queens, the city is looking to replace a 13-block area that is home to scrap metal yards and auto shops with a waterfront shopping district to complement a new stadium for the New York Mets.

New York City's landscape has been remade over and over again, and in the process hundreds of thousands of New Yorkers have lost their private property so that the government can build roads, bridges, public housing, parks, playgrounds, and hospitals.

The concept of eminent domain—and debate surrounding the practice—dates back to the founding of the nation.

"Eminent domain means the power of the crown over his or her domain," said Dwight Merriam, author of the book *Eminent Domain Use and Abuse*. "The theory is that the government really owns all of the property and can take it back whenever it wants."

The nation's founders tried to address the issue in the Fifth Amendment to the U.S. Constitution, which guarantees citizens "just compensation" when private property is taken for "public use."

But what exactly is a "public use"?

Until the case of Berman vs. Parker in 1954, the Supreme Court ruled that it was for such clearly public physical structures as bridges, highways, schools, and train tracks.

Today, in an era when government and private developers often work closely with one another, the term "public use" is used for sports stadiums, corporate headquarters, office buildings, museums, and even shopping malls.

New York's Eminent Domain Powers

In New York State, eminent domain can be used to remove areas of "blight"—which means deteriorating, vacant, or obsolete buildings or even oddly shaped parcels of land. Historically, the courts and lawmakers have used the term "blight" rather liberally.

For 40 years, "master builder" Robert Moses, made use of the power to level entire neighborhoods for projects like the West Side highway, Lincoln Center, and the Triborough Bridge.

An entire downtown neighborhood, including a string of small electronics shops known as "Radio Row," was demolished to make way for the World Trade Center.

In the 1980s, the city and state condemned property in Times Square to rid the area of sex shops and other abandoned buildings. Currently, on 43rd Street, the New York Times is building a new headquarters on a property obtained through eminent domain.

In 2001, the state took over several buildings on Wall Street in order to make way for an expansion of the New York Stock Exchange, an idea which never became a reality.

And recently in Harlem, a dozen businesses were demolished to make way for a Home Depot.

The Kelo vs. New London Case

The issue of eminent domain gained a new level of attention last summer when the United States Supreme Court ruled that the government could use eminent domain to take away private property and then sell it to a private developer.

In the case, known as Kelo vs. New London, the court ruled in a 5 to 4 vote that the city of New London, Connecticut, could take the property of 15 homeowners for the purpose of economic development. The city plans to transfer the property to developers who will build office space, a hotel, housing, and a riverfront esplanade.

The Kelo case has sparked new debate among legal and planning experts.

Some say that while eminent domain is appropriate to build schools or hospitals, it should not benefit private developers, because it can too easily abused.

"We never hear that eminent domain should be used to take a Hyatt and build mixed-income housing," said Susan Fainstein, a professor of urban studies at Columbia University. "It is always about taking property away from poor people and give it to someone who is much better off."

Others say that if a project produces tax revenue and jobs, economic development can be considered legitimate "public purpose."

"We shouldn't think that these projects are 'bad' just because they are the work of private developers," said Jerilyn Perine, who served as housing commissioner under Mayor Michael Bloomberg.

Backlash against Eminent Domain

Concern over the Kelo case has also inspired a flurry of legislation at the national and local level.

In Congress, a bill, dubbed the "Private Property Rights Protection Act of 2005, has already passed the House and is awaiting a vote in the Senate. It would withhold federal aid from states that Congress believes abuse eminent domain.

In New York, there are several bills being considered in Albany, including a package of legislation drafted by Assembly member Richard Brodsky which would slow down local eminent domain proceedings, create an ombudsman to oversee the use of the law, and require 150 percent of market value be paid for private property that the government takes over. This week, the New York City Council will hold hearings on the subject.

And recently opponents of eminent domain claimed victory when the U.S. Court of Appeals ruled that the city of Port Chester, New York, failed to properly alert a businessman of his right to challenge an eminent domain decision before the government seized his four buildings to make way for a convenience store. The court's decision, some said, was a warning to local governments who may be tempted to take private property without properly notifying the people who own it.

Three Current Eminent Domain Projects in New York City

While the experts debate how eminent domain should be used, residents and businesses in neighborhoods where it is being considered struggle to preserve the future of their communities.

Atlantic Yards and Prospect Heights, Brooklyn

In December 2003, developer Bruce Ratner, along with Mayor Michael Bloomberg and Governor George Pataki, unveiled plans for a massive project in downtown Brooklyn, known as the "Atlantic Yards." The latest version of the plan would build a Frank Gehry designed basketball arena for the New Jersey Nets and 16 skyscrapers with office space and 7,300 apartments.

In order to acquire the 22 acres of land needed for the project, New York's Empire State Development Corporation is planning to use the government's power of eminent domain to condemn two parcels of land.

Opponents of eminent domain say that the state would take over approximately 53 properties. Local groups, which oppose the plan, say more than 330 residents, 33 businesses with 235 employees, and a 400 person homeless shelter will be displaced by the project.

And Daniel Goldstein, who works for the group Develop Don't Destroy and lives in the area of the proposed development, warns that the definition of "blight" could apply to any neighborhood in the city.

"On any six square block in this city you will find a property that might be 'dilapidated' or 'structurally unsound' or 'vacant,' and all throughout the city nearly every property could be considered 'economically underutilized,'" said Goldstein.

However some in the area, including many local officials, have praised the development, in particular for the "community benefits agreement" with neighborhood representatives that promises that 50 percent of the 4,500 rental apartments will go to low and middle-income residents, with 10 percent of these set aside for seniors. The project also sets aside 35 percent of the jobs for minority workers and another 10 percent for women.

But even some supporters of the project, like Assembly member Roger Green, question the use of eminent domain.

"Under the definition of blight, as related to poverty or environmental degradation, this definition is not related to Prospect Heights," Green said at recent state hearing.

Columbia University Expansion, Manhattanville

Last summer, Anne Whitman, who runs a moving company out of her building on Broadway and 129th Street, received a letter from Columbia University informing her that the institution planned to build a biotech research center where her business stands.

Columbia offered to help Whitman find a single-floor building outside of Manhattan; she rejected the offer.

"Since then," Whitman said, "it has been all out war."

Columbia University plans to spend $5 billion over the next 25 years to build a new campus in upper Manhattan. The 18-acre complex would stretch from West 125th Street to West 133rd Street between 12th Avenue and Broadway and would house biotech research facilities, a building for its art school, student and faculty housing, and administrative buildings.

The university says the campus will create 14,500 permanent jobs in the area.

Columbia hopes to convince area residents and businesses that there is a mutually acceptable resolution. Failing that, it has suggested that the state could use eminent domain to transfer control of these properties.

However, local businesses, community board members, and students at Columbia University oppose the plan and criticize its approach to the negotiations with the community.

For some of the area's landowners, the talk of eminent domain has poisoned negotiations.

"They say 'deal with us now or deal with the state later,'" said Whitman, who also sits on Community Board Nine. "It's like having a gun to your head."

Willets Point, Queens

For decades, city planners have had their eye on Willets Point, a 13-block area on a peninsula on the Flushing River that is home to scrap metal yards and auto shops.

In the 1960s, Robert Moses attempted to force out the local business owners to make way for the World's Fair. In the 1990s, the New York Mets wanted to build a new stadium on the land. Recently, some have proposed a new stadium for the New York Jets football team or facilities for the now-defunct 2012 Olympic bid on the grounds. All of these plans failed.

Now, the city is determined to transform the area to include an attractive waterfront shopping and residential enclave, which would complement another proposed stadium for the New York Mets.

Although the city will not discuss the details of its plans at the current time, scrap metal yard owners fear that eminent domain may be used to move them out.

"Sounds to me like they're going to pull a sneak attack," said Richard Musick, president of the Willets Point Business Association.

There is little doubt that the area—which is riddled with large potholes and abandoned cars, and even lacks plumbing in some areas—will meet the definition of "blight." And some local officials, like Councilmember John Liu expresses confidence that the owners "will be given fair compensation, and relocated, if necessary."

But the scrap metal and auto shop owners say that it will be nearly impossible to find other neighborhoods that would welcome their businesses.

Critical Thinking

1. What is eminent domain? Is it constitutional or is it against the U.S. Constitution? What exactly does the U.S. Constitution say about eminent domain?

2. How is the present-day controversy over eminent domain really a controversy over what constitutes "public use"? How do local governments today use eminent domain powers for more than the taking of property necessary to build a road or a university campus?

3. What did the Supreme Court in its Kelo decision rule about the local use of eminent domain by local governments for economic development—is it allowable or not?

4. New York has been more moderate than other states in its reaction to the Kelo decision. How have the states generally responded in the wake of the Court's Kelo ruling?

Reprinted with permission from *Gotham Gazette*, December 12, 2005. Copyright © 2005 by Gotham Gazette, an online publication on New York policy and politics. www. gothamgazette.com

UNIT 4
Citizen Participation

Unit Selections

Learning Outcomes

After reading this unit, you should be able to:

- Recognize Jane Jacobs' contribution to cities and how her advocacy and work changed the nature of urban planning.

- Propose a strategy that effectively builds citizen engagement instead of one that gives only lip-service to citizen participation without really providing citizens with the tools and opportunities for citizen participation.

- Identify community development corporations (CDCs), explain how they work, and report on their contributions to building better poor-people's and working-class communities.

Student Website

www.mhhe.com/cls

Internet References

E-Governance Institute: Citizen Participation
    http://andromeda.rutgers.edu/~egovinst/Website/citizenspg.htm
National Civic Review
    www.ncl.org/publications/ncr
Shelterforce
    www.shelterforce.org

Citizen participation is based on the democratic notion that people should have a say in the making of decisions that affect their lives. In cities, citizen participation represents an attempt to open up decision-making processes that were once the preserve of growth coalition interests and bureaucratic actors.

To a great extent, cities over the last half century have witnessed a citizen participation revolution. In the 1950s and early 1960s, urban renewal and highway programs actually harmed urban neighborhoods, destroying communities and displacing thousands of people from their homes (Article 17, "Jane Jacobs' Radical Legacy"). Public officials soon began to recognize the dangers of top-down decision making and the importance of gaining the active participation of persons whose lives are being the most affected. Much like private business, local government has come to see the virtues of listening and responding to "customers'" concerns.

Yet, citizen participation is not easy to achieve. Residents are often disinterested in municipal affairs and too busy to participate. For their part, bureaucratic officials are resistant when it comes to bending to the view of citizens who may lack technical knowledge and formal training. Even public officials who value citizen involvement will, at times, cut participatory processes short. In order to "get things done," bureaucrats will try to circumvent the seemingly endless haggling, debates, and delays that can characterize participatory processes.

The City of Seattle, with its strong traditions of neighborhood engagement and grassroots action, has the reputation of a city that does participation right (Article 18, "Neighbor Power: Building Community the Seattle Way"). As the Seattle experience shows, extensive citizen involvement does not always come about naturally. Instead, the local government committed extensive resources to informing and mobilizing residents, providing various forms of assistance in its outreach to community groups. The city provided staff and technical assistance to neighborhood groups as they formulated a community vision. The city also ceded to community groups new authority over neighborhood projects. As the Seattle experience demonstrates, citizen participation has its best chance of succeeding in cases where city leaders genuinely believe in the importance of mobilizing the citizens' voice and where city agencies provide staff, technical

© CDC/Cade Martin

training, of other support resources to community groups. Citizens will participate in neighborhood governance when given real decision-making authority, as opposed to merely dispensing advice and recommendations that municipal officials are free to ignore.

One piece of good news for U.S. cities over the last few decades has been the rise of **Community Development Corporations (CDCs),** neighborhood-oriented groups that engage in **bridge-building** initiatives with private and governmental partners. CDCs work with a variety of public agencies and private and nonprofit organizations in order to bring new investment in affordable housing, job training, and better health and social services to a community in need. CDCs have had their greatest success in building and rehabilitating housing for low-income renters—and, in some cases, even for low-income buyers. "New Life in Newark" (Article 19) describes how one CDC helped to bring a sense of hope to the core area of one of the nation's most troubled big cities, Newark, New Jersey. While CDCs engage in political protest activities when necessary, they devote most of their time to finding the necessary financial support and to building housing and delivering the health and jobs services that poorer communities so desperately need.

Jane Jacobs' Radical Legacy

Sometimes a book can change history. Books often influence ideas, but only rarely do they catalyze activism.

PETER DREIER

In the 1960s, a handful of books triggered movements for reform. These include Michael Harrington's *The Other America* (1962), which inspired the war on poverty; Rachel Carson's *Silent Spring* (1962), which helped galvanize the environmental movement; Betty Friedan's *The Feminine Mystique* (1963), the manifesto of modern feminism; Ralph Nader's *Unsafe at Any Speed* (1965), which made its author a household name and precipitated the rise of the consumer movement; and Charles Hamilton and Stokely Carmichael's *Black Power* (1967), which signaled the civil rights movement's transformation toward black separatism.

Jane Jacobs' 1961 book, *The Death and Life of Great American Cities,* belongs in this pantheon. Perhaps more than anyone else during the past half century, Jacobs changed the way we think about livable cities. Indeed, it is a mark of her impact that many people influenced by her ideas have never heard of her. Her views have become part of the conventional wisdom, if not always part of the continuing practice, of city planning.

The 1950s was the heyday of urban renewal, the federal program that sought to wipe out urban "blight" with the bulldozer. Its advocates were typically downtown businesses, developers, banks, major daily newspapers, big-city mayors and construction unions—what John Mollenkopf would later call the "growth coalition" and Harvey Molotch would label the "growth machine." Most planners and architects at the time joined the urban renewal chorus. It was, after all, their bread and butter. Moreover, they convinced themselves that big development projects would "revitalize" downtown business districts, stem the exodus of middle-class families to suburbs and improve the quality of public spaces.

Jacobs, a journalist, was self-taught. She had no college degree. This may have been liberating, because she was unencumbered by planning orthodoxy, although she carefully read and thoroughly critiqued the major thinkers in the field. Had she studied architecture or urban planning when she was college age (in the 1930s and 1940s), she would have been taught the value of top-down planning and modernist mega-projects. Instead, she learned about cities by observing and doing. In the 1950s, she wrote a series of articles in *Fortune* magazine (later

the basis for *The Death and Life of Great American Cities*) that said, essentially, cities are for people.

When Robert Moses, New York's planning czar and perhaps the most powerful unelected city official of the 20th century, proposed building a highway bisecting Jacobs' Greenwich Village neighborhood, she sprung into action, mobilizing her neighbors to challenge and confront the bulldozer bully in the name of human-scale, livable communities. She was no armchair liberal. She was fully engaged in her community and in the battle to save it. For her efforts, she was arrested and jailed. Her courageous efforts helped catalyze a broader grassroots movement against the urban renewal bulldozer, first in New York and then around the country.

She persisted even as Moses and other powerful figures tried to vilify her. Eventually, her dissenting ideas found a wider audience. In 1969, Mayor John Lindsay killed Moses' expressway plan. In other cities, mayors and planning agencies began to rethink the bulldozer approach to urban renaissance. In 1974, President Nixon canceled the urban renewal program.

Jacobs' book became required reading in planning and urban studies programs. She was hailed for her visionary writing and activism. But she refused to accept sainthood, turning down honorary degrees from more than 30 institutions. She always gave credit to the ordinary people on the front lines of the battle over the future of their cities.

Jacobs was a thinker and a doer who had a profound influence on two distinct, but overlapping, groups: city planners and community organizers. She is best known for her impact on city planning. She was among the most articulate voices against "slum clearance," high-rise development, highways carved through urban neighborhoods and big commercial projects.

Cities, she believed, should be untidy, complex and full of surprises. Good cities encourage social interaction at the street level. They are pedestrian friendly. They favor walking, biking and public transit over cars. They get people talking to each other. Residential buildings should be low-rise and should have stoops and porches. Sidewalks and parks should have benches. Streets should be short and wind around neighborhoods. Livable neighborhoods require mixed-use buildings—especially first-floor retail and housing above. She saw how "eyes on the street" could make neighborhoods safe as well as supportive, prefiguring an idea that later got the name "social capital." She favored corner stores over big chains. She liked newsstands and pocket parks where people can meet casually. Cities, she believed, should foster a mosaic of architectural styles and heights. And they should allow people from different income, ethnic, and racial groups to live in close proximity.

Although many developers and elected officials still favor the top-down approach, most planners and architects have absorbed Jacobs' lessons. Advocates of "smart growth" and "new urbanism" claim Jacobs' mantle, although she would no doubt dispute some of their ideas, particularly the failure of these approaches to make room for poor and working class folks. In later writings, Jacobs touted the role of cities as the engines of economic prosperity. In doing so, she anticipated arguments against unfettered suburban sprawl, recent debates about the reliance of suburbs on healthy cities, and the new wave of thinking about regionalism.

More importantly, perhaps, Jacobs paved the way for what became known as "advocacy planning." Starting in the 1960s, a handful of urban planners chose to side with residents of low-income urban neighborhoods against the power of city redevelopment agencies that pushed for highways, luxury housing, expansion of institutions such as hospitals and universities, corporate-sponsored mega projects, and government subsidies for sports complexes and convention centers.

Based in universities or in small nonprofit firms, advocate planners played an important role in battles over development in most major cities. They provided technical skills (and sometimes political advice) for community groups engaged in trench warfare against displacement and gentrification. At first isolated within the profession, advocate planners soon moved from the margins to the mainstream—or at least became enough of a force to have a serious impact on urban planning education. These activist planners worked for advocacy consulting firms (such as Urban Planning Aid), community groups and university planning departments (such as Pratt Institute's Center for Community and Environmental Development), and as oppositional "guerillas" inside municipal planning agencies or even, as recounted in Norm Krumholz and Pierre Clavel's book, *Reinventing Cities: Equity Planners Tell Their Stories* (1994) for progressive neighborhood-oriented mayors.

Often overlooked is Jacobs' influence on community organizing. Most histories of community organizing trace its origins and evolution to the settlement houses of the Progressive Era, to Saul Alinsky's efforts (starting in the late 1930s in Chicago), to adapt labor organizing strategies to community problems, and to the tactical creativity of the civil rights movement. But Jacobs' activist work showed people around the country that they could fight the urban renewal bulldozer—and win.

The upsurge of neighborhood organizing that emerged in the 1960s and 1970s was triggered by the initial battles against urban renewal, or what some critics called "Negro removal." By leading the fight in New York City, the nation's largest city and media center, Jacobs inspired people in New York and other cities to organize to stop the destruction of their communities and to find more community-friendly ways to achieve such goals as improving housing. They won some battles and lost others, but many of them persisted to gain increasing influence over plans by city governments and private developers for their neighborhoods. Out of this cauldron emerged new leaders, new organizations and new issues—such as the fight over bank redlining, tenants rights and rent control, neighborhood crime, environmental racism and underfunded schools. Some groups that were founded to protest against top-down plans began thinking about what they were for. Hundreds of community development corporations (CDCs) emerged out of these efforts. National networks of community organizations, such as ACORN, the Industrial Areas Foundation, PICO and National Peoples Action, and thousands of other independent community organizing groups, unwittingly built on Jacobs' efforts.

In 1981, Harry Boyte chronicled this revival of grassroots activism in his book, *The Backyard Revolution.* Even though it, and many subsequent books about community organizing, don't acknowledge (and may even be unaware of) Jacobs' influence, these activists were (and still are) standing on her shoulders as well as those of Jane Addams, Saul Alinsky and Ella Baker. Jacobs is mentioned once, in passing, in Peter Medoff and Holly Sklar's fascinating book, *Streets of Hope,* about the Dudley Street Neighborhood Initiative, that brought together residents of Boston's Roxbury ghetto, along with local churches, social agencies and other institutions, to rebuild their community as an "urban village" from the bottom up, starting in the 1980s. Few if any of DSNI's leaders, or foundation allies, had ever heard of her. But it is unlikely that Medoff, DSNI's first director, who graduated from Columbia's urban planning program, had not been influenced—directly (by reading her book) or indirectly (by studying with professors familiar with Jacobs' writing and activism)—by the activist author of *The Death and Life of Great American Cities.*

A fierce critic of Moses' efforts to decimate New York neighborhoods, Jacobs was equally opposed to President Johnson's plans to destroy Vietnamese villages. Always an activist, she marched in anti-war rallies. In 1968, Jacobs moved with her husband and children from New York City to Toronto, triggered by her anti-war sentiments. She didn't want their two draft-age sons to have to go to Vietnam.

She had a profound influence on city planning and community activism in her adopted country. There, too, she did battle with powerful forces who pushed for highways over public transit, and large scale projects over people-oriented neighborhoods. As she did in the U.S., she helped lead the fight to preserve neighborhoods and stop expressways, including the proposed Spadina Expressway that would have cut right through the heart of her own Annex neighborhood (where she lived until her death in a three-story brick building) as well as parts of downtown. Soon after moving to Toronto, she wrote a newspaper article critical of city planners for their plans to "Los Angelize" Toronto, which she described as "the most hopeful and healthy city in North America, still unmangled, still with options." It is difficult to know how much of Canada's success in creating more humane cities is due to Jacobs' influence, but many Canadian politicians, planners and advocates give her credit.

One unfortunate side effect of the battle against urban renewal in the United States was a knee-jerk opposition to government efforts to improve cities, a sentiment that lingers on. We see this in the growing antagonism to the use of eminent domain. Rather than see it as a tool that could be wielded for good or evil—depending on whether a city regime is progressive, liberal or conservative—many people in the U.S. view the tool itself as the enemy.

Canadians, too, battled against their country's version of urban renewal. But they, like Jacobs, did not view elected officials or government actions with the same degree of suspicion, as mean-spirited and heartless. They oppose government officials when they are in the pockets of private developers and businesses or refuse to listen to the voices of ordinary people. During Jacobs' years in Canada, municipal and provincial governments were often controlled by the Liberal Party and the progressive New Democratic Party—both to the left of the liberal wing of the Democratic Party in the U.S. The two Canadian parties had close ties to labor unions, environmentalists, women's rights advocates and community activists.

Canada has a similar economy and distribution of wealth to the U.S., but it provides a much wider and generous array of government-sponsored social insurance and safety net provisions to cushion the harshness of poverty. The U.S.'s stingy social programs have only a minor impact in reducing the poverty rate, while programs in Canada have a dramatic impact in lifting children, low-wage workers and the elderly out of poverty. Not surprisingly, compared with the U.S., Canada has a much smaller poverty rate, a higher proportion of subsidized housing, more mixed-income neighborhoods, less economic segregation and fewer homeless people. It also has safer cities, greater reliance on public transit, lower levels of pollution and traffic congestion and stronger downtown and neighborhood commercial districts.

Jacobs was a true "public intellectual," who put her ideas into practice. She loved cities and urban neighborhoods. She was fearless and feisty. She was a moralist, who believed that people had a responsibility to the greater good, and that societies and cities existed to bring out the best in people.

Critical Thinking

1. How did Jane Jacobs view major urban projects, including slum clearance and urban renewal programs?
2. According to Jacobs, what makes a city livable? Do major urban rebuilding projects enhance or destroy the characteristics of a good city?
3. What is advocacy planning? How does it differ from top-down planning?

PETER DREIER, an NHI board member, is E.P. Clapp Distinguished Professor of Politics and director of the Urban & Environmental Policy program at Occidental College in Los Angeles. He is coauthor of *Place Matters: Metropolitics for the 21st Century* and several other books.

Neighbor Power: Building Community the Seattle Way

Carmen Sirianni

In their 1993 book *The Rebirth of Urban Democracy,* Jeffrey Berry, Kent Portney, and Ken Thomson showed that communities with citywide systems of neighborhood associations in the 1970s and 1980s manifested many characteristics of what the authors described as "strong democracy." On questions of efficacy and citizens' learning, these communities compared favorably to cities with various forms of independent community organizing but without similar levels of government support. Their findings were quite convincing and anchored in an impressive analytic framework. But for many, these findings were counterintuitive: How could institutionalized systems of participation empower citizens more than some of the best forms of independent organizing to come out of the Saul Alinsky grassroots tradition?

The questions still linger, since the data in *Rebirth* were from the 1980s and some of these systems appeared to become sclerotic in the 1990s, while the most innovative models in community organizing—especially faith-based organizing in networks such as the Industrial Areas Foundation, the Pacific Institute of Community Organizing, and the Gamaliel Foundation—began to demonstrate their real potential for extensive leadership development and partnerships only after 1990. In *Civic Innovation in America,* Lewis Friedland and I argued that at least some of these citywide systems continued to innovate, combining neighborhood empowerment with new forms of grassroots watershed partnerships and restoration, community policing, dispute resolution, participatory planning, youth empowerment, and more. In addition, some of the more recent citywide systems, such as Seattle, showed a distinctive innovativeness, while also learning from cities such as Portland and St. Paul.

In *Neighbor Power: Building Community the Seattle Way,* Jim Diers provides the first detailed account of just how innovative the system of neighborhood empowerment in Seattle actually has been. Diers, himself an organizer in the Alinsky tradition during the 1970s, became the first director of Seattle's new Department of Neighborhoods (DON) in the late 1980s and saw it through an impressive period of capacity building for more than a decade. Now at the University of Washington, Diers has written a beautiful and highly readable account of what has clearly been inspired work by a very diverse array of

neighborhood residents and activists, working in collaboration with city staff, several mayors, and the city council. Though not an academic book, *Neighbor Power* provides a very careful and detailed analysis of the design principles and practices of Seattle's system. Although Seattle's political culture, economy, and demographics are not those of Everycity, USA, every mayor and city manager, as well as every neighborhood staff member and citizen leader should read this important book. It provides a model of the kind of visionary pragmatism that all our cities need if they are to become true laboratories of democracy in the twenty-first century. It also shows how city government can become a key player in civic renewal.

The vision behind Seattle's innovative strategies has been the use of city government to catalyze civic initiative for productive and collaborative solutions to problems without simultaneously undermining the independence of community organizations. Central to this vision is the idea that wise investments by the city enable and motivate citizens to mobilize their own assets and create public value far beyond what municipal staff and tax dollars alone could do. Seattle took its first steps in creating a system of formal neighborhood representation in 1987–1988, when it established district councils and the City Neighborhood Council, both of which represented citizens, and the Office of Neighborhoods, which provided city staff to support their work. In 1989, with a modest $150,000, a Neighborhood Matching Fund was established, which soon was granted an Innovations in Government Award from the Ford Foundation and Kennedy School of Government. Soon the concept began to spread to other cities. The fund was expanded to a high of $4.5 million in 2001. The core idea is simple: the city awards grants for neighborhood-generated projects that commit to matching these funds with their own in-kind contributions, cash, and donated labor.

To qualify, projects must be neighborhood-based and groups applying must have open membership and be democratically governed. Initially, the groups also had to be neighborhood-based, but to counteract the under-representation of immigrants and communities of color in many neighborhood organizations eligibility was extended to ethnic associations and similar groups. Projects must be time delimited, or have distinct phases that can be broken down into separate components. Ongoing programs are not eligible, nor can funds cover operating costs such as rent or staff salaries. Proposals can go to the Small and Simple Projects Fund, with a current limit of $15,000 and a quick monthly turnaround, or they can go to the Large Projects Fund, with a current cap of $100,000. The City Neighborhood Council, made up of neighborhood representatives from each of the thirteen district councils into which neighborhoods have been clustered, reviews proposals on a competitive basis for quality and feasibility, and according to criteria that represent core values shared by citizens and the city: civic participation, diversity, self-help, sustainability, and collaboration. It is the intent of the matching fund not only to yield products of visible public value, but also to build civic capacities that will continue to bear fruit in myriad other ways.

The vision behind Seattle's innovative strategies has been the use of city government to catalyze civic initiative for productive and collaborative solutions to problems without simultaneously undermining the independence of community organizations.

One cannot walk through the neighborhoods of Seattle today without seeing ample evidence of the collaborative work of its citizens as a result of the matching funds. In its first fifteen years, more than twenty-five hundred projects have been completed: new and renovated playgrounds, restored streams and wetlands, reforested hillsides and ravines, community centers and gardens, public art and sculpture. Much of this work is intended to provide civic education as well: the history of specific neighborhoods and ethnic communities, campaigns for diversity and social justice, dynamics of ecological sustainability. It very clearly represents the public work of a citizenry creating public space and a public culture. The fund's projects have elicited active involvement from several tens of thousands of citizens. Many existing organizations have seen an increase in membership, and a good number of new civic groups have been created as the result of an ad hoc effort that was first enabled by a matching grant.

When local residents resisted top-down planning in the mid-1990s, to meet the requirements of the state's growth management act Diers convened some 250 neighborhood leaders to develop a collaborative planning process that would devolve powers downward but also hold local citizens accountable for fair and effective deliberative processes, as well as substantive growth targets. This represents what Archon Fung, in his important book on community policing and local school councils in Chicago (still further evidence of the potential for civic innovation of city government itself), calls "accountable autonomy." The new Neighborhood Planning Office, headed by Karma Ruder, oversaw the process in which neighborhoods were free to identify their own scope of work and proceed in holistic fashion, rather than having to tailor their planning to the functions of various city departments. They could also hire their own planners and were aided by the planning office in contracting for services.

During the initial phase, neighborhoods were eligible for $10,000 to help them define a vision and involve the broad community and all major stakeholders through public meetings and surveys. Each neighborhood was accountable to the planning office for developing a detailed outreach plan that would engage the full diversity of its residents. Were minorities and recent immigrants represented? Youth? People with disabilities? Were affected businesses and other institutions at the table? The planning office also supplied an "outreach tool kit" with ideas and resources (for example, language translation) for helping engage those who might normally fall under the radar screen and to address needs that might be specific to such groups. Once the city was assured that the initial outreach was broadly democratic and that the scope of proposed planning made sense, the neighborhood was eligible for $60,000 to $100,000 to conduct the second phase of actual planning.

If there is one overriding analytic lesson in the book, it is that it may be time to "bring the state back in."

Neighborhoods chose to focus on various mixes of housing, open space, transportation, public safety, human services, and business district revitalization. The planning committee of each neighborhood presented options at an "Alternatives Fair" to which the entire community was invited. This elicited fresh ideas and modifications and drew in additional people to help plan and do further outreach. When a draft was finally ready, it was mailed to all households in the neighborhood, as well as to all businesses and property owners, who either voted for or against the plan on an enclosed ballot or at an open meeting. Further revisions were then possible and the final plan was sent to the mayor's Strategic Planning Office for review. This enabled the executive to advise the city council, whose Neighborhoods Committee reviewed each plan and then held a public hearing in the neighborhood to determine whether the community did, in fact, have general consensus on the proposals. Between twenty thousand and thirty thousand residents participated in the various public meetings, land-use walks, planning workshops, door-knocking campaigns, surveys, and other events at one time or another. As a result of the iterative process based on broad outreach and continual revision, as well as the opportunity the neighborhood leaders had to consult with relevant departments throughout, most plans yielded consensus among all the actors involved, though in some instances the city council's Neighborhoods Committee did have to mediate disputes. All neighborhoods produced plans that accommodated growth as envisioned by state law, but did so in a way they felt they could control. The city council approved all the plans in 1998 and 1999.

In order to facilitate implementation, mayor Paul Schell (1998–2001) decentralized various city departments into six sectors (overlapping police precincts and most neighborhood district councils) so that their local units could work collaboratively with each other and with the neighborhood stewardship groups that succeeded the planning committees in each of the thirty-seven affected areas. Stewardship groups worked with an interdepartmental team to ensure that multiple plan components, available resources, and agency regulations were well integrated; sector managers hired by DON could assist in leveraging other resources from developers and foundations. Stewardship groups could continue to clarify the vision, prioritize recommendations, and hold the city accountable for following through—and all plans and periodic implementation updates are available on the department's Website (www.ci.seattle.wa.us/neighborhoods) in a striking degree of democratic transparency. The mayor also expanded the matching fund to enable groups to get started on some projects. But since this was still far from enough money to implement the more than four thousand recommendations contained in the plans (with a target completion date of 2014), the city placed on the ballot a series of bond and levy measures that represented common requests in the neighborhood plans. Citizens passed a library bond measure to fund new building, expansion, and renovation for several dozen branch libraries, as well as a new downtown library. They voted similar measures for community centers, parks and open space, with an overall total of $470 million, more than 90 percent of which was for specific recommendations in the neighborhood plans. Citizens also voted to renew the low-income housing levy. Since the city had been willing to invest in democracy during the planning process, citizens were willing to invest their own tax money in making their neighborhood visions become reality.

The role of government as civic capacity builder has been relatively neglected.

In this wonderful book, Diers covers various other components of Seattle's innovative system, including its engagement of citizens with developmental disabilities and its extensive P-Patch community gardening program, which is as popular with immigrant, ethnic, and racial minorities and public housing tenants as it is with white middle-class renters and homeowners. His short portraits of projects, as well as one longer case study of holistic community development, provide a sense of the richness of civic work made possible by city staff and elected officials committed to grassroots democracy, and clearly show that there are, indeed, creative ways to combine the best of Madisonian representation, administrative accountability, and participatory democracy. As I know from my own interviews with neighborhood activists and professional staff in Seattle, the author's leadership was critical to building this infrastructure and establishing the relational foundation upon which it rests. He also assembled the staff—with the commitment of several mayors and city council members (especially Richard Conlin, a consistent champion) to really invest in staff capacity—who were able to help train other staff and a broad array of citizens to do complex relational work, planning, and assets-based community development within and across various neighborhoods, civic associations, and agencies.

Much of the recent debate on civic renewal in the United States has focused on diffuse forms of social capital, trust, and the benefits of our classic multitiered civic associations. The role of government as civic capacity builder has been relatively neglected. Although we might continue to argue the relative merits (and mixes) of independent community organizing and city-supported leadership development, there can no longer be any doubt that city government has the capability, if it so chooses, to help develop the kinds of civic leadership skills needed by citizens and agency professionals alike to grapple with a broad range of public problems in a creative and collaborative fashion. If there is one overriding analytic lesson in the Diers book, as in *The Rebirth of Urban Democracy* and *Empowered Participation*, it is that it may be time to "bring the state back in."

Notes

Berry, J., Pormey, K., and Thomson, K. *The Rebirth of Urban Democracy.* Washington, D.C.: Brookings, 1993.

Fung, A. *Empowered Participation: Reinventing Urban Democracy.* Princeton, N.J.: Princeton University Press, 2004.

Sirianni, C., and Friedland, L. A. *Civic Innovation in America.* Berkeley, Calif.: University of California Press, 2001.

Critical Thinking

1. It is not always easy to get community residents—especially poorer residents—to participate in community meetings and public affairs. How has the City of Seattle attempted to promote citizen participation? Detail the exact steps that Seattle has taken to support neighborhood empowerment.

Carmen Sirianni is professor of sociology and public policy at Brandeis University.

From *National Civic Review*, vol. 94, issue 3, Fall 2005, pp. 59–63. Copyright © 2005 by The National Civic League. Reprinted by permission of John Wiley & Sons.

New Life in Newark

Father Linder has built a small empire that offers services government has been unable to provide.

ALAN EHRENHALT

Forty years ago this month, police in Newark beat up a black cab driver in a traffic dispute, touching off one of the worst urban riots in American history. When it ended, after five days, 23 people had been killed, 725 had been injured, and much of the city's Central Ward was in ruins.

A few months later, Father William Linder created the New Community Corporation, a nonprofit entity aimed at restoring inner-city Newark through social services, grassroots entrepreneurship, and a commitment to personal and spiritual renewal. Father Linder was 32 years old at that time, a street-smart New Jersey idealist steeped in the civil rights movement, the community organizing theories of the 1960s, and the social liberalism that was beginning to permeate the American Catholic church. His organization was one of dozens of similarly structured Community Development Corporations (CDCs) that sprouted quickly in troubled cities all around the country.

Even in his most expansive moments, it's unlikely that Father Linder could have envisioned what New Community eventually became. Today, at 71, he presides over an organization that employs 1,800 people, runs more than 3,000 units of housing, two charter schools and a nursing home, operates training programs for cooks, auto mechanics and practical nurses, and owns property whose market value is probably more than half a billion dollars.

"There's no city in the United States where a community development corporation has had a more profound influence," says Richard Roper, a Newark urban policy consultant and long-time student of CDCs. "Father Linder has built a small empire that offers services government has been unable to provide."

More than this, Newark as a whole is showing signs of life. Commercial buildings are going up downtown, chain stores are reviving the long-dead shopping district, and there is more residential construction in the Central Ward right now than anywhere else in the city.

There is, however, another side to the story. In the 40 years since New Community launched its operations, the statistics on poor people in Newark have barely budged at all. The poverty rate is 27 percent, unemployment hovers around 13 percent and per capita income is stuck near the bottom among major American cities. If the goal of New Community was to transform the life of the inner city through grassroots economic development—and in large part, it was—that effort has failed.

That sobering reality applies to nearly all of the roughly 4,000 community development corporations throughout the country, big ones such as NCC and small ones that exist in every urban area. They have become experts at delivering social services to the poor, often as providers of last resort. What they have not done is lift many community residents out of poverty.

This is more than just an abstract issue. CDCs depend on foundations and other private sources—as well as government grants, loans and tax credits—to keep them going financially. In the past five years, the funders have begun to lose some of their earlier enthusiasm about what CDCs might accomplish. The Ford Foundation, which single-handedly financed many of the early efforts in the 1960s and '70s, has cut back dramatically. Even the Local Initiatives Support Corporation, spun off by Ford in the 1980s expressly for the purpose of backing CDCs, has grown much more selective. These and other foundations have become interested in "microlending"—the small, direct loans to individual entrepreneurs that have produced widely publicized success stories in Asia and Africa. Some of them regard CDCs as middlemen they would rather bypass.

One stark result of this was the abrupt closing last year of the National Congress for Community Economic Development, the umbrella organization that promoted the interests of CDCs in Washington and around the country. Faced with declining philanthropic interest, the NCCED simply ran out of money.

The big CDCs, at least, are not going to disappear. New Community Corporation is the largest nonprofit housing provider in the state of New Jersey and one of the largest employers in the city of Newark. The interesting question is whether it can move beyond its historic role of social service provider in a demoralized city into a new position as a partner to private interests in a city that has begun to recover.

NCC, despite its size and influence, has suffered from many of the difficulties that have plagued CDCs elsewhere. A fair number of its 3,000 housing units, built as long ago as the early 1970s, are in serious disrepair. Their maintenance problems have been exacerbated by the organization's insistence on accepting even the most dysfunctional city residents as tenants. Overall, the housing program is struggling with a current operating shortfall of about $300,000. "We've had about five bad years in a row," Father Linder says.

Even in the best years, NCC doesn't make a profit, won't make a profit, and, in the opinion of its founder, shouldn't make a profit. Father Linder believes one of the unfortunate illusions in the early days of the movement was that a successful CDC could generate enough economic development to pay for its operations on a continuing basis. "All the community groups began to think they could make money," Father Linder says. "They thought CDCs might be a gold mine." More than three decades later, they have been stripped of that illusion.

NCC, however, has advantages unavailable to most organizations of its kind. Its properties in the Central Ward are worth a fortune. In the 1970s, Father Linder was buying up 50 × 100-foot lots for $500. Virtually any of those lots can now be sold for more than $100,000, most of them for considerably more. When cash flow becomes a serious problem, NCC can simply dispose of some of its holdings. There is little doubt that the organization could survive for years, and continue to provide the social safety net Father Linder still cherishes, simply by managing its real estate assets.

But that points to what may be the fundamental dilemma about NCC and its future: how to operate in an urban environment dramatically different from the one that prevailed a generation ago.

Many of NCC's problems are directly related to the improving economics of the city in which it is located. One reason the workforce development program has trouble finding promising cooks and auto mechanics is that the best candidates often can get paying jobs. NCC is left trying to coach the more problematic recruits, those with serious criminal or substance-abuse histories.

Nor is NCC likely to remain the housing giant it became in the 1990s. As properties close or are sold off, there is virtually nothing available in the Central Ward to replace them. "The private sector is pushing them aside," says Dennis Gale, an urban affairs specialist at the downtown Newark campus of Rutgers University. "Most of the available lots have been developed or are being held by speculators for appreciation."

Given where the city was even a decade ago, few would decry these changes. But they point to a slimmed down and reconfigured New Community Corporation, and in fact that is already happening. At the start of this decade, NCC had annual revenues of about $200 million. Now, it is closer to $120 million.

Father Linder doesn't plan to get out of real estate development altogether, but he acknowledges that the future for NCC lies in partnerships with private developers, helping to plan the affordable component of projects whose other units will sell or rent at high-priced market rates.

A lot of this is feasible because NCC is on speaking terms with local government again. During the last few years of Mayor Sharpe James' 20-year administration, Father Linder was not welcome at City Hall, and any project that required city approval was simply a non-starter. "Our growth in size was a problem," Father Linder admits. "We were a threat." Cory Booker, the mayor who succeeded James last year, considers the organization to be a friend.

So New Community Corporation has a future—even as it seems haunted by the realization that much of what it hoped for in the early days never came to pass. Newark isn't reviving because inner-city residents created an entrepreneurial juggernaut; it's reviving thanks to investors and affluent new residents coming in from the outside. Father Linder's constituency in the Central Ward was poor in 1970; it's poor now. The real success stories are people who straightened themselves out, got good jobs and moved away.

In the end, perhaps the most important legacy of Father William Linder and the New Community Corporation will be that they provided a modicum of peace and stability to a place that was in serious danger of becoming an urban wasteland. They didn't generate economic renewal; they didn't attract the investors from Manhattan; but it may have been due to them that when the investors showed up, there was a city to invest in.

It's entirely possible, of course, that Newark would be showing signs of life now even if Father Linder hadn't chosen to take a stand in 1967. But it may be just as well that the above scenario was never put to the test. The New Community Corporation didn't save Newark. But it may have kept it alive.

Critical Thinking

1. What is a community development corporation (CDC)? What do CDCs do?
2. What specific benefits did Father William Lender and the New Community Corporation bring Newark?
3. What are the limitations of CDCs?

UNIT 5

School Choice and School Reform

Unit Selections

Learning Outcomes

After reading this unit, you should be able to:

- Identify charter schools and explain what makes a charter school different from a regular public school.

- Identify the advocates and opponents of charter schools and other school choice programs.

- Evaluate the successes, limitations, and criticisms of charter schools.

- Assess the degree of racial segregation/integration that currently exists in the nation's public schools.

Student Website

www.mhhe.com/cls

Internet References

Brookings Institution: School Choice; School Vouchers; Charter Schools; Urban and Inner-city Schools
www.brookings.edu/topics/school-choice.aspx
www.brookings.edu/topics/school-vouchers.aspx
www.brookings.edu/topics/charter-schools.aspx
www.brookings.edu/topics/urban-and-inner-city-schools.aspx

Center for Education Reform
www.edreform.com

Center for School Reform at the Heartland Institute
www.heartland.org/schoolreform-news.org/index.html

Civil Rights Project, UCLA
www.civilrightsproject.ucla.edu

National Center on School Choice, Vanderbilt University
www.vanderbilt.edu/schoolchoice/research-home.html

School Choice, Wisconsin
www.schoolchoiceinfo.org

Thomas B. Fordham Institute
www.fordhaminstitute.org/template/index.cfm

For many city and suburban residents, "the schools" comprise the focal point of their interest in local government. Dissatisfied with the state of public schooling, local citizens have looked with great hope to a number of educational reforms.

One set of reform measures embraces the idea of **choice,** where parents and children are given increased options; they need not take what an underperforming and irresponsive public school has to offer. School **vouchers,** for instance, give participating families a certificate that they can use to choose the school their child will attend. The vouchers increase parental options; a child no longer needs to attend the local public school.

But how much choice vouchers really give a parent depends on the size of the voucher and the willingness of private, church-related, and suburban schools to enroll a child for the amount of the voucher (plus whatever additional amount a parent can afford to pay if **add-ons** are allowed). Advocates argue that vouchers give parents increased ability to find a school that matches a child's needs. Critics, however, contend that a voucher plan is dangerous, that it will exacerbate urban inequality by draining funds from the public schools and allowing the exodus of the best students and the most active parents. Students who are left behind will find that they are in public schools that have become under-resourced **dumping grounds** of hopelessness.

A system of **tax credits** can also help spur educational choice. A parent can choose to enroll a student in a private school, pay tuition, and then use the amount paid in tuition to calculate a reduction in the taxes that the family would normally pay the government at the end of the year. While such a system promotes choice, it also suffers from obvious dangers. As conventionally administered, a tax credit only helps a family that is sufficiently well off financially that it can afford to pay private school tuition and wait for partial reimbursement to be claimed later in the form of a tax reduction. A tax credit also does not mean very much to poor families who owe the government little in taxes.

The creation of **charter schools** offers a more popular and pragmatic alternative to vouchers and tax credits. A charter academy is a special or innovative school established by the state (that is, given a state charter). Charter schools are freed from numerous state rules and regulations in order to promote greater flexibility in curriculum and teaching. More than 5,000 charter schools have been created across the United States.

Charters schools, like vouchers and tax credits, can also create a new atmosphere of **competition** that will spur the remaining public schools to better performance. Faced with the prospect of a continued loss of a number of children and tax dollars to voucher and charter schools, the public schools will respond with a new sense of urgency, dismissing teachers who do not teach and finding new ways to be creative, efficient, and considerate of the concerns voiced by parents.

But do choice programs deliver the benefits—especially the educational gains—that their enthusiasts promise? According to critics, choice schools seldom produce dramatic increases in student achievement. The test scores of students in voucher and charter school programs differ only a little, if at all, from the scores of equivalent students in the public schools.

© SW Productions / Getty Images

John Witte and his colleagues (Article 20, "The Performance of Charter Schools in Wisconsin") compare the educational outcomes in charter schools and more traditional public schools in Wisconsin, which has a strong history of offering choice programs. Witte found generally positive, but not overwhelmingly or uniformly positive, results for charter schools. Even where charter schools do show some gains in working with at-risk students, the charter approach provides no "magic bullet" or cure for the ills of public education. Gail Robinson (Article 21, "Charter Schools") surveys the new popularity of charter schools in New York City, and similarly seeks to assess where they have met their goals and where they fail to live up to their promises.

Aggressive school reform often runs into powerful resistance. Adrian Fenty, the African-American mayor of Washington D.C. lost reelection in 2010, partly as a result of the education reforms he helped put in place, including the dismissal of hundreds of teachers that led to the opposition of the teacher's union and even criticisms from a large number of citizens in the Black community (Article 22, "D.C. School Reform in Question after Mayor Fenty's Loss").

One much-debated consequence of choice programs concerns their potential impact on racial integration. Advocates claim that choice programs will actually lead to greater integration, that parents will be willing to send their children to racially-mixed classrooms when students share an interest and when a school offers a quality program and engaged teaching. Critics, however, respond that choice programs allow one more opportunity for **white flight,** for whites (and others) to leave integrated classrooms, undermining the gains in classroom diversity that have been achieved over the years (Article 23, "With More Choice Has Come Resegregation").

School integration efforts have also been limited by public ballot initiatives (such as Proposition 209 in California) and a series of court decisions that strictly limit or even ban the use of race as a factor in school assignments. These restrictions come at a time when the statistics point not to racial integration progress but to a **resegregation** of public schools and classrooms. Localities terminated school busing and other desegregation efforts as soon as the courts permitted them to do so.

School integration efforts have been halted even in cases where substantial racial integration has not been achieved (Article 24, "Here Comes the Neighborhood" also see Article 26, "The UCLA Civil Rights Project State of Segregation: Fact Sheet, 2007").

The Supreme Court has even set limits on the ability of local school districts to voluntarily undertake plans for racial diversity. In 2007, a sharply divided Court struck down the efforts by Seattle and Louisville to use the program of specialized **magnet schools** for integration, ruling that the system unconstitutionally gave too much emphasis to an applicant's race in deciding just which students would gain entrance to the system's more elite schools (Article 25, "Schools Seek New Diversity Answers after Court Rejects Race as Tiebreaker"). The 5-member majority saw the classification of people by their race, even for such a noble purpose as promoting racial diversity, as an impermissible discrimination against white applicants, a discrimination not allowed by the "equal protection clause" of the 14th Amendment. Civil rights advocates argued that the Court had stood the meaning of the 14th Amendment on its head and had set back the struggle for racial equality (Article 27, "Joint Statement of Nine University-Based Civil Rights Centers on Today's Supreme Court Rulings on Voluntary School Desegregation: McFarland v. Jefferson Country Public Schools & Parents Involved in Community Schools v. Seattle School District No. 1").

Today, local educators and civil rights activists face quite a conundrum: What steps can a school district taken to promote racial integration and diversity in public classrooms, given the sharp confines imposed by public opinion and Supreme Court rulings?

The Performance of Charter Schools in Wisconsin

JOHN WITTE, DAVID WEIMER, ARNOLD SHOBER, AND PAUL SCHLOMER

Research on school choice has exploded since its modest beginning less than two decades ago. In addition to producing general works on the benefits or pathologies of a competitive marketplace for education, scholars have devoted substantial attention to two other questions: First, does the academic performance of students who exercise choice improve? Second, does school choice improve the performance and accountability of the traditional public system overall?

School choice takes four forms: intra-district choice, which allows students to go to any traditional public school of their choosing; inter-district choice, which extends that choice across district boundaries; charter schools; and voucher schools. Much scholarly interest has focused on the most controversial form, voucher schools, in which parents receive public money to send their children to private schools. Though few public voucher programs operate, a large number of studies assess their impact. These studies have produced little consensus.

School choice based on charter schools has been less politically controversial. Charter schools are public schools that operate under a management contract. A charter school submits to the requirements of a contract with its authorizing agency in exchange for exemptions from many of the rules and regulations that govern traditional public schools. In theory, if a school does not meet the obligations of its charter, then the authorizing agency will revoke the contract and close the school. If choice and competition work, then poor quality schools will not be tolerated. Most advocates of charter schools see improved educational performance as the primary goal, although other cite the importance of additional goals, such as competition. Regardless, charter schools have gained advocates across the political spectrum. Both the Republican and Democratic parties called for more charter schools across the country in 2000 and in 2004. And, as of September 2006, more than 3,900 charter schools were open in 41 states and the District of Columbia.

Research on the relative effectiveness of charter over traditional schools has not been without controversy, however. National-level studies have reported advantages, disadvantages, and mixed results. At times, the debate among researchers has spilled to the pages of the *New York Times* and been described as a "dustup". State-level studies offer conflicting assessments for Michigan, North Carolina, and California. Two unpublished studies that consider Wisconsin in the context of national studies based on National Assessment of Educational Progress data suggest some advantages for charters.

We assess the performance of charter schools in Wisconsin at both the individual student and school levels. Our data come from two sources: first, data on individual students in Milwaukee in charter and traditional schools for the academic years 1998–99 through 2001–02; second, school-level state data on standardized tests in the fourth and eighth grades for two academic years, 2000–01 and 2001–02. For the school-level data, we apply a statistical analysis that harnesses the plethora of publicly available aggregated data generated by the No Child Left Behind law. We believe this method will help scholars improve their analyses of schools, especially when performance data on individual students are not available.

We find generally positive results for the effects of charter schools relative to traditional schools.

We find generally positive results for the effects of charter schools relative to traditional schools, although not uniformly so. Both individual-student and school-level analyses show this relative advantage for charter schools, although for one year, eighth-grade results favor traditional public schools. Our school-level analyses suggest that charter schools attain their advantage primarily by moving poorly performing students to proficiency rather than moving proficient students to advanced levels.

Our analyses suggest that charter schools attain their advantage primarily by moving poorly performing students to proficiency rather than moving proficient students to advanced levels.

Charter Schools in Wisconsin

Despite Wisconsin's leadership in school choice initiatives, including the nation's first voucher program, laws facilitating charter schools developed slowly. The initial authorization in 1993 allowed only 20 schools statewide. Subsequent laws removed this restriction and, more importantly, allowed several universities, the City of Milwaukee, a technical college, and school districts to issue charters. By the 2002–03 school year, the number of charter schools had risen to 130, with more than 19,000 enrolled students, approximately 2 percent of all public school students in Wisconsin. Charter schools in Milwaukee, Wisconsin's largest city, enroll minority students at approximately the same rate as traditional schools, while charter schools elsewhere in the state tend to enroll somewhat higher percentages of minorities. Charter schools in Milwaukee have about one-quarter fewer free-lunch qualified students than traditional schools. This trend is consistent with the tendency of charter schools to use the free-lunch program less than traditional schools. In addition, high schools make up a disproportionately large share of charter schools, and high school students in general are less likely to participate in the free-lunch program. A 2005 study of California charters found that those created by conversion of existing traditional schools to charter status were more effective than newly created charters, and that those with a higher proportion of instruction in traditional classroom settings were more effective. As more than two-thirds of Wisconsin charter schools are startups rather than conversions, they should be somewhat disadvantaged. Although our data do not allow us to assess in detail the method of instruction in charters, we were able to estimate that about half of Wisconsin charter schools were directed primarily toward at-risk students. In all of the 19 charter schools we visited throughout the state during the course of the study, school personnel sought to improve the achievement of at-risk students, often outside of traditional classroom settings. Consequently, the deck seems stacked against finding an advantage for Wisconsin charters relative to traditional schools.

Assessing Charter School Performance

Analyzing performance of charter schools presents numerous challenges. First, as with all studies of performance at the elementary level, very few quantitative measures exist other than standardized test scores. Attendance varies little in any setting. Small children go to school, and when they do not, it usually relates to illness. Behavioral measures also vary little and unpredictably, based on school-level philosophies. Increasingly, students are not graded until the higher elementary grades. Thus, we have to rely on standardized tests as indicators of student performance. Other measures, such as parental involvement and satisfaction, were not available for this study and have rarely been available in other studies.

At the middle school level, measures other than test scores begin to be useful, although they are also very limited. Students increasingly are given "at-risk" placements in specialty schools. We control for those schools in our estimates of achievement. However, we judge that behavioral data (suspension rates), attendance, and other measures of dysfunctional school action are still very sporadic and come under the purview of the principal. Thus, at the middle school level, we believe a control on the type of school (as at-risk or not) will measure some level of disadvantage. We question the reliability of other measures of performance beyond test results.

We are not as confident about using test data to measure the success of students in charter high schools, most of which provided specialized education for at-risk students, many of whom are severely at-risk. For example, several charter schools, in Milwaukee and outside, were "last chance" schools for students who were in legal custody, rehab programs, or had been expelled from other schools. Often these schools were, in the words of one administrator, "schools to teach kids how to go to school." The preparation of students to return to more traditional schools usually had minor academic components and much more emphasis on "life skills," self-discipline, and avoidance of adverse behaviors. Outside of Milwaukee, all charter high schools had some at-risk component, and, therefore, less emphasis on academics. That was not true of Milwaukee, so we included ninth- and 10th-graders in our individual student-level analyses. Because of the high percentage of at-risk charter high schools across the state, we limit the statewide school-level analysis to fourth and eighth grade.

Student-Level Performance of Charter and Non-charter Schools in Milwaukee

We obtained individual student test data for the Milwaukee school district, including students in its charter schools. With these data, we performed conventional statistical analyses, using administratively available data to control for student characteristics, and various value-added specifications that take advantage of repeated test data for each student.

Results confirm that charter school students in most grades appear to be performing better than students in traditional schools.

Results

Overall, the results confirm that charter school students in most grades appear to be performing better than students in traditional schools. These effects are quite robust across all races, with very positive effects for whites and Hispanics. With the exception of some black students, being in a charter school produces positive effects relative to students in traditional schools in Milwaukee, with Hispanics and whites showing the largest gains.

The test data and our analysis suggest that the largest advantages of charter schools lie in gains for math. We are not certain why this occurs, but case studies in Milwaukee indicate that a number of the charter schools emphasized science, math, or technology. In breaking down test results by grade, we find that charter schools students do modestly less well in grades 3, 4, and 10, compared to students in traditional, non-charter schools. The explanation for grades 3 and 4 may be that students have spent less time in charters in those grades and so do not begin to realize the benefits of being in charter schools until they reach grade 5. For 10th-graders, the explanation may be that charter high schools are more likely to be for at-risk students, and so their curricula do not focus as much on academic subjects.

School-Level Performance of Charter and Non-Charter Schools

Analyzing school performance in terms of levels of proficiency offers several advantages. First, policymakers seem to be enamored with judging schools, not necessarily students. The No Child Left Behind law, the standards movement, and most charter laws are clear examples. In view of this, we must get better at school-level analyses. Second, privacy laws increasingly impede access to student-level data for evaluations, even if sanitized of student identity, unless political authorities (states, school boards) agree to release such data. Third, the standards movement has affected data and testing; students and schools must meet certifiable levels of performance against clearly stated standards for grades and subjects. These performance standards do not necessarily have to adhere to population "norms" based simply on the distribution of test scores across comparable populations, which puts students up against other students. Rather, performance standards serve as the goal and the club to assure that students achieve appropriate levels of proficiency.

Wisconsin has changed the testing protocol to adhere to federal law that stipulates that schools must be judged against state standards. Therefore, we apply a technique to estimate a school-level model based on performance criteria. Because these types of performance criteria have national scope, we think the method we demonstrate has utility beyond the assessment of charter schools. As the method considers differences along the performance spectrum rather than just central tendencies, it offers more nuanced assessments of school performance.

For each school, the Wisconsin Department of Instruction reports for five subject areas the proportions of fourth- and eighth-graders who achieve four levels of performance: minimal, basic, proficient, and advanced. Our analysis of these data takes into account variation in school characteristics such as a specialized pedagogical approach, pupil-teacher ratios, or differences in the student body.

Results

The fourth-grade results show that charter schools had lower proportions of students performing at the minimal and basic levels for all subjects in 2000–01 and 2001–02. The results differed, however, for the advanced category. In four subjects in 2000–01, non-charter schools had higher proportions of students in the advanced category. There appeared to be no clear differences with respect to the advanced category between types of schools in 2001–02.

School control variables had the expected effects. The higher the percentage of black, free-lunch, and disabled students in a school, the greater the number of students who tested at the minimal or basic categories. The percentage of disabled students had a greater effect than the percentage of poor or black students.

Results for eighth graders were very different in 2000–01, with non-charter schools doing better than charters. For language arts, this included every performance category. Non-charter schools had fewer students in minimal and basic, and more in advanced. The situation dramatically reversed in 2001–02. The results favored charter schools, except for social studies. As with the fourth-grade results, charter schools seemed to do better at getting students out of the minimal and basic categories, rather than pushing them into advanced (although that occurred for language arts and social studies).

What happened in the two very different eighth grade years? The answer comes from looking very carefully at the schools in each year. First, in the first year (2000–01), when traditional schools outperformed charter schools, only 12 charter schools reporting test data. Five other charter schools did not. Two of these schools were charters in 2000–01 but did not begin eighth grade until the next year. Two others had too few students tested either overall or in subcategories of students. The other, for unknown reasons, reported only national percentile rankings in 2000–01. When we look at these five "missing schools" in the next year, they had better scores than the reporting schools in 2000–01 by well over 3 national percentile rankings on all the tests but one. Second, and more important, the schools tested in both years simply improved on their prior years' scores. This does not indicate that eighth graders are doing uniformly better in charter schools, but it explains the deviations and suggests further tracking is required.

We find that traditional schools had a greater proportion of students in the advanced level than did charter schools. This means that charter schools seem to be making their inroads by bringing students out of the minimal and basic levels in proportions higher than we would expect based on school characteristics; traditional schools seem to hold an advantage in bringing students up to the advance level in proportions higher than we would expect based on school characteristics. In view of the aggregate student populations served by charter versus traditional students, this pattern should be expected and applauded.

One could reasonably argue that controlling for school-level demographics does not adequately control for unmeasured selectin bias. One possible way to get at this using our method would be to analyze aggregate results for different races or for poor or non-poor students as determined by free-lunch status. In Wisconsin, with its small school sizes and small populations of minority students in many schools, attempts to do this dropped out too many schools. However, because No Child Left Behind requires publishing these breakdown aggregates, we recommend this kind of analysis when possible.

Conclusions

Charter schools clearly provide additional options for students and families not only in Wisconsin's one large city, Milwaukee, but also in a number of other medium-sized cities and towns throughout the state. In many districts, charters offer the major alternative to the traditional systems that are in place and operating quite satisfactorily for many families. It is also clear that charter schools offer options to students who do not match the overall demographic makeup of the districts in which they reside. This creates more diverse student populations in these schools.

With the exception of one eighth-grade cohort, we believe that, subject to the cautions already raised, the achievement test results for schools in Wisconsin should be interpreted as favoring charter schools. In Milwaukee, charter school students consistently outperformed traditional students. The effects were largest for Hispanic and white students, larger in math, and most pronounced in grades 5 through 9. Analysis of statewide data that control for school characteristics indicates that charter schools did better than traditional public schools at ensuring that students achieve at the proficient level of performance. Finally, our finding are generally consistent with other studies using National Assessment of Educational Progress aggregated data, in which Wisconsin charter school students did very well, and better than charter schools in all but one other state.

Why might this be the case? We offer two reasons. First, local school boards authorize most charter schools in Wisconsin—and all of them in our study. According to a 2005 National Center for Education Statistics study, district-authorized charters perform better than schools authorized by state boards, colleges, or other entities. Further, charter schools authorized by school boards, with no controls for differing school populations, were slightly better than all other public schools.

Second, we offer a qualitative reason. In most of the apparently successful charter schools we visited, strong leadership was evident. Not only did local superintendents enthusiastically support the school, but so did school boards and other district officials. Within these successful schools, two forms of leadership were apparent—often not by the same person. One person, or a small group of people, was inspirational and instrumental in starting the school and shaping its initial vision. Equally important was a competent, day-to-day administrator. Certainly other reasons exist, but future research on charter schools is necessary for us to understand what is in the black box and whether these explanations also fit the experiences of schools in other states.

Critical Thinking

1. What exactly is a charter school? How does a charter school differ from a normal public school?
2. How do charter schools differ from the more controversial program of school vouchers?

3. What does the evidence show about the educational impact of charter schools in Wisconsin? Do charter schools lead to better student learning and higher scores on achievement tests?

JOHN WITTE and **DAVID WEIMER** are professors of public affairs and political science at the La Follette School of Public Affairs at the University of Wisconsin-Madison, where Paul Schlomer is a doctoral candidate in political science. Arnold Shober is an assistant professor of political science at Lawrence University. The authors thank Martin Carnoy for helpful advice and the U.S. Department of Education for financial support. The findings and conclusions reported are the sole responsibility of the authors. A longer, more detailed version of this article appears in the summer 2007 issue of the Journal of *Policy Analysis and Management*, volume 26, no. 3.

Charter Schools

GAIL ROBINSON

The school playground is cramped, the day is bleak and chilly, but the kindergarten students are having fun, and one boy in particular resists going back inside. "You haven't made good choices," two teachers tell him. To his more cooperative classmates, the teachers say, "*You* have made good choices."

The use of the phrase "good choices" is no accident. "We believe in creating a democratic society where our children feel they have a choice," said school leader Rita Danis.

But "choice" holds another meaning at UFT Charter Elementary, a new school in the East New York section of Brooklyn run by the teachers union. It is a charter school. As such it is key to Mayor Michael Bloomberg and Chancellor Joel Klein's campaign to give city parents more choices about where to send their children to school.

While Bloomberg has set more requirements for public schools, he has, in an apparent contradiction, sought to encourage charter schools, which function outside of those rules. He hopes to more than double the number of charter schools in the city, from 47 to 100. "It's time to clear away the barriers to the creation of charter schools," Bloomberg said in a recent speech.

But charter schools, such as One World in Astoria and Carl Icahn in the Bronx, educate only about one percent of city public school students and only four percent in the nation as a whole. So why have they attracted so much attention? And why do some people think they can help solve New York City's education problems?

The Appeal of Charters

Charter schools receive public money but are independently and privately run. Though they must comply with certain state regulations and health and safety rules, they do not have to operate under union contracts, and they exist largely outside the Department of Education bureaucracy.

The charter school movement began in the 1970s, the brainchild of Ray Budde, a professor of education at the University of Massachusetts. He suggested that individual teachers could be given contracts, which he dubbed charters, to explore new approaches. United Federation of Teachers president Albert Shanker then expanded the idea to call for granting entire schools charters (with union approval). The first charter school in the U.S. opened in St. Paul, Minnesota, in 1992. Today about 580,000 students in the country attend 2,400 charter schools.

But New York was slow to embrace charter schools. The legislature finally approved them in 1998 as part of a political deal. Governor George Pataki agreed to support a legislative pay raise if the lawmakers approved charters. The bill included a rigorous application process for charter schools and a ceiling on the number of new charter schools.

As Pataki hailed the bill's passage, he noted that dozens of state schools were considered to be failing. "We're telling the parents in those neighborhoods, you have no choice but to send your child to a school that we know fails. Well, now they're going to have an option," Pataki said, "and I think all the schools are going to be better because of that."

Seven years later, New York City's 47 charter schools have a total of about 12,000 students—compared with about 1.1 million in conventional public schools. (Charter schools are considered public schools too.) Fifteen of the 47, including the UFT school, opened this fall. The vast majority are elementary schools and many are small, with fewer than 200 pupils.

A Choice or a Drain?

While much of the adamant opposition to charters has faded, conflicts remain over their performance and how they should be controlled and regulated. In many ways, these disputes come down to a battle over who should control education, what some have likened to a "power struggle."

Charter schools offer parents choice, particularly in poorer neighborhoods. But they also provide a counterweight to the so-called "educrats" and unions, often derided by Bloomberg and others. The lack of the union and of longtime school administrators holds particular appeal for many on the political right. It is no coincidence that one of the leading academic proponents of charter schools is the Goldwater Institute in Arizona—named for the founder of the modern American conservative moment.

"I see charter schools as, first, a source of needed education options for disadvantaged kids otherwise stuck in failing district schools and unable to afford private schools; second, a source of important external pressure on traditional school systems (and private schools); and, third, a preview of things to come for public education as a whole," as the big bureaucracies lose much of their power said Chester Finn, a charter school advocate.

Charter schools also benefit from being contrasted with vouchers, which give parents money to spend on their children's education as they see fit. "Instead of pushing private school vouchers that funnel scarce dollars away from the public schools, we will support public school choice, including charter schools and magnet schools that meet the same high standards as other schools," said the Democratic Party platform for 2004.

"The educational establishment has been willing to allow charters in some state just to forestall vouchers," Clint Bolick of the Alliance for School Choice told the *New York Times*.

Those who remain opposed argue that charter schools drain energy and resources from the public schools, while only educating a tiny percentage of kids. As evidence, some point to Albany, where the public school system has lost more than 1,000 students and must spend about $10 million a year on charters.

Instead of moving to create a new parallel school system, "parents are interested in improving the schools that they have," said David Ernst, spokesman for the state Schools Board Association.

Do Charters Work?

Most New York City charter schools have existed for only a few years, if that, and so information about their performance remains sketchy.

In general, the results appear promising. For example, on eighth grade tests, where the city's regular public school students tend to stumble, charter school students did better, according to figures compiled by the Center for Charter School Excellence.

But nationally the statistics are murkier. The first study comparing students in regular schools with those in charters, released in August 2004, found that charter school students often did not perform as well as students in regular public schools. Finn called the results "dismayingly low" and called for those overseeing charters to be more demanding.

On the most recent National Assessment of Education Progress test, charter school students did not do as well as public school students. They did, however, narrow the gap between the two types of schools. This prompted a pro charter group, the National Alliance for Public Charter Schools, to say the scores showed "real progress for charter schools," while the American Federation of Teachers declared that charters "continue to lag behind regular public schools."

What Parents Want

To many New York City parents, such arguments are academic. They are dissatisfied with their local public school and want something better for their child but cannot afford private school.

The city's charter schools are concentrated in poorer neighborhoods. Ninety percent of their students are black or Latino, and almost three quarters come from families poor enough that they qualify for a free school lunch. But the students are less likely than their regular school counterparts to need special education services, according to a state report.

Parents of students at the UFT school only have to look to I.S. 292, the public junior high school that resides in the same building as the charter school, to see what they are up against. Although a new principal has reportedly tried to turn the school around, in 2004, 28 percent of its eighth graders failed to meet even minimum state standards in reading.

And some charters offer services that go far beyond what public schools provide. At Harlem Day Charter, for example, students can stay at school until 5:30 P.M. at no charge. Some of that time is devoted to a program where artists supervise students in projects such as a felt mural showing how to count in Swahili. A fourth grade classroom boasts a bank of new computers, and a room set aside for parents offers computers as well as books that might be of interest. And the school takes advantage of a foundation program where students go to a local Barnes and Noble and get to spend $50 each on books of their own choosing.

Charter schools can adjust their programs to meet the wishes of parents in the community. And so many of the city charter schools stress academic basics, feature strict disciplinary codes and require uniforms. Some are single sex schools. Seth Andrew, who has applied to launch a charter school called *Democracy Prep* first looked at lots of other charter schools. He was particularly impressed by those that set "incredibly high expectations with plans for college for all kids"—expectations that extend to behavior as well as academics.

To parents such an approach seems to have appeal. The charters select students by lottery and most, if not all, have more applicants than they can accept.

How Do They Do It?

Harlem Day receives slightly over $9,000 per student from the Department of Education, less than the public schools receive for each child. But, many say, money goes further in charter schools.

For one, new charter schools do not have to be unionized. "The big Kahuna is the union contract," said Peter Murphy, director of policy for the New York State Charter School Association. "The contract dictates things beyond wages and salaries" and takes away the school leader's ability to manage.

And charter school teachers may make less than their public school counterparts or work longer hours.

It seems clear that the UFT launched its charter school partly to rebut the contention that a UFT contract hampers education. Instead, union officials blame the school bureaucracy for excess costs. They say that administrative expenses take up 11 percent of most schools' budgets; at the UFT school, that figure is four percent.

But cost savings are only part of the story. Most charter schools raise money to supplement what they get from the city. Educating a student at the Harlem Day costs $3,400 to $4,000 more than the school receives from the city, said its director, Keith Meacham. But real estate developer Benjamin Lambert founded the school, and he and his brother Henry Lambert have helped it find space and money. And the Carl Icahn School in the South Bronx got a $3 million facility from the businessman for whom it is named.

Flexibility contributes to the success of charter schools, according to Paula Gavin, executive director of the city Center for Charter School Excellence. But, in addition, she said, the schools benefit from having a clear mission and a drive to fulfill that mission. They are small, Gavin said—"not just class size, but the overall school is smaller. The size of the school allows individual attention." And,

she said, charters must be accountable for what they do and do not do.

Spreading Reform

New York City and state do more than many other cities and states to promote charter schools. The city provides some schools with space in Department of Education buildings and recently launched a $250 million program to help other charters build their own homes. It has also established the New York City Center *for Charter School Excellence* in partnership with several foundations to help charter applicants and to assist existing schools.

Charter school advocates praise many things about New York state's charter law. But they do not like the cap, which limits the number of new charter schools in the entire state to 100, with 50 for the city. As of last month, some 42 schools were competing for the remaining 16 spots left for charters statewide.

The original rationale for the cap was that the state should be sure charter schools would work before launching too many of them. But now that charters have a track record, charter proponents say, the cap has outlived any use it might have once had.

Bloomberg wants the state to eliminate the cap entirely and give him the authority to create charter schools without going to the state. Others call for doubling the cap to 200.

Supporters of charter schools would also like to see the government boost its allocation for each child in a charter school. "At the end of the day, they're all our children," said Mimi Corcoran, executive director of Beginning with Children Foundation, an early sponsor of charters.

But, while every child's future is important, won't spending money for charters still leave behind the vast majority of students who remain in regular public schools?

Supporters say no, contending that competition from charter schools may spur public schools to do better. Charters can, the argument goes, function as laboratories, developing techniques public schools can adopt. For example, said Corcoran, charters developed the idea of lead teachers, paying senior teachers extra money to remain in the classrooms rather than go into administration. Now that concept has been incorporated into the new union contract.

But many of the approaches used in charter schools, such as smaller class size, have already proved successful. Public schools simply don't have the money or the freedom to implement them.

"Our members envy the autonomy charter schools have," said Ernst of the school boards association. While the state frees charter school from many regulations, he said, it subjects public schools to requirements that are "costly, onerous, time consuming and not always in line with good educational process."

Similarly, while Bloomberg and Klein encourage charters to be independent, they have imposed a uniform curriculum on most regular public schools, increased standardized testing and, critics charged, micromanaged teachers and principals.

Brian Ferguson, the principal of One World, is reluctant to set up a conflict between charters and more conventional public schools. "I'm sort of always leery to say that we're doing it and the public schools aren't doing it, because that's not the case," he said. "I think that we're both trying to get from each other what the best practices are for educating our children."

Critical Thinking

1. What arguments can be made in favor of charter schools?
2. What possible criticisms can be made against charter schools? How can critics argue that school choice programs, including charter schools, may have undesirable impacts?
3. Do charter schools work? What does the evidence from New York show? What do national statistics show?
4. How do inner-city parents, especially African-American and Latino parents, generally feel about charter schools?
5. How do charter schools save money? Should their approach to cost savings be applauded or criticized?

D.C. School Reform in Question after Mayor Fenty's Loss

Julianne Hing

When Washington, D.C. mayor Adrian Fenty lost his primary in a major upset against city council chairman Vincent Gray on Tuesday night, the immediate question for many was not what would happen to the young black mayor once hailed as a Democratic party rising star. It was: what will happen to his hard-charging school chief Michelle Rhee?

Since Tuesday, Gray has repeatedly ducked the question, saying he will not comment on personnel issues until after the November election. Gray and Rhee have clashed over the years, and the local teachers' union backed Gray, who noted during his campaign that he's interested in working "with parents and teachers," a group of folks that Rhee has been at odds with in her short tenure. Rhee, for her part, has had to tamp down rumors that she's already stepped down, though she acknowledged Wednesday evening that she "absolutely" felt guilty for Fenty's loss. She also has made it clear Wednesday night that she's uninterested in compromising her reform agenda for a new mayor.

The question for the rest of the country is: where aggressive, pro-testing and pro-teacher accountability school reforms are concerned, how much are parents and teachers willing to handle?

Michelle Rhee has served as chancellor of the D.C. public school system since 2007, when she was installed by Mayor Fenty. The turnover rate for her job is high and chancellors in the failing school district have rarely lasted long. But Rhee, a self-styled education reform crusader with a take no prisoners attitude, was determined to stay. Or at least shake things up.

Within her first 18 months on the job, Rhee dismissed 270 teachers, shut down almost two dozen schools and dramatically consolidated the district's administrative offices. She's pushed an agenda demanding that teachers' job security depend on their students' test scores, a model of so-called "accountability" that's slowly being adopted by the rest of the country, in part at the urging of the Obama administration. She's since made it a yearly practice to fire teachers whose student test scores prove unsatisfactory. This summer Rhee fired 241 teachers and put another 737 on probation. And Rhee instituted a teacher evaluation system called IMPACT where student test scores counted for as much as 50 percent of a teacher's job performance. Rhee was also responsible for negotiating a controversial and unprecedented teacher contract that weakened teacher tenure in favor of higher salaries and bonuses upfront. Unsurprisingly, the national American Federation of Teachers union poured in a lot of money to unseat Fenty.

Rhee's one of the most public faces of a controversial model of local education reform called mayoral control, where school chiefs appointed by mayors push aggressive policies and operate with near full autonomy because they don't have to answer to school boards. Department of Education Secretary Arne Duncan is himself a former school chief who ran Chicago's public schools with the backing of his mayor Richard Daley. He and President Obama have offered high praise for Rhee. Tuesday's election and the fallout from Fenty's loss has allowed the rest of the country to re-evaluate a model of education reform that's got lots of people talking, but perhaps not a whole lot of actual support from voters. Already, school chiefs operating under mayoral control in other cities who've been sheltered from city politics are looking at D.C. with wariness. New York City schools chancellor Joel Klein told *Time*: "The vote on Fenty will be opportunistically misused by the opponents of real school reform." But it wasn't just Rhee's style, it was also the substance of her demands that got her in trouble.

While it's true that Adrian Fenty, once praised as a suave, smart young politician on the rise, had problems that were much bigger than Rhee alone, she acknowledged that her aggressive nature (if not her policies) showed a level of tone deafness she now regrets. According to a *Washington City Paper poll,* Fenty polled well with white D.C. voters who have kids in the DCPS, and who are newer residents in the rapidly gentrifying city. But he lost support with longtime black residents, who were generally not opposed to school reform, but hated Rhee's yearly mass firings.

With Fenty out of the picture, it's not just Rhee's job that's on the line—though two of her allies on the D.C. city council are lobbying for her to stick around till the end of the 2010–2011 school year. The question for the rest of the country remains how much support education reform initiatives have at the local level. At the end of the day, who outside the Obama administration and hard-driving reformers wants the brand of change that they're pushing?

Critical Thinking

1. Who in the District of Columbia were the most active opponents of school reform as administered by Mayor Adrian Fenty and his chosen schools' chancellor Michelle Rhee?

2. How did Fenty lose re-election? Which parts of Washington D.C. voted for him? In which parts did he suddenly lose support? Explain why these constituencies were no longer enthusiastic supporters of Fenty?

With More Choice Has Come Resegregation

Board's challenge: Reconcile imbalance with least parental uproar.

LESLIE FULBRIGHT AND HEATHER KNIGHT

A school-assignment system established in 2001 to give San Francisco parents more choice has resegregated many schools across San Francisco.

After years of warnings that the assignment system was unsuccessful in its attempt to comply with a court order mandating integrated schools, the Board of Education now wants to fix that problem without angering parents of all ethnicities who want good schools close to home.

Many parents have made it clear that they will flee to private schools or the suburbs if they don't get a public school they like, but school board members have said that having segregated schools is indefensible.

The seven elected board members now have the unenviable task of balancing these dueling interests. No longer subject to court-ordered desegregation after 23 years, board members say they are determined to address the problem of resegregated schools by creating a new student-assignment system.

Board members say they hope to have a new plan in place by August and use it for the first time in the 2007–08 school year.

"The board has to make a huge decision. They're asking all the right questions, and some of the answers are mutually exclusive," said Ruth Grabowski, who runs the Parent Advisory Council to the school board. "There are so many different possible solutions. The issues are heartbreaking to me."

The district has been coping with segregation since the 1970s, when the NAACP sued the school district, saying African American and Latino students were not getting an equal education. In a 1982 settlement, the district agreed that no school would have more than 45 percent from one ethnicity and that each school would be represented by at least four ethnic groups. The district achieved this by assigning students to schools and busing some across the city.

Court Challenge

This system, in turn, was challenged in 1994 when Chinese American families sued the district in a case called Ho vs. San Francisco Unified, saying their children were being kept out of their preferred schools simply because of their ethnicity. By the time the Ho case was settled in 1999, African Americans had dwindled to about 10,000, or 16 percent of enrollment, and Chinese Americans had become the largest group, with more than 18,000 students, or 28 percent.

This school year, 32 percent of San Francisco Unified students are Chinese American, 9 percent from other Asian groups (Filipino, Japanese American and Korean American), 13 percent African American, 22 percent Latino, 9 percent white and 12 percent from other nonwhite groups, district data shows. By comparison, San Francisco's whole school-age population was 44 percent Asian and Pacific Islander, 12 percent black, 23 percent white and 19 percent Latino of any race in 2003, according to a U.S. census estimate.

The 1999 settlement forbade the use of race in school assignments, and two years later the district created a "diversity index" to comply. The index assigns students based on social and economic factors but not race. Those factors are poverty, mother's education, English skill, home language and academic performance of the student's previous school. Parents submit a wish list of up to seven schools, and if there's space, their child will get into one of those schools without being subjected to the diversity index.

But the district has applied the diversity index only at schools with too many enrollment requests. So while the system has increased choices for parents, it has also resegregated dozens of schools, especially in poor neighborhoods.

The number of racially identifiable public schools in San Francisco has jumped by two-thirds in the past four years, according to the last annual report of Stuart Biegel, the UCLA professor appointed to monitor the district's desegregation efforts until the court order expired in December.

Biegel found that in close to 50 of the district's 113 schools, 60 percent or more of students in any grade were from a single racial or ethnic group. The district, he said, had undergone "severe resegregation."

Recent Warning

In a 2004 report, Biegel warned the district that racial groups were becoming isolated.

U.S. District Court Judge William Alsup agreed and in November of last year halted the 22-year-old consent decree that mandated integration. He called it a failure.

The system "has not achieved diversity in any meaningful sense," Alsup wrote. "It has allowed, if not fostered, resegregation. The court has pleaded with the parties to fix the diversity index. They have not."

The resegregated schools also show a distinct pattern of academic underachievement. With the rare exception—such as George R. Moscone Elementary in the Mission, which is heavily Latino and scores tremendously well—schools with low-income students who are predominantly Latino or African American score poorly.

Experts say segregation contributes to the disparity because it typically means low-income black and Latino students are stuck in schools with the highest teacher turnover and the lowest rates of parental involvement.

"It is not simply a change in the skin color of students in a school, but is systematically linked to inequality," said Gary Orfield, the director of Harvard's Civil Rights Project, who has studied the phenomenon nationwide.

The current system, however, satisfies many parents because it allows their children to get into schools of their choice.

For the 2006–07 school year, 84 percent of families got one of their top seven choices. The other 16 percent were assigned to a school they didn't want. They could accept it, try again in the second round or bail out of the public schools altogether.

Other Considerations

Not all parents are determined to send their children to neighborhood schools. Many want the choice of a top-performing school, one with a unique language program, or one near their workplace.

Yet the school board is opposed to segregated schools and has been meeting over the past several months to brainstorm solutions.

The board's options include applying the diversity index at all schools, using race as a factor in school assignments or crafting separate assignment systems for students of different ages.

Commissioner Dan Kelly has been a strong proponent of adding race back into the assignment system and has criticized his fellow board members for ignoring the problem as it worsened.

"We should have been dealing with this for years," Kelly said. "The resegregation is accelerating dramatically."

Some school board members criticize the current diversity index system because schools with few requests—typically in black and Latino neighborhoods—have no mechanism to ensure diversity of any kind.

"The board should have foreseen that the index would be unequal if only applied at selective schools," said school board member Eric Mar. "It has led to African Americans and Latinos concentrated in low-income schools, where there is tremendous racial isolation."

But board members disagree about whether to apply the diversity index to all schools.

School board President Norman Yee, who opposes that plan, said he does not want to force people to attend unpopular schools in order to diversify them. "Saying to everybody, 'You have to go there,' doesn't make any sense," he said, noting it could drive even more white and middle-class families out of the public schools.

Hard Line

Mar said it's a price that must be paid, even though it could drive families out. "It may have the impact of getting them to choose a private school, but that's their choice," he said. Six of the seven board members say they want to restore race as a factor in assigning students to schools.

Though Mar, Yee, Kelly, Sarah Lipson, Mark Sanchez and Jill Wynns told *The Chronicle* that integration can't be achieved without taking race into account, they have not committed to actually putting a race-based assignment system into play. Eddie Chin, historically the group's strongest proponent of neighborhood schools, said he has not yet decided whether he will support using race.

Whether or not the board eventually agrees, restoring race may not be easy.

Proposition 209, which California voters approved in 1996, prohibits public agencies from using race in making decisions about education, employment or contracting. San Francisco schools escaped its provisions between 1996 and 1999 only because the district was under a federal desegregation order that required it to use race in making such decisions.

Now, however, the board is talking with lawyers behind closed doors about whether there may be a way to legally consider race in school assignments, several board members confirmed. Several said they would like to adopt something similar to Seattle's assignment system, which uses race as a tie-breaker in assigning students to popular high schools.

The Ninth U.S. Circuit Court of Appeals in San Francisco upheld Seattle's system last fall after parents sued claiming the system violated their 14th Amendment right to equal protection.

David Levine, the lawyer for the Chinese American families who settled with the San Francisco schools in 1999, said the district would leave itself open to another lawsuit if it adopts a new race-based system.

"California law takes the use of race off the table—it's just clear as can be," Levine said. "The schools have all these financial problems, and to waste money on lawyers defending something that's not defensible, it seems like a monumental waste of money."

Legal Battles

But other districts have won court battles over Prop. 209. An Alameda County judge found Berkeley's voluntary desegregation plan did not violate the ban on racial preferences. Superior Court Judge James Richman ruled that the measure allows race to be used in integrating public schools.

Berkeley's plan, which requires enrollment at each school to come within five percentage points of the district's breakdown overall, was fair because in addition to race it considered parent choice, residence and socioeconomics, Richman ruled.

Some San Francisco board members say race is the only way to achieve integration and they are committed to finding a way to take it into account.

"Prop. 209 does not change the United States Constitution," Wynns said.

Kelly added, "We can't ignore the fact that there is still serious segregation in San Francisco. We're not a colorblind society, and it's difficult for us to talk about it in a rational, calm way, but we do need to do that. We do need to acknowledge that racial segregation is a very serious problem for this nation and for our city."

Sanchez said he supports adding race as a tie-breaker and would also like to give enrollment preference to students who live in public housing. He also wants to see Lowell High and the School of the Arts—which use selective admissions processes and are exempt from the diversity index—added into the general assignment pool.

Some board members, though, believe there should be at least some classroom seats set aside for neighborhood students, and a hybrid system incorporating neighborhood preference and diversity preference could be a compromise.

Separate Systems

The board is also considering devising different assignment systems for elementary schools, middle schools and high schools, Yee said. The group has toyed with emphasizing neighborhood schools for younger students, who cannot easily traverse the city on their own, and promoting a diversity system for older students, Yee said.

Myong Leigh, the district's director of policy and planning, is working with the board to develop the new plan. He said it's too soon to say exactly what it will look like.

"All that stuff is in the soup—it's still being discussed," he said.

Parents are split as to whether race should be added back into the student assignment plan.

Dori Lange is convinced it would work, by forcing schools to integrate and then reducing academic disparities. If busing children across town is the only solution, then the district must do it, she said, even if more parents may flee.

"I think they should put race back in," said Lange, whose 6-year-old son attends Rosa Parks Elementary in the Western Addition. "The top-tier schools are basically private schools at this point, and many others are doing poorly.

"The families who really need help continue to get assigned to crappy schools in bad neighborhoods."

Omar Khalif, who is a candidate for school board in November, lives in Bayview-Hunters Point and has four daughters.

Khalif said he's so happy he's "over the moon" with the education his girls are receiving in neighborhood schools and thinks busing to integrate schools is overrated. Two of his daughters attended a middle school across town for a while, but he said the family felt unwelcome and the girls' grades suffered.

"Some African American families are choosing schools on the west side because they have good test scores—what, do they think their children will learn by osmosis?" he said.

If school districts around the country still haven't figured out how to develop integrated, high-performing schools for children of all races more than a half-century after the U.S. Supreme Court's Brown vs. Board of Education decision outlawing "separate but equal" education, they probably never will, Khalif said.

"How have you not figured it out after 50 years?" Khalif asked. "We've developed the Internet. We've sent people to the moon, and we can't figure this one out."

Critical Thinking

1. How has the racial and ethnic complexity of San Francisco affected the city's ability to promote school integration?
2. What does Prop. 209 in California reveal about public opinion when it comes to the use of race in school assignments?
3. What does the statistical data reveal regarding racial isolation in San Francisco schools? Is the racial integration of the city's schools improving or diminishing?

Here Comes the Neighborhood

Charlotte and the resegregation of America's public schools.

DAMIEN JACKSON

Darius Swann remembers the blazing cross that illuminated the night sky outside his window at Johnson C. Smith University in Charlotte. The year was 1966, and Swann, an African-American theology professor, had recently initiated a lawsuit against the Charlotte-Mecklenburg school system after his 6-year-old son was denied admission to a nearby elementary because he was black. "There's always a certain amount of danger whenever you take a stand," says the Presbyterian minister.

Around that time, Swann recalls, the homes of several of the city's African-American leaders were firebombed. "It drove home the point that such issues were deeply embedded in the psyche of the community," he says. "People were willing to resort to extreme measures."

Swann was willing to go pretty far himself. For more than a decade, Swann pursued his case in the courts. The lawsuit that bore his name, *Swann v. Charlotte-Mecklenburg Board of Education,* concluded successfully when a U.S. District Court judge ordered the creation of a more racially diverse school district. Later affirmed by the Supreme Court in 1971, Swann is commonly recognized as the case that "put the teeth" in the earlier *Brown v. Board of Education* decision by instituting timely and practical ways of combating separate and unequal education, such as busing and race-conscious student assignments. The case changed the face of American education in the 20th century, as the nation's school districts followed its lead toward increasing integration.

More than two decades later, that face is changing back. A recent study by Gary Orfield of the Civil Rights Project at Harvard University shows that more than 70 percent of the nation's African-American students currently attend predominantly minority schools, or schools where more than half the students are minority. (Close to 76 percent of Latinos attend schools with non-white majorities.) Though this growing trend can be attributed, in part, to declining public school enrollment by whites, the study reveals that the typical white public school student is educated in an institution that is 80 percent white.

Since 1995, 45 school districts across the country have been declared "unitary"—that is, sufficiently desegregated—and had their federal desegregation orders rescinded by the courts. Challenges by critics of court-ordered desegregation have sparked recent or ongoing court battles in school districts in a majority of states, including Alabama, Florida, Massachusetts, Michigan and Pennsylvania.

The trend toward resegregation is particularly pronounced in the South, a region where most of the Swann-based remedies for integrating schools were focused. Between 1988 and 1998, the percentage of blacks in majority white schools dropped from 43.5 to 32.7 percent. "There's something really bad happening," Orfield told a recent national conference on school resegregation at the University of North Carolina in Chapel Hill. "It's related to race. And it's getting worse."

Charlotte, which less than two decades ago boasted one of the most integrated school systems in the country, is rapidly heading toward resegregation. In 1999, the Swann decision was overturned by U.S. District Court Judge Robert Potter, a busing critic, who declared the Charlotte-Mecklenburg school district to be unitary.

The ruling resulted from a lawsuit brought by white advocates of "neighborhood schools"—an assignment model that prioritizes attendance in a student's own neighborhood. Given that neighborhoods in and around Charlotte, like elsewhere, are largely divided along racial and ethnic lines, neighborhood school models make it virtually impossible for districts to avoid resegregation.

"There's absolutely nothing wrong with integrated schools," says Paul Haisley, a Charlotte accountant and outspoken advocate of neighborhood schools. "But if it means a kid is going to leave his own neighborhood to spend an hour on a school bus each day, is it really worth it? I don't think so."

A majority of the Charlotte-Mecklenburg School Board was opposed to Potter's ruling—including all four African-American members—and it crafted a plan that tried to stem resegregation. The "school choice" plan allows parents to pick from a number of area schools within their "choice zone," with transportation provided. If they desire a school outside of their zone, they are responsible for their own transportation.

The plan prioritizes school choice for students whose home schools have high concentrations of poor students, and gives more funds to such schools. "Parents were leaving the system," contends Haisley, referring to the "white flight" commonly associated with increasing minority enrollment in a school district. "This plan was the best way of empowering parents and ensuring they had a choice."

Many African-Americans are less optimistic. "No community in America has ever been able to achieve separate but equal," says Arthur Griffin, a member of the school board who opposed the plan and Potter's ruling. Even with the new plan and a commitment from Charlotte's education, political and business leadership to equalize funding in majority-black city schools, Griffin believes school resegregation, along with its associated disparities, is just a matter of time. In the year since the plan has been in place, the number of elementary schools with more than 90 percent minority enrollment has already increased from nine to 16.

Orfield's study provides a broader interpretation. Not unlike the disparities that produced the *Brown* decision a half-century ago, the nation's majority-minority schools are commonly "isolated by race and poverty" while offering "vastly unequal educational opportunities" than their majority-white counterparts. This stark reality—based largely in historically segregated housing patterns, white flight and an inequitable reliance on local property taxes for school funding—provides an unhealthy prognosis for a large-scale return to neighborhood schools in African-American communities across the country.

"Philosophically, I support the concept of neighborhood schools," says Griffin, who feels all students should have quality schools close to home. "Unfortunately, all neighborhoods are not created equal."

They never were. For a decade after the *Brown* decision in 1954, widespread southern resistance to integration by local school boards kept the vast majority of African-American students in the South in segregated schools. The passage of the 1964 Civil Rights Act stepped up the federal enforcement of desegregation orders and, by 1968, transformed the region into one where a quarter of all southern black students attended majority white schools.

After taking office in 1968, however, President Richard Nixon largely abandoned the enforcement of desegregation requirements, appointing four Supreme Court justices known for their pro-segregation leanings. The court issued a number of key decisions substantially limiting the scope and impact of school desegregation. *Keyes v. Denver* (1973) hampered plaintiffs in de facto segregated systems by requiring proof of "intentionally segregative school board actions in a meaningful portion of a school system." *Milliken v. Bradley* (1974) forbade such inter-district remedies to segregation as transferring students between predominantly black inner-cities and predominantly white suburbs.

Even so, earlier federal and local commitments, combined with the Swann decision, continued the trend toward integration. By 1988, the percentage of African-American students attending majority-white schools in the South peaked near 44 percent.

But this peak also marked a sharp turning point. The number of integrated southern schools steadily declined as a result of strong opposition to desegregation policy from the Reagan administration, which repealed federal desegregation assistance programs and advocated the end of relevant court orders. By the '90s, Supreme Court appointments by Reagan and George Bush Sr. had created a judicial majority committed to doing just that. In a number of key cases—including *Board of Education of Oklahoma City v. Dowell* and *Freeman v. Pitts*—the high court elected to end existing desegregation orders by making it easier to declare school systems unitary. It was irrelevant, the court further ruled, if the termination of such orders led to the resegregation of these school systems.

While capitalizing on an increasing political backlash to busing (yet not necessarily to integration), critics have often characterized school desegregation as a failed policy. Sociologist Roslyn Mickelson offers evidence to the contrary. The UNC-Charlotte professor, who spent years examining the academic impact of desegregation and related policies on students in Charlotte-Mecklenburg's public schools, found that "the more time both black and white students spent in desegregated elementary schools, the greater their academic achievement."

Her study highlights the positive effects of a desegregated setting on such current indicators of achievement as high school advanced placements and standardized test scores. It also reveals that "the higher the percent of blacks in a school, the lower the percent of the school's teachers who are fully credentialed, are experienced, and who possess master's degrees."

Mickelson concludes that the likely resegregation of the Charlotte-Mecklenburg schools "does not bode well for black children's education prospects." As the district returns to segregated neighborhood schools, she writes, "we can anticipate that racial antagonisms and racial gaps in achievement and attainment will grow."

While most black Charlotte residents say they should have access to good schools in their own neighborhoods, and some of them insist the burden of busing was placed disproportionately on their black children, most are quick to clarify that such sentiment does not reflect abandonment of the ideals of desegregation. "The customary line has been that we need to keep diversity in our schools," says Blanche Penn, a parent leader and the director of the West Charlotte Community Center. "I haven't heard anyone say otherwise."

Apparently, Charlotte residents are still largely committed to the concepts of integration and equity in funding. Griffin and other pro-desegregation African-Americans were recently re-elected to the school board by substantial margins over white advocates of neighborhood schools.

Even so, says Stoney Sellers, a prominent Charlotte businessman and community activist, it's ultimately a question of limited resources in a rapidly growing city. "At some point, as the growth continues, will the community choose school equity first, or will the money follow the development of all the new schools we're building?" Sellers asks. "Seven to 10 years down the road, how will our communities look then?"

"I am more concerned that a child is succeeding rather than if that child is in a diverse setting or not," says Lindalyn Kakadelis, a former school board member and teacher in Charlotte, who argues that diversity is an imprecise term "since we're almost at a point in America where white is a minority." Kakadelis says "the bottom line is student achievement," and she's "so tired of people making excuses" for low achievers and acting like "victims" of poverty and other social ills. "What I'm for," she adds, is "pushing everybody to succeed in their own schools."

"We know it's not just about integration or sitting in the same classrooms with whites," Sellers counters. His concerns are educational quality, the distribution of resources and academic achievement. "School desegregation wouldn't have meant much if there had been no impact on educational achievement."

"If we had the money, the certified teachers and everything we needed in our neighborhood schools, then I wouldn't have a problem with segregated schools," Penn says. "But we know that's not going to happen. The resources follow the folks with the money."

For Penn, it's back to the future. "Putting kids back in neighborhood schools brings back memories," she says, recalling her own experiences as a teen-age student at all-black West Charlotte High. "We got all the old, leftover books." She quickly adds that the African-American community "doesn't want leftovers."

Swann, who no longer lives in Charlotte, acknowledges the irony of his desire 30 years ago for his son to attend a white school in his own neighborhood. He contends that, for African-Americans, neighborhood schools are less significant because neighborhoods now reflect "proximity as opposed to a real community. A lot of people don't even know their neighbors."

Even so, without solutions to the current trend, African-Americans could find themselves with leftovers again. But despite the increasingly conservative tone of the country and its judicial system, new attempts at maintaining diversity in the public schools are afoot. A number of systems—including North Carolina's Wake County Schools, which includes Raleigh, the capital—are considering socioeconomic status in school assignments. In San Francisco, schools are using a "diversity index"

that accounts for economic status, parental education levels and the number of languages spoken at a student's home. Similar approaches are being tried in Manchester, Connecticut, and La Crosse, Wisconsin.

But for some there's a bottom line. "Integrated neighborhoods produce integrated schools," says Steve Johnston, executive director of the Charlotte-based Swann Fellowship. The nonprofit organization, named for Swann and his wife Vera, was formed in 1997 to advance the value of diversity in public education.

Johnston contends that until white people and the institutions they control pay equitable wages to people of color and allow for the kind of educational institutions that can produce economic parity, the onus will always be on whites to make neighborhoods and schools integrated. "Economic diversity in housing patterns will create diverse schools," he says.

To Johnston, the solution is simple. "We can wait until we're all brown, or we can work at living together."

Swann adds: "I believe that the public school is the most important element in the transformation of a society. If the schools can change, then so can it."

Critical Thinking

1. How did the U.S. Supreme Court in its 1971 *Swann v. Charlotte-Mecklenburg Board of Education* decision make the city of Charlotte a symbol in the fight for school integration? What exactly did the Court rule in *Swann?*

2. What does the more recent statistical evidence reveal about Charlotte's schools? Are Charlotte's schools and other schools in the South becoming increasingly integrated or resegregated?

3. How have more recent court decisions affected the racial integration efforts started as a result of *Swann?*

4. How did the Supreme Court's 1974 *Millikin v. Bradley* decision and 1990s decision in *Board of Education of Oklahoma City v. Dowell* affect the prospects for school integration?

DAMIEN JACKSON is a writer in North Carolina. This story was produced under the George Washington Williams Fellowship for Journalists of Color, a project sponsored by the Independent Press Association.

Schools Seek New Diversity Answers after Court Rejects Race as Tiebreaker

JESSICA BLANCHARD AND CHRISTINE FREY

More magnet schools. More money to underperforming schools or ones that are largely segregated. Weighing whether a student comes from a poor or wealthy family.

These will likely be among the next batch of solutions the Seattle School District turns to as it attempts to foster diversity and create equally strong schools citywide.

With the racial tiebreaker portion of its school assignment plan shot down Thursday by the U.S. Supreme Court, Seattle district officials vowed to find another way to promote diversity in a city where schools and neighborhoods are still fairly segregated.

Wary of a potential court ruling against it, the Seattle School District has not been using the racial tiebreaker system.

"We have had a racially neutral student assignment system for the past five years, and our fears of having schools become more segregated have become fulfilled," said Gary Ikeda, the district's general counsel.

The high court's 5–4 decision, which struck down racial aspects of student assignment plans in Seattle and Louisville, Ky., brought to a close the lengthy legal battle that has been called the most crucial public education case since the landmark 1954 *Brown v. Board of Education* school desegregation decision.

Because the Seattle district has not used the racial tiebreaker since 2001 and next year's school assignments have already been set, the ruling won't have an immediate impact here.

It could, however, jeopardize similar voluntary desegregation plans in hundreds of districts nationwide. And it will force the Seattle district to come up with alternative methods to encourage racial diversity as it revamps its student assignment plan this summer.

To do so, however, the district will have to rethink and likely expand its idea of diversity. Perhaps when determining school assignments, the district could instead consider a student's economic background, or whether they're a recent immigrant or a special-needs student, for example.

"This ruling leaves us open to pursue diverse schools as a goal," said School Board member Michael DeBell. "And we'll be looking to define diversity more broadly."

How that goal is achieved, however, makes a difference. In his majority opinion, Chief Justice John Roberts wrote that classifying students by race only perpetuated the unequal treatment that the Brown ruling sought to extinguish.

"The way to stop discrimination on the basis of race is to stop discriminating on the basis of race," Roberts wrote.

The ruling applies to school districts that aren't under a court order to remove the vestiges of past discrimination.

Justice Anthony Kennedy sided with the court's four most conservative members in rejecting the Louisville and Seattle plans, but in a concurring opinion suggested race may be used as part of a district's broader plan to diversify schools.

Justice Stephen Breyer and the three more liberal members of the court strongly disagreed. In a sharp dissent, Breyer wrote that the ruling would "threaten the promise" of Brown and warned, "this is a decision that the court and the nation will come to regret."

Federal appeals courts had upheld the Seattle and Louisville plans after some parents sued. The Bush administration took the parents' side, arguing that racial diversity is a noble goal but can be sought only through race-neutral means.

The tiebreaker was part of a School Board decision in 1997 to allow the district's 46,000 students to attend a school of their choice. That assignment plan was intended to replace the district's widely unpopular mandatory busing program and return to a neighborhood schools assignment plan, so students could attend school closer to home.

School officials considered a student's race as one of several tiebreakers at popular schools; their race was a factor if the student's attendance would help bring the high school closer to the districtwide average of about 40 percent white students. The tiebreaker helped some minority students get into predominately white high schools, and vice versa.

A student with a sibling at a school got first priority; a student's race was the second tiebreaker, followed by the distance a student lived from the school.

But the plan had critics, including those parents whose students were denied seats at the high school of their choice based on their race. They formed Parents Involved in Community Schools and sued the district in 2000, claiming the racial tiebreaker policy was unfair and violated students' civil rights.

Kathleen Brose, the group's president, fought back tears Thursday as she discussed her victory.

"It's been seven years. A lot of people have moved on, but I don't want another parent to go through what I did—what we did," she said at a news conference.

Her daughter Elisabeth, now 22, wanted to attend Ballard High School, the closest high school to their Magnolia home. But she wasn't able to get a seat there, nor at her second or third choices. She finally ended up at Ingraham High, and later transferred to The Center School when it opened at the Seattle Center. The move was upsetting to the girl, who missed attending high school with her middle school friends, Brose said.

The school district's policy also affected students of color, said Seattle attorney Harry Korrell, who represented the parents. Some who wanted to attend Franklin High, their neighborhood school, were turned away because the district gave those seats to white students in an attempt to balance the school's racial mix.

The lawsuit challenged only the use of the racial tiebreaker for high school assignments, but the district in 2002 suspended the use of the tiebreaker for all schools while the case worked its way through the courts.

Seattle district officials, who have long maintained the racial tiebreaker is necessary and that racial diversity is a laudable goal within public schools, did not waver in that stance Thursday.

At an otherwise somber press conference, they portrayed the ruling as an endorsement of the importance of diversity in public schools.

"I don't believe it's a matter of winning or losing," outgoing Seattle Superintendent Raj Manhas said. "The high court affirmed that diversity matters. . . . That's fundamental."

Enrollment records show the racial makeup at some Seattle high schools has changed since the district suspended the use of the racial tiebreaker. Ballard High's student population has become whiter, for example, while Cleveland High has seen a jump in the percentage of black students.

Seattleites have long recognized that "the opportunity to learn with friends and peers from other races and backgrounds is a valuable part of the American educational experience," Manhas said. "We will be looking at all options available to us."

The idea of a socioeconomic tiebreaker has gained momentum in recent months, with some parents arguing it's a fairer way to determine which students need extra academic support and resources, and that poverty and race are often intertwined.

Still, it will be a challenge to integrate schools without being able to consider a student's race, said Mark Long, an assistant professor of public affairs at the University of Washington.

"Nothing correlates with race like race," he said. "Anytime you try to use some proxy indicator for race to lead to more

diversity for a group of students, you're going to have more difficulty doing that."

Sharon Rodgers, president of the Seattle Council PTSA, said the goal should be to work to make all Seattle schools strong.

"Until we get all our schools to be top performing, whether we use one tiebreaker or another, we're just changing the particular population of students that are assigned to low performing schools," she said.

Key Dates

- **July 2000:** A group of Seattle parents called Parents Involved in Community Schools sues the Seattle school district for using race as a tiebreaker in assigning students to high schools.
- **Spring 2001:** The Seattle district halts the use of the tiebreaker while the case works its way through the courts.
- **April 6, 2001:** U.S. District Court Judge Barbara Rothstein says the policy doesn't violate the U.S. Constitution or anti-affirmative action Initiative 200.
- **April 16, 2002:** The 9th U.S. Circuit Court of Appeals says the policy is illegal under I-200 and the district must stop using it.
- **April 2002:** Ballard Principal David Engle announces his resignation to protest the ruling, saying it will "further intensify the racial divide in this city."
- **June 17, 2002:** The federal court withdraws its own decision and asks the state Supreme Court to consider the issue first.
- **June 26, 2003:** The state Supreme Court upholds the use of race as a tiebreaker.
- **Oct. 20, 2005:** The full 9th Circuit upholds the district's use of race as a tiebreaker.
- **Dec. 4, 2006:** The Seattle case and a similar case from Kentucky are argued before the U.S. Supreme Court.
- **June 28, 2007:** The U.S. Supreme Court rules against Seattle's use of race to determine school assignment.

Critical Thinking

1. What is a magnet school? Why have so many school districts turned to magnet schools as opposed to school busing and other programs for racial integration?

2. What exactly did the U.S. Supreme Court rule in its decision concerning the use of magnet schools as part of a program intended to produce voluntary integration?

From *Seattle Post-Intelligencer*, June 29, 2007. Copyright © 2007 by Hearst Seattle Media LLC. Reprinted by permission. www.seattlepi.com

The UCLA Civil Rights Project State of Segregation

Fact Sheet, 2007

Public school enrollment has undergone a dramatic transformation since the Civil Rights Era and is multiracial.

- Latino students are now the largest group of minority students in the public schools (19%); Latino students comprise over a third of students in the West (36%).
- Black students are 17% of all public school students and are more than a quarter of students in the South.
- The West now has a minority of white students (47%) and the South soon will (50%).

Students in the largest three racial groups typically attend schools in which less than half the students are from other races than themselves.

- White students are more isolated than students from any other racial/ethnic background. They go to schools, on average, where only one out of five students are from different racial groups. This gives white students very little opportunity to reap the benefits of integrated schools.
- Asian students are the most integrated group of students, although some subgroups of Asian students experience high levels of segregation.

Black students in the South for decades were more integrated than black students in any region of the country, although segregation levels for black students in the South have been rising rapidly since the late 1980s.

High—and growing—percentages of black and Latino students attend schools with high percentages of minority students.

- Nearly three-quarters of black & Latino students (73% and 77%, respectively) attend predominantly minority schools, or schools where more than half of students are nonwhite.

- Almost 40% of black and Latino students (38% and 39%, respectively) attended racially isolated minority schools in which less than ten percent of students are white. Research shows that such schools are also very likely to be schools where more than half of students come from low-income families and have difficulty retaining highly qualified teachers.
- The percentage of black and Latino students attending both types of segregated schools has increased in the last fifteen years. Segregation levels are highest in the Northeast.

Why should we care about segregated schools? A great deal of social science evidence regarding the benefits of integrated schools and the harms of segregated schools is summarized in an *amicus* brief filed with the Supreme Court in October 2006; see "Brief of 553 American Social Scientists" at www.civilrightsproject.ucla.edu/research/deseg/amicus_parents_v_seatle.pdf.

Critical Thinking

1. What does the data show? Describe the racial/ethnic make-up of the school that the typical African-American or Latino student attends.
2. Students from which ethnic/racial background are the most "isolated;" that is, they attend schools with relatively few members of other racial groups?

For further information, please visit The Civil Rights Project website at www.civilrightsproject.ucla.edu/. Statistics taken from "Racial Transformation and the Changing Nature of Segregation" by Gary Orfield and Chungmei Lee. Data analyzed is from the U.S. Department of Education's Common Core of Data, 2003–04.

Joint Statement of Nine University-Based Civil Rights Centers on Today's Supreme Court Rulings on Voluntary School Desegregation

McFarland v. Jefferson County Public Schools & Parents Involved in Community Schools v. Seattle School District No. 1

This morning, the U.S. Supreme Court acknowledged the well-documented benefits of racially and ethnically diverse schools, but severely limited the very tools school districts need to achieve integration and avoid segregation.

Ironically, today's decision comes at a time when, more than ever, social science research offers powerful evidence of the strong benefits of diversity for students, communities, and a democratic society. Similarly, research has also long demonstrated the detrimental effects of segregation and its ever-present attendant, concentrated poverty, in our public schools on educational opportunity, race relations and the psychological development of young people.

Public policy, thus, should encourage rather than hamstring local educators who have come to recognize both the benefits of desegregation and racial/economic diversity and the harmful effects of segregation. Like educators in Louisville and Seattle, so many local educators across the country had voluntarily taken action to foster diverse learning experiences in public schools, usually through choice-based programs that allow parents greater opportunities to choose their children's schools. Educators took such actions voluntarily and not because any court had ordered "busing" or "mandatory" desegregation.

Today's decision striking down the student assignment plans in these two districts is inconsistent with the ever-growing body of research accumulated during a half century in studies of both segregated and desegregated schools. The ruling comes at a time when school segregation rates for racial minority students are rising in every region of the nation following earlier Supreme Court decisions leading to the termination of desegregation court orders. It is a trend lamented by experienced educators who have not merely studied the research, but who have decades of on-the-ground experience with the harm of racial and economic segregation.

Although today's ruling is a disappointment, the majority of the Court recognized that integration is a compelling interest and that there are some legally acceptable techniques including zoning and site selection and that choice plans that consider multiple factors could be upheld with appropriate educational justification. In reviewing today's decision, it appears that several avenues for maintaining diversity are still open and legally permissible. Also, courts generally grant communities time to come into compliance with rulings such as this.

Each one of our centers, located across the nation, pledges to work in the coming months and years with educators and advocates in local communities who wish to foster integration, avoid segregation and keep the uniquely American aspiration of Brown alive. Permissible options may include race-conscious efforts that do not single out any one student on the basis of his or her race such as siting schools in areas that would naturally draw students from a mixture of racial/ethnic backgrounds or magnet schools that have special programs that draw students from different backgrounds. Some communities have crafted assignment plans that bring together students from various geographic areas of cities (or metropolitan areas) into individual schools. Similarly, under the No Child Left Behind Act, children in schools in need of improvement are permitted transfer to other schools within their district. If interdistrict transfers were permitted, this too, might be lead to greater racial and economic diversity.

School districts under existing court orders to remedy racial discrimination are not affected by this ruling. Districts should continue to thoughtfully consider the consequences of ending their desegregation plans given today's decision. School districts should also investigate the experience of other districts, the consequences of abandoning integration policies, and carefully consider all their options before deciding how to change their existing policies. We will make every effort to put districts in touch with legal and educational experts from their region to think about ways to comply with the Court decision with the least adverse consequences.

Similarly, we will collaboratively document the effects of the Court ruling on rates of segregation, student achievement, graduation rates and the nature of educational opportunity in what we expect will be an increasing number of racially segregated schools. Just as important, our centers will continue to study and report on what is known about how to construct successful multiracial schools. In our increasingly multiracial, multiethnic and multilinguistic nation, it is more crucial than ever that we continue to develop and promote working models of educational institutions that approximate the larger society students will someday join. Although the Court has spoken, the American people and their elected representatives have not yet responded. When they do, it is our hope and firm belief that today's decision will be regarded as ill-reasoned, ill-advised, but not insurmountable obstacle to realizing our cherished ideal of a vibrant integrated society.

A variety of academic institutions and research organizations, including the American Educational Research Association and the American Psychological Association, had submitted briefs to the Court in these cases about the benefits of diversity and harms of segregation. The general findings bear repeating.

Generally, students in segregated, high-poverty schools—disproportionate numbers of whom are African-American, Latino and economically disadvantaged—are taught by less qualified, less experienced teachers. The course offerings in such schools are generally severely limited, including a lack of college preparatory instruction often required for college entry and the levels of academic competition are usually not nearly as rigorous as a student would experience in predominantly middle-class more diverse schools. Further, these schools have far lower relative graduation rates (research strongly suggests that concentrated poverty and segregation itself—as independent variables—contribute to low relative graduation rates). Such schools are often overwhelmed with myriad social problems that are symptoms of poverty. In addition, both white and nonwhite students lose increasingly critical opportunities to deepen understanding of complex social and political issues and to prepare for successful life, work and citizenship in our profoundly changing society. Research demonstrates that racially and ethnically mixed schools promote cross-racial understanding in ways not possible in segregated school environments, making integrated student bodies essential ingredients in preparing children for citizenship and work in a society where whites are projected to be a minority group by 2050.

In the 2004–05 school year, more than 42 percent of students in our public schools are nonwhite. Our two largest regions—the South and West—have a markedly multiracial enrollment with white students in the minority. Experience has long shown that increased racial segregation brings with it increased economic segregation. In many cases, it also brings linguistic segregation.

Cutting off remedies to segregation, in the manner that the Court has done today, will not make these inequalities disappear. There exists no evidence that current educational policies will significantly reduce the large racial and economic gaps in achievement and graduation rates. The concomitant rise of segregation and educational inequality has long been evident in districts that had been forced by lower federal courts to drop desegregation policies. Civil rights groups and local communities will, and should, aggressively pursue every permissible route to provide more equitable opportunities for students in resegregated schools.

The nation's highest court upheld the sham of Plessy v. Ferguson's "separate but equal" doctrine for 58 years until it held in Brown v. Board of Education that it was unworkable where schools were concerned. As a result of today's decision, and in light of the Supreme Court's devastating 1973 holding in Rodriguez, that there is no Constitutional right to equal funding of public education, the Court more deeply institutionalizes "separate and unequal" for minority children.

As Justice Douglas observed in 1974, dissenting in Milliken v. Bradley, limiting the scope of permissible desegregation "puts the problem of [minorities] and our society back to the period that antedated the 'separate but equal' regime of Plessy v. Ferguson." The legal standard now, it seems, is "separate but nothing." This policy accepts racial and ethnic inequality and leaves minorities at the mercy of state and local politics, in much the same way we did before Brown. As segregation deepens, communities and citizens should closely monitor what happens to achievement, graduation levels, college access and persistence, and success in adult life.

Brown v. Board of Education has long been widely celebrated as the greatest Supreme Court decision of the last century. It recognized that "separate but equal" was a legal fiction and it was the trigger for the dismantling of hundreds of apartheid laws of the Southern and Border states. After Congress enacted the 1964 Civil Rights Act and the Supreme Court in Green v. New Kent County supported mandatory and comprehensive desegregation, the schools in the South became the most integrated in the nation for the next third of a century. The legacy of the widely celebrated Brown decision, though, has been undermined in a series of Supreme Court decisions over the past three decades which includes today's ruling. We have already lost much of the progress in desegregation achieved in the last 40 years for black students. Latino students, now our largest minority group face even more extreme isolation and educational inequality, often facing triple segregation by ethnicity, poverty, and language.

When the Court handed down Plessy v. Ferguson in 1896, there were no civil rights research centers in the nation's great universities documenting the negative results. A small cadre of dedicated lawyers and scholars at the preeminent historically black Howard University Law School, aided by a few researchers led to the legal theories and cases that culminated with the triumph of Brown.

The national debate on this issue is far from over. Today, ever more researchers and advocates are watching. As civil-rights research centers, we consider it our duty to carefully document the consequences of today's ruling and to assist school districts struggling with decisions about what direction to take now. We stand even more strongly committed to making the aspiration of equal life chances, most clearly manifest in the Brown decision, alive in our time.

Signatories

The Civil Rights Project, Harvard University and University of California at Los Angeles

Center for Civil Rights Center, University of North Carolina School of Law

Institute for Race and Poverty, University of Minnesota

The Chief Justice Earl Warren Institute on Race, Ethnicity and Diversity, University of California at Berkeley

Charles Hamilton Houston Institute for Race and Justice, Harvard University

Center on Democracy in a Multiracial Society, University of Illinois at Urbana Champaign

Center for Multicultural Education, University of Washington

Kirwan Institute for the Study of Race and Ethnicity, Ohio State University

Campaign for Educational Equity, Teachers College, Columbia University

Critical Thinking

1. Why do the civil rights centers raise the specter of "separate but equal," a system of segregation that the U.S. Supreme Court struck down in its widely celebrated 1954 *Brown v. Board of Education* decision?

2. What do civil rights advocates mean when they argue that recent Court decisions represent a return to *Plessy?*

UNIT 6
Policing and Crime

Unit Selections

Learning Outcomes

After reading this unit, you should be able to:

- Differentiate between the "law enforcement" and "order maintenance" jobs of the police.

- Propose steps that police departments can take to reduce citizens' fears and to increase the support that the public extends to the police.

- Explain how the broken-windows approach to policing differs from more traditional policing approaches.

- Explain how community-oriented policing differs from more traditional policing approaches.

- Explain how community-oriented policing forms new partnerships in the fight for law and order.

- Understand the skepticism and reluctance that more traditional officers often have for community-oriented policing.

Student Website

www.mhhe.com/cls

Internet References

Prof. Wesley G. Skogan Home Page: Community Policing; Crime and Disorder
www.skogan.org

The Urban Institute, Policing and Crime Prevention
www.urban.org/center/jpc/projects/Policing-and-Crime-Prevention.cfm

For a community to thrive, it must maintain a reasonable level of public safety. Businesses will be attracted to safe environments. Neighborhoods—rich and poor alike—demand protection.

But how does a city reduce crime and promote respect for the law and the maintenance of public order? There are no easy answers to the questions of how to decrease crime and improve public safety.

One fairly innovative approach seeks to alter police priorities as officers decide just how to approach the great many tasks expected of them. Typically, law enforcement officials concentrate their energies on the most important matters, pursuing major criminals, drug dealers, and violent offenders, overlooking many small infractions of the law as officers just don't have the time or person-power to enforce every detail of every law. Actually, if officers tried to enforce every law (on speeding, on alcohol consumption in public, on littering, etc.), a large portion of the public would be displeased, as citizens would wind up paying more frequent fines, facing larger premiums for auto insurance, and having to spend more time in court appearances.

Broken-windows policing seeks to reverse the usual order of things by having the police pay greater attention to the small things (Article 28, "Broken Windows"). According to the broken-windows theory, as detailed in the classic writings of James Q. Wilson, a community's tolerance of small-level disorders (say, of graffiti spray-painted on walls or of turnstile jumpers who refuse to pay the fare in the subway, or of "squeegee" window washers who demand a dollar from a driver for "cleaning" (often, running a dirty rag across) the windows of an automobile stopped at a traffic light) only serves to communicate the wrong message, that disrespect for the law and public civility is tolerated. Sending the wrong message creates an atmosphere that undermines public safety and leads to further "urban decay." When small infractions are tolerated, a miscreant learns that he can "get away" with misbehavior, an attitude that may lead to more serious law breaking. In contrast, when law enforcement officials crack down on the "small stuff," they send a clear message that respect for the law, community norms, and public order is demanded. The broken-windows approach has one additional important advantage; officers often find that when they stop and hold persons on minor charges they often find persons who are also wanted for more serious offenses.

The broken-windows approach was one of the tools that New York Mayor Rudy Giuliani and police chief Robert Kelly used in turning around the image of New York as a wild city where the streets were out of control. Giuliani and Kelly claimed that the broken-windows approach led to a dramatic reduction in crime, producing corresponding gains in the city's livability that improved the city's business climate and poured the foundation for the city's economic renewal (Article 29, "How an Idea Drew People Back to Urban Life"). Critics, however, argue that broken-windows policing receives too much credit for the drop in crime that was reported. Crime fell nationwide as the crack cocaine epidemic receded. Crime fell in communities across the nation, even in those that had not adopted

© David R. Frazier Photolibrary, Inc.

the broken-windows approach. Other critics, including libertarians, worried that such aggressive police enforcement of minor crimes might intrude on individual freedoms and violate civil rights and civil liberties.

Community policing represents another important innovation in law enforcement. The idea of community policing stems from the recognition that the police, acting by themselves, cannot successfully enforce the law. Instead, law enforcement officials need the cooperation of citizens and business owners who will install locks and alarm systems, turn on outdoor lights at night, and direct the police to areas of illegal activity and situations where citizens feel in danger. Community policing seeks to build a **partnership** between law enforcement officials and the public, where citizens freely communicate with officers and direct them to community problems. **Beat meetings,** where community members regularly meet and discuss problems and priorities with officers they have come to know, are an important feature of community policing. While many officers recognize the importance of establishing an informed working relationship with the community, other more "old guard" officers see community meetings as "social work" and a diversion from more serious law enforcement activities.

Both broken-windows and community policing require the devotion of officers' time and a commitment of resources that are in short supply, especially in difficult financial times. Police departments are often successful in fighting off the threat of deep cutbacks when a city first confronts fiscal difficulty. But in times of economic recession and a slow-growth economy, municipal fiscal problems persist over years and eventually force new economies in police department operations. It remains to be seen if municipal and police leaders truly value broken-windows and community policing or if they regard these innovations as frills than can be cut in bad fiscal times renewal (Article 30, "200 Cops to be Reassigned from Community Policing").

The Police and Neighborhood Safety

Broken Windows

JAMES Q. WILSON AND GEORGE L. KELLING

In the mid-1970s, the state of New Jersey announced a "Safe and Clean Neighborhoods Program," designed to improve the quality of community life in twenty-eight cities. As part of that program, the state provided money to help cities take police officers out of their patrol cars and assign them to walking beats. The governor and other state officials were enthusiastic about using foot patrol as a way of cutting crime, but many police chiefs were skeptical. Foot patrol, in their eyes, had been pretty much discredited. It reduced the mobility of the police, who thus had difficulty responding to citizen calls for service, and it weakened headquarter's control over patrol officers.

Many police officers also disliked foot patrol, but for different reasons: it was hard work, it kept them outside on cold, rainy nights, and it reduced their chances for making a "good pinch." In some departments, assigning officers to foot patrol had been used as a form of punishment. And academic experts on policing doubted that foot patrol would have any impact on crime rates; it was, in the opinion of most, little more than a sop to public opinion. But since the state was paying for it, the local authorities were willing to go along.

Five years after the program started, the Police Foundation, in Washington, D.C., published an evaluation of the foot-patrol project. Based on its analysis of a carefully controlled experiment carried out chiefly in Newark, the foundation concluded, to the surprise of hardly anyone, that foot patrol had not reduced crime rates. But residents of the foot-patrolled neighborhoods seemed to feel more secure than persons in other areas, tended to believe that crime had been reduced, and seemed to take fewer steps to protect themselves from crime (staying at home with the doors locked, for example). Moreover, citizens in the foot-patrol areas had a more favorable opinion of the police than did those living elsewhere. And officers walking beats had higher morale, greater job satisfaction, and a more favorable attitude toward citizens in their neighborhoods than did officers assigned to patrol cars.

These findings may be taken as evidence that the skeptics were right—foot patrol has no effect on crime; it merely fools the citizens into thinking that they are safer. But in our view, and in the view of the authors of the Police Foundation study (of whom Kelling was one), the citizens of Newark were not fooled at all. They knew what the foot-patrol officers were doing, they knew it was different from what motorized officers do, and they knew that having officers walk beats did in fact make their neighborhoods safer.

But how can a neighborhood be "safer" when the crime rate has not gone down—in fact, may have gone up? Finding the answer requires first that we understand what most often frightens people in public places. Many citizens, of course, are primarily frightened by crime, especially crime involving a sudden, violent attack by a stranger. This risk is very real, in Newark as in many large cities. But we tend to overlook or forget another source of fear—the fear of being bothered by disorderly people. Not violent people, nor, necessarily, criminals, but disreputable or obstreperous or unpredictable people: panhandlers, drunks, addicts, rowdy teenagers, prostitutes, loiterers, the mentally disturbed.

What foot-patrol officers did was to elevate, to the extent they could, the level of public order in these neighborhoods. Though the neighborhoods were predominantly black and the foot patrolmen were mostly white, this "order-maintenance" function of the police was performed to the general satisfaction of both parties.

One of us (Kelling) spent many hours walking with Newark foot-patrol officers to see how they defined "order" and what they did to maintain it. One beat was typical: a busy but dilapidated area in the heart of Newark, with many abandoned buildings, marginal shops (several of which prominently displayed knives and straight-edged razors in their windows), one large department store, and, most important, a train station and several major bus stops. Though the area was run-down, its streets were filled with people, because it was a major transportation center. The good order of this area was important not only to those who lived and worked there but also to many others, who had to move through it on their way home, to supermarkets, or to factories.

The people on the street were primarily black; the officer who walked the street was white. The people were made up of "regulars" and "strangers." Regulars included both "decent folk" and some drunks and derelicts who were always there but who "knew their place." Strangers were, well, strangers, and viewed suspiciously, sometimes apprehensively. The officer—call him Kelly—knew who the regulars were, and they knew him. As he saw his job, he was to keep an eye on strangers, and make certain that the disreputable regulars observed some informal but widely understood rules. Drunks and addicts could sit on the stoops, but could not lie down. People could drink on side streets, but not at the main intersection. Bottles had to be in paper bags. Talking to, bothering, or begging from people waiting at the bus stop was strictly forbidden. If a dispute erupted between a businessman and a customer, the businessman was assumed to be right, especially if the customer was a stranger. If a stranger loitered, Kelly would ask him if he had any means of support and what his business was; if he gave unsatisfactory answers, he was sent on his way. Persons who broke the informal rules, especially those who bothered people waiting at bus stops, were arrested for vagrancy. Noisy teenagers were told to keep quiet.

These rules were defined and enforced in collaboration with the "regulars" on the street. Another neighborhood might have different rules, but these, everybody understood, were the rules for *this* neighborhood. If someone violated them, the regulars not only turned to Kelly for help but also ridiculed the violator. Sometimes what Kelly did could be described as "enforcing the law," but just as often it involved taking informal or extralegal steps to help protect what the neighborhood had decided was the appropriate level of public order. Some of the things he did probably would not withstand a legal challenge.

A determined skeptic might acknowledge that a skilled foot-patrol officer can maintain order but still insist that this sort of "order" has little to do with the real sources of community fear—that is, with violent crime. To a degree, that is true. But two things must be borne in mind. First, outside observers should not assume that they know how much of the anxiety now endemic in many big-city neighborhoods stems from a fear of "real" crime and how much from a sense that the street is disorderly, a source of distasteful, worrisome encounters. The people of Newark, to judge from their behavior and their remarks to interviewers, apparently assign a high value to public order, and feel relieved and reassured when the police help them maintain that order.

Second, at the community level, disorder and crime are usually inextricably linked, in a kind of developmental sequence. Social psychologists and police officers tend to agree that if a window in a building is broken *and is left unrepaired,* all the rest of the windows will soon be broken. This is as true in nice neighborhoods as in run-down ones. Window-breaking does not necessarily occur on a large scale because some areas are inhabited by determined window-breakers whereas others are populated by window-lovers; rather, one unrepaired broken window is a signal that no one cares, and so breaking more windows costs nothing. (It has always been fun.)

Philip Zimbardo, a Stanford psychologist, reported in 1969 on some experiments testing the broken-window theory. He arranged to have an automobile without license plates parked with its hood up on a street in the Bronx and a comparable automobile on a street in Palo Alto, California. The car in the Bronx was attacked by "vandals" within ten minutes of its "abandonment." The first to arrive were a family—father, mother, and young son—who removed the radiator and battery. Within twenty-four hours, virtually everything of value had been removed. Then random destruction began—windows were smashed, parts torn off, upholstery ripped. Children began to use the car as a playground. Most of the adult "vandals" were well-dressed, apparently clean-cut whites. The car in Palo Alto sat untouched for more than a week. Then Zimbardo smashed part of it with a sledgehammer. Soon, passersby were joining in. Within a few hours, the car had been turned upside down and utterly destroyed. Again, the "vandals" appeared to be primarily respectable whites.

Untended property becomes fair game for people out for fun or plunder, and even for people who ordinarily would not dream of doing such things and who probably consider themselves law-abiding. Because of the nature of community life in the Bronx—its anonymity, the frequency with which cars are abandoned and things are stolen or broken, the past experience of "no one caring"—vandalism begins much more quickly than it does in staid Palo Alto, where people have come to believe that private possessions are cared for, and that mischievous behavior is costly. But vandalism can occur anywhere once communal barriers—the sense of mutual regard and the obligations of civility—are lowered by actions that seem to signal that "no one cares."

We suggest that "untended" behavior also leads to the breakdown of community controls. A stable neighborhood of families who care for their homes, mind each other's children, and confidently frown on unwanted intruders can change, in a few years or even a few months, to an inhospitable and frightening jungle. A piece of property is abandoned, weeds grow up, a window is smashed. Adults stop scolding rowdy children; the children, emboldened, become more rowdy. Families move out, unattached adults move in. Teenagers gather in front of the corner store. The merchant asks them to move; they refuse. Fights occur. Litter accumulates. People start drinking in front of the grocery; in time, an inebriate slumps to the sidewalk and is allowed to sleep it off. Pedestrians are approached by panhandlers.

At this point it is not inevitable that serious crime will flourish or violent attacks on strangers will occur. But many residents will think that crime, especially violent crime, is on the rise, and they will modify their behavior accordingly. They will use the streets less often, and when on the streets will stay apart from their fellows, moving with averted eyes, silent lips, and hurried steps. "Don't get involved." For some residents, this growing atomization will matter little, because the neighborhood is not their "home" but "the place where they live." Their interests are elsewhere; they are cosmopolitans. But it will matter greatly to other people, whose lives derive meaning and satisfaction from local attachments rather than worldly involvement; for them, the neighborhood will cease to exist except for a few reliable friends whom they arrange to meet.

Such an area is vulnerable to criminal invasion. Though it is not inevitable, it is more likely that here, rather than in places where people are confident they can regulate public behavior by informal controls, drugs will change hands, prostitutes will solicit, and cars will be stripped. That the drunks will be robbed by boys who do it as a lark, and the prostitutes' customers will be robbed by men who do it purposefully and perhaps violently. That muggings will occur.

Among those who often find it difficult to move away from this are the elderly. Surveys of citizens suggest that the elderly are much less likely to be the victims of crime than younger persons, and some have inferred from this that the well-known fear of crime voiced by the elderly is an exaggeration: perhaps we ought not to design special programs to protect older persons; perhaps we should even try to talk them out of their mistaken fears. This argument misses the point. The prospect of a confrontation with an obstreperous teenager or a drunken panhandler can be as fear-inducing for defenseless persons as the prospect of meeting an actual robber; indeed, to a defenseless person, the two kinds of confrontation are often indistinguishable. Moreover, the lower rate at which the elderly are victimized is a measure of the steps they have already taken—chiefly, staying behind locked doors—to minimize the risks they face. Young men are more frequently attacked than older women, not because they are easier or more lucrative targets but because they are on the streets more.

Nor is the connection between disorderliness and fear made only by the elderly. Susan Estrich, of the Harvard Law School, has recently gathered together a number of surveys on the sources of public fear. One, done in Portland, Oregon, indicated that three fourths of the adults interviewed cross to the other side of a street when they see a gang of teenagers; another survey, in Baltimore, discovered that nearly half would cross the street to avoid even a single strange youth. When an interviewer asked people in a housing project where the most dangerous spot was, they mentioned a place where young persons gathered to drink and play music, despite the fact that not a single crime had occurred there. In Boston public housing projects, the greatest fear was expressed by persons living in the buildings where disorderliness and incivility, not crime, were the greatest. Knowing this helps one understand the significance of such otherwise harmless displays as subway graffiti. As Nathan Glazer has written, the proliferation of graffiti, even when not obscene, confronts the subway rider with the "inescapable knowledge that the environment he must endure for an hour or more a day is uncontrolled and uncontrollable, and that anyone can invade it to do whatever damage and mischief the mind suggests."

In response to fear, people avoid one another, weakening controls. Sometimes they call the police. Patrol cars arrive, an occasional arrest occurs, but crime continues and disorder is not abated. Citizens complain to the police chief, but he explains that his department is low on personnel and that the courts do not punish petty or first-time offenders. To the residents, the police who arrive in squad cars are either ineffective or uncaring; to the police, the residents are animals who deserve each other. The citizens may soon stop calling the police, because "they can't do anything."

The process we call urban decay has occurred for centuries in every city. But what is happening today is different in at least two important respects. First, in the period before, say World War II, city dwellers—because of money costs, transportation difficulties, familial and church connections—could rarely move away from neighborhood problems. When movement did occur, it tended to be along public-transit routes. Now mobility has become exceptionally easy for all but the poorest or those who are blocked by racial prejudice. Earlier crime waves had a kind of built-in self-correcting mechanism: the determination of a neighborhood or community to reassert control over its turf. Areas in Chicago, New York, and Boston would experience crime and gang wars, and then normalcy would return, as the families for whom no alternative residences were possible reclaimed their authority over the streets.

Second, the police in this earlier period assisted in that reassertion of authority by acting, sometimes violently, on behalf of the community. Young toughs were roughed up, people were arrested "on suspicion" or for vagrancy, and prostitutes and petty thieves were routed. "Rights" were something enjoyed by decent folk, and perhaps also by the serious professional criminal, who avoided violence and could afford a lawyer.

This pattern of policing was not an aberration or the result of occasional excess. From the earliest days of the nation, the police function was seen primarily as that of a night watchman: to maintain order against the chief threats to order—fire, wild animals, and disreputable behavior. Solving crimes was viewed not as a police responsibility but as a private one. In the March, 1969, *Atlantic,* one of us (Wilson) wrote a brief account of how the police role had slowly changed from maintaining order to fighting crimes. The change began with the creation of private detectives (often ex-criminals), who worked on a contingency-fee basis for individuals who had suffered losses. In time, the detectives were absorbed into municipal police agencies and paid a regular salary; simultaneously, the responsibility for prosecuting thieves was shifted from the aggrieved private citizen to the professional prosecutor. This process was not complete in most places until the twentieth century.

In the 1960s, when urban riots were a major problem, social scientists began to explore carefully the order-maintenance function of the police, and to suggest ways of improving it—not to make streets safer (its original function) but to reduce the incidence of mass violence. Order-maintenance became, to a degree, coterminous with "community relations." But, as the crime wave that began in the early 1960s continued without abatement throughout the decade and into the 1970s, attention shifted to the role of the police as crime-fighters. Studies of police behavior ceased, by and large, to be accounts of the order-maintenance function and became, instead, efforts to propose and test ways whereby the police could solve more crimes, make more arrests, and gather better evidence. If these things could be done, social scientists assumed, citizens would be less fearful.

A great deal was accomplished during this transition, as both police chiefs and outside experts emphasized the crime-fighting function in their plans, in the allocation of resources, and in deployment of personnel. The police may well have become better crime-fighters as a result. And doubtless they remained aware of their responsibility for order. But the link between order-maintenance and crime-prevention, so obvious to earlier generations, was forgotten.

That link is similar to the process whereby one broken window becomes many. The citizen who fears the ill-smelling drunk, the rowdy teenager, or the importuning beggar is not merely expressing his distaste for unseemly behavior; he is also giving voice to a bit of folk wisdom that happens to be a correct generalization—namely, that serious street crime flourishes in areas in which disorderly behavior goes unchecked. The unchecked panhandler is, in effect, the first broken window. Muggers and robbers, whether opportunistic or professional, believe they reduce their chances of being caught or even identified if they operate on streets where potential victims are already intimated by prevailing conditions. If the neighborhood cannot keep a bothersome panhandler from annoying passersby, the thief may reason, it is even less likely to call the police to identify a potential mugger or to interfere if the mugging actually takes place.

Some police administrators concede that this process occurs, but argue that motorized-patrol officers can deal with it as effectively as foot-patrol officers. We are not so sure. In theory, an officer in a squad car can observe as much as an officer on foot; in theory, the former can talk to as many people as the latter. But the reality of police–citizen encounters is powerfully altered by the automobile. An officer on foot cannot separate himself from the street people; if he is approached, only his uniform and his personality can help him manage whatever is about to happen. And he can never be certain what that will be—a request for directions, a plea for help, an angry denunciation, a teasing remark, a confused babble, a threatening gesture.

In a car, an officer is more likely to deal with street people by rolling down the window and looking at them. The door and the window exclude the approaching citizen; they are a barrier. Some officers take advantage of this barrier, perhaps unconsciously, by acting differently if in the car than they would on foot. We have seen this countless times. The police car pulls up to a corner where teenagers are gathered. The window is rolled down. The officer stares at the youths. They stare back. The officer says to one, "C'mere." He saunters over, conveying to his friends by his elaborately casual style the idea that he is not intimidated by authority. "What's your name?"

"Chuck." "Chuck who?" "Chuck Jones." "What you doing, Chuck?" "Nothin." "Got a P.O. [parole officer]?" "Nah." "Sure?" "Yeah." "Stay out of trouble, Chuckie." Meanwhile, the other boys laugh and exchange comments among themselves, probably at the officer's expense. The officer stares harder. He cannot be certain what is being said, nor can he join in and, by displaying his own skill at street banter, prove that he cannot be "put down." In the process, the officer has learned almost nothing, and the boys have decided the officer is an alien force who can safely be disregarded, even mocked.

Our experience is that most citizens like to talk to a police officer. Such exchanges give them a sense of importance, provide them with the basis for gossip, and allow them to explain to the authorities what is worrying them (whereby they gain a modest but significant sense of having "done something" about the problem). You approach a person on foot more easily, and talk to him more readily, than you do a person in a car. Moreover, you can more easily retain some anonymity if you draw an officer aside for a private chat. Suppose you want to pass on a tip about who is stealing handbags, or who offered to sell you a stolen TV. In the inner city, the culprit, in all likelihood, lives nearby. To walk up to a marked patrol car and lean in the window is to convey a visible signal that you are a "fink."

The essence of the police role in maintaining order is to reinforce the informal control mechanisms of the community itself. The police cannot, without committing extraordinary resources, provide a substitute for that informal control, on the other hand, to reinforce those natural forces the police must accommodate them. And therein lies the problem.

Should police activity on the street be shaped, in important ways, by the standards of the neighborhood rather than by the rules of the state? Over the past two decades, the shift of police from order-maintenance to law-enforcement has brought them increasingly under the influence of legal restrictions, provoked by media complaints and enforced by court decisions and departmental orders. As a consequence, the order-maintenance functions of the police are now governed by rules developed to control police relations with suspected criminals. This is, we think, an entirely new development. For centuries, the role of the police as watchmen was judged primarily not in terms of its compliance with appropriate procedures but rather in terms of its attaining a desired objective. The objective was order, an inherently ambiguous term but a condition that people in a given community recognized when they saw it. The means were the same as those the community itself would employ, if its members were sufficiently determined, courageous, and authoritative. Detecting and apprehending criminals, by contrast, was a means to an end, not an end in itself; a judicial determination of guilt or innocence was the hoped-for result of the law-enforcement mode. From the first, the police were expected to follow rules defining that process, though states differed in how stringent the rules should be. The criminal-apprehension process was always understood to involve individual rights, the violation of which was unacceptable because it meant that the violating officer would be acting as a judge and jury—and that was not his job. Guilt or innocence was to be determined by universal standards under special procedures.

Ordinarily, no judge or jury ever sees the persons caught up in a dispute over the appropriate level of neighborhood order. That is true not only because most cases are handled informally on the street but also because no universal standards are available to settle arguments over disorder, and thus a judge may not be any wiser or more effective than a police officer. Until quite recently in many states, and even today in some places, the police make arrests on such charges as "suspicious person" or "vagrancy" or "public drunkenness"—charges with scarcely any legal meaning. These charges exist not because society wants judges to punish vagrants or drunks but because it wants an officer to have the legal tools to remove undesirable persons from a neighborhood when informal efforts to preserve order in the streets have failed.

Once we begin to think of all aspects of police work as involving the application of universal rules under special procedures, we inevitably ask what constitutes an "undesirable person" and why we should "criminalize" vagrancy or drunkenness. A strong and commendable desire to see that people are treated fairly makes us worry about allowing the police to rout persons who are undesirable by some vague or parochial standard. A growing and not-so-commendable utilitarianism leads us to doubt that any behavior that does not "hurt" another person should be made illegal. And thus many of us who watch over the police are reluctant to allow them to perform, in the only way they can, a function that every neighborhood desperately wants them to perform.

This wish to "decriminalize" disreputable behavior that "harms no one"—and thus remove the ultimate sanction the police can employ to maintain neighborhood order—is, we think, a mistake. Arresting a single drunk or a single vagrant who has harmed no identifiable person seems unjust, and in a sense it is. But failing to do anything about a score of drunks or a hundred vagrants may destroy an entire community. A particular rule that seems to make sense in the individual case makes no sense when it is made a universal rule and applied to all cases. It makes no sense because it fails to take into account the connection between one broken window left untended and a thousand broken windows. Of course, agencies other than the police could attend to the problems posed by drunks or the mentally ill, but in most communities—especially where the "deinstitutionalization" movement has been strong—they do not.

The concern about equity is more serious. We might agree that certain behavior makes one person more undesirable than another, but how do we ensure that age or skin color or national origin or harmless mannerisms will not also become the basis for distinguishing the undesirable from the desirable? How do we ensure, in short, that the police do not become the agents of neighborhood bigotry?

We can offer no wholly satisfactory answer to this important question. We are not confident that there *is* a satisfactory answer, except to hope that by their selection, training, and supervision, the police will be inculcated with a clear sense of the outer limit of their discretionary authority. That limit, roughly, is this—the police exist to help regular behavior, not to maintain the racial or ethnic purity of a neighborhood.

Consider the case of the Robert Taylor Homes in Chicago, one of the largest public-housing projects in the country. It is home for nearly 20,000 people, all black, and extends over ninety-two acres along South State Street. It was named after a distinguished black who had been, during the 1940s, chairman of the Chicago Housing Authority. Not long after it opened, in 1962, relations between project residents and the police deteriorated badly. The citizens felt that the police were insensitive or brutal; the police, in turn, complained of unprovoked attacks on them. Some Chicago officers tell of times when they were afraid to enter the Homes. Crime rates soared.

Today, the atmosphere has changed. Police–citizen relations have improved—apparently, both sides learned something from the earlier experience. Recently, a boy stole a purse and ran off. Several young persons who saw the theft voluntarily passed along to the police information on the identity and residence of the thief, and they did this publicly, with friends and neighbors looking on. But problems persist, chief among them the presence of youth gangs that terrorize residents and recruit members in the project. The people expect the police to "do something" about this, and the police are determined to do just that.

But do what? Though the police can obviously make arrests whenever a gang member breaks the law, a gang can form, recruit, and congregate without breaking the law. And only a tiny fraction of gang-related crimes can be solved by an arrest; thus, if an arrest is the only recourse

for the police, the residents' fears will go unassuaged. The police will soon feel helpless, and the residents will again believe that the police "do nothing." What the police in fact do is to chase known gang members out of the project. In the words of one officer, "We kick ass." Project residents both know and approve of this. The tacit police–citizen alliance in the project is reinforced by the police view that the cops and the gangs are the two rival sources of power in the area, and that the gangs are not going to win.

None of this is easily reconciled with any conception of due process or fair treatment. Since both residents and gang members are black, race is not a factor. But it could be. Suppose a white project confronted a black gang, or vice versa. We would be apprehensive about the police taking sides. But the substantive problem remains the same: how can the police strengthen the informal social-control mechanisms of natural communities in order to minimize fear in public places? Law enforcement, per se, is no answer. A gang can weaken or destroy a community by standing about in a menacing fashion and speaking rudely to passersby without the law.

We have difficulty thinking such matters, not simply because the ethical and legal issues are so complex but because we have become accustomed to thinking of the law in essentially individualistic terms. The law defines *my* rights, punishes *his* behavior, and is applied by *that* officer because of *this* harm. We assume, in thinking this way, that what is good for the individual will be good for the community, and what doesn't matter when it happens to one person won't matter if it happens to many. Ordinarily, those are plausible assumptions. But in cases where behavior that is tolerable to one person is intolerable to many others, the reactions of the others—fear, withdrawal, flight—may ultimately make matters worse for everyone, including the individual who first professed his indifference.

It may be their greater sensitivity to communal as opposed to individual needs that helps explain why the residents of small communities are more satisfied with their police than are the residents of similar neighborhoods in big cities. Elinor Ostrom and her co-workers at Indiana University compared the perception of police services in two poor, all-black Illinois towns—Phoenix and East Chicago Heights—with those of three comparable all-black neighborhoods in Chicago. The level of criminal victimization and the quality of police–community relations appeared to be about the same in the towns and the Chicago neighborhoods. But the citizens living in their own villages were much more likely than those living in the Chicago neighborhoods to say that they do not stay at home for fear of crime, to agree that the local police have "the right to take any action necessary" to deal with problems, and to agree that the police "look out for the needs of the average citizen." It is possible that the residents and the police of the small towns saw themselves as engaged in a collaborative effort to maintain a certain standard of communal life, whereas those of the big city felt themselves to be simply requesting and supplying particular services on an individual basis.

If this is true, how should a wise police chief deploy his meager forces? The first answer is that nobody knows for certain, and the most prudent course of action would be to try further variations on the Newark experiment, to see more precisely what works in what kinds of neighborhoods. The second answer is also a hedge—many aspects of order-maintenance in neighborhoods can probably best be handled in ways that involve the police minimally, if at all. A busy, bustling shopping center and a quiet, well-tended suburb may need almost no visible police presence. In both cases, the ratio of respectable to disreputable people is ordinarily so high as to make informal social control effective.

Even in areas that are in jeopardy from disorderly elements, citizen action without substantial police involvement may be sufficient. Meetings between teenagers who like to hang out on a particular corner and adults who want to use that corner might well lead to an amicable agreement on a set of rules about how many people can be allowed to congregate, where, and when.

Where no understanding is possible—or if possible, not observed—citizen patrols may be a sufficient response. There are two traditions of communal involvement in maintaining order. One, that of the "community watchmen," is as old as the first settlement of the New World. Until well into the nineteenth century, volunteer watchmen, not policemen, patrolled their communities to keep order. They did so, by and large, without taking the law into their own hands—without, that is, punishing persons or using force. Their presence deterred disorder or alerted the community to disorder that could not be deterred. There are hundreds of such efforts today in communities all across the nation. Perhaps the best known is that of the Guardian Angels, a group of unarmed young persons in distinctive berets and T-shirts, who first came to public attention when they began patrolling the New York City subways but who claim now to have chapters in more than thirty American cities. Unfortunately, we have little information about the effect of these groups on crime. It is possible, however, that whatever their effect on crime, citizens find their presence reassuring, and that they thus contribute to maintaining a sense of order and civility.

The second tradition is that of the "vigilante." Rarely a feature of the settled communities of the East, it was primarily to be found in those frontier towns that grew up in advance of the reach of government. More than 350 vigilante groups are known to have existed; their distinctive feature was that their members did take the law into their own hands, by acting as judge, jury, and often executioner as well as policeman. Today, the vigilante movement is conspicuous by its rarity, despite the great fear expressed by citizens that the older cities are becoming "urban frontiers." But some community-watchmen groups have skirted the line, and others may cross it in the future. An ambiguous case, reported in *the Wall Street Journal,* involved a citizens' patrol in the Silver Lake area of Belleville, New Jersey. A leader told the reporter, "We look for outsiders." If a few teenagers from outside the neighborhood enter it, "we ask them their business," he said. "If they say they're going down the street to see Mrs. Jones, fine, we let them pass. But then we follow them down the block to make sure they're really going to see Mrs. Jones."

T hough citizens can do a great deal, the police are plainly the key to order-maintenance. For one thing, many communities, such as the Robert Taylor Homes, cannot do the job by themselves. For another, no citizen in a neighborhood, even an organized one, is likely to feel the sense of responsibility that wearing a badge confers. Psychologists have done many studies on why people fail to go to the aid of persons being attacked or seeking help, and they have learned that the cause is not "apathy" or "selfishness" but the absence of some plausible grounds for feeling that one must personally accept responsibility. Ironically, avoiding responsibility is easier when a lot of people are standing about. On streets and in public places, where order is so important, many people are likely to be "around," a fact that reduces the chance of any one person acting as the agent of the community. The police officer's uniform singles him out as a person who must accept responsibility if asked. In addition, officers, more easily than their fellow citizens, can be expected to distinguish between what is necessary to protect the safety of the street and what merely protects its ethnic purity.

But the police forces of America are losing, not gaining, members. Some cities have suffered substantial cuts in the number of officers available for duty. These cuts are not likely to be reversed in the near future. Therefore, each department must assign its existing officers with great care.

Some neighborhoods are so demoralized and crime-ridden as to make foot patrol useless; the best the police can do with limited resources is respond to the enormous number of calls for service. Other neighborhoods are so stable and serene as to make foot patrol unnecessary. The key is to identify neighborhoods at the tipping point—where the public order is deteriorating but not unreclaimable, where the streets are used frequently but by apprehensive people, where a window is likely to be broken at any time, and must quickly be fixed if all are not to be shattered.

Most police departments do not have ways of systematically identifying such areas and assigning officers to them. Officers are assigned on the basis of crime rates (meaning that marginally threatened areas are often stripped so that police can investigate crimes in areas where the situation is hopeless) or on the basis of calls for service (despite the fact that most citizens do not call the police when they are merely frightened or annoyed). To allocate patrol wisely, the department must look at the neighborhoods and decide, from first-hand evidence, where an additional officer will make the greatest difference in promoting a sense of safety.

One way to stretch limited police resources is being tried in some public-housing projects. Tenant organizations hire off-duty police officers for patrol work in their buildings. The costs are not high (at least not per resident), the officer likes the additional income, and the residents feel safer. Such arrangements are probably more successful than hiring private watchmen, and the Newark experiment helps us understand why. A private security guard may deter crime or misconduct by his presence, and he may go to the aid of persons needing help, but he may well not intervene—that is, control or drive away—someone challenging community standards. Being a sworn officer—a "real cop"—seems to give one the confidence, the sense of duty, and the aura of authority necessary to perform this difficult task.

Patrol officers might be encouraged to go to and from duty stations on public transportation and, while on the bus or subway car, enforce rules about smoking, drinking, disorderly conduct, and the like. The enforcement need involve nothing more than ejecting the offender (the offense, after all, is not one with which a booking officer or a judge wishes to be bothered). Perhaps the random but relentless maintenance of standards on buses would lead to conditions on buses that approximate the level of civility we now take for granted on airplanes.

But the most important requirement is to think that to maintain order in precarious situations is a vital job. The police know this is one of their functions, and they also believe, correctly, that it cannot be done to the exclusion of criminal investigation and responding to calls. We may have encouraged them to suppose, however, on the basis of our oft-repeated concerns about serious, violent crime, that they will be judged exclusively on their capacity as crime-fighters. To the extent that this is the case, police administrators will continue to concentrate police personnel in the highest-crime areas (though not necessarily in the areas most vulnerable to criminal invasion), emphasize their training in the law and criminal apprehension (and not their training in managing street life), and join too quickly in campaigns to decriminalize "harmless" behavior (though public drunkenness, street prostitution, and pornographic displays can destroy a community more quickly than any team of professional burglars).

Above all, we must return to our long-abandoned view that the police ought to protect communities as well as individuals. Our crime statistics and victimization surveys measure individual losses, but they do not measure communal losses. Just as physicians now recognize the importance of fostering health rather than simply treating illness, so the police—and the rest of us—ought to recognize the importance of maintaining, intact, communities without broken windows.

Critical Thinking

1. What are the consequences of a broken window that is left unrepaired? How does an "untended" broken window lead to more serious neighborhood problems?
2. How can the broken-windows metaphor be applied to policing? On what sort of activities should police focus if they wish to increase order maintenance in a neighborhood?
3. How does the broken-windows emphasis on order maintenance in a community differ from more traditional policing approaches?

JAMES Q. WILSON is Shattuck Professor of Government at Harvard and author of *Thinking About Crime*. **GEORGE L. KELLING,** formerly director of the evaluation field staff of the Police Foundation, is currently a research fellow at the John F. Kennedy School of Government at Harvard.

How an Idea Drew People Back to Urban Life

Twenty years after 'Broken Windows,' James Q. Wilson assesses the theory.

JAMES Q. WILSON

Two decades ago, George Kelling and I published an article in the *Atlantic Monthly* entitled "Broken Windows: The Police and Neighborhood Safety." Maybe it was the catchy title, maybe it was the argument, but for some reason the phrase and maybe the idea spread throughout American policing, and now is being taken up by the police in many other countries. Today, I sometimes hear a police official explain to me that they have adopted the "broken windows" strategy as if I had never heard of it.

The idea was simple. Citizens want public order as much as they want crime reduced, and so the police ought to worry about public disorder as much as they worry about catching crooks. Disorder arises from minor offenses such as aggressive panhandling, graffiti sprayed on the outside of buildings, alcoholics wandering the streets, and hostile teenagers hanging around bus stops and delicatessens.

Even though chasing away or arresting people who did these things may not do much to reduce crime immediately and in any event would constitute at best a minor pinch that police officers rarely took seriously and that courts were likely to ignore, recreating public order would do two things: Convince decent citizens that they and not some hostile force were entitled to use the streets and (perhaps) reduce crime over time by inducing good people and discouraging bad ones from using the streets.

The idea arose from Mr. Kelling's study of the effects of foot patrol on crime and public attitudes in New Jersey. He worked for the Police Foundation as it carried out a rigorous evaluation of foot patrol in Newark when Hubert Williams was the police chief. The neighborhoods where the experiment took place were largely inhabited by blacks and the officers who did the patrolling were largely white. The theory was that foot patrol would make the streets safer.

By and large, police chiefs did not believe this; after all, an officer on foot could not do much to chase a burglar in a car, and besides thieves could easily avoid the streets where foot patrol officers were walking. Police officers did not much care for foot patrol either. Standing outside on a cold or rainy night

in Newark was a lot less pleasant than sitting in a warm patrol car, and the arrests you were likely to make while on foot would probably be of small-time offenders that would not do much to advance your police career.

The research showed that the police chiefs were right: Foot patrol did not cut crime. But it showed something else as well: The citizens loved it.

Explaining this puzzle is why we wrote the article. Were the citizens just fooling themselves by liking foot patrol? Did the whole project mean that the cops got better public relations just by conning the voters? Or maybe the citizens were right. Maybe they valued public order as much as they valued less crime. Perhaps public order would later on reduce the chances of crime rates rising if enough good folk used the streets and fewer roughnecks did.

We think the citizens were right. Getting rid of graffiti, aggressive panhandling, and wandering drunks made the citizens happier and increased their support for the police. Moreover, the cops on foot actually liked the work because they got to meet a lot of decent people and learn how they thought instead of just getting out of a patrol car to arrest a crook. We went on to offer the speculation—and at the time it was only a guess—that more orderly neighborhoods would, over the long haul, become less dangerous ones.

Our idea survived the predictable onslaught. Many civil rights organizations began to protest against efforts to control panhandling. Such efforts, they argued, were directed at the poor, blacks and the homeless. The ACLU filed suits in some cities against aspects of broken-windows policing. They must have forgotten, or perhaps they never knew, that broken-windows policing was first tested in poor black neighborhoods that enthusiastically endorsed it.

Civil libertarians also complained that stopping begging in the New York subways denied people free speech, and even got a federal judge to agree with them. But the appeals court threw out the argument because begging was not speech designed to convey a message, it was simply solicitation for money.

Slowly our idea grew until now it is hard to find a police department that does not claim to practice community-oriented policing and follow a broken-windows strategy. Just what the police chief means by these terms is not always very clear; to some extent, these words have become buzz phrases, backed up by a federal government policy of giving money to cities if they practice community policing, somehow defined.

In 1996, Mr. Kelling and his wife, Catherine Coles, published a book, "Fixing Broken Windows," that reviewed what has been done by Robert Kiley, David Gunn, and William Bratton to restore decency and safety to the New York subways and Bratton's later efforts to cut crime citywide after he became commissioner of the New York Police Department. Similar efforts took place in Baltimore, San Francisco, and Seattle.

The New York Transit Authority experience was especially telling. Long before he became the NYPD commissioner, Mr. Bratton, working with Messrs. Kiley and Gunn, had cut crime dramatically in the city's subways by holding his subordinates accountable for reducing offenses and getting rid of the graffiti. The people and the editorial writers cheered and in time the number of cops on duty underground could be safely cut.

Everyone in New York will recall the key steps whereby the subway success became the whole city's achievement. Rudolph Giuliani got elected mayor after a tough anti-crime campaign. One of the first things the NYPD did after he took office was to emphasize a policy begun by former police commissioner Raymond Kelly (who is now commissioner again) to get tough on "squeegee-men," males who extort money from motorists by pretending to wash (and sometimes spitting on) their car windows. Traditionally, officers would at best give only tickets to squeegeers, who would usually ignore the tickets or at worst pay a small fine. But then the NYPD began issuing warrants for the arrest of squeegee-men who ignored their tickets. Getting the warrant for non-appearance meant jail time for the recipient, and suddenly squeegee harassment stopped.

It may have been a little thing, but every New York motorist noticed it. Almost overnight, the city seemed safer. No one can say it was safer from serious crime, but it appeared safer and the people loved it.

After Mr. Giuliani took office, the crime rate plummeted. Lots of criminologists think that this happened automatically or as a result of some demographic change. No doubt serious crime fell in a lot of cities, but it fell faster and more in New York than almost anywhere else.

I do not assume that broken-windows policing explains this greater drop. Indeed, my instinct is to think that Mr. Bratton's management style, and especially his effort to hold precinct commanders accountable by frequently reviewing their performance in rigorous CompStat hearings, was the chief factor.

But Mr. Kelling has gathered a lot of evidence that a broken-windows strategy also made a difference. He measured that strategy by counting the number of misdemeanor arrests in New York precincts and showing that an increase in such arrests was accompanied by a decrease in serious crime, even in areas where unemployment rates rose, drug use was common, and the number of young men in their crime-prone years had increased.

So maybe a broken-windows strategy really does cut crime. But we know that it draws people back into urban life. And that is no trivial gain.

Critical Thinking

1. How did enforcement under broken-windows policing help to establish new standards of public conduct, of just what would and would not be tolerated in New York City?

2. According to Wilson, how did broken-windows enforcement help to change the public culture in New York, paving the way for the city's economic comeback?

MR. WILSON is an emeritus professor at UCLA and a lecturer at Pepperdine University.

200 Cops to be Reassigned from Community Policing

FRAN SPIELMAN AND FRANK MAIN

Mayor Daley said Thursday he wants to take the police out of community policing to put 200 more officers on the street.

Daley said Chicago's Alternative Policing Strategy, known as CAPS, was conceived as a civilian-run program in the 1990s but now involves many more uniformed officers than was originally intended.

"Over 200 police officers or more were assigned to CAPS over years—lieutenants and sergeants and patrolmen. In some districts, they had 8 to 10 or 12 people assigned to CAPS. . . . All the sudden, a civilian thing . . . went to a Police Department [program]. That was not the concept," the mayor said.

The decision to yank the officers out of community policing comes three months after Daley asked Ron Holt, the police officer father of a 16-year-old gunned down on a CTA bus, to breathe new life into the CAPS program.

"When Ron took it over, he couldn't believe how many police officers were assigned and transferred over many years into it. It became a huge amount of police officers," the mayor said.

"It was originally a civilian thing with the cooperation of a commander—not to have all policemen assigned to it," Daley said. "You put the policemen on the street. . . . He wants to take it back to its original belief."

A two-year-hiring slowdown has left the Chicago Police Department more than 2,300 officers short of its authorized strength, counting vacancies, medical leave and limited duty.

In light of that shortage, which triggered a police protest this week, Holt said the move makes sense.

"The citizens have spoken. They have complained about not enough police presence. They want more police presence in their neighborhoods," Holt said.

"When you have a large number of police officers—enough to reassign to districts—you have to adhere to the concerns of the community. We are not getting rid of all the police. We are putting some police officers back onto the street. They're going to be replaced with organizers and staff members who work for the CAPS office."

Critics contend the program is being decimated. Holt denied that.

"You have a lot of people who have complained unfairly. Some with political motives, some who have become complacent, some who are afraid for change," he said.

In 1993, Chicago launched the nation's largest experiment with community policing, which calls for citizens and police to work together to solve crimes and identify neighborhood problems before they escalate into crimes.

Two years ago, Daley gutted Chicago's community policing budget and reduced its staff by 25 percent—a cost-cutting move that left the 15-year-old crime fighting program "almost dead," critics contended.

That followed Police Supt. Jody Weis' decision to stop paying overtime to police officers to attend monthly beat meetings or community policing functions.

Police spokesman Roderick Drew said the changes will not take place immediately.

He said it's no different that what the department has already been doing in other areas: moving officers from desk duty to the street.

"Obviously the mayor has been committed to it for years," Drew said. "You have to work smarter with existing resources. The duties will fall to those who remain plus civilians."

The city's budget does not make it clear that hundreds of officers are working in the CAPS program.

The budget lists 53 employees in the CAPS "project office," including a commander, lieutenant, six sergeants and 39 officers.

There's also a 54-employee CAPS "implementation office" headed by Holt. The budget does not specify if any of those positions are held by cops.

Critical Thinking

1. What is community-oriented policing (more simply known as community policing)? How does it differ from traditional policing?

2. Why do many more traditional police officers resist a city's move to community-oriented policing?

UNIT 7

A Suburban Nation: Suburban Growth, Diversity, and the Possibilities of "New Urbanism" and "New Regionalism"

Unit Selections

Learning Outcomes

After reading this unit, you should be able to:

- Describe the evolution of suburbia.
- Differentiate between communalism and autonomy, two quite different and often antagonistic political attitudes that are often associated with suburban living.
- Propose policies that can aid First Suburbs that are experiencing decline.
- Explain how the architects of New Urbanism seek to reinvigorate a sense of community that many observers feel is missing in suburbia.
- Describe the major principles of New Urbanism and explain how New Urbanists seek to better alternatives to conventional suburbs.
- Assess the New Urbanism, exploring both its potential and its limits.
- Identify the opportunities for creative coalition-building that may exist among cities and suburbs.
- Explain and illustrate how the New Regionalism differs from the Old Regionalism.
- Show how Portland, Oregon, has attempted to battle suburban sprawl and to promote reinvestment in the central city and older suburbs.
- Assess the ability—or inability—of the New Regionalism to promote regional cooperation and to contain sprawled development.

Student Website

www.mhhe.com/cls

Internet References

The Brookings Institution: First Suburbs
www.brookings.edu/topics/first-suburbs.aspx

Congress for a New Urbanism
www.cnu.org

First Suburbs Coalition
www.marc.org/firstsuburbs

National Geographic Magazine, Urban Sprawl
http://ngm.nationalgeographic.com/ngm/data/2001/07/01/html/ft_20010701.3.html

Newurbanism.org
www.newurbanism.org

Sierra Club, Stopping Sprawl
www.sierraclub.org/sprawl

Smart Communities Network: Urban Growth Boundaries
www.smartcommunities.ncat.org/landuse/urban.shtml

Sprawl Watch Clearinghouse
www.sprawlwatch.org

The United States is a suburban nation. As first reported in the 1970 census, the number of Americans who live in suburbs surpasses the number in central cities. In the year 2000, 62 percent of the entire United States population lived in suburban areas.

Lang, LeFurgy, and Nelson (Article 31, "The Six Suburban Eras of the United States") trace the history of U.S. suburban development. Initially, communities on the edge of cities were quite small and largely rural, not really suburbs as much as **protosuburbs** that lacked any strong connection to the central city. In the early 1900s, population pressures and advances in transportation led cities to expand, in a process that transformed rural hamlets and farming centers into **streetcar suburbs.** The automobile led to the rapid growth of affluent **bedroom communities** during post-World War II years. Continuing advances in telecommunications and transportation led to the emergence of the **New Metropolis,** with the complexes of office parks, shopping galleries, and entertainment centers of **edge cities** and **technoburbs** providing new competition for the central city and older, more established suburbs.

The 1950s stereotype of suburbia as a mass of faceless and boring bedroom communities is no longer true; in fact, it was never totally accurate. Contemporary suburbia encompasses a **diversity of communities:** leafy and wealthy bedroom communities; working- and middle-class communities with rows of tract housing; gritty industrial suburbs centered around factories; **minority suburbs** with large concentrations of South Asian, East Asian, African-American, and Latino populations; booming edge cities and too-quickly-growing residential communities that suffer from overcrowded schools; and even **disaster suburbs** where conditions are not all that different from the troubled central cities that they border. David Brooks (Article 32, "Patio Man and the Sprawl People: America's Newest Suburbs") observes the diversity of communities and political attitudes that can be found in contemporary suburbia. While some residents try to make suburbs the reincarnation of the American small town where members of a community look out for one another, Brooks' **patio man,** by contrast, resents communitarian pressure and governmental regulation—even regulations imposed by local government. Such residents see government action—and high taxes—as violations of their freedom and intrusions into the privacy they enjoy in their homes and back yards. While many academics, social critics, and even popular filmmakers continue to castigate the insularity and shallowness of suburban life (see the Academy Award-winning film *American Beauty*), Brooks reminds us that a great many people enjoy life in the suburbs and value the independence and privacy that suburban living affords.

Brooks describes the general prosperity of many **exurban communities,** the **boomburbs** and the fast-growing **sprinkler cities** of the American Southwest. These communities, however, often have very little in common with America's **first suburbs,** the older or **inner-ring communities** located adjacent to the central city. As Bruce Katz and Robert Puentes of The Brookings Institution describe (Article 33, "Affluent, but Needy [First Suburbs]"), at one time many of these older communities were once quite well off and prestigious, the home of a region's factory owners, bankers, and other members of the local elite.

Today, these communities suffer an aging infrastructure, job losses, population stagnation, a rise in housing vacancies, and closed shops that dot once-thriving shopping strips. Americans, especially younger families, no longer value these aging communities but instead seek newer and larger houses at a greater distance from the city center. Businesses, too, have moved out to suburban locations along a metropolitan area's **ring road** or perimeter highway. Today, it is no longer just the center city but also older suburbs that suffer economic decline. Katz and Puentes urge the adoption of policies to prevent the nation's first suburbs from sliding further downhill.

As previously noted, many residents enjoy suburban living. Yet others find suburban life rather sterile and boring. Others are disappointed that they failed to discover the sense of community that they had hoped to find in suburbia. For many, life in the suburbs is too faceless and overly dominated by the automobile. Many suburbanites barely know their neighbors.

A group of American urban planners sought to reshape suburbia and break the isolation that too often engulfs suburban life. The planners proposed designs that would promote human interaction and a restored sense of community. Their ideas, known as the school of **New Urbanism,** have been widely copied around the world.

Simply put, New Urbanism seeks to build living environments that promote neighborliness and caring. New Urbanism also seeks **sustainable development,** ecologically-sound practices and patterns of growth that pose a viable alternative to continued urban sprawl (Article 34, "Principles of New Urbanism"). New Urban communities feature: homes built close to the street, often with front porches; houses built close to one another and to stores and other community facilities to promote **walkability;** few driveway cuts that impair walkability and the ability to know one's neighbors; traffic-calming measures that reduce speed, making streets safer for leisurely pedestrian activity; **dense or clustered development** to preserve **open space;** interesting architecture; and mixed-income development to promote a sense of community that extends beyond caring only for persons who resemble one's self.

The New Urbanism has succeeded in building wonderful communities, Yet, The New Urbanism does not really provide a viable alternative that will stem suburban sprawl (Article 35, "The New Urbanism: A Limited Revolution"). Few Americans choose to live in New Urban communities. They prefer large detached homes and the convenience of the automobile. Despite the success of a few New Urban communities, for the most part developers will continue to build, and Americans will continue to buy, homes in more conventional suburbs, with a continued reliance on the automobile.

The design principles of the New Urbanism have also been applied in the inner city, as part of the effort to transform public housing and their surrounding neighborhoods. Chicago and other cities used the federal assistance provided by the **HOPE VI program** to tear down the most distressed high-rise public housing towers, replacing them with new low-rise units. In order to break the isolation of the ghetto, the new developments, where possible, included a mix of housing at various income levels, not just units for the very poor. The subsidized low-income housing units were "blended in" and made to look indistinguishable from market-rate units. The newly built developments were certainly quite an improvement over the dilapidated housing they replaced. But in many cities, only a lucky few of the former housing tenants were able to move into new mixed-income developments. Fearing displacement, the poor in Chicago and other cities protested the conversion (Article 36, "HOPE VI and the New Urbanism: Eliminating Low-Income Housing to Make Mixed-Income Communities").

In the **fragmented metropolis,** each community enjoys the autonomy to decide when it will pursue its own interests and just when it will cooperate with others. No single city or suburb enjoys the scope of action that allows it to effectively deal with a region's economic decline, air pollution, or other complex urban problems that can only be fought by comprehensive action that extends beyond the borders of any one city. Many urbanists call for a greater **regionalism.** They note the advantages that come when services are provided on a large-scale basis and when cities and suburbs work together in developing a mass transit system, in marketing a region to bring new jobs to the metropolis, and in joint efforts to combat air pollution and other problems that transcend local borders.

In the 1950s and 1960s, numerous academic experts and planners sought to restructure local governments by creating new **metropolitan governments** with the power to plan and govern in the entire region's interest, without actions being thwarted by the parochial concerns of each self-serving locality. A few important **city-county consolidations** or mergers occurred, most notably in greater Jacksonville, Nashville, Indianapolis, and, most recently, Louisville. New metropolitan governing bodies or empowered counties were created in Miami, Minneapolis-St. Paul, and Seattle. None of the metropolitan governments, however, were given full governing authority over the region. Across the country, suburbs fought metropolitan restructuring plans; suburbanites were quite unwilling to give up their autonomy and cede powers to a strong metropolitan government.

In more recent years, the **old regionalism** of regional restructuring has largely ground to a halt. Regional reformers have come to recognize the extreme difficulty—oftentimes the near political impossibility—of creating new metropolitan governments. As a consequence, a new school of thought, the **new regionalism,** has emerged. The new regionalists do not seek to create new metropolitan governing bodies as much as they seek opportunities for sustained problem-solving collaborative action among the existing communities in the metropolis. The New Regionalism seeks to create new incentives and forums to promote joint action across city and suburban boundary lines. The New Regionalism is often business-led, with the Chambers of Commerce and other local business councils pushing for new visions and plans to reshape and guide a region's future economic development.

Myron Orfield argues that the opportunities for joint city-suburban action are greater than is usually recognized (Article 37, "Regional Coalition-Building and the Inner Suburbs"). Once the diversity of suburbia is recognized, the opportunities **for creative coalition building** become more apparent. Declining inner-ring suburbs and low property-tax-base working-class communities have suffered as economic growth has largely been concentrated in its **favored quarter communities,** the better-off residential areas and more prestigious edge cities and technoburbs that home buyers and private businesses prefer. Orfield argues that central cities, aging first suburbs, and low-resource working-class communities can work together to fight for their fair share of new investment and infrastructure support and other governmental aid. The dividing line in the metropolis no longer needs to be one of all suburbs versus the central city. A coalition of communities that seeks to direct growth back toward the urban core may even find support among environmentalists and rural organizations who want to preserve farmland. Orfield even raises the possibility of **regional tax-base sharing,** a program enacted in the Twin Cities region which helps to ensure that all area communities receive a share of the benefits from a region's new growth and development. Orfield also observes the special role that churches and faith-based groups can play in pushing for more equitable patterns of regional growth.

Fred Siegel, however, counters that regionalism is not always very desirable (Article 38, "Is Regional Government the Answer?"). Siegel argues that many Americans do not want a regional government with the power to channel where growth occurs and hence limit where they can live or buy a home. Americans are reluctant to place control over land use and other important matters in the hands of large-scale metropolitan governments and regional bureaucracies.

Does the New Regionalism work? Given the political impossibility of creating strong, new metropolitan-wide governments, collaborative action may be all that is possible. But exactly what incentives need to be given so that cities and suburbs will show a willingness to work together collaboratively in the fight against sprawled development and other urban problems?

The Six Suburban Eras of the United States

ROBERT LANG, JENNIFER LEFURGY, AND ARTHUR C. NELSON

Introduction

The Metropolitan Institute at Virginia Tech (MI) proposes a timeline to show the flow of suburban eras and types. The timeline defines six periods of U.S. suburban development in order to establish more common base years for historical data analysis. As the field of suburban studies matures into a formal academic sub-discipline, these suggested eras can help guide research projects.

The current standard split in suburban history, proposed by New Urbanists such as Andres Duany, offers a rather crude division into pre- and post–World War II periods (Duany, Plater-Zyberk, and Speck 2000). But this simple pre/post-war dichotomy is a caricature of suburban history. It can be argued that one suburban era actually spans the immediate pre- and post-war decades, which are labeled "Mid-Century Suburbs" (or the years 1930 to 1970) in this note. In addition, the post-war period is now so long, at 60 plus years, that it too can be divided into eras. Consider, for example an article by Robert Lang, Edward Blakely, and Meghan Gough (2005) that looks at the "new suburban metropolis" period from 1970 to 2010.

This timeline is not meant to be definitive. There are no clean breaks in history. Thus the timeline is depicted as a meandering river to indicate the continuous flow of events. The dates show stops along the way where the river course shifts, implying a directional change in history.

This note divides American suburban history into six eras. It finds that the United States is now in the fifth era and will soon enter a sixth one. The timeline also indicates some exemplar suburbs of each period and touches on key political changes and technological innovations. However, this argument does not subscribe to the notion of technological or economic determinism. Previous efforts to categorize historic eras focused especially on advances in transit technology (Stern and Massengale 1981), but multiple forces propel suburban change, and this proposed timeline also considers how cultural influences shaped the course of evolution.

The timeline reflects current thinking on the suburbs and incorporates the work of many historians including James Borchert (1996), Robert Fishman (1987, 1990), Dolores Hayden (2003), Kenneth Jackson (1985), Chester Liebs (1985), Richard Longstreth (1998, 1999), and Sam Bass Warner, Jr. (1962, 1972). The understanding of the three later eras is driven mostly by the current work of researchers at MI and the Brookings Institution's Metropolitan Policy Program. The labels attached to these eras were developed by MI and reflect its conceptualization of how the suburbs have evolved since the mid-19th century.

Before 1850: Proto Suburbs

Prior to 1850, U.S. suburbs were mostly extensions of cities (Jackson 1985, Warner 1972). They featured street plans and housing that closely resembled the urban core. In this era, the urban fringe featured dense row houses that abruptly give way to open fields and farms. However, some historians have documented the fact that the residents of early U.S. suburbs such as Brooklyn already had a different demographic character than residents of the central city (Jackson 1985). At first, these borderlands were poorer than the core. But with the introduction of ferry service around New York harbor, neighborhoods such as Brooklyn Heights emerged that catered to middle-income commuters. Henry Binford (1988) finds a similar development pattern at the fringe of Boston in the first half of the 19th century.

The earliest distinctly non–urban looking suburbs began in the United Kingdom in the early 19th century (Fishman 1987). They appeared first in London (Clapham Common—1800) and later Manchester (Victoria Park—1830s). These same kinds of "picturesque" suburbs did not emerge in the United States until the second half of the 19th century.

1850 to 1890: Town and Country Suburbs

The notion of suburbs as distinct physical places from cities became evident in the United States by the 1850s (Fishman 1987). The earliest documented English-style American suburb was Llewellyn Park, NJ, designed by Frederick Law Olmsted in 1857. Olmsted's work captured in design and spirit an entire mid-19th century U.S. movement that elevated domesticity and the nuclear family. This movement, along with the picturesque landscape architecture, had its roots in England.

But note that we do not refer to this suburban era as "picturesque" as some others have (Hayden 2003). That is because these suburbs are only part of the suburban story of the period. The flip side of the affluent picturesque places was a more moderate-income and city-like suburb based on horse-drawn streetcars (Hayden 2003). These streetcars were a big improvement over horse-drawn omnibuses because they were faster and carried more load (Warner 1962). They helped change the course of urban development in places such as New York, where suburbs now spread north on Manhattan Island instead of only crossing the East River to Brooklyn (Jackson 1985).

The horse-drawn streetcar suburbs were much denser and more traditionally urban that their picturesque counterparts—thus they were the "town" in the "town and country suburbs." But they also were now distinct from the urban core. In places such as the Jamaica Plains neighborhood of Boston, the architecture began to shift in the 1850s from the tight row houses such as those found on Beacon Hill to a looser configuration with side alleys (Warner 1962). In many cases, the houses were fully detached but remained on small narrow lots. To a modern eye, this does not seem as important a distinction, but it signaled a much larger change. Also note that many of the "town" suburbs had been annexed by the central city and appeared for all intents and purposes to be "urban neighborhoods" (Rusk 1993). Yet in the context of the mid-to-late 19th century American metropolis, these places were suburbs. The best example of a neighborhood built in this style was Gross Park in Chicago, dating from the 1880s (Hayden 2003).

1890 to 1930: Streetcar Suburbs

By the late 1880s, the first electric streetcars—or trolleys—were in use. The trolleys were a turbo version of the horse-drawn streetcars (Warner 1962). They were much bigger and faster and helped spread development for miles past the old urban core. Many of the trends that began in the horse-drawn era were greatly accentuated and extended by trolleys—the suburban houses spread out more (especially in places such as Los Angeles) and differences between the look and feel of the edge and the core grew (Fishman 1987). The streetcars so dominated the construction and speculation of this period that many historians use them to label this suburban era (Warner 1962). Suburban diversity, which began in earlier eras, continues and intensifies with the emergence of large-scale residential "city suburbs" (Borchert 1996).

Suburban retail and commercial districts also began to change radically in the streetcar suburbs (Liebs 1985). The old, dense form of Main Street now took on an elongated appearance. Storefronts stretched to reflect the fact that people might now window shop from a fast-moving trolley. These extended main streets, also referred to as "taxpayer strips," were the forerunner of the auto-based strip (Liebs 1985; Lang, LeFurgy, and Hornburg 2005). Many of these places exist today, threading through the edges of central cities and older suburbs, and are to the modern eye "traditional looking." But in their era, these strips represented a sharp break with commercial districts in the urban core.

Automobiles were invented around the same time as trolleys, but had much less immediate impact on urban development in the early years of the 20th century. They were expensive, hard to store, and poorly accommodated in urban places. Yet the streetcars began to loosen up the American metropolis so effectively that cars began to find navigating suburbs easier with each passing year. The first commercial districts to begin building parking lots were the trolley-based taxpayer strips. By the 1920s, the west side of Los Angeles began to develop fully auto-based shopping (Longstreth 1998, 1999).

1930 to 1970: Mid-Century Suburbs

Key developments during this era include the creation of Federal Housing Administration loans in the 1930s, which greatly improved middle-income access to suburban housing, and the beginning of the interstate highways in 1956 (Jackson 1985). Suburban architecture grew even more distinct from both traditional urban and even earlier suburbs (Hayden 2003). The dominant housing type was the one-story ranch-style home with a minimally classic exterior and a modern open floor plan. The scale of development expanded, especially after World War II in projects such as Levittown and Lakewood (Hayden 2003). The modest suburban shopping centers of the early 20th century exploded into massive malls that, beginning in 1956, were mostly enclosed and climate-controlled (Liebs 1985).

The New Urbanists, such as Andres Duany (Duany, Plater-Zyberk, and Speck 2000) and James Kunstler (1993), argue that a clean break in history exists between the pre- and post-World War II eras. In their view, all development before the war was pedestrian-oriented and traditional in form. After the war came an auto-dominated environment of subdivisions and shopping malls. However, the historical literature does not support this simplistic view (Harris 1988) and instead indicates that many early 20th century suburbs began a slow, decades-long adoption of automobiles (Liebs 1985). By the 1930s, cars were poised to significantly remake the American metropolis, but first a depression and then war greatly slowed the pace of urban change (Jackson 1985). Yet in the few places that still grew during the depression and war, such as the Los Angeles and Washington, DC, regions, the car made its mark (Longstreth 1998, 1999). These places, along with select parts of suburban New York, contain many examples of 1930s auto suburbs complete with proto tract-style subdivisions and early auto-oriented shopping centers.

Thus, a new suburban style emerged at the mid-20th century. This style existed both immediately before and after the war. There is just so much more development occurring after the war, that Mid-Century Suburbs were said to have a "post-war" style.

1970 to 2010:
New Metropolis Suburbs

The interstate beltways, constructed mostly in the 1960s, paved the way for a boom in suburban commercial development by the 1970s. A new suburban-dominated metropolis emerged during this period (Fishman 1990; Sharpe and Wallock 1994). The amount of suburban office space surpassed that of central cities, giving rise to Edge Cities and even more commonly Edgeless Cites (Lang 2003)—a more sprawling style of commercial development. Suburbs now typically had the region's balance of people, shopping, and business, yet they maintained a distinct non-urban look (Lang, Blakely and Gough 2005). They became cities in function, but not in form (Fishman 1990; Lang 2003).

The suburbs also grew diverse (Lang and LeFurgy 2006). The 1965 reform in immigration law led to a surge in the foreign-born population of the United States by the 1980s. The cities no longer had a monopoly on attracting immigrants. By the first decade of the 21st century, the suburbs equaled cities as immigrant magnets (Frey 2003). The suburbs also attracted growing numbers of nontraditional households, including single and even gay residents (Brekhus 2003; Frey and Berube 2003). In fact, the suburbs grow so diverse in this era that a whole new language was needed to describe the multiple types of communities and their complicated forms of development.

The suburban split between upscale and more modest development, detectable even in the 19th century, intensified in this era (Orfield 1997, 2002). Many older suburbs from the streetcar, and even mid-century, periods were in decline (most town and country era suburbs have been annexed by central cities). The amount of suburban poverty dramatically increased in places that fall outside the "favored quarter" (Leinberger 1997), or the most affluent wedge of the metropolis. Places in the favored quarter boomed. Newer suburbs at the edge of the region featured "McMansions" as the average house size in new construction nearly doubled from 1970 to the end of the century (Lang and Danielsen 2002). Closer-in suburbs within this quarter became cosmopolitan and competed directly with fashionable urban neighborhoods for the region's arts and intellectual communities (Lang, Hughes, and Danielsen 1997).

2010 and beyond:
Megapolitan Suburbs

A new suburban era may emerge after 2010. It likely will be characterized by an enlarging exurban belt that stretches so far from the original urban core that its residents may have a choice of directions in which to commute. For example, people living around Fredericksburg, VA, 50 miles south of Washington, DC, now have the option of commuting south to Richmond or north to the District of Columbia or booming Northern Virginia. The commuter sheds in the "Megapolitan Suburbs" will link up vast networks of cities (Carbonell and Yaro 2005). The scale of the building also will be enormous as the nation adds at least 30 million new residents each decade until mid-century (Nelson 2004).

Lang and Dhavale (2005) developed a new trans-metropolitan geography that labels vast urban zones "Megapolitan Areas." The first one emerged in the Northeast between Maine and Virginia (Gottmann 1961), but now nine others reach into all regions of the United States. By 2005, Megapolitans captured more than two in three Americans, and the share will grow significantly by 2050 (Lang and Dhavale 2005).

A wave of suburban gentrification will occur post-2010, especially in the favored quarter. Many of the new developments will intensify the urban look and feel of many suburbs. A new urbanity will sweep the suburbs—they will still not look like traditional cities, but may incorporate more urban elements than Edge Cities of the past. Many first-generation Edge Cities will lose their edge as traditional cores revive and more distant suburbs explode with new development (Lang 2003). The scale of urbanity may shift away from mega projects in the suburbs—like Edge Cities—and into smaller scale town centers. The new town centers will have less concentrated office space than Edge Cities, but will be more mixed-use and pedestrian-oriented than the current form of suburban commercial development.

References

Binford, Henry, C. 1988. *The First Suburbs: Residential Communities on the Boston Periphery, 1815–1860.* Chicago: University of Chicago Press.

Borchert, James. 1996. Residential City Suburbs: The Emergence of a New Suburban Type, 1880–1930. *Journal of Urban History* 22: 283–307.

Brekhus, Wayne. 2003. *Peacocks, Chameleons, Centaurs: Gay Suburbia and the Grammar of Social Identity.* Chicago: University of Chicago Press.

Carbonell, Armando and Robert Yaro. 2005. American Spatial Development and the New Megalopolis. *Landlines* 17(2): 2–5.

Duany, Andres, Elizabeth Plater-Zyberk, and Jeff Speck. 2000. *Suburban Nation.* New York: North Point Press.

Fishman, Robert. 1987. *Bourgeois Utopias: The Rise and Fall of Suburbia.* New York: Basic Books.

Fishman, Robert. 1990. America's New City: Megalopolis Unbound. *Wilson Quarterly* 14(1): 24–45.

Frey, William. 2003. Melting Post Suburbs: A Study of Suburban Diversity. In Bruce Katz and Robert E. Lang (eds.), *Redefining Cities and Suburbs: Evidence from Census 2000,* Volume I, pp. 155–180. Washington, DC: Brookings Institution Press.

Frey, William and Alan Berube. 2003. City Families and Suburban Singles: An Emerging Household Story. In Bruce Katz and Robert E. Lang (eds.), *Redefining Cities and Suburbs: Evidence from Census 2000,* Volume I, pp. 257–288. Washington, DC: Brookings Institution Press.

Gottmann, Jean. 1961. *Megalopolis: The Urbanized Northeastern Seaboard of the United States.* New York: Twentieth-Century Fund.

Harris, Richard. 1988. American Suburbs: A Sketch of a New Interpretation. *Journal of Urban History* 15: 98–103.

Hayden, Dolores. 2003. *Building Suburbia: Green Fields and Urban Growth, 1820.* New York: Vintage Books.

Jackson, Kenneth. 1985. *Crabgrass Frontier: The Suburbanization of the United States.* New York: Oxford University Press.

Kunstler, James H. 1993. *Geography of No-where: The Rise and Decline of America's Man-made Landscape.* New York: Free Press.

Lang, Robert. 2003. *Edgeless Cities: Exploring the Elusive Metropolis.* Washington, DC: Brookings Institution.

Lang, Robert E. and Karen A. Danielsen. 2002. Monster Homes. *Planning* (5): 2–7.

Lang, Robert and Dawn Dhavale. 2005. "Beyond Megalopolis: Exploring America's New "Megapolitan" Geography." Census Report Series: 05:01. Alexandria, VA: Metropolitan Institute at Virginia Tech.

Lang, Robert E. and Jennifer LeFurgy. 2006. *Boomburbs: The Rise of America's Accidental Cities.* Washington, DC: Brookings Institution Press.

Lang, Robert E., Edward J. Blakely, and Meghan Z. Gough. 2005. Keys to the New Metropolis: America's Big, Fast-Growing Suburban Counties. *Journal of the American Planning Association* 71(4): 381–391.

Lang, Robert E., James W. Hughes, and Karen A. Danielsen. 1997. Targeting the Suburban Urbanites: Marketing Central City Housing. *Housing Policy Debate* 8(2): 437–470.

Lang, Robert, Jennifer LeFurgy, and Steven Hornburg. 2005. From Wall Street to Your Street: New Solutions for Smart Growth Finance. Coral Gables, FL: Funders' Network for Smart Growth and Livable Communities.

Leinberger, Christopher. 1997. The Favored Quarter; Where the Bosses Live, Jobs and Development Follow. *Atlanta Journal Constitution,* June 8.

Liebs, Chester. 1985. *Main Street to Miracle Mile: American Roadside Architecture.* Boston: Little, Brown.

Longstreth, Richard. 1998. *City Center to Regional Mall: Architecture, the Automobile, and Retailing in Los Angeles, 1920–1950.* Cambridge, MA: MIT Press.

Longstreth, Richard. 1999. *The Drive-In, the Supermarket, and the Transformation of Commercial Space in Los Angeles, 1914–1941.* Cambridge, MA: MIT Press.

Nelson, Arthur C. 2004. Toward a New Metropolis: The Opportunity to Rebuild America. Washington, DC: Brookings Institution Metropolitan Policy Program Survey Series (December).

Orfield, Myron. 1997. *Metro Politics: A Regional Agenda for Community and Stability.* Washington, DC: The Brookings Institution Press.

Orfield, Myron. 2002. *American Metropolitics.* Washington, DC: The Brookings Institution Press.

Rusk, David. 1993. *Cities Without Suburbs.* Washington, DC: Woodrow Wilson Center Press.

Sharpe, William and Leonard Wallock. 1994. Bold New City or Built-Up 'Burb? Redefining Contemporary Suburbia. *American Quarterly* 46(1): 1–30.

Stern, Robert A.M. and John M. Massengale. 1981. The Anglo-American Suburb, Architectural Design Profile 37, Vol. 51, No. 10/11. New York: St. Martin's Press.

Warner, Sam Bass, Jr. 1962. *Streetcar Suburbs: The Process of Growth in Boston, 1870–1900.* Cambridge, MA: Harvard University Press.

Critical Thinking

1. Explain how a series of transportation and technological advancements led to the growth of suburbia.

2. How do Edge Cities differ from a more sprawling style of suburban development of an earlier era?

ROBERT E. LANG is the Director of the Metropolitan Institute at Virginia Tech and is an Associate Professor in the school's Urban Affairs and Planning Program. He is also co-editor of *Opolis*. **JENNIFER LEFURGY** is the Deputy Director of the Metropolitan Institute at Virginia Tech. Along with Robert Lang, she is authoring *Boomburbs: The Rise of America's Accidental Cities* for the Brookings Institution Press. She is also doctoral candidate in Virginia Tech's Urban Affairs and Planning program. **ARTHUR C. NELSON** is professor and founding director of Virginia Tech's Urban Affairs and Planning Program at the Alexandria Center. He was formerly professor of city and regional planning, and public policy at Georgia Tech and adjunct professor of law at Georgia State University.

Patio Man and the Sprawl People
America's Newest Suburbs

David Brooks

I don't know if you've ever noticed the expression of a man who is about to buy a first-class barbecue grill. He walks into a Home Depot or Lowe's or one of the other mega hardware complexes and his eyes are glistening with a faraway visionary zeal, like one of those old prophets gazing into the promised land. His lips are parted and twitching slightly. Inside the megastore, the grills are just past the racks of affordable-house plan books, in the yard-machinery section. They are arrayed magnificently next to the vehicles that used to be known as rider mowers but are now known as lawn tractors, because to call them rider mowers doesn't really convey the steroid-enhanced M-1 tank power of the things.

The man approaches the barbecue grills and his face bears a trance-like expression, suggesting that he has cast aside all the pains and imperfections of this world and is approaching the gateway to a higher dimension. In front of him are a number of massive steel-coated reactors with names like Broilmaster P3, The Thermidor, and the Weber Genesis, because in America it seems perfectly normal to name a backyard barbecue grill after a book of the Bible.

The items in this cooking arsenal flaunt enough metal to suggest they have been hardened to survive a direct nuclear assault, and Patio Man goes from machine to machine comparing their features—the cast iron/porcelain coated cooking surfaces, the 328,000-Btu heat-generating capacities, the 1,600-degree-tolerance linings, the multiple warming racks, the lava rock containment dishes, the built-in electrical meat thermometers, and so on. Certain profound questions flow through his mind. Is a 542-square-inch grilling surface really enough, considering that he might someday get the urge to roast an uncut buffalo steak? Though the matte steel overcoat resists scratching, doesn't he want a polished steel surface on his grill so he can glance down and admire his reflection as he is performing the suburban manliness rituals, such as brushing tangy sauce on meat slabs with his right hand while clutching a beer can in an NFL foam insulator ring in his left?

Pretty soon a large salesman in an orange vest who looks like a human SUV comes up to him and says, "Howyadoin'," which is, "May I help you?" in Home Depot talk. Patio Man, who has so much lust in his heart it is all he can do to keep from climbing up on one of these machines and whooping rodeo-style with joy, manages to respond appropriately. He grunts inarticulately and nods toward the machines. Careful not to make eye contact at any point, the two manly suburban men have a brief exchange of pseudo-scientific grill argot that neither of them understands, and pretty soon Patio Man has come to the reasoned conclusion that it really does make sense to pay a little extra for a grill with V-shaped metal baffles, ceramic rods, and a side-mounted smoker box. Plus the grill he selects has four insulated drink holders. All major choices of consumer durables these days ultimately come down to which model has the most impressive cup holders.

Patio Man pays for the grill with his credit card, and is told that some minion will forklift his machine over to the loading dock around back. It is yet another triumph in a lifetime of conquest shopping, and as Patio Man heads toward the parking lot he is glad once again that he's driving that Yukon XL so that he can approach the loading dock guys as a co-equal in the manly fraternity of Those Who Haul Things.

He steps out into the parking lot and is momentarily blinded by sun bouncing off the hardtop. The parking lot is so massive that he can barely see the Wal-Mart, the Bed Bath & Beyond, or the area-code-sized Old Navy glistening through the heat there on the other side. This mall is in fact big enough to qualify for membership in the United Nations, and is so vast that shoppers have to drive from store to store, cutting diagonally through the infinity of empty parking spaces in between.

As Patio Man walks past the empty handicapped and expectant-mother parking spots toward his own vehicle, wonderful grill fantasies dance in his imagination: There he is atop the uppermost tier of his multi-level backyard patio/outdoor recreation area posed like an admiral on the deck of his destroyer. In his mind's eye he can see himself coolly flipping the garlic and pepper T-bones on the front acreage of his new grill while carefully testing the citrus-tarragon trout filets that sizzle fragrantly in the rear. On the lawn below he can see his kids, Haley and Cody, frolicking on the weedless community lawn that is mowed twice weekly by the people who run Monument Crowne Preserve, his town-home community.

Haley, 12, is a Travel Team Girl, who spends her weekends playing midfield against similarly pony-tailed, strongly calved soccer marvels. Cody, 10, is a Buzz Cut Boy, whose naturally blond hair has been cut to a lawn-like stubble and dyed an almost phosphorescent white. Cody's wardrobe is entirely derivative of fashions he has seen watching the X-Games.

In his vision, Patio Man can see the kids enjoying their child-safe lawn darts with a gaggle of their cul de sac friends, a happy gathering of Haleys and Codys and Corys and Britneys. It's a brightly colored scene: Abercrombie & Fitch pink spaghetti-strap tops on the girls and ankle length canvas shorts and laceless Nikes on the boys. Patio Man notes somewhat uncomfortably that in America today the average square yardage of boys' fashion grows and grows while the square inches in the girls' outfits shrink and shrink, so that while the boys look like tent-wearing skateboarders, the girls look like preppy prostitutes.

Nonetheless, Patio Man envisions his own adult softball team buddies lounging on his immaculate deck furniture watching him with a certain moist envy in their eyes as he mans the grill. They are fit, sockless men in dock siders, chinos, and Tommy Bahama muted Hawaiian shirts. Their wives, trim Jennifer Aniston women, wear capris and sleeveless tops that look great owing to their many hours of sweat and exercise at Spa Lady. These men and women may not be Greatest Generation heroes, or earthshaking inventors like Thomas Edison, but if Thomas Edison had had a Human Resources Department, and that Human Resources Department had organized annual enrichment and motivational conferences for mid-level management, then these people would have been the marketing executives for the back office outsourcing companies to the meeting-planning firms that hooked up the HR executives with the conference facilities.

They are wonderful people. And Patio Man can envision his own wife, Cindy, a Realtor Mom, circulating amongst them serving drinks, telling parent-teacher conference stories and generally spreading conviviality while he, Patio Man, masterfully runs the grill—again, to the silent admiration of all. The sun is shining. The people are friendly. The men are no more than 25 pounds overweight, which is the socially acceptable male paunch level in upwardly mobile America, and the children are well adjusted. It is a vision of the sort of domestic bliss that Patio Man has been shooting for all his life.

And it's plausible now because two years ago Patio Man made the big move. He pulled up stakes and he moved his family to a Sprinkler City.

Sprinkler Cities are the fast-growing suburbs mostly in the South and West that are the homes of the new style American Dream, the epicenters of Patio Man fantasies. Douglas County, Colorado, which is the fastest-growing county in America and is located between Denver and Colorado Springs, is a Sprinkler City. So is Henderson, Nevada, just outside of Las Vegas. So is Loudoun County, Virginia, near Dulles Airport. So are Scottsdale and Gilbert, Arizona, and Union County, North Carolina.

The growth in these places is astronomical, as Patio Men and their families—and Patio retirees, yuppie geezers who still like to grill, swim, and water ski—flock to them from all over. Douglas County grew 13.6 percent from April 2000 to July 2001, while Loudoun County grew 12.6 percent in that 16-month period. Henderson, Nevada, has tripled in size over the past 10 years and now has over 175,000 people. Over the past 50 years, Irving, Texas, grew by 7,211 percent, from about 2,600 people to 200,000 people.

The biggest of these boom suburbs are huge. With almost 400,000 people, Mesa, Arizona, has a larger population than Minneapolis, Cincinnati, or St. Louis. And this sort of growth is expected to continue. Goodyear, Arizona, on the western edge of the Phoenix area, now has about 20,000 people, but is projected to have 320,000 in 50 years' time. By then, Greater Phoenix could have a population of over 6 million and cover over 10,000 square miles.

Sprinkler Cities are also generally the most Republican areas of the country. In some of the Sprinkler City congressional districts, Republicans have a 2 or 3 or 4 to 1 registration advantage over Democrats. As cultural centers, they represent the beau ideal of Republican selfhood, and are becoming the new base—the brains, heart, guts, and soul of the emerging Republican party. Their values are not the same as those found in either old-line suburbs like Greenwich, Connecticut, where a certain sort of Republican used to dominate, or traditional conservative bastions, such as the old South. This isn't even the more modest conservatism found in the midwestern farm belt. In fact, the rising prominence of these places heralds a new style of suburb vs. suburb politics, with the explosively growing Republican outer suburbs vying with the slower-growing and increasingly Democratic inner suburbs for control of the center of American political gravity.

If you stand on a hilltop overlooking a Sprinkler City, you see, stretched across the landscape, little brown puffs here and there where bulldozers are kicking up dirt while building new townhomes, office parks, shopping malls, AmeriSuites guest hotels, and golf courses. Everything in a Sprinkler City is new. The highways are so clean and freshly paved you can eat off them. The elementary schools have spic and span playgrounds, unscuffed walls, and immaculate mini-observatories for just-forming science classes.

The lawns in these places are perfect. It doesn't matter how arid the local landscape used to be, the developers come in and lay miles of irrigation tubing, and the sprinklers pop up each evening, making life and civilization possible.

The roads are huge. The main ones, where the office parks are, have been given names like Innovation Boulevard and Entrepreneur Avenue, and they've been built for the population levels that will exist a decade from now, so that today you can cruise down these flawless six lane thoroughfares in traffic-less nirvana, and if you get a cell phone call you can just stop in the right lane and take the call because there's no one behind you. The smaller roads in the residential neighborhoods have pretentious names—in Loudoun County I drove down Trajan's Column Terrace—but they too are just as smooth and immaculate as a blacktop bowling alley. There's no use relying on a map to get around these places, because there's no way map publishers can keep up with the construction.

The town fathers try halfheartedly to control sprawl, and as you look over the landscape you can see the results of their ambivalent zoning regulations. The homes aren't spread out with quarter-acre yards, as in the older, close-in suburbs. Instead they are clustered into pseudo-urban pods. As you scan the horizon you'll see a densely packed pod of townhouses, then a stretch of a half mile of investor grass (fields that will someday contain 35,000-square-foot Fresh-Mex restaurants but for now are being kept fallow by investors until the prices rise), and then another pod of slightly more expensive detached homes just as densely packed.

The developments in the southeastern Sprinkler Cities tend to have Mini-McMansion Gable-gable houses. That is to say, these are 3,200-square-foot middle-class homes built to look like 7,000-square-foot starter palaces for the nouveau riche. And on the front at the top, each one has a big gable, and then right in front of it, for visual relief, a little gable jutting forward so that it looks like a baby gable leaning against a mommy gable.

These homes have all the same features as the authentic McMansions of the mid-'90s (as history flows on, McMansions come to seem authentic), but significantly smaller. There are the same vaulted atriums behind the front doors that never get used, and the same open kitchen/two-story great rooms with soaring palladian windows. But in the middle-class knockoffs, the rooms are so small, especially upstairs, that a bedroom or a master-bath suite would fit inside one of the walk-in closets of a real McMansion.

In the Southwest the homes tend to be tile and stucco jobs, with tiny mousepad lawns out front, blue backyard spas in the back, and so much white furniture inside that you have to wear sunglasses indoors. As you fly over the Sprinkler Cities you begin to see the rough pattern—a little pseudo-urbanist plop of development, a blank field, a plop, a field, a plop. You also notice that the developers build the roads and sewage lines first and then fill in the houses later, so from the sky you can see cul de sacs stretching off into the distance with no houses around them.

Then, cutting through the landscape are broad commercial thoroughfares with two-tier, big-box malls on either side. In the front tier is a line of highly themed chain restaurants that all fuse into the same Macaroni Grill Olive Outback Cantina Charlie Chiang's Dave & Buster's Cheesecake Factory mélange of peppy servers, superfluous ceiling fans, free bread with olive oil, and taco salad entrees. In the 21st-century migration of peoples, the food courts come first and the huddled masses follow.

Then in the back row are all the huge, exposed-air-duct architectural behemoths, which are the big-box stores.

Shopping experiences are now segregated by mood. If you are in the mood for some titillating browsing, you can head over to a Lifestyle Center, which is one of those instant urban streetscapes that developers put up in suburbia as entertainment/retail/community complexes, complete with pedestrian zones, outdoor cafés, roller rinks, multiplexes, and high-attitude retail concepts such as CP Shades, a chain store that masquerades as a locally owned boutique.

If you are buying necessities, really shopping, there are Power Malls. These are the big-box expanses with Wal-marts, K-Marts, Targets, price clubs, and all the various Depots (Home, Office, Furniture, etc.). In Sprinkler Cities there are archipelagoes of them—one massive parking lot after another surrounded by huge boxes that often have racing stripes around the middle to break the monotony of the windowless exterior walls.

If one superstore is in one mall, then its competitor is probably in the next one in the archipelago. There's a Petsmart just down from a Petco, a Borders nearby a Barnes & Noble, a Linens 'n' Things within sight of a Bed Bath & Beyond, a Best Buy cheek by jowl with a Circuit City. In Henderson, there's a Wal-Mart superstore that spreads over 220,000 square feet, with all those happy greeters in blue vests to make you feel small-town.

There are also smaller stores jammed in between the mega-outlets like little feeder fish swimming around the big boys. On one strip, there might be the ostentatiously unpretentious Total Wine & More, selling a galaxy of casual Merlots. Nearby there might be a Michaels discount women's clothing, a bobo bazaar such as World Market that sells raffia fiber from Madagascar, Rajasthani patchwork coverlets from India, and vermouth-flavored martini onions from Israel, and finally a string of storefront mortgage bankers and realtors serving all the new arrivals. In Sprinkler Cities, there are more realtors than people.

People move to Sprinkler Cities for the same reasons people came to America or headed out West. They want to leave behind the dirt and toxins of their former existence—the crowding and inconvenience, the precedents, and the oldness of what suddenly seems to them a settled and unpromising world. They want to move to some place that seems fresh and new and filled with possibility.

Sprinkler City immigrants are not leaving cities to head out to suburbia. They are leaving older suburbs—which have come to seem as crowded, expensive, and stratified as cities—and heading for newer suburbs, for the suburbia of suburbia.

One of the problems we have in thinking about the suburbs is that when it comes to suburbia the American imagination is motionless. Many people still have in their heads the stereotype of suburban life that the critics of suburbia established in the 1950s. They see suburbia as a sterile, dull, Ozzie and Harriet retreat from the creative dynamism of city life, and the people who live in the suburbs as either hopelessly shallow or quietly and neurotically desperate. (There is no group in America more conformist than the people who rail against suburbanites for being conformist—they always make the same critiques, decade after decade.)

The truth, of course, is that suburbia is not a retreat from gritty American life, it is American life. Already, suburbanites make up about half of the country's population (while city people make up 28 percent and rural folk make up the rest), and America gets more suburban every year.

According to the census data, the suburbs of America's 100 largest metro areas grew twice as fast as their central cities in the 1990s, and that was a decade in which many cities actually reversed their long population slides. Atlanta, for example, gained 23,000 people in the '90s, but its suburbs grew by 1.1 million people.

Moreover, newer suburbs no longer really feed off cities. In 1979, 74 percent of American office space was located in cities, according to the Brookings Institution's Robert Puentes. But now, after two decades in which the biggest job growth has been in suburban office parks, the suburbs' share of total office space has risen to 42 percent. In other words, we are fast approaching a time when the majority of all office space will be in the suburbs, and most Americans not only will not live in cities, they won't even commute to cities or have any regular contact with city life.

Encompassing such a broad swath of national existence, suburbs obviously cannot possibly be the white-bread places of myth and literature. In reality, as the most recent census shows, suburbs contain more non-family houses—young singles and elderly couples—than family households, married couples with children. Nor are they overwhelmingly white. The majority of Asian Americans, half of Hispanics, and 40 percent of American blacks live in suburbia.

And so now there are crucial fault lines not just between city and suburb but between one kind of suburb and another. Say you grew up in some southern California suburb in the 1970s. You graduated from the University of Oregon and now you are a systems analyst with a spouse and two young kids. You're making $65,000 a year, far more than you ever thought you would, but back in Orange County you find you can't afford to live anywhere near your Newport Beach company headquarters. So your commute is 55 minutes each way. Then there's your house itself. You paid $356,000 for a 1962 four-bedroom split level with a drab kitchen, low ceilings, and walls that are chipped and peeling. Your mortgage—that $1,800 a month—is like a tapeworm that devours the family budget.

And then you visit a Sprinkler City in Arizona or Nevada or Colorado—far from the coast and deep into exurbia—and what do you see? Bounteous roads! Free traffic lanes! If you lived here you'd be in commuter bliss—15 minutes from home on Trajan's Column Terrace to the office park on Innovation Boulevard! If you lived here you'd have an extra hour and a half each day for yourself.

And those real estate prices! In, say, Henderson, Nevada, you wouldn't have to spend over $400,000 for a home and carry that murderous mortgage. You could get a home that's brand new, twice the size of your old one, with an attached garage (no flimsy carport), and three times as beautiful for $299,000. The average price of a single-family home in Loudoun County, one of the pricier of the Sprinkler Cities, was $166,824 in 2001, which was an 11 percent increase over the year before. Imagine that! A mortgage under 200 grand! A great anvil would be lifted from your shoulders. More free money for you to spend on yourself. More free time to enjoy. More Freedom!

Plus, if you moved to a Sprinkler City there would be liberation of a subtler kind. The old suburbs have become socially urbanized. They've become stratified. Two sorts of people have begun to move in and ruin the middle-class equality of the development you grew up in: the rich and the poor.

There are, first, the poor immigrants, from Mexico, Vietnam, and the Philippines. They come in, a dozen to a house, and they introduce an element of unpredictability to what was a comforting milieu. They shout. They're less tidy. Their teenage boys seem to get involved with gangs and cars. Suddenly you feel you will lose control of your children. You begin to feel a new level of anxiety in the neighborhood. It is exactly the level of anxiety—sometimes intermingled with racism—your parents felt when they moved from their old neighborhood to the suburbs in the first place.

And then there are the rich. Suddenly many of the old ramblers are being knocked down by lawyers who proceed to erect 4,000-square-foot arts and crafts bungalows with two-car garages for their Volvos. Suddenly cars in the neighborhoods have window and bumper stickers that never used to be there in the past: "Yale," "The Friends School," "Million Mom March." The local stores are changing too. Gone are the hardware stores and barber shops. Now there are Afghan restaurants, Marin County bistros, and environmentally sensitive and extremely expensive bakeries.

And these new people, while successful and upstanding, are also . . . snobs. They're doctors and lawyers and journalists and media consultants. They went to fancy colleges and they consider themselves superior to you if you sell home-security systems or if you are a mechanical engineer, and in subtle yet patronizing ways they let you know it.

I recently interviewed a woman in Loudoun County who said she had grown up and lived most of her life in Bethesda, Maryland, which is an upscale suburb close to Washington. When I asked why she left Bethesda, she hissed "I hate it there now" with a fervor that took me by surprise. And as we spoke, it became clear that it was precisely the "improvements" she hated: the new movie theater that shows only foreign films, the explosion of French, Turkish, and new wave restaurants, the streets choked with German cars and Lexus SUVs, the doctors and lawyers and journalists with their educated-class one-upmanship.

These new people may live in the old suburbs but they hate suburbanites. They hate sprawl, big-box stores, automobile culture. The words they use about suburbanites are: synthetic, bland, sterile, self-absorbed, disengaged. They look down on people who like suburbs. They don't like their lawn statuary, their Hallmark greeting cards, their Ethan Allen furniture, their megachurches, the seasonal banners the old residents hang out in front of their houses, their untroubled attitude toward McDonald's and Dairy Queen, their Thomas Kinkade fantasy paintings. And all the original suburbanites who were peacefully enjoying their suburb until the anti-suburban suburbanites moved in notice the condescension, and they do what Americans have always done when faced with disapproval, anxiety, and potential conflict. They move away. The pincer movements get them: the rich and the poor, the commutes and the mortgages, the prices and the alienation. And pretty soon it's Henderson, Nevada, here we come.

George Santayana once observed that Americans don't solve problems, they just leave them behind. They take advantage of all that space and move. If there's an idea they don't like, they don't bother refuting it, they just go somewhere else, and if they can't go somewhere else, they just leave it in the past, where it dies from inattention.

And so Patio Man is not inclined to stay and defend himself against the condescending French-film goers and their Volvos. He's not going to mount a political campaign to fix the educational, economic, and social woes that beset him in his old neighborhood. He won't waste his time fighting a culture war. It's not worth the trouble. He just bolts. He heads for the exurbs and the desert. He goes to the new place where the future is still open and promising. He goes to fresh ground where his dreams might more plausibly come true.

The power of this urge to leave and create new places is really awesome to behold. Migration is not an easy thing, yet every year 43 million Americans get up and move. And it sets off a chain reaction. The migrants who move into one area push out another set of people, who then migrate to another and push out another set of people, and so on and so on in one vast cycle of creative destruction. Ten years ago these Sprinkler Cities didn't really exist. Fifteen years ago the institutions that dot them hadn't been invented. There weren't book superstores or sporting goods superstores or Petsmart or Petco, and Target was just something you shot arrows at. And yet suddenly metropolises with all these new stores and institutions have materialized out of emptiness.

It's as if some Zeus-like figure had appeared out of the ether and slammed down a million-square-foot mall on the desert floor, then a second later he'd slammed down a 5,000-person townhome community, then a second later an ice rink and a rec center and soccer fields and schools and community colleges. How many times in human history have 200,000-person cities just materialized almost instantaneously out of nowhere?

The people who used to live in these empty places don't like it; they've had to move further out in search of valleys still pristine. But the sprawl people just love it. They talk to you like born-again evangelists, as if their life had undergone some magical transformation when they made the big move. They talk as if they'd thrown off some set of horrendous weights, banished some class of unpleasant experiences, and magically floated up into the realm of good climate, fine people, job opportunities, and transcendent convenience. In 2001, Loudoun County did a survey of its residents. Ninety-eight percent felt safe in their neighborhoods. Ninety-three percent rated their county's quality of life excellent or good. Only a third of the county's residents, by the way, have lived there for more than 10 years.

These people are so happy because they have achieved something that human beings are actually quite good at achieving. Through all the complex diversity of society, they have managed to find people who want pretty much the same things they want.

This is not to say they want white Ozzie and Harriet nirvana. The past 40 years happened. It never occurs to them to go back before rock, rap, women working, and massive immigration. They don't mind any of these things, so long as they complement the core Sprinkler City missions of orderly living, high achievement, and the bright seeking of a better future.

Recently three teams from the Seneca Ridge Middle School in Loudoun County competed in the National Social Studies Olympiad. The fifth grade team finished fifth out of 242 teams, while the eighth grade team finished twenty-third out of 210. Here are some of the names of the students competing for Loudoun: Amy Kuo, Arshad Ali, Samanth Chao, Katie Hempenius, Ronnel Espino, Obinna Onwuka, Earnst Ilang-Ilang, Ashley Shiraishi, and Alberto Pareja-Lecaros. At the local high school, 99 percent of seniors graduate and 87 percent go on to higher education.

When you get right down to it, Sprinkler Cities are united around five main goals:

- *The goal of the together life.* When you've got your life together, you have mastered the complexities of the modern world so thoroughly that you can glide through your days without unpleasant distractions or tawdry failures. Instead, your hours are filled with self-affirming reminders of the control you have achieved over the elements. Your lawn is immaculate. Your DVD library is organized, and so is your walk-in closet.

Your car is clean and vacuumed, your frequently dialed numbers are programmed into your cell phone, your telephone plan is suited to your needs, and your various gizmos interface without conflict. Your wife is effortlessly slender, your kids are unnaturally bright, your job is rewarding, your promotions are inevitable, and you look great in casual slacks.

You can thus spend your days in perfect equanimity, the Sprinkler City ideal. You radiate confidence, like a professional golfer striding up the 18th fairway after a particularly masterful round. Compared with you, Dick Cheney looks like a disorganized hothead. George W. Bush looks like a self-lacerating neurotic. Professionally, socially, parentally, you have your life together. You may not be the most intellectual or philosophical person on the planet, but you are honest and straightforward. You may not be flamboyant, but you are friendly, good-hearted, and considerate. You have achieved the level of calm mastery of life that is the personality equivalent of the clean and fresh suburban landscape.

- *The goal of technological heroism.* They may not be stereotypical rebels, and nobody would call them avant-garde, but in one respect many Sprinkler City dwellers have the souls of revolutionaries. When Patio Man gets out of his Yukon, lowers his employee-badge necklace around his neck, and walks into his generic office building, he becomes a technological radical. He spends his long workdays striving to create some technological innovation, management solution, or organizing system breakthroughs that will alter the world. Maybe the company he works for has one of those indecipherable three-initial names, like DRG Technologies or SER Solutions, or maybe it's got one of those jammed together compound names that were all the rage in the 1990s until WorldCom and MicroStrategy went belly up.

Either way, Patio Man is working on, or longs to be working on, a project that is new and revolutionary. And all around him there are men and women who are actually achieving that goal, who are making that leap into the future. The biotech revolution is being conducted in bland suburban office parks by seemingly unremarkable polo-shirt-and-chino people at firms like Celera and Human Genome Sciences. Silicon Valley is just one long string of suburban office parks jutting out from San Jose. AOL is headquartered in Loudoun County. You walk down a path in a Sprinkler City corporate center and it leads you to a company frantically chasing some market-niche innovation in robotics, agricultural engineering, micro-technology, or hardware and software applications.

There are retail-concept revolutionaries, delivery-system radicals, market-research innovators, data-collection pioneers, computer-game Rembrandts, and weapons-systems analysts. They look like bland members of some interchangeable research team, but many of them are deeply engrossed in what they consider a visionary project, which if completed will help hurtle us all further into the Knowledge Revolution, the Information Millennium, the Age of MicroTechnology, the Biotech Century, or whatever transplendent future it is you want to imagine. They have broken the monopoly that cities used to have, and they have made themselves the new centers of creativity.

- *The goal of relaxed camaraderie.* The critics of suburbia believe that single-family homeowners with their trimmed yards and matching pansies are trying to keep up with the Joneses. But like most of what the critics assert, that's completely wrong. Sprinkler City people are competitive in the marketplace and on the sports field, but they detest social competition. That's part of why these people left inner-ring suburbs in the first place.

They are not emulating the rich; they are happy to blend in with each other. One of the comforts of these places is that almost nobody is far above you socially and almost nobody is far below. You're all just swimming in a pond of understated success.

So manners are almost aggressively relaxed. Everybody strives overtime to not put on airs or create friction. In style, demeanor, and mood, people reveal the language and values they have in common. They are good team members and demonstrate from the first meeting that they are team-able. You could go your entire life, from home to church to work to school, wearing nothing but Lands' End—comfortable, conservative, non-threatening activewear for people with a special fondness for navy blue. The dominant conversational tone is upbeat and friendly, like banter between Katie Couric and Matt Lauer on the "Today" show. The prevailing style of humor is ironic but not biting and owes a lot to ESPN's "SportsCenter."

- *The goal of the active-leisure lifestyle.* Your self-esteem is based on your success at work, but since half the time it's hard to explain to people what the hell it is you do, your public identity is defined by your leisure activities. You are the soccer family, engrossed by the politics and melodrama of your local league, or you are the T-ball coach and spend your barbecue conversations comparing notes on new $200 titanium bat designs (there's a new bat called The Power Elite—even C. Wright Mills has been domesticated for the Little League set). You are Scuba Woman and you converse about various cruises you have taken. You are Mountain Bike Man and you make vague references to your high altitude injuries and spills. Or you are a golfer, in which case nobody even thinks of engaging you in conversation on any topic other than golf.

Religion is too hot a subject and politics is irrelevant, so if you are not discussing transportation issues—how to get from here to there, whether the new highway exit is good or bad—you are probably talking about sports. You're talking about your kids' ice hockey leagues, NBA salary levels, or the competition in your over-70 softball league—the one in which everybody wears a knee brace and it takes about six minutes for a good hitter to beat out a double. Sports sets the emotional climate of your life. Sports provides the language of easy camaraderie, self-deprecating humor, and (mostly) controlled competition.

- *The goal of the traditional, but competitive, childhood.* Most everything in Sprinkler Cities is new, but much of the newness is in the service of tradition. The families that move here are trying to give their children as clean and upright and traditional a childhood as they can imagine. They're trying to move away from parents who smoke and slap their kids, away from families where people watch daytime TV shows about transvestite betrayals and "My Daughter is a Slut" confessions, away from broken homes and, most of all, away from the company of children who are not being raised to achieve and succeed.

They are trying to move instead to a realm of clean neighborhoods, safe streets, competitive cheerleading, spirit squads, soccer tots academies, accelerated-reader programs, and adult-chaperoned drug-free/alcohol-free graduation celebrations.

For the fifth consecutive year, the Henderson, Nevada, high school Marine Corps Junior ROTC squad has won the National Male Armed Drill Team championship. The Female Unarmed Drill Team has come in first six out of the past eight years. In Loudoun County the local newspaper runs notices for various travel team tryouts. In one recent edition, I counted 55 teams announcing their tryouts, with names like The Loudoun Cyclones, the Herndon Surge, the Loudoun Volcanoes. (It's not socially acceptable to name your team after a group of people anymore, so most of the teams have nature names.) As you drive around a Sprinkler City you see SUVs everywhere with cheers scrawled in washable marker on the back windows: "Go Heat!" "#24 Kelly Jones!" "Regional Champs!"

The kids spend their days being chaperoned from one adult-supervised activity to another, and from one achievement activity to the next. They are well tested, well trophied, and well appreciated. They are not only carefully reared and nurtured, they are launched into a life of high expectations and presumed accomplishment.

The dominant ideology of Sprinkler Cities is a sort of utopian conservatism. On the one hand, the people who live here have made a startling leap into the unknown. They have, in great numbers and with great speed, moved from their old homes in California, Florida, Illinois, and elsewhere, to these brand new places that didn't really exist 10 years ago. These places have no pasts, no precedents, no settled institutions, very few longstanding groups you can join and settle into.

Their inhabitants have moved to towns where they have no family connections, no ethnic enclaves, and no friends. They are using their imaginations to draw pictures for themselves of what their lives will be like. They are imagining their golf club buddies even though the course they are moving near is only just being carved out of the desert. They are imagining their successful children's graduation from high school, even though the ground around the new school building is still rutted with the tracks of construction equipment. They are imagining outings with friends at restaurants that are now only investor grass, waiting to be built.

And when they do join groups, often the groups turn out to be still in the process of building themselves. The migrants join congregations that meet in school basements while raising the money to construct churches. They go to office parks at biotech companies that are still waiting to put a product on the market. They may vote, or episodically pay attention to national politics, but they don't get drawn into strong local party organizations because the local organizations haven't been built.

But the odd thing is that all this imaginative daring, these leaps into the future, are all in the service of an extremely conservative ideal. You get the impression that these people have fled their crowded and stratified old suburbs because they really want to live in Mayberry. They have this image of what home should be, a historical myth or memory, and they are going to build it, even if it means constructing an old fashioned place out of modern materials.

It's going to be morally upstanding. It's going to be relaxed and neighborly. It's going to be neat and orderly. Sprinkler City people seem to have almost a moral revulsion at disorder or anything that threatens to bring chaos, including out-of-control immigration and terrorist attacks. They don't think about the war on terror much, let alone some alleged invasion of Iraq, but if it could be shown that Saddam Hussein presented a threat to the good order of the American homeland, then these people would support his ouster with a fervor that would take your breath away. "They have strong emotions when dealing with security," says Tom Tancredo, a congressman from suburban Denver. "Border security, the security of their families, the security of their neighborhoods."

Of course, from the moment they move in, they begin soiling their own nest. They move in order to get away from crowding, but as they and the tens of thousands like them move in, they bring crowding with them. They move to get away from stratification, snobbery, and inequality, but as the new towns grow they get more stratified. In Henderson, the $200,000 ranch homes are now being supplemented by gated $500,000-a-home golf communities. People move for stability and old fashioned values, but they are unwilling to accept limits to opportunity. They are achievement oriented. They are inherently dynamic.

For a time they do a dance about preserving the places they are changing by their presence. As soon as people move into a Sprinkler City, they start lobbying to control further growth. As Tancredo says, they have absolutely no shame about it. They want more roads built, but fewer houses. They want to freeze the peaceful hominess of the town that was growing when they moved there five minutes before.

But soon, one senses, they will get the urge to move again. The Hendersons and the Douglas Counties will be tomorrow what the Newport Beaches and the Los Altoses and the White Plainses are today, places where Patio Man no longer feels quite at home. And the suburban middle-class folks in these places will again strike out as the avant-garde toward new places, with new sorts of stores and a new vision of the innocent hometown.

So the dynamism and volatility will continue—always moving aggressively toward a daring future that looks like an imagined picture of the wholesome past, striving and charging toward that dream of the peaceful patio, the happy kids, the slender friends, and, towering over it all, the massive barbecue grill.

Critical Thinking

1. Where does Patio Man live? What are the political attitudes of Patio Man that can be seen as typical of a great many suburbanites?

2. The concept of "suburbia" often masks a surprising diversity of communities. What different types of suburbs can you identify?

DAVID BROOKS is a senior editor at *The Weekly Standard*.

Affluent, but Needy (First Suburbs)

As they grow and change, the nation's first suburbs, Nassau County included, show signs of stress ahead.

BRUCE KATZ AND ROBERT PUENTES

The problems of America's older, inner-ring first suburbs, Nassau County being among the most prominent, are finally beginning to draw national attention. And not a moment too soon. Warning signs loom.

A new analysis of statistics comparing population growth and demographic changes in these areas from 1950 to 2000, to be formally released by the Brookings Institution this week, shows that across the country first suburbs are undergoing a series of changes that threaten their ability to remain vital and prosperous communities during the long term.

While still largely affluent and suburban in character, these places, which are adjacent to central cities and were identified as standard metropolitan areas by 1950, are beginning to take on some of the characteristics of urban areas. An influx of lower-income minority and foreign-born residents means that, like cities, these first suburbs increasingly will need more state and federal aid to keep up with a growing need for social services and affordable housing.

At the moment, however, they fall through the cracks in a nation where government assistance has been directed for years at urban or rural areas. As Sen. Hillary Clinton said in a speech last month at Adelphi University, "Long Island is the victim of its own success."

Nassau, as we all know, possesses major assets—proximity to New York City, extensive parkland and beaches, quality neighborhoods, a large number of highly educated residents with high income levels and a highly developed transportation network for commuting to the city. Its home values are among the highest in the nation. But a number of trends suggest that stress lies ahead.

The population has remained stagnant since the 1960s in terms of size, yet is much more diverse than even 20 years ago. Racially, the nonwhite percentage of the population has grown nearly 15 percent since 1970; the percentage of foreign-born has more than doubled, and the elderly population has risen nearly 400 percent since 1950, compared with the U.S. average of 185 percent.

Amid great wealth, growing pockets of poverty and communities of poorer and older residents are presenting needs that weren't an issue in earlier years, when incomes and education levels were not as dissimilar as they are today. A county built as a haven for young, middle-class families with automobiles, most of whom who could afford single-family houses, is now home to a growing population with limited access to cars, a need for cheaper housing and a greater need for social services in order to succeed as members of the community.

Just as we have seen in cities, as their numbers increase, foreign-born populations will put new demands on schools unaccustomed to non-English speakers and on health care systems designed to serve much smaller numbers of lower-income clients. The growing numbers of elderly also will need more health and social services.

Across the country, other first-ring suburbs such as Newark's Essex County, Chicago's Cook County, Seattle's King County and Atlanta's Fulton County also are dealing daily with these issues. The risk for the nation is that their relatively small local governments—which not only have to serve a changing population but maintain an aging system of highways and bridges—will leave them vulnerable to a rapid decline once they start to run out of resources. The suburbs' underdiversified commercial bases add to the risk.

As Nassau County Executive Thomas Suozzi warned in his State of the County address last year, "We have stopped growing. America's first suburb has reached middle age. We now have little open space left to grow, and we want to preserve what we have left. Meanwhile, traffic worsens, and under current zoning laws we can't redevelop those places that could sustain more density. With no new construction or new business, with rising expenses and a flat tax base, local government will be forced to raise property taxes even further or dramatically cut existing services. To continue on that course would be a catastrophe for Nassau. It would mean not simply no new business, but a loss of business and a shrinking tax base to pay higher and higher taxes."

The long-run problem Nassau faces is really a national problem, and it deserves a national solution.

You'd expect the first suburbs to have the political clout to demand one. They are home to about 20 percent of the nation's population. In some states like Maryland, Connecticut and New Jersey, about half the residents live in first suburbs. New York State, the city and first suburban populations together constitute a super majority: Two-thirds of all New Yorkers live in these places. At least a third of congressional districts represent all or part of first suburbs.

The trouble is that these suburbs are not organized to deliver on this political power. Rather, they operate independently or as part of a vast suburban bloc. We tend to think of Nassau and Suffolk as a bloc, for instance, even though most of Suffolk County is a good deal newer.

As a consequence, first suburbs are caught in a policy blind spot between the benefaction long directed toward central cities for problems like housing and economic investment and the new attention being lavished on fast-growing outer suburbs, where demands for new infrastructure and services take precedence.

The first suburbs are often not poor enough to participate in economic programs like empowerment zones or other housing and urban redevelopment efforts. They are frequently too small to qualify for direct funding. With populations less than 50,000, for example, Garden City, Wantagh, West Hempstead and others are not entitled to receive direct funding from the federal Community Development Block Grant program, which pays for improving housing, streets, infrastructure and downtowns.

What can the first suburbs do to get the attention they need from federal and state governments?

First, they need to encourage more research that can help state and federal policy makers understand the urgency of the demographic and market trends in first suburbs and re-envision how these places can continue to thrive. Unfortunately, scant data exist. Institutions such as Hofstra University have begun to fill this gap—in Hofstra's case, with its new Center for Suburban Studies—as have metropolitan organizations in places like Philadelphia and St. Louis. Much more research is needed in many localities.

Second, these first suburbs need to build coalitions and share experiences and lessons, in order to develop and articulate an agenda that focuses specifically on their needs. Successful regional alliances have emerged in Cuyahoga County, near Cleveland, and in Los Angeles County. Some leaders like Suozzi are seeking to build alliances statewide.

The groundwork for reform already is being laid in a number of areas:

On the federal level, Sen. Clinton and Rep. Peter King (R-Seaford) have introduced the Suburban Core Opportunity, Restoration and Enhancement Act in the Senate and House. This bill would set aside $250 million for first

Changing with Age

Nassau and older suburbs are developing differently from cities and newer suburbs.

Nassau County

Percent change in population, 1950–2000 **98.4**
Percentage point change in share of population other than non-Hispanic white, 1980–2000 **14.7**
Percent change in foreign-born population, 1970–2000 **108.5**
Percent change in population age 65 and older, 1950–2000 **398.3**
Percent change in population younger than 15, 1970–2000 **−28.8**

First Surburbs

Percent change in population, 1950–2000 **161.3**
Percentage point change in share of population other than non-Hispanic white, 1980–2000 **17.0**
Percent change in foreign-born population, 1970–2000 **263.7**
Percent change in population age 65 and older, 1950–2000 **341.7**
Percent change in population younger than 15, 1970–2000 **1.7**

Primary Cities

Percent change in population, 1950–2000 **5.3**
Percentage point change in share of population other than non-Hispanic white, 1980–2000 **15.8**
Percent change in foreign-born population, 1970–2000 **138.1**
Percent change in population age 65 and older, 1950–2000 **44.3**
Percent change in population younger than 15, 1970–2000 **−13.1**

Newer Surburbs

Percent change in population, 1950–2000 **75.1**
Percentage point change in share of population other than non-Hispanic white, 1980–2000 **10.8**
Percent change in foreign-born population, 1970–2000 **208.2**
Percent change in population age 65 and older, 1950–2000 **131.1**
Percent change in population younger than 15, 1970–2000 **32.5**

United States

Percent change in population, 1950–2000 **86.0**
Percentage point change in share of population other than non-Hispanic white, 1980–2000 **10.4**
Percent change in foreign-born population, 1970–2000 **223.4**
Percent change in population age 65 and older, 1950–2000 **185.2**
Percent change in population younger than 15, 1970–2000 **4.1**

suburbs nationwide to help fund reinvestment and revitalization projects.

Several states, including Pennsylvania, Michigan and Illinois, are directing infrastructure dollars to cities and established suburbs. This gives priority to the maintenance and rehabilitation needs of existing infrastructure before building new.

Efforts are under way to foster cooperation between first suburbs and central cities. Cleveland's new mayor has promised, for example, to create a post in his administration to oversee regional issues.

First suburbs in Pittsburgh's Allegheny County and Boston's Middlesex County are collaborating to jointly assemble parcels of land with uniform tax rates, codes and streamlined approvals to encourage redevelopment.

Such federal, state and regional efforts are still early in formation and, to date, limited in effect. They raise the potential, however, of first suburbs' flexing their political muscle.

Whether Nassau County and the other first suburbs will emerge as a powerful, focused and disciplined force remains one of the great political questions of a young century.

Critical Thinking

1. What is a First Suburb?

2. How do the conditions of a First Suburb generally differ from those of the suburb in which Patio Man lives?

3. Are there opportunities for city-suburban political alliances? What sort of suburbs would find it in their interest to form an alliance with central cities? On what issues?

Principles of New Urbanism

The principles of New Urbanism can be applied increasingly to projects at the full range of scales from a single building to an entire community.

1. Walkability

- Most things within a 10-minute walk of home and work.
- Pedestrian friendly street design (buildings close to street; porches, windows & doors; tree-lined streets; on street parking; hidden parking lots; garages in rear lane; narrow, slow speed streets).
- Pedestrian streets free of cars in special cases.

2. Connectivity

- Interconnected street grid network disperses traffic & eases walking.
- A hierarchy of narrow streets, boulevards, and alleys.
- High quality pedestrian network and public realm makes walking pleasurable.

3. Mixed-Use & Diversity

- A mix of shops, offices, apartments, and homes on site. Mixed-use within neighborhoods, within blocks, and within buildings.
- Diversity of people—of ages, income levels, cultures, and races.

4. Mixed Housing

A range of types, sizes and prices in closer proximity.

5. Quality Architecture & Urban Design

Emphasis on beauty, aesthetics, human comfort, and creating a sense of place; Special placement of civic uses and sites within community. Human scale architecture & beautiful surroundings nourish the human spirit.

6. Traditional Neighborhood Structure

- Discernable center and edge.
- Public space at center.
- Importance of quality public realm; public open space designed as civic art.
- Contains a range of uses and densities within 10-minute walk.
- Transect planning: Highest densities at town center; progressively less dense towards the edge. The transect is an analytical system that conceptualizes mutually reinforcing elements, creating a series of specific natural habitats and/or urban lifestyle settings. The Transect integrates environmental methodology for habitat assessment with zoning methodology for community design. The professional boundary between the natural and man-made disappears, enabling environmentalists to assess the design of the human habitat and the urbanists to support the viability of nature. This urban-to-rural transect hierarchy has appropriate building and street types for each area along the continuum.

7. Increased Density

- More buildings, residences, shops, and services closer together for ease of walking, to enable a more efficient use of services and resources, and to create a more convenient, enjoyable place to live.
- New Urbanism design principles are applied at the full range of densities from small towns, to large cities.

8. Smart Transportation

- A network of high-quality trains connecting cities, towns, and neighborhoods together.
- Pedestrian-friendly design that encourages a greater use of bicycles, rollerblades, scooters, and walking as daily transportation.

9. Sustainability

- Minimal environmental impact of development and its operations.
- Eco-friendly technologies, respect for ecology and value of natural systems.
- Energy efficiency.
- Less use of finite fuels.
- More local production.
- More walking, less driving.

10. Quality of Life
Taken together these add up to a high quality of life well worth living, and create places that enrich, uplift, and inspire the human spirit.

Benefits of New Urbanism
1. Benefits to Residents
Higher quality of life; Better places to live, work, & play; Higher, more stable property values; Less traffic congestion & less driving; Healthier lifestyle with more walking, and less stress; Close proximity to main street retail & services; Close proximity to bike trails, parks, and nature; Pedestrian friendly communities offer more opportunities to get to know others in the neighborhood and town, resulting in meaningful relationships with more people, and a friendlier town; More freedom and independence to children, elderly, and the poor in being able to get to jobs, recreation, and services without the need for a car or someone to drive them; Great savings to residents and school boards in reduced busing costs from children being able to walk or bicycle to neighborhood schools; More diversity and smaller, unique shops and services with local owners who are involved in community; Big savings by driving less, and owning fewer cars; Less ugly, congested sprawl to deal with daily; Better sense of place and community identity with more unique architecture; More open space to enjoy that will remain open space; More efficient use of tax money with less spent on spread out utilities and roads.

2. Benefits to Businesses
Increased sales due to more foot traffic & people spending less on cars and gas; More profits due to spending less on advertising and large signs; Better lifestyle by living above shop in live-work units—saves the stressful & costly commute; Economies of scale in marketing due to close proximity and cooperation with other local businesses; Smaller spaces promote small local business incubation; Lower rents due to smaller spaces & smaller parking lots; Healthier lifestyle due to more walking and being near healthier restaurants; More community involvement from being part of community and knowing residents.

3. Benefits to Developers
More income potential from higher density mixed-use projects due to more leasable square footage, more sales per square foot, and higher property values and selling prices; Faster approvals in communities that have adopted smart growth principles resulting in cost/time savings; Cost savings in parking facilities in mixed-use properties due to sharing of spaces throughout the day and night, resulting in less duplication in providing parking; Less need for parking facilities due to mix of residences and commercial uses within walking distance of each other; Less impact on roads/traffic, which can result in lower impact fees; Lower cost of utilities due to compact nature of New Urbanist design; Greater acceptance by the public and less resistance from NIMBYS; Faster sell out due to greater acceptance by consumers from a wider product range resulting in wider market share.

4. Benefits to Municipalities
Stable, appreciating tax base; Less spent per capita on infrastructure and utilities than typical suburban development due to compact, high-density nature of projects; Increased tax base due to more buildings packed into a tighter area; Less traffic congestion due to walkability of design; Less crime and less spent on policing due to the presence of more people day and night; Less resistance from community; Better overall community image and sense of place; Less incentive to sprawl when urban core area is desirable; Easy to install transit where it's not, and improve it where it is; Greater civic involvement of population leads to better governance.

Ways to Implement New Urbanism
The most effective way to implement New Urbanism is to plan for it, and write it into zoning and development codes. This directs all future development into this form.

New Urbanism Is Best Planned at All Levels of Development
- The single building.
- Groups of buildings.
- The urban block.
- The neighborhood.
- Networks of neighborhoods.
- Towns.
- Cities.
- Regions.

Increasingly, regional planning techniques are being used to control and shape growth into compact, high-density, mixed-use neighborhoods, villages, towns, and cities. Planning new train systems (instead of more roads) delivers the best results when designed in harmony with regional land planning—known as Transit Oriented Development (TOD). At the same time, the revitalization of urban areas directs and encourages infill development back into city centers.

Planning for compact growth, rather than letting it sprawl out, has the potential to greatly increase the quality of the environment. It also prevents congestion problems and the environmental degradation normally associated with growth.

Obstacles to Overcome
The most important obstacle to overcome is the restrictive and incorrect zoning codes currently in force in most municipalities. Current codes do not allow New Urban-

ism to be built, but do allow sprawl. Adopting a TND ordinance and/or a system of 'smart codes' allows New Urbanism to be built easily without having to rewrite existing codes.

An equally important obstacle is the continuous road building and expansion taking place in every community across America. This encourages more driving and more sprawl which has a domino effect increasing traffic congestion across the region. Halting road projects and building new train systems helps reverse this problematic trend. Read more.

"Only when humans are again permitted to build authentic urbanism—those cities, towns, and villages that nurture us by their comforts and delights—will we cease the despoiling of Nature by escaping to sprawl"—Andres Duany.

Critical Thinking

1. How does New Urbanism seek to build better suburban communities?

2. List what you think are the four most important guiding principles of New Urbanism.

From NewUrbanism.org, 2008. Copyright © 2008 by New Urbanism. Reprinted by permission. www.newurbanism.org

The New Urbanism:
A Limited Revolution

Myron A. Levine

The New Urbanism "is arguably the most influential movement in city design in the last half-century."[1] New Urbanist developers and planners have reacted against the environmental degradation and the perceived lost sense of communal life in suburbia. The New Urbanism seeks to build better suburbs—sustainable communities that offer alternatives to reliance on the automobile. The New Urbanism embraces the more efficient use of land, reducing the vast acreage that is lost to wide roadways, access ramps and a sea of parking lots that surround suburban shopping malls and office gallerias. Just as significantly, New Urbanist design seeks to re-inject a sense of community into suburbia reestablishing the small-town connections among citizens that, as critics charge, have been lost to privatization of lives in backyards and big houses separated by side yards and driveways.

The New Urbanism promises a better alternative to the traditional suburb. But just how realistic and viable is this new and better vision of suburbia? Before this question can be answered, we must first review the core principles and promises of the New Urbanist movement.

The Guiding Principles of the New Urbanism[2]

In its attempt to offer an alternative to both the sprawl and anomie of suburbia, the New Urbanism emphasizes such principles as compact development, walkable communities, identifiable town centers, and the integration of suburban communities in regional mass-transit systems. New Urbanists seek to get Americans out of their cars and back on the streets and in touch with their neighbors. Conventional suburbs, designed for the convenience of the automobile, place virtually insurmountable barriers in the way of walking. Homes are located far from commercial destinations. High schools and office centers are situated on virtual islands surrounded by acres of parking that are not easily traversable on foot. Multi-lane highways and access ramps are nearly impossible for pedestrians to cross; they pose virtual moats that separate one office building and retail development from another. The workers in a suburban

office tower simply cannot walk to a café or convenience store; they have no alternative but to get into their cars and drive across one parking lot into another. The highway- and parking-dominated landscape of suburbia further lacks visual attractions and walkable destinations; it is "an incredibly boring place to walk."[3]

New Urbanist design encourages people to return to the streets. Homes can be built close to sidewalks and located within a five-minute walk to schools, convenience stores, and other key facilities that serve as neighborhood focal points. Town homes and apartments are included in suburban developments, as their existence helps to provide the population densities needed to support walkable neighborhood facilities and town centers. With more people walking and with more homes being built with front porches (town homes can even share porches) located close to the street, residents are encouraged to interact and learn and care about their neighbors.

Front porches also help to restore the "eyes" that watch over streets, making streets safe and free of crime. In commercial areas, "live-works," where owners reside above their stores, help to restore 24-hour-a-day surveillance and a sense of life necessary for the vitality of shopping areas. Just as walkability can be promoted (and the sense of suburban isolation reduced) by having homes located close to one another with parking moved to the rear, stores are similarly located, one abutting another in order to promote walking.

Narrow and tree-lined streets, lower speed limits, and the preservation of on-street parallel parking to protect pedestrians in shopping districts from the flow of automobile traffic and various other traffic calming measures, all serve to make communities more walkable. A conventional street grid, as opposed to dead-end suburban *cul-de-sacs,* further allows residents to choose from a variety of paths, adding to the interest of walking from one destination to another. Walkways and bike paths provide pleasant alternatives to the automobile.

The New Urbanism also emphasizes the construction of attractive, old-style town centers with cafés and interesting shops that serve to promote a leisurely, community lifestyle. Where central facilities require automobile access, parking is pushed to rear garages so that pedestrian-friendly shopping and an environment conducive to civic activity can be maintained in the town center.

New Urbanists emphasize diversity as an alternative to the insularity of life in more conventional (especially exclusive) suburbs, where homogeneity is rigidly enforced through zoning. At its visionary best, the New Urbanism seeks to blend well-designed and visually-attractive apartments into communities with single-family homes. New Urbanists even accept subsidized housing, again stressing the "blending in" concept so that the subsidized units are made part of the community as their appearance is not easily distinguishable from market-rate apartments. These New Urbanist principles have also been applied to the creation of better public housing environments in Chicago, Atlanta, Baltimore, Pittsburg, Charlotte, and other cities across the nation.[4]

New Urbanist communities are not meant to be isolated developments. Rather the New Urbanism seeks an environmentally sustainable vision of communities embedded in a larger metropolis As a result, New Urbanists propose greater residential densities around a rail station, with the goal of establishing a transit-oriented village that provides shopping and other conveniences as well as a mass-transit connection to work.[5] In Portland, Oregon, transit stations have served as the nodes for new development and pedestrian-friendly activity. The sustainability of New Urbanist communities enmeshed in their larger surroundings depends, to a great extent, on the existence of a well-funded and functioning regional mass transit system.

Preliminary evidence from Orenco Station, an affluent New Urban subdivision in Portland, shows that residents exhibit a higher sense of community or "within-neighborhood cohesion" than do the residents of more typical Portland communities. Orenco Station citizens, however, do not exhibit any great sense of responsibility to citizens who live outside, beyond the borders of the local community.[6] The question remains as to what extent New Urbanist design can truly increase a community's stock of social capital.

Limitations and Criticisms of the New Urbanism

Does the New Urbanism provide a viable alternative to conventional suburban development? Can the New Urbanism, as celebrated as it is, reshape suburbia?

One obvious limitation is that the New Urbanism cannot greatly alter patterns of land use that have taken root over time. New Urbanist developers and planners have been most successful where they have had the freedom to design new housing developments according to their community-oriented principles; but, overall, they have not been able to greatly reduce automobile commutes, as residents choose to travel to jobs, shopping centers, and strip malls located outside the borders of the ideal New Urban community.

The New Urbanism creates highly desirable communities for those who choose, and those with the buying power, to live in them. But the New Urbanism lacks the ability to change the suburban preference of the vast majority of Americans. Homeowners in conventional suburbs express a great deal of satisfaction with their lives. As a result, the vast majority of Americans can be expected to continue to use their buying power to purchase big homes with spacious backyards and a sense a privacy; they are satisfied with the escape and exclusiveness that affluence and the automobile have placed within their grasps.

Not only does the New Urbanism lack the power to reverse the suburban housing choices that most Americans have made, but also this architectural and design movement does little to alter the provision of road-building subsidies and homeowner tax breaks that continue to promote sprawl development. As a result, New Urban developments often fail to attract the population densities necessary to support neighborhood facilities and thriving town centers.

Compared to most New Urban developments, Celebration, Florida, is noteworthy for its attractive town center with a town hall, bank, post office, upscale grocery store, theater, trendy cafés, and a lakeshore path; yet, the residents of Celebration routinely drive to supermarkets, shopping malls, power stores, and restaurants in the suburban shopping strips beyond its borders. Celebration, like other New Urban communities, lacks the population density to support major stores of its own. For a long while, Celebration was able to maintain its town center only as a result of the subsidized store leases offered by the Disney Corporation.[7]

In Kentlands, Maryland (located within Gaithersburg, a suburb of Washington, D.C.), there was no deep-pockets Disney Corporation to subsidize store leases. In Kentlands and similar communities, developers had to respond to market forces, compromising New Urbanist ideals where the market required. Indeed, Kentlands Square is like any other strip mall, only a bit more aesthetically pleasing. The stores facing the parking area have proved economically viable; but vacancies quickly appeared in areas of the center that were not visible to, or easily accessible from, the parking lot.[8]

Constrained by market forces and reliant on private developers, the New Urbanism has not produced communities with great social balance. Seaside, Florida, in the state's panhandle, is a New Urban community much celebrated for its small-town appearance—white picket fences, front porches, gabled roots, narrow streets, walkways to the beach, homes of architectural distinction, public spaces, and striking beach pavilions. The setting for Jim Carrey's film, *The Truman Show,* Seaside is pleasant and attractive. But Seaside fails to represent an authentic revival of small-town life. Seaside is little more than a fashionable beachfront community, with housing that sells at high prices attesting to the community's aesthetically-pleasing qualities. Seaside's homes mainly cater to short-term vacationers, not permanent town residents.

The decline in federal subsidies for the new construction of subsidized housing has seriously impaired the ability of New Urbanist developers to achieve their ideal vision of social balance. In the absence of government subsidies to build extensive affordable housing, New Urbanist developers have found that their efforts to design ideal communities are still highly constrained by a market in which many homebuyers value exclusivity and distance from lower classes. Even where New Urban communities have offered affordable housing, the lower-income units tend to be relatively few and are usually separated from the more high-status and attractive residential developments. As a result of these constraints, New Urbanists "are producing only slightly less exclusive suburbs than the ones they dislike."[9]

Celebration, Florida, developed by the Disney Corporation, is not strictly a New Urban community yet is noteworthy for a number of its New Urban design features. As already noted, the development, just south of Disney World, contains an attractive, upscale town center with cafés, a theater, and a community store, but no full-scale supermarket. The development also contains different neighborhoods with different housing styles. Yet, Celebration has only the most limited class diversity. Disney did not support the construction of affordable housing within the community; instead, the developer chose to meet its obligations under state law by contributing to a fund to assist people with rents and housing down payments outside of Celebration's borders. Celebration's housing is priced beyond the reach of the area's Hispanic service workers: "It's true that Celebration does have some mix of housing, but it's a mixing of the upper class."[10] Despite its aesthetically pleasing appearance, in important ways, Celebration is not all that different from other exclusive suburbs.

"You Say You Want a Revolution, Well, You Know, We All Want to Change the World."

—The Beatles

Regardless of the shortcomings and incompleteness of the New Urbanism, the residents of New Urban communities often express great satisfaction with their lives—with biking and hiking trails, with the sense of freedom that comes with the ability of children to walk safely to schools and recreation, and with the sense of community that they report they have found. Homeowners in Celebration, for instance, report that they value community and neighborliness: "You *can* be isolated in Celebration, but unlike in traditional suburbs, you have to work at it."[11]

Overall, the New Urbanism offers a relative few citizens, who desire it, a more aesthetically-pleasing alternative to the conventional suburb. The movement, however, falls short of achieving its goal of offering residents a revival of small-town community life with a respect for true social diversity. The goal of having a community in which residents "live, work, shop, and play in close proximity" is "more theory than reality," especially as New Urbanists have been unable to build at high densities and have failed to counter Americans' automobile-oriented lifestyles.[12] The New Urban communities that have been built fall far short of the ideal vision of compact, socially-balanced, mixed-use, transit-oriented communities. Instead, New Urbanists have succeeded in building only "a slightly reconfigured suburb," an "automobile-oriented subdivision dressed up to look like a small pre-car-centered town."[13]

The practitioners of the New Urbanism have created a number of highly desirable communities. Residents often express great satisfaction with life there. Still, the movement, despite the overstated claims of its enthusiasts, promises no great reshaping of suburbia. While the New Urbanism does offer a more sustainable alternative to the conventional suburb, it is a choice that the great majority of Americans will resist. Rather than revolutionize suburbia, the New Urbanism poses only the smallest of counterweights to continued sprawl.

Notes

1. Alex Marshall, *How Cities Work: Suburbs, Sprawl, and the Roads Not Taken* (Austin, TX; University of Texas Press, 2000), p. xix.

2. For a good review of the guiding principles of The New Urbanism, see Andres Duany, Elizabeth Plater-Zyberk, and Jeff Speck, *Suburban Nation: The Rise of Sprawl and the Decline of the American Dream* (New York: North Point Press, 2000); Peter Katz, *The New Urbanism: Toward an Architecture of Community* (New York: McGraw-Hill, 1994); Congress for The New Urbanism, *Charter of The New Urbanism* (New York: McGraw-Hill, 2000); Calthorpe and Fulton, *The Regional City.*

3. Duany et al, *Suburban Nation,* p. 30.

4. Calthorpe and Fulton, *The Regional City,* pp. 253–265; Janet L. Smith, "HOPE VI and The New Urbanism, Eliminating Low-Income Housing to Make Mixed-income Communities," *Planner's Network* 151 (Spring 2002): 22–25; Sabrina Deitrick and Cliff Ellis, "New Urbanism in the Inner City: A Case Study of Pittsburgh," *Journal of the American Planning Association* 70, 4 (Autumn 2004); 426–442.

5. Michael Bernick and Robert Cervero, *Transit Villages in the 21st Century* (New York: McGraw-Hill, 1997); Peter Newman and Jeffrey Kenworthy, *Sustainability and Cities: Overcoming Automobile Dependence* (Washington, DC: Island Press, 1999).

6. Bruce Podobnik, "The New Urbanism and the Generation of Social Capital: Evidence from Orenco Station," *National Civic Review* 91, 3 (Fall 2002): 245–55. F. Kaid Benfield, Jutka Terris and Nancy Vorsanger, *Solving Sprawl: Models of Smart Growth in Communities across America* (Washington, DC: Island Press, 2001) present Orenco Station as a model "smart growth" community. Also see Thomas H. Sander, "Social Capital and The New Urbanism: Leading a Civic Horse to Water?" *National Civic Review* 91, 3 (Fall 2002): 213–34.

7. Marshall, *How Cities Work,* pp. 8–14.

8. Alexander Garvin, *The American City: What Works, What Doesn't,* 2nd ed. (New York: McGraw-Hill, 2002), pp. 415–416.

9. Susan F. Fainstein, "New Directions in Planning Theory," *Urban Affairs Review* 35(4), (March 2000), p. 464.

10. Marshall, p. 27. For a more detailed and nuanced discussion of life in Celebration, see Douglas Frantz and Catherine Collins, *Celebration, U.S.A.: Living in Disney's Brave New Town* (New York: Owl Books/Henry Holt, 2000), pp. 74–77 and 219–225.

11. Frantz and Collins, *Celebration, U.S.A.,* p. 313; also see pp. 255–56.

12. Garvin, *The American City: What Works, What Doesn't,* pp. 336–337.

13. Marshall, *How Cities Work,* pp. xx and 6. Also see Alex Krieger, "Arguing the Against' Position: The New Urbanism as a Means of Building and Rebuilding Our Cities," in *The Seaside Debates: A Critique of The New Urbanism,* ed. Todd W. Bressi (Rizzoli, 2002), pp. 51–58. For a defense of The New Urbanism that attempts to rebut many of the critiques, see Cliff Ellis, "The New Urbanism: Critiques and Rebuttals," *Journal of Urban Design* 7, 3 (2002): 261–291. For a most useful overview of The New Urbanism movements, the international reach of The New Urbanism, and the potential and limitations inherent in The New Urbanism, see Jill Grant, *Planning the Good Community: The New Urbanisms in Theory and Practice* (London: Routledge, 2006).

Critical Thinking

1. What are the limitations of the New Urbanism? Despite its admirable ideas, why won't the New Urbanism lead to a revolution that reshapes suburbia?

HOPE VI and the New Urbanism

Eliminating Low-Income Housing to Make Mixed-Income Communities

JANET L. SMITH

Chicago's public housing is testimony to a long history of struggle between poor people and politicians. The latest contest is over the Chicago Housing Authority's (CHA) Plan for Transformation, which aims to reduce the existing unit count from 38,000 to 25,000. Fifty-one buildings—most of them high-rise—are slated for demolition. Some developments are being cleared entirely and replaced with new, mixed-income communities.

This public housing "transformation" hinges on a narrowly constructed argument that high-rise, high-density sites are inherently bad. Embracing the rhetoric of new urbanists (NU), transformation plans around the country are promoting mixed-use and mixed-income development at a neighborhood scale. In practice, however, they are resulting in the net loss of low-income housing units.

For the Department of Housing and Urban Development (HUD), the CNU's approach is a means to reduce the concentration of poverty: transforming "the projects" into communities will encourage higher-income working families to live in redeveloped sites. But with all the talk of community building and building new communities, it is still not clear who is to benefit. Preliminary findings from a national study of HOPE VI being completed by the Urban Institute indicate a real disconnect between policy and practice. While policy speaks of creating communities for families, the reality is that many of these redeveloped sites do not house the original families that were displaced. Many families *chose* to live in the private sector with vouchers, but many others had *no choice,* since the development they moved out of offered fewer replacement housing units.

In the transformation of public housing, NU is not categorically the culprit. Rather, the NU principles are used to justify reducing the number of public housing units overall. Instead of dismissing it wholesale, activist planners need to capitalize on the NU climate, particularly the promotion of mixed-income housing, to push for more, not less, affordable public and private housing in all our communities.

Learning from Cabrini Green

Reducing the number of public housing units in order to make redeveloped sites "mixed-income" is an issue in Chicago, where most of the plans call for only one-third of the units to be public housing, with the rest either "affordable" (80–120 percent of area median income (AMI)) or market-rate. At Cabrini Green, one of the city's best known sites, residents fought in court to ensure that those who wanted to stay could be included in the new community that the city envisioned for them. They also fought to get more control over the process to ensure that replacement housing be built first and that demolition happens afterwards, whenever possible. Their view—and the one expressed here—is that while the physical design is important to residents, having enough replacement public housing is essential to the success of housing plans. Otherwise, this "new urbanism" is just another form of displacement of poor people.

While Cabrini Green is a unique case, it offers strategies and principles planners and community activists can employ to ensure that current residents get *mixed in* rather than *out* of these new public housing communities.

Located within walking distance of some of the most expensive real estate in the city, Cabrini Green was the first HOPE VI grant in Chicago. Chicago received a $50 million HOPE VI grant in 1994 to redevelop a portion of the 3,600 unit site. Initially the CHA had made an agreement with the Local Advisory Council (LAC)—the elected leadership for tenants–to demolish 660 units, rebuilding 493 new units of public housing and issuing 167 housing assistance vouchers in place of the balance of the units.

Soon after the plan was approved, the federal government took over the CHA. Two buildings containing 398 units were demolished and no replacement units were provided. A Request For Proposals (RFP) was issued to replace what was going to be torn down. None of the responses fully met the minimum criteria of the RFP in regard to reducing density and providing the appropriate number of replacement units on-site, so the city of Chicago declared all the plans inappropriate. Soon afterward, the City and CHA entered into "private" meetings to compose an alternative strategy, producing the *Near North Redevelopment Plan* and the corresponding Tax Increment Financing (TIF) district. The plan was to demolish 1,300 public housing units and produce 2,300 new units in a larger geographic area (340 acres compared to ten acres in the original proposal). Only 700 units would be public housing, and half of those would be for "working poor." In response to this plan, residents filed a lawsuit against both the city and the CHA on the grounds that the plan was prejudicial to their interests. Residents were outraged because the plan, besides violating the previous development agreement with the LAC, was to demolish more buildings and move more residents permanently off-site. In the spring of 1997, a federal judge stopped CHA from demolishing anything more until this conflict was resolved.

Cabrini Green Tenants Win in Court

While TIFs are controversial—especially in Chicago, where there are more than 110 districts and several new ones proposed—the city's decision to create a TIF significantly expanded the development site. This was an important factor in the ruling on the tenant's lawsuit against the CHA in the summer of 1998, which gave the LAC substantial control over the development process and the outcome of the demolition of the remaining six buildings. The court ordered the CHA to build 895 public housing-eligible units in the *HOPE VI Planning Area,* which was now defined by the boundaries of the TIF and not just the public housing site. Furthermore, demolition could not begin until at least one-third of the replacement units were underway, funds and sites for another 400 units were secured, and proposal(s) were received for rebuilding remaining units on the CHA land. The LAC also negotiated to reduce down to less than forty percent of AMI (about $30,000) the income levels in "affordable housing" units subsidized with Low Income Housing Tax Credits, which made more units available to current public housing residents. The LAC will serve as co-developer of the site, and shall comprise half of the review panel.

While the consent decree was appealed and later revised to reduce resident control from fifty-one percent to fifty percent, the final settlement was still considered a victory by tenants since it both maintained the policy that units had to be built prior to demolition, and gave them substantial, although not sole, control over the redevelopment process. To date, the first phase of development is nearly completed: 350 units have resulted, one-third of which are public housing. Phase two will begin shortly. All stages have been controlled by the LAC and the developer to ensure that the outcomes meet the requirements of the lawsuit. Based on accounts from both partners, residents and the developer appear to be working well together. In addition, a group of residents has been working to convert their building, which is not slated for demolition, to a limited equity co-op.

Transformative Strategies

Clearly, a bigger vision of transformation is needed in the US—one that is not just driven by new urbanist design ideas. We need *transformative strategies.* Similar to the notion of transformative community planning that Marie Kennedy describes in her Planners Network working paper, the goal should be to put real control in the hands of the people we are planning with to help them identify and implement real alternatives. These may or may not include NU design ideas. The NU principles used in public housing plans should be broadened to include the areas outside of public housing. Transformative strategies should include three principles: clear outcomes, expanded space and public control.

Clear Outcomes

An outcomes component to the housing plan, similar to the one negotiated in the Cabrini Green case, will ensure that all residents are provided a unit if they choose to return. It will also help meet future needs for affordable housing. The premise here is that residents generally want to return to the site once it is redeveloped. However, the goal should always be to maximize the number of public housing units to meet current and future demand, even if there are residents who do not choose to return to the neighborhood. While not legally binding, these outcomes can then function as guiding principles for negotiating how, when and where units will be built.

Expanded Space

Expanding the space of public housing means changing the scale of redevelopment to include more than just the original site. This avoids the need to challenge federal limits on how many units can be built back on-site. More importantly, however, it is a means to open up adjacent communities, especially in locations like Cabrini Green, where the surrounding housing development was also income segregated. In this case, however, the income levels of people surrounding Cabrini were well above the city median, and depending on how you drew the boundaries, the neighborhood was already a mixed-income community. Mechanisms to produce affordable housing, whether publicly or privately owned, can be part of the plan. For example, in a development adjacent to Cabrini Green but in the TIF district, the city required a set-aside of eleven percent "affordable" units. While still out of the price range for most (up to 120 percent of AMI), the set-aside is a step in the right direction, and is now being pushed by a citywide coalition. In addition, two strategies should be considered that are not in widespread use but have proven effective: inclusionary zoning, which requires a proportion of a development to be affordable, and linkage programs, which generate funds to produce affordable housing from development exactions.

Public Control

A public control component is critical to ensuring that public housing is first part of the mix and, once built, remains in the public domain and affordable. Many different strategies could be used to keep public investment accessible and affordable to low-income families: land trusts, which keeps the land in the public domain; reciprocal agreements, a method already used in public housing, which requires developers to keep housing affordable for a long period of time; and limited equity cooperatives like the ones being pursued by tenants in Cabrini, which help very low-income tenants become owners and keep property off the speculative market. Public control may also include resident management, which ensures that tenants also control the property, but this should be up to residents to decide.

These strategies aim to empower residents, but not simply by making tenants into property owners. As Bill Peterman describes in his book *Neighborhood Planning and Community-Based Development,* a progressive view of empowerment means giving residents real control. In public housing transformation this means that residents really make decisions about the future of their developments and really have control over the resources needed to implement them. The strategies outlined here aim to reduce the power of private partners in public-private partnerships—the sanctioned means to fund neighborhood revitalization and community development in the US these days. While we work on getting more public funding for affordable housing (e.g., a National Housing Trust Fund), there is an immediate need to re-position the public in these partnerships. We know that efforts by planners to control development do not necessarily discourage private investment. The key is to make known the return on investment and the public's quid pro quo. The assumption should be that high-quality and durable public housing is a good investment. If NU design principles are a means to ensuring public housing development, then we should consider how to capitalize on the movement so that there is more, not less, public housing built in our communities.

While this may appear opportunistic and idealistic, the logic here is that well-designed mixed-income communities are not fundamentally bad. It's the underlying assumptions and processes used to produce them that we should worry about, especially when they are used to reduce housing options for people who already have few. Equally important, however, planners need to look beyond the sites of public housing to produce these new mixed communities. NU principles can be good rules to plan by, but only if adhered to in all forms of development and in all places.

Why is HUD only promoting the mixing of uses and incomes in public housing when it is clearly needed everywhere? There is no reason to stop at the public housing border and every reason to look beyond the public housing sites in central cities to fashion mixed-income communities as the new urbanists propose. Given the spatial patterns created by a long history of segregation by race, ethnicity and income, planners should add a principle to the new urbanist mantra: do not endorse the new urbanist experiment *unless* it is uniformly implemented in all development.

Critical Thinking

1. What were the goals of the HOPE VI program? How did HOPE VI improve public-housing communities?

2. What ideas did HOPE VI borrow from the New Urbanism?

3. Why did many of the residents of Cabrini Green public housing vigorously oppose HOPE VI and the Chicago Housing Authority's plans to build attractive mixed-income developments that would transform a housing project that had gained such notoriety?

JANET L. SMITH is assistant professor in the Urban Planning and Policy Program at the University of Illinois at Chicago.

Regional Coalition-Building and the Inner Suburbs

MYRON ORFIELD

In response to growing social and economic polarization, between 1993 and 1997 Minnesota's Twin Cities jump-started a long-dormant regional debate. In three years, the area reorganized its regional planning council, moving it from a $40-million-a-year coordinating agency to a $600-million-a-year regional governance structure for transit and transportation, sewers, land use, airports, and housing policy. It enacted an important regional affordable-housing bill, strengthened the regional land-use system, and the legislature passed (but the governor vetoed) a major addition to regional tax-base sharing and a measure to elect the Metropolitan Council, a regional planning and operating agency. Energy for regional reform is growing.

In the process of reenergizing regionalism and ranging metropolitan issues on our negotiating table, we have discovered that our problems are not unique and that the suburban monolith, thought to prevent all progress on regional issues, is a myth. Every metropolitan region in the United States faces the same problems. Coalition-building efforts that emphasize the links between core cities and suburbs can bring about reforms to increase equity for an entire region.

Local Metropolitan Subregions

Over generations of urban growth, four distinct types of suburban communities have emerged in the Twin Cities metropolitan area.

The "inner suburbs" are a collection of fully developed working- and middle-class communities just outside the inner city, where 26 percent of the metropolitan population lives. Many of these communities are beginning to feel the effects of socioeconomic changes spreading outward from the city and are ill equipped to handle new problems. Politically, the inner suburbs house a mix of Democrats and Republicans.

Middle-class, and particularly working-class, inner suburbs are less stable than central cities for economic, organizational, and cultural reasons. Older suburbs are often a collection of smaller houses without a significant commercial industrial base and without the central city's amenities, significant police force and social welfare presence.

"Mid-developing suburbs," the low-tax-capacity but developing suburbs beyond the beltways, tend to be extensions of middle- and working-class neighborhoods. These rapidly developing communities, with a property tax base resting mainly on inexpensive single-family homes and apartment buildings, have insufficient resources to support basic public services. The older suburbs and mid-developing suburbs are classic swing districts, leaning toward Democrats on economic issues and Republicans on social issues.

The "commercial high-tax-capacity developing suburbs" in the Twin Cities form the "favored quarter" of the area's south and west. To the east lie the "residential, high-tax capacity developing suburbs," with a broad, rich property tax base and comparatively few socioeconomic needs. The crime rate is low in the south and west, and even lower in the east.

More than half the cities in this area had smaller concentrations of poor children at the end of the decade than at the beginning, possibly as a result of local zoning and metropolitan transportation policies restrictive to poor residents. Over time, households that cannot make it over suburban housing barriers tend to collect in the central cities and the older suburbs. The high-tax capacity suburbs have a median household income almost twice as high as in the central cities, 23 percent higher than in the inner ring, and 10 percent higher than in the mid-developing suburbs. They have about one-third more tax wealth than the other subregions.

Income Polarization and Politics

Underlying this spatial polarization has been the polarization of household income. Throughout the United States in the 1980s, those in the bottom three quintiles of household income lost ground, those in the fourth stayed even, and those in the top fifth saw their household income increase by nearly one-third.

These shifts in income have exacerbated tension between people in the second and third economic quintiles and those on the bottom. In the late 1960s, in older, larger regions of the country, poor people had rolled into these suburbs, fleeing the declining core city. People in the second- and third-quintile groups felt a deep threat to the value of their houses—their main assets—and to their neighborhoods—the center of their world. As residents resisted these incursions, they aligned with more conservative economic and political forces than their economic circumstances would normally indicate. These increasingly conservative, working class inner suburbanites outside of large cities feared for their homes and neighborhoods. Their racism was wrong, but their fear that disorderly metropolitan change would severely hurt their communities was well founded.

Spatial and income polarizations marry in unpredictable and angry politics. In the older, more divided regions of the country, the divide-and-conquer tactics of 1960s politics succeeded in working-class city neighborhoods and older suburbs undergoing social changes. In his book *Middle Class Dreams,* Stan Greenberg writes of the inner suburbs, the land of the second and third quintiles. While central cities have traditionally voted Democratic and white-collar suburbs Republican, many people in the middle groups, who had voted for Kennedy in 1960 and Johnson in 1964, switched to Nixon and the Republicans by 1968. These communities of middle-class whites, raised with the union movement and the New Deal, now had homes and neighborhoods to protect—homes and communities directly in the path of metropolitan decline.

Although this trend continued with the "Reagan revolution" of the 1980s, in 1992, during an economic recession, the middle class supported Bill Clinton and, to some degree, Ross Perot. In Minnesota, the lowest three income quintiles supported Clinton, but in declining numbers as income rose; George Bush's strength lay in the top two quintiles. Perot took 20 percent of the vote of each group. The central cities, inner suburbs, and low-tax-capacity suburbs went Democratic in both statewide and legislative elections; the affluent, high-tax capacity suburbs supported Bush and the Republicans. But in 1994, many middle-income voters throughout the country again turned to the Republican Party, not so much because of the inherent force of the Contract with America—which few voters had even heard of—but perhaps because their economic prospects were not improving.

In the end, spatial polarization and income polarization augment each other. As social and economic polarization spreads throughout the Twin Cities, instability is growing. The intensity of debate on schools and crime is a good indicator of the scope and depth of middle-class anxiety. It is the rapid increase of poor children in local schools, however, that sounds the first warning of imminent middle-class flight.

In another part of suburbia, in their insulated, exclusive neighborhoods, people in the upper quintiles have watched those in the lower and mid-quintiles fighting among themselves. The more they have fought, the more insulated and affluent the top economic group has become. In some ways, the desperate struggle for exclusivity in the affluent suburbs is part and parcel an effort by the upper class to reduce its responsibilities to society in terms of a progressive tax policy. As the privileged have less and less contact with those less fortunate, their attitudes harden. Their intensely exclusive zoning practices may be a last-ditch effort to act through municipal government before opting for private "gated" communities, as the affluent have already done in many older, more polarized regions of the United States—and in the third world.

In light of this polarization of residential areas, the challenges of regionalism are substantial:

- To unite the central cities with the middle- and lower middle-class voters in the declining and low-property tax value suburbs;
- To show them that tax-base sharing lowers their taxes and improves local services, particularly schools; and
- To convince them that fair housing will limit their commitment to poor citizens to manageable regional standards and thereby stabilize residential change in their communities.

For middle-class inner suburban neighborhoods—which have their fair share of the region's poor residents already—regionalism promises to limit their commitment to affordable housing and end overwhelming waves of poor people arriving from the city. Once inner-suburban legislators understand this message, they can become powerfully supportive. For years, however, they have campaigned against the city in elections. At the outset, these inner suburbs are not disposed to believe that an alliance with their previous enemy is either wise or politically expedient.

Coalition Building in the Twin Cities

In the Twin Cities, the coalition built to pass recent fair housing and tax-base sharing bills included suburban leaders, church groups, environmental advocates, 'good government' groups, and concerned citizens. Though each group traditionally had different agendas, the issue of fiscal equity brought them together. Some of the older suburbs supported this legislation because they were overburdened with affordable housing and believed their decline would be more precipitous unless the newer suburbs stepped up to the plate. The churches supported it because of the moral dimension: many higher-income communities—particularly job rich communities—have restrictive zoning laws that keep large classes of people from social and economic opportunity. Environmental advocates supported the legislation because affordable housing gets people closer to jobs and requires less commuting. 'Good government' groups backed the measure for all these reasons, but with less passion than those with a more direct stake in the process.

As the debate continued over three legislative sessions, which heightened public awareness on these issues, a particularly restrictive Twin Cities suburb, Maple Grove, went through convulsions over the siting of an affordable housing project. The scenes on the evening news, much like the early civil rights movement, galvanized the public and local officials in support of a plan to equitably distribute tax burdens and benefits throughout the region. Finally, after the governor vetoed two bills, came the Livable Communities Act of 1995.

The Fair Tax Base Act was designed to redistribute taxes collected from high valued homes in the region. The bill would benefit 83 percent of the area's population. These communities, particularly the property-poor northern suburbs, unified with the central cities to support this measure, and along the way religious and 'good government' groups joined in. The issue was intensely controversial, as the high-property wealth suburbs—about one fourth of the region—strongly opposed the bill. However, self-interest and strong public policy carried the day, and the legislature approved the bill after a lengthy debate. Although it was vetoed in 1995, it signaled the growing strength of the coalition and led to a significantly more equitable school funding formula, and the Minneapolis and Saint Paul school districts are now spending significantly more per student than the suburban averages.

Such issues are difficult and controversial but of mutual concern to inner-cities and suburbs. And efforts to find solutions that will unite communities within the Twin Cities region hold lessons for other regions facing similar circumstances.

Lessons in Coalition Building
Understand the Region's Demographics and Make Maps

Develop the most accurate and comprehensive picture of the region possible. Look for the declining older, low tax-base developing, and favored-quarter suburbs. Understand the local fiscal equity issue and the local barriers to affordable housing. Measure road spending and land use. Finance and conduct regional studies, and seek other regions' studies. Bring in the best scholars from area universities.

Use color maps to show trends. Politicians, newspaper reporters, citizens groups, and other potential allies will not necessarily read reports or speeches, but they will look at color maps, over and over again.

Reach Out and Organize on a Personal Level

Political reform is about ideas, but individuals who organize others bring it about. Political persuasion is about selling an idea to another person or group that has power. Once regional trends are satisfactorily described, some individual or group of people has to reach out, person to person, to make contact with the individuals and groups affected by these trends. Do not announce problems and disparities until after meeting with the groups who will be affected by your work.

Invite broad input from these individuals. Then lay out broad themes and the areas where regional progress is necessary—namely, affordable housing, tax-base sharing, and land-use planning. Talk about the experience of other states. Engage all affected constituencies in crafting legislation. This gives them all ownership and allows for adjustment to the peculiarities of the local terrain they know best—economic, physical, cultural, and political.

Build a Broad, Inclusive Coalition

The coalition should stress two themes: It is in the long-term interest of the entire region to solve the problems of polarization, and it is in the immediate short-term interest of the vast majority of the region. The first argument is important for the long haul; the second gets the ball rolling.

A regional agenda, at the beginning, finds few elected altruistic supporters. The early political support for regional reform in the Twin Cities came entirely from legislators who believed their districts would benefit immediately or soon from part or all of our policy package.

"It's the Older Suburbs, Stupid"

Regional reformers should tape this message to their mirrors: The inner and low-tax-base suburbs are the pivot point in American politics and are the reformers' key political allies. They were instrumental in electing Presidents Nixon, Carter, Reagan, and Clinton and an endless procession of officials in state office. The support of these suburbs alters the political dynamics. When regionalism becomes a suburban issue, it becomes possible. As long as regionalism is portrayed as a conflict between city and suburbs, the debate is over before it starts.

Do not accept early rejection by working-class, inner, older suburbs. These communities have been polarized for over a generation. Residential turnover and the growing impoverishment of their communities, the downturn in the U.S. economy for low-skilled workers, and relentless class- and raced-based political appeals have made many residents callous. Underneath they will soon realize that they need regionalism to have healthy, stable communities. They will come around as they come to see that a better future is possible, their alternatives are limited, cooperation will produce measurable benefits, and they have long-term, trustworthy friends in those who promote regionalism.

Reach into the Central Cities to Make Sure the Message Is Understood

Central cities have a volatile political landscape. Without person-to-person contact in the inner city, the message will be misunderstood. Regionalism, if misperceived, threatens the power base of officials elected by poor, segregated constituencies. In this light, as in the older suburbs, the patterns of regional polarization must be reemphasized and the hopelessness of the present course revealed. Metropolitan reforms must not be presented as alternatives to existing programs competing for resources and power. Instead, they need to be seen as complements that would gradually reduce overwhelming central-city problems to manageable size and provide resources for community redevelopment through metropolitan equity. Fair housing is not an attempt to force poor minority communities to disperse but to allow individuals to choose—whether to remain or seek opportunity, wherever it may be.

Seek the Religious Community

Politicians and arguments appealing to people's self-interest can move the agenda forward in the city and older suburbs, but they will not build a base of understanding of affluent communities, whose determined opposition will slow progress. Churches and other houses of worship and religious organizations can bring a powerful new dimension to the debate—the moral dimension. How moral is it, they will ask, to divide a region into two communities, one prospering and enjoying all the benefits of metropolitan citizenship while the other bears most of its burdens? How moral is it to strand the region's poor people on a melting ice cube of resources at the region's core or to destroy forests and farmland while older cities decline? Churches will broaden the reach of a regional movement. They can provide a legitimacy for its message in distrustful blue-collar suburbs, and understanding and a sense of responsibility and fair play in more affluent ones. Without the churches, the Twin Cities housing bill would not have been signed.

Seek the Philanthropic Community, Established Reform Groups, and Business Leaders

Every day philanthropic organizations face the consequences of regional polarization, and their mission statements are often in line with regional reform. They can be important sources of financing for research and nonprofit activities in support of regional solutions. The League of Women Voters can be helpful, as can the National Civic League and established reform groups. These groups can confer establishment respectability to the regional cause. Many of these groups, by themselves, have been working on regional reform for a generation. Seek their counsel as well as their support. Business leaders, particularly in the central business district and the older suburbs, can also be helpful and influential.

Include Distinct but Compatible Issues and Organizations

In addition to the churches, communities of color have a deep stake in this agenda, as do land use groups and a broad variety of environmental organizations that can reach into affluent suburbia. Women's and senior citizens' organizations, for example, want a variety of housing types in all communities for single mothers and retired people who cannot remain in their homes. These groups also want better transit. Regionalism is a multifaceted gemstone. In the power of its comprehensive solutions, it can show a bright face to many different constituencies to build broad support.

With the Coalition, Seek Media Attention

Using factual information, suburban officials, churches, philanthropists, reform groups, and business leaders, seek out editorial boards, which by necessity must have a broad, far-reaching vision for the region. Reporters who have covered the same political stories over and over will be interested in something new and potentially controversial. They will like the maps, and straightforward news releases without too much theoretical discussion will get the message across.

Prepare for Controversy

Over the years professional regionalists have explained away Minnesota's and Oregon's success with reforms as being the result of people having reached some happy consensus. This is not true. Each reform was a tough battle, and each group of leaders had to build coalitions to weather intense opposition and controversy. This is how any important reform in politics comes about—from labor reform, to civil rights, to the women's movement. Reform never happens effortlessly or overnight. It entails building coalitions, creating power, and engaging in strenuous political struggle.

The agenda sketched here to deal with growing regional instability and disparities will evolve in the negotiation, reformulation, and synthesis that make up the political process. Essential to this discussion is the realization that our metropolitan areas are suffering from a set of problems too massive for an individual city to confront alone—the same problems that have caused the decline and death of some of our largest urban centers. Unless we concentrate on finding new solutions, we can expect no better outcome in the future.

Critical Thinking

1. How does New Regionalism differ from the Old Regionalism that dominated metropolitan reform in the 1960s and 1970s?

2. What is a metropolitan region's "favored quarter" communities?

3. What types of communities in a metropolitan area might find it in their interest to join together in building a coalition to fight for policies that better address their needs?

MYRON ORFIELD is an adjunct professor of law at the University of Minnesota and Minnesota state representative, 612-296-9281. This article has been adapted from *Metropolitics: A Regional Agenda for Community and Stability,* Brookings Institution/Lincoln Institute for Land Policy 1997.

Is Regional Government the Answer?

Fred Siegel

Suburban sprawl, the spread of low-density housing over an ever-expanding landscape, has attracted a growing list of enemies. Environmentalists have long decried the effects of sprawl on the ecosystem; aesthetes have long derided what they saw as "the ugliness and banality of suburbia"; and liberals have intermittently insisted that suburban prosperity has been purchased at the price of inner-city decline and poverty. But only recently has sprawl become the next great issue in American public life. That's because suburbanites themselves are now calling for limits to seemingly inexorable and frenetic development.

Slow-growth movements are a response to both the cyclical swings of the economy and the secular trend of dispersal. Each of the great postwar booms have, at their cyclical peak, produced calls for restraint. These sentiments have gained a wider hearing as each new upturn of the economy has produced an ever widening wave of exurban growth. A record 96 months of peacetime economic expansion has produced the strongest slow-growth movement to date. In 1998, anti-sprawl environmentalists and "not-in-my-backyard" slow-growth suburbanites joined forces across the nation to pass ballot measures restricting exurban growth.

Undoubtedly, the loss of land and the environmental degradation produced by sprawl are serious problems that demand public attention. But sprawl also brings enormous benefits as well as considerable costs. It is, in part, an expression of the new high-tech economy whose campus-like office parks on the periphery of urban areas have driven the economic boom of the 1990s. And it's sprawl that has sustained the record rise in home ownership. Sprawl is not some malignancy to be summarily excised but, rather, part and parcel of prosperity. Dealing with its ill effects requires both an understanding of the new landscape of the American economy and a willingness to make subtle trade-offs. We must learn to curb its worst effects without reducing the wealth and freedom that permit sprawl to develop.

Rising incomes and employment, combined with declining interest rates, have allowed a record number of people, including minority and immigrant families, to purchase homes for the first time. Home ownership among blacks, which is increasingly suburban, has risen at more than three times the white rate; a record 45 percent of African Americans

owned their own homes in 1998. Nationally, an unprecedented 67 percent of Americans are homeowners.

Sprawl is part of the price we're paying for something novel in human history—the creation of a mass upper middle class. Net household worth has been increasing at the unparalleled annual rate of 10 percent since 1994, so that while in 1970, only 3.2 percent of households had an annual income of $100,000 (in today's dollars), by 1996, 8.2 percent of American households could boast a six-figure annual income. The new prosperity is reflected in the size of new homes, many of whose owners no doubt decry the arrival of still more "McMansions" and new residents, clogging the roads and schools of the latest subdivisions. In the midst of the 1980's boom, homebuilders didn't have a category for mass-produced houses of more than 3,000 square feet: By 1996, one out of every seven new homes built was larger than 3,000 square feet.

Today's Tenement Trail

Sprawl also reflects upward mobility for the aspiring lower-middle class. Nearly a half-century ago, Samuel Lubell dedicated *The Future of American Politics* to the memory of his mother, "who pioneered on the urban frontier." Lubell described a process parallel to the settling of the West, in which families on "the Old Tenement Trail" were continually on the move in search of a better life. In the cities, they abandoned crowded tenements on New York's Lower East Side for better housing in the South Bronx, and from there, went to the "West Bronx, crossing that Great Social Divide—the Grand Concourse—beyond which rolled true middle-class country where janitors were called superintendents."

Today's "tenement trail" takes aspiring working- and lower-middle class Americans to quite different areas. Kendall, Florida, 20 miles southeast of Miami, is every environmentalist's nightmare image of sprawl, a giant grid carved out of the muck of swamp land that encroaches on the Everglades. Stripmalls and mega-stores abound for mile after mile, as do the area's signature giant auto lots. Yet Kendall also represents a late-twentieth-century version of the Old Tenement Trail. Kendall, notes the *New Republic*'s Charles Lane, is "the Queens of the late twentieth century," a place where immigrants are buying into America. Carved out of the palmetto wilderness, its population exploded from roughly 20,000 in 1970 to 300,000 today. Agricultural in the 1960s, and a hip place for young whites in the 1970s, Kendall grew increasingly Hispanic in the 1980s, as Cubans, Nicaraguans, and others who arrived with very little worked their way up. Today, it's half Hispanic and a remarkable example of integration. In most of Kendall, notes University of Miami geographer Peter Muller, "You can't point to a white or Latino block because the populations are so intermixed."

Virginia Postrel, the editor of *Reason,* argues that the slow-growth movement is animated by left-wing planners' hostility to suburbia. Others mock slow-growthers as elitists, as in the following quip:

Q: What's the difference between an environmentalist and a developer?

A: The environmentalist already has his house in the mountains.

But, in the 1990s, slow-growth sentiment has been taking hold in middle- and working-class suburbs like Kendall, as development turns into overdevelopment and traffic congestion becomes a daily problem.

Regional Government

One oft-proposed answer to sprawl has been larger regional governments that will exercise a monopoly on land-use decisions. Underlying this solution is the theory—no doubt correct—that sprawl is produced when individuals and townships seek to maximize their own advantage without regard for the good of the whole community. Regionalism, however, is stronger in logic than in practice. For example, the people of Kendall, rather than embracing regionalism, are looking to slow down growth by *seceding* from their regional government. Upon examination, we begin to see some of the problems with regional government.

Kendall is part of Metro-Dade, the oldest major regional government, created in 1957. The largest of its 29 municipalities, Miami, the fourth poorest city in the United States, has 350,000 people; the total population of Metro-Dade is 2 million, 1.1 million of whom live in unincorporated areas. In Metro-Dade, antisprawl and antiregional government sentiments merge. Despite county-imposed growth boundaries, residents have complained bitterly of overdevelopment. The county commissioners—many of whom have been convicted of, or charged with, corruption—have been highly receptive to the developers who are among their largest campaign contributors. As one south Florida resident said of the developers, "It's a lot cheaper to be able to buy just one government." The south Florida secessionists want to return zoning to local control where developers' clout is less likely to overwhelm neighborhood interests.

When Jane Jacobs wrote, in *The Death and Life of Great American Cities,* that "the voters sensibly decline to federate into a system where bigness means local helplessness, ruthless oversimplified planning and administrative chaos," she could have been writing about south Florida. What's striking about Metro-Dade is that it has delivered neither efficiency nor equity nor effective planning while squelching local self-determination.

The fight over Metro-Dade echoes the conflicts of an earlier era. Historically, the fight over regional versus local government was an important, if intermittent, issue for many cities from 1910 to 1970. From about 1850 to 1910, according to urban historian Jon Teaford, suburbanites were eager to be absorbed by cities whose wealth enabled them to build the water, sewage, and road systems they couldn't construct on their own. "The central city," he explains, "provided superior service at a lower cost." But, in the 1920s, well before race became a central issue, suburbanites, who had increasingly sorted themselves out by ethnicity and class, began to use special-service districts and innovative financial methods to provide their own infrastructure and turned away from unification. Suburbanites also denounced consolidation as an invitation to big-city, and often Catholic, "boss rule" and as a threat to "self-government."

In the 1960s, as black politicians began to win influence over big-city governments, they also joined the anticonsolidation chorus. At the same time, county government, once a sleepy extension of rural rule, was modernized, and county executives essentially became the mayors of full-service governments administering what were, in effect, dispersed cities. But they were mayors with a difference. Their constituents often wanted a balance between commercial development, which constrained the rise of taxes, and the suburban ideal of family-friendly semirural living. When development seemed too intrusive, suburban voters in the 1980s, and again in the 1990s, have pushed a slow-growth agenda.

The New Regionalism

In the 1990s, regionalism has been revived as an effort to link the problem of sprawl with the problem of inner-city poverty. Assuming that "flight creates blight," regionalists propose to recapture the revenue of those who have fled the cities and force growth back into older areas by creating regional or metropolitan-area governments with control over land use and taxation.

The new regionalism owes a great deal to a group of circuit-riding reformers. Inspired by the arguments of scholars like Anthony Downs, one of the authors of the Kerner Commission report, and sociologist William Julius Wilson of Harvard, as well as the example of Portland, Oregon's metro-wide government, these itinerant preachers have traveled to hundreds of cities to spread the gospel of regional cooperation. The three most prominent new regionalists—columnist

Neil Peirce, former Albuquerque mayor David Rusk, and Minnesota state representative Myron Orfield—have developed a series of distinct, but overlapping, arguments for why cities can't help themselves, and why regional solutions are necessary.

Peirce, in his book *Citistates,* plausibly insists that regions are the real units of competition in the global economy, so that there is a metro-wide imperative to revive the central city, lest the entire area be undermined. Less plausibly, Orfield in *Metropolitics* argues that what he calls "the favored quarter" of fast-growing suburbs on the periphery of the metro area have prospered at the expense of both the central city and the inner-ring suburbs. In order [for] both to revive the central city and save the inner suburbs from decline, Orfield proposes that these two areas join forces, redistributing money from the "favored quarter" to the older areas. Rusk argues, in *Baltimore Unbound,* that older cities, unable to annex the fast growing suburbs, are doomed to further decline. He insists that only "flexible cities"—that is, cities capable of expanding geographically and capturing the wealth of the suburbs—can truly deal with inner-city black poverty. Regionalism, writes Rusk, is "the new civil rights movement."

There are differences among them. Orfield and, to a lesser degree, Rusk operate on a zero-sum model in which gain for the suburbs comes directly at the expense of the central city. Peirce is less radical, proposing regional cooperation as the means to a win-win situation for both city and the surrounding region. But they all share a desire to disperse poverty across the region and, more importantly, recentralize economic growth in the already built-up areas. The latter goal is consistent with both the environmental thrust of the antisprawl movement and the push for regional government. In a speech to a Kansas City civic organization, Rusk laid out the central assumption of the new regionalism. "The greater the fragmentation of governments," he asserted, "the greater the fragmentation of society by race and economic class." Fewer governments, argue the new regionalists, will yield a number of benefits, including better opportunities for regional cooperation, more money for cash-strapped central cities, less racial inequality, less sprawl, and greater economic growth. However, all of these propositions are questionable.

Better Policies, Not Fewer Governments

Consider Baltimore and Philadelphia, cities that the regionalists have studied thoroughly. According to the 1998 *Greater Baltimore State of the Region* report, Philadelphia has 877 units of local government (including school boards)—or 17.8 per 100,000 people. Baltimore has only six government units of any consequence in Baltimore City and the five surrounding counties—or 2.8 per 100,000 people. Greater Baltimore has fewer government units than any other major metro area in the United States. As a political analyst told me: "Get six people in a room, and you have the government of 2,200 square miles, because the county execs have very strong powers." We might expect considerable regional cooperation in Baltimore, but not in Philadelphia. Regionalism has made no headway in either city, however. The failure has little to do with the number of governments and a great deal to do with failed policy choices in both cities.

Rusk does not mention the many failings of Baltimore's city government. He refers to the current mayor, Kurt Schmoke, just once and only to say that Baltimore has had "excellent political leadership." In Rusk's view, Baltimore is "programmed to fail" because of factors entirely beyond its control, namely, the inability to annex its successful suburbs. In the ahistorical world of the regionalist (and here, Peirce is a partial exception), people are always pulled from the city by structural forces but never pushed from the city by bad policies.

Baltimore is not as well financed as the District of Columbia, which ruined itself despite a surfeit of money. But Baltimore, a favorite political son of both Annapolis and Washington, has been blessed with abundant financial support. Over the past decade, Schmoke has increased spending on education and health by over a half-billion dollars. He has also added 200 police officers and spent $60 million more for police over the last four years. "His greatest skill," notes the *Baltimore Sun,* "has been his ability to attract more federal and state aid while subsidies diminished elsewhere." But, notwithstanding these expenditures, middle-class families continue to flee the city at the rate of 1,000 per month, helping to produce the sprawl environmentalists decry.

Little in Baltimore works well. The schools have been taken over by the state, while the Housing Authority is mired in perpetual scandal and corruption. Baltimore is one of the few cities where crime hasn't gone down. That's because Schmoke has insisted, contrary to the experiences of New York and other cities, that drug-related crime could not be reduced until drug use was controlled through treatment. The upshot is that New York, with eight times more people than Baltimore, has only twice as many murders. Baltimore also leads the country in sexually transmitted diseases. These diseases have flourished among the city's drug users partly owing to Schmoke's de facto decriminalization of drugs. According to the Centers for Disease Control and Prevention (CDC), Baltimore has a syphilis rate 18 times the national average, 3 or 4 times as high as areas where the STD epidemic is most concentrated.

Flexible Cities

Rusk attributes extraordinary qualities to flexible cities. He says that they are able to both reduce inequality, curb sprawl, and maintain vital downtowns. Rusk was the mayor of

Albuquerque, a flexible city that annexed a vast area, even as its downtown essentially died. The reduced inequality he speaks of is largely a statistical artifact. If New York were to annex Scarsdale, East New York's average income would rise without having any effect on the lives of the people who live there. As for sprawl, flexible cities like Phoenix and Houston are hardly models.

A recent article for *Urban Affairs Review,* by Subhrajit Guhathakurta and Michele Wichert, showed that within the elastic city of Phoenix, inner-city residents poorer than their outer-ring neighbors are subsidizing the building of new developments on the fringes of the metropolis. While sprawl is correlated with downtown decline in Albuquerque, in Phoenix it's connected with what *Fortune* described as "the remarkable rebound of downtown Phoenix, which has become a chic after-dark destination as well as a residential hot spot." There seems to be no automatic connection between regionalism and downtown revival.

Orfield's *Metropolitics* provides another version of an over-determined structuralist argument. According to him, the favored quarter is sucking the inner city dry, and, as a result, central-city blight will inevitably engulf the older first-ring suburbs as well. He is right to see strong pressures on the inner-ring suburbs, stemming from an aging housing stock and population as well as an influx of inner-city poor. But it is how the inner-ring suburbs respond to these pressures that will affect their fate.

When Coleman Young was mayor of Detroit, large sections of the city returned to prairie. But the inner-ring suburbs have done fairly well precisely by not imitating Detroit's practice of providing poor services at premium prices. "Much like the new edge suburbs," explains the *Detroit News,* "older suburbs that follow the proven formula of promoting good schools, public safety and well-kept housing attract new investment." Suburban Mayor Michael Guido sees his city's well developed infrastructure as an asset, which has already been bought and paid for. "Now," says Mayor Guido, "it's a matter of maintenance . . . and we offer a sense of history and a sense of community. That's really important to people, to have a sense of belonging to a whole community rather than a subdivision."

Suburb Power

City-suburban relations are not fixed; they are various depending on the policies both follow. Some suburbs compete with the central city for business. In south Florida, Coral Gables more than holds its own with Miami as a site for business headquarters. Southfield, just outside Detroit, and Clayton, just outside St. Louis, blossomed in the wake of the 1960s' urban riots and now compete with their downtowns. Aurora, with a population of more than 160,000 and to the east of Denver, sees itself as a competitor, and it sees regional efforts at growth management as a means by which the downtown Denver elite can ward off competition.

Suburban growth can also help the central city. In the Philadelphia area, economic growth and new work come largely from the Route 202 high-tech corridor in Chester County, west of the city. While the city has lost 57,000 jobs, even in the midst of national economic prosperity, the fast growing Route 202 companies have been an important source of downtown legal and accounting jobs. At the same time, the suburbs are creating jobs for residents that the central city cannot produce, so that 20 percent of city residents commute to the suburbs while 15 percent of people who live in the suburbs commute to Philadelphia.

The "new regionalists" assume that the prosperity of the edge cities is a function of inner-city decline. But, in many cities, it is more nearly the case that suburban booms are part of what's keeping the central-city economy alive. It is the edge cities that have taken up the time-honored urban task of creating new work.

According to *INC* magazine, the 500 fastest growing small companies are all located in suburbs and exurbs. This is because local governments there are very responsive to the needs of start-up companies. These high-tech hotbeds, dubbed "nerdistans" by Joel Kotkin, are composed of networks of companies that are sometimes partners, sometimes competitors. They provide a pool of seasoned talent for start-ups, where engineers and techies who prefer the orderly, outdoor life of suburbia to the crowds and disorder of the city can move from project to project. Henry Nicholas, CEO of Broadcom, a communications-chip and cable-modem maker, explained why he reluctantly moved to Irvine: "It's hard to relocate techies to LA. It's the congestion, the expensive housing—and there's a certain stigma to it."

Imagine what the United States would be like if the Bay Area had followed the New York model. In 1898, New York created the first regional government when it consolidated all the areas of the New York harbor—Manhattan, Brooklyn, Queens, the Bronx, and Staten Island—into the then-largest city in the world. The consolidation has worked splendidly for Manhattan, which thrives as a capital of high-end financial and legal services. But over time, the Manhattan-centric economy based on high taxes, heavy social spending, and extensive economic regulation destroyed Brooklyn's once vital shipping and manufacturing economy.

In 1912, San Francisco, the Manhattan of Northern California, proposed to create a unified regional government by incorporating Oakland in the East Bay and San Jose in the South. The plan for a Greater San Francisco was modeled on Greater New York and called for the creation of self-governing boroughs within an enlarged city and county of San Francisco. East Bay opposition defeated the San Francisco expansion in the legislature, and later attempts at consolidation in 1917, 1923, and 1928 also failed. But had San Francisco with its traditions of high taxation and heavy regulation succeeded, Silicon Valley might never have become one of the engines of the American economy.

Similarly, it's no accident that the Massachusetts Route 128 high-tech corridor is located outside of the boundaries of Boston, even as it enriches the central city.

The Portland Model

The complex and often ironic history of existing regional governments has been obscured by the bright light of hope emanating from Portland. It seems that in every generation one city is said to have perfected the magic elixir for revival. In the 1950s, it was Philadelphia; today, it's Portland. In recent years, hundreds of city officials have traveled to Portland to study its metropolitan government, comprehensive environmental planning, and the urban-growth boundary that has been credited with Portland's revival and success.

While there are important lessons to be learned from Portland, very little of its success to date can be directly attributed to the growth boundary, which was introduced too recently and with boundaries so capacious as not yet to have had much effect. Thirty-five percent of the land within the boundary was vacant when it was imposed in 1979. And, at the same time, fast growing Clark County, just north of Portland but not part of the urban-growth boundary, has provided an escape valve for potential housing pressures. The upshot, notes demographer Wendell Cox, is that even with the growth boundary, Portland still remains a relatively low-density area with fewer people per square mile than San Diego, San Jose, or Sacramento.

Portland has also been run with honesty and efficiency, unlike Metro-Dade. Blessed with great natural resources, Portland—sometimes dubbed "Silicon forest," because chipmakers are drawn to its vast quantities of cheap clean water—has conserved its man-made as well as natural resources. A city with more cast-iron buildings than any place outside of Manhattan, it has been a leader in historic preservation. Time and again, Portland's leadership has made the right choices. It was one of the first cities to reconnect its downtown with the riverfront. Portland never built a circumferential freeway. And, in the 1970s, under the leadership of mayor Neil Goldschmidt, the city vetoed a number of proposed highway projects that would have threatened the downtown.

In 1978, Portland voters, in conjunction with the state government, created the first directly elected metropolitan government with the power to manage growth over three counties. Portland metro government has banned big-box retailers, like Walmart and Price Club, on the grounds that they demand too much space and encourage too much driving. This is certainly an interesting experiment well worth watching, but should other cities emulate Portland's land-management model? It's too soon to say.

Good government is always important. But aside from that, it's hard to draw any general lessons from the Portland experience. The growth boundaries may or may not work, and

there's certainly no reason to think that playing with political boundaries will bring good government to Baltimore.

Living with Sprawl

What then is to be done? First, we can accept the consensus that has developed around preserving open space, despite some contradictory effects. The greenbelts around London, Portland, and Baltimore County pushed some development back toward the city and encouraged further sprawl as growth leapfrogged the open space. The push to preserve open space is only likely to grow stronger as continued growth generates both more congestion and more wealth, which can be used to buy up open land.

Secondly, we can create what Peter Salins, writing in *The Public Interest,*[1] described as a "level playing field" between the central cities and the suburbs. This can be done by ending exurban growth subsidies for both transportation as well as new water and sewer lines. These measures might further encourage the revival of interest in old fashioned Main Street living, which is already attracting a new niche of home buyers. State and local governments can also repeal the land-use and zoning regulations that discourage mixed-use development of the sort that produces a clustering of housing around Main Street and unsubsidized low-cost housing in the apartments above the streets' shops.

Because of our strong traditions of local self-government, regionalism has been described as an unnatural act among consenting jurisdictions. But regional cooperation needn't mean the heavy hand of all-encompassing regional government. There are some modest, but promising, experiments already under way in regional revenue sharing whose effects should be carefully evaluated. Allegheny County, which includes Pittsburgh, has created a Regional Asset District that uses a 1 percent sales tax increase to support cultural institutions and reduce other taxes. The Twin Cities have put money derived from the increase in assessed value of commercial and industrial properties into a pot to aid fiscally weaker municipalities. Kansas and Missouri created a cultural district that levies a small increase in the sales tax across the region. The money is being used to rehabilitate the area's most treasured architectural landmark, Kansas City's Union Station.

Cities and suburbs do have some shared interests, as in the growing practice of reverse commuting which links inner-city residents looking to get off welfare with fast growing suburban areas hampered by a shortage of labor. Regionalism can curb sprawl and integrate and sustain central-city populations if it reforms the misguided policies and politics that have sent the black and white middle class streaming out of cities like Baltimore, Washington, and Philadelphia. Regional co-operation between the sprawling high-tech suburbs and the central cities could modernize cities that are in danger of being left further behind by the digital economy. In that vein, the District of Columbia's Mayor Anthony Williams has seized on the importance of connecting his welfare population with the fast growing areas of Fairfax County in Northern Virginia. The aim of focused regional policies, argues former HUD Undersecretary Marc Weiss, should be economic, not political, integration.

Sprawl isn't some malignancy that can be surgically removed. It's been part and parcel of healthy growth, and curbing it involves difficult tradeoffs best worked out locally. Sprawl and the movement against sprawl are now a permanent part of the landscape. The future is summed up in a quip attributed to former Oregon Governor Tom McCall, who was instrumental in creating Portland's growth boundary. "Oregonians," he said, "are against two things, sprawl and density."

Note

1. "Cities, Suburbs, and the Urban Crisis," *The Public Interest,* No. 113 (Fall 1993).

Critical Thinking

1. Why do most Americans continue to resist the idea of regional government and even extensive New Regional collaboration?

2. In what ways can the establishing of strong regional institutions be considered less than desirable?

3. What is the Portland Model? What actions did Portland take in its effort to contain sprawl and promote core city revitalization?

From *The Public Interest* by Fred Siegel, Fall 1999, pp. 85–98.

UNIT 8

Toward Sustainable Cities and Suburbs?

Unit Selections

Learning Outcomes

After reading this unit, you should be able to:

- Explain what is meant by "sustainability" and why urban and suburban development in the United States is often viewed as unsustainable.

- Propose effective measures that would reduce the destructiveness of wildfires, recognizing the political difficulty of getting some of the measures passed.

- Identify the various "hidden" ways by which the United States encourages automobile use and suburban development, especially when contrasted to the policies of European nations that seek to reduce gasoline consumption and contain urban sprawl.

- Propose a reasonable plan for reducing highway congestion.

- Explain how London's system of congestion pricing works and is enforced.

- Assess the various arguments for and against a system of congestion pricing that would impose a steep fee on an automobile that enters certain parts of a city during peak hours.

Student Website

www.mhhe.com/cls

Internet References

The Brookings Institution: Transportation
   www.brookings.edu/topics/transportation.aspx
Green Cities
   http://greencities.com
Our Green Cities, featuring Dr. Kent Portney, Tufts University
   http://ourgreencities.com
Resources For the Future (RFF): Transportation and Urban Land
   www.rff.org/Focus_Areas/Pages/Transportation_and_Urban_Land.aspx
Sierra Club
   www.sierraclub.org/sprawl
Smart Growth America
   http://smartgrowthamerica.org
Sprawl & Growth
   www.plannersweb.com/articles/sprawl-articles.html
Sustainable Cities
   http://sustainablecities.net

Rising gasoline and energy prices have only served to heighten the prominence that cities and suburbs are giving to questions of **sustainability:** Are patterns of urban and suburban development ecologically sound? Can urban living patterns be sustained over time? Hundreds of cities have already enacted ordinances promoting **(LEED Leadership in Energy and Environmental Design) standards** in building construction, practices that conserve energy and water, minimize runoff and ground water contamination, and create incentives for the re-use of recycled and older building materials.

But questions of urban sustainability go beyond matters of energy consumption in new construction. Mike Davis (Article 39, "Firebugs: Build It in California's Foothills, and It Will Burn") points to the ecological blindness of building—and rebuilding—points out that developers and home buyers have often been blind to the natural ecology, with the results that houses in California and other states have been built in virtual **fire zones,** areas where weather conditions produce perpetual droughts, almost guaranteeing the repeat occurrence of devastating fires. Davis argues against the construction of new homes in such ecologically hostile areas and that government insurance programs be changed to end the hidden subsidies that promote such ecologically unwise construction. Developers and home owners in such vulnerable areas must also pursue more fire-resistant construction, for instance, sacrificing leafy green foliage for improved safety. Local authorities must also ensure that the roads leading to newly developed areas are wide enough to allow access by fire trucks.

There are alternatives to the American-style, automobile-dominated urban development. Freiburg, Germany, (Article 40, "New German Community Models Car-Free Living") has created a pedestrian- and mass-transit-oriented living community where automobiles are largely unwanted. Parking is limited, ride-sharers are given free transit passes, and biking is promoted by an extensive network of safe cycling paths. In cities in Germany and throughout Europe, **car-sharing programs** make automobiles available to persons who value city living and who require a car only for weekend shopping trips and the occasional escape to the countryside. Such Zip-Car and car-sharing arrangements are just beginning to emerge in San Francisco and the Bay Area, where some residents find that they only require a car on infrequent occasions.

Anthony Downs (Article 41, "Traffic: Why It's Getting Worse, What Government Can Do") applies the perspective of an economist to show why reducing urban traffic is not as simple as it sometimes appears. When a government builds roads and undertakes other measures to alleviate traffic congestion, traffic flow improves, but only for a short time. Other commuters soon find it convenient to use the road. In a short while, traffic fills the road, and drivers once again sit in traffic jams. Downs seeks to identify the various tools that government can use to limit, but not eliminate, urban traffic problems.

London, Stockholm, and a number of European and Asian cities have resorted to a system of **congestion pricing** to reduce traffic overcrowding and maintain a more healthy and pleasant central city. Under a system of congestion pricing, drivers pay a steep fee to bring their cars into the busiest parts of the city. The fee can vary with the time of day and the day of the week to reduce traffic at peak hours. New computerized camera

© Photodisc / Getty Images

and digital technology makes it relatively easy to detect and bill drivers who bring cars into the city (and heavily penalize owners who fail to pay the daily entrance fee). The goal of congestion pricing is really very simple; the high fees seek to reduce the flow of automobiles, returning city centers to the people who live, work, and shop there.

Many businesses resist the imposition of fees, fearing that such charges will scare off customers or make it difficult for them to attract good workers from the suburbs (Article 42, "Is Congestion Pricing Ready for Prime Time?"). But the advocates of congestion pricing respond that the centers of London and Stockholm have thrived economically despite the imposition of commuting charges. Still, when New York Mayor Michael Bloomberg sought to bring the system of congestion pricing to his city, the New York State legislature refused to allow the city to do so.

Various governmental policies in the United States serve to promote the purchase of large homes and sprawled patterns of development (a point that Article 49, "Are Europe's Cities Better?," explores further). A much different set of governmental policies can promote more sustainable patterns of development.

155

Firebugs: Build It in California's Foothills, and It Will Burn

MIKE DAVIS

Following last autumn's disastrous wildfires in Southern California, Governor Pete Wilson warned of "an army of arsonists lurking in our foothills." The governor was right. The arsonists are the developers and homeowners who built in a tinderbox, and the policymakers who allowed them to do so.

Southern California is a fire ecology in exactly the same sense that it is a land of sunshine. Its natural ecosystems—coastal sage, oak savanna, and chaparral—have coevolved with wildfire. Periodic burning is necessary to recycle nutrients and germinate seeds.

The indigenous Californians were skilled fire-farmers. They used the firestick to hunt rabbits, cultivate edible grasses, increase browse for deer, thin mistletoe from oaks, and produce better stalks for basketry. Their careful annual burnings usually prevented fire catastrophe by limiting the accumulation of fuel.

But aboriginal ecologists also understood that some areas are spectacularly prone to regular conflagration. What is now Los Angeles, for example, they called "Valley of the Smokes." Malibu Canyon is a huge bellows that seasonally fans hot, dry Santa Ana winds to near-hurricane velocities. Major fires here are frequent (five since 1930) and, as the board of inquiry into the disastrous 1970 Malibu blaze acknowledged, "impossible to control."

Modern Southern California, however, built on the belief that even the most elemental forces can be mastered, refuses to concede anything to the laws of nature. Yet as Stephen Pyne emphasizes in his magisterial pyrohistory, *Fire in America* (1982), Southern California's deadly foothill firestorms of the 20th century are, in fact, the ironic consequence of massive expenditure on fire suppression.

In a famous study, geographer Richard Minnich once compared the fire histories of eastern San Diego County and adjacent Baja California. Hundreds of millions of dollars have been spent on fire suppression in San Diego's increasingly urbanized backcountry, while a natural fire-cycle has been tolerated in Baja's wild hill areas. As a result, only San Diego County has experienced out-of-control firestorms.

Prescriptive burning (after the aboriginal model) has been practiced successfully in local national forests for decades. It is precluded in most Southern California foothills by the sheer density of housing and the threat of lawsuits from powerful homeowners' associations. They are the principal political constituency for the continuation of costly and quixotic efforts at "total fire suppression."

Since the end of World War II, at least 50,000 high-priced homes have been constructed in Southland foothills and mountains. More than communion with nature, these homes represent—as design critic Reyner Banham recognized—a search for absolute "thickets of privacy" outside the fabric of common citizenship and urban life. Hillside homebuilding, in these cases, has despoiled the natural heritage of the majority for the sake of an affluent minority. The beautiful coastal-sage and canyon-riparian ecosystems of the Santa Monica Mountains have now been supplanted by castles and "guard-gate prestige." Elsewhere in Southern California, tens of thousands of acres of oak and walnut woodland have been destroyed by bulldozers to make room for similar posh developments.

Despite a season of horrifying firestorms, dozens of new hillside tracts remain under construction. In the foothills above Monrovia, for example, several hundred venerable oak trees have been cut down for the sake of overscaled (and combustible) faux chateaux. In Altadena a favorite glen is being transformed into a "total-security" gated suburb complete with its own private school.

Instead of protecting "significant ecological areas" as required by law, county planning commissions in Southern California have historically been the malleable tools of hillside developers. Furthermore, studies have shown that property taxes on remote foothill homes are seldom sufficient to pay for the ordinary public services they require. Society as a whole is conscripted to carry the enormous costs of defending hillside developments from inevitable natural hazards. Over the last half-century, several billion dollars of general revenue have been expended on flood-control and fire fighting efforts focused specifically on elite foothill society.

There has been no comparable investment in the fire, toxic, or earthquake safety of the inner city. Instead, we tolerate two systems of hazard prevention, separate and unequal. The Los Angeles Times recently exposed the scandal of unenforced fire laws in midtown MacArthur Park neighborhoods where dozens have died in tenement fires—many more, after all, than tragically lost their lives in this fall's firestorms.

But these underlying ecological and social-justice issues seldom surface in public debate about the wildfire problem. Following the lead of Governor Wilson, conservative politicians instead treat fire ecology as a criminal conspiracy of arsonists and environmentalists. Thus Representative David Dreier (R-Calif.) has introduced a bill that would impose the federal death penalty on arsonists, while his colleague Ken Calvert (R-Calif.) wants to radically amend the Endangered Species Act, which he blames for the incineration of several dozen homes in Riverside County.

According to Calvert and his supporters in the powerful Riverside Building Industry Association, federal regulations designed to protect the habitat of the Stephens kangaroo rat prevented homeowners from clearing tall brush. In fact, the U.S. Fish and Wildlife Service encourages the mowing of grasses surrounding homes for fire safety; the problem is that homeowners find mowing too troublesome, preferring simply to rototill their ecosystem under.

Similarly, the tiny California gnatcatcher has been indicted for the Laguna Hills firestorm (in which 15 percent of the total remaining gnatcatcher population perished), while environmentalists have been characterized as "arson's fifth column" on Orange County talk radio. Such "green-baiting" is a useful diversion from any consideration of the social costs of hillside development. It is also the opening salvo in a major political offensive to unleash further pyromanic suburbanization. Local governments are now under tremendous pressure from developers to "clear a firebreak through cumbersome environmental regulations." Taxpayers are being asked to finance expensive fleets of water-scooping aircraft—the latest in a long line of supposed "technological fixes" for California wildfire—to protect new and rebuilt hillside homes.

It won't work. Unless the rest of the state is paved (90 percent of California's coastal sage has already been lost try to suppress all fires), the worse the inevitable infernos will be. At a minimum, the latest fire season dramatically demonstrates the need for an immediate moratorium on further hillside development. "Fire zoning" should be established to ensure that foothill homeowners pay a fairer share of the costs of protecting their own homes. Land-use restrictions in defense of endangered ecosystems should be reinforced, not deregulated.

Finally, environmentalists need to forge a more explicit common cause with inner-city residents. We should lobby for equal enforcement of the fire code in every part of the community, with harsh sanctions against criminally negligent landlords. The loss of human life and property to natural disasters is tragic wherever it happens, but our sympathy for the victims should not extend to letting them play with fire.

Critical Thinking

1. According to Mike Davis, why have wildfires in California been so destructive and costly?
2. Why have governmental authorities in California failed to fully enforce laws that would protect fragile ecological areas?

MIKE DAVIS is the author of *City of Quartz: Excavating the Future of Los Angeles* (London: Routledge, Chapman & Hill, 1990).

From *Sierra*, vol. 79, No. 2, March/April 1994. Copyright © 1994 by Mike R. Davis. Reprinted by permission of the author.

New German Community Models Car-Free Living

Isabelle de Pommereau

It's pickup time at the Vauban kindergarten here at the edge of the Black Forest, but there's not a single minivan waiting for the kids. Instead, a convoy of helmet-donning moms—bicycle trailers in tow—pedal up to the entrance.

Welcome to Germany's best-known environmentally friendly neighborhood and a successful experiment in green urban living. The Vauban development—2,000 new homes on a former military base 10 minutes by bike from the heart of Freiburg—has put into practice many ideas that were once dismissed as eco-fantasy but which are now moving to the center of public policy.

With gas prices well above $6 per gallon across much of the continent, Vauban is striking a chord in Western Europe as communities encourage people to be less car-dependent. Just this week, Paris unveiled a new electric tram in a bid to reduce urban pollution and traffic congestion.

"Vauban is clearly an offer for families with kids to live without cars," says Jan Scheurer, an Australian researcher who has studied the Vauban model extensively. "It was meant to counter urban sprawl—an offer for families not to move out to the suburbs and give them the same, if better quality of life. And it is very successful."

There are numerous incentives for Vauban's 4,700 residents to live car-free: Carpoolers get free yearly tramway passes, while parking spots—available only in a garage at the neighborhood's edge—go for € 17,500 (US $23,000). Forty percent of residents have bought spaces, many just for the benefit of their visiting guests.

As a result, the car-ownership rate in Vauban is only 150 per 1,000 inhabitants, compared with 430 per 1,000 inhabitants in Freiburg proper.

In contrast, the US average is 640 household vehicles per 1,000 residents. But some cities—such as Davis, Calif., where 17 percent of residents commute by bike—have pioneered a car-free lifestyle that is similar to Vauban's model.

Vauban, which is located in the southwestern part of the country, owes its existence, at least in part, to Freiburg—a university town, like Davis—that has a reputation as Germany's ecological capital.

In the 1970s, the city became the cradle of Germany's powerful antinuclear movement after local activists killed plans for a nuclear power station nearby. The battle brought energy-policy issues closer to the people and increased involvement in local politics. With a quarter of its people voting for the Green Party, Freiburg became a political counterweight in the conservative state of Baden-Württemberg.

At about the same time, Freiburg, a city of 216,000 people, revolutionized travel behavior. It made its medieval center more pedestrian-friendly, laid down a lattice of bike paths, and introduced a flat rate for tramways and buses.

Environmental research also became a backbone of the region's economy, which boasts Germany's largest solar-research center and an international center for renewable energy. Services such as installing solar panels and purifying wastewater account for 3 percent of jobs in the region, according to city figures.

Little wonder then, that when the French Army closed the 94-acre base that Vauban now occupies in 1991, a group of forward-thinking citizens took the initiative to create a new form of city living for young families.

"We knew the city had a duty to make a plan. We wanted to get as involved as possible," says Andreas Delleske, then a physics student who led the grass-roots initiative that codesigned Vauban. "And we were accepted as a partner of the city."

In 1998, Freiburg bought land from the German government and worked with Delleske's group to lay out a master plan for the area, keeping in mind the ecological, social, economic, and cultural goals of reducing energy levels while creating healthier air and a solid infrastructure for young families. Rather than handing the area to a real estate developer, the city let small homeowner cooperatives design and build their homes from scratch.

In retrospect, "It would have been much simpler to give a big developer a piece of land and say, 'Come back five years later with a plan,'" says Roland Veith, the Freiburg city official in charge of Vauban.

But the result is a "master plan of an ecological city . . . unique in its holistic approach," says Peter Heck, a professor of material-flow management at Germany's University of Trier, pointing out that this was a community-wide effort involving engineers, politicians, city planners, and residents—not just an environmental group's pilot program.

Today, rows of individually designed, brightly painted buildings line streets that are designed to be too narrow for cars. There are four kindergartens, a Waldorf school, and plenty of playgrounds—a good thing, because a third of Vauban's residents are under age 18, bucking the trend in a graying country.

As Germany's population ages—and shrinks—experts say Vauban's model will become more important as officials increasingly tailor-make communities in an effort to attract citizens.

"We have fewer young people. What you need now is a good quality of life with good services, a good infrastructure for kids and older people," says Thomas Schleifnecker, a Hannover-based urban planner.

Across Europe, similar projects are popping up. Copenhagen, for instance, maintains a fleet of bikes for public use that is financed through advertising on bicycle frames.

But what makes Vauban unique, say experts, is that "it's as much a grass-roots initiative as it is pursued by the city council," says Mr. Scheurer. "It brings together the community, the government, and the private sector at every state of the game."

As more cities follow Vauban's example, some see its approach taking off. "Before you had pilot projects. Now it's like a movement," says Mr. Heck. "The idea of saving energy for our landscape is getting into the basic planning procedure of German cities."

Critical Thinking

1. What policies in Germany seek to limit reliance on the automobile?
2. How does Vauban, Germany, promote car-free living?

From *The Christian Science Monitor,* December 20, 2006. Copyright © 2006 by Isabelle de Pommereau. Reprinted by permission of the author.

Traffic: Why It's Getting Worse, What Government Can Do

ANTHONY DOWNS

Rising traffic congestion is an inescapable condition in large and growing metropolitan areas across the world, from Los Angeles to Tokyo, from Cairo to Sao Paolo. Peak-hour traffic congestion is an inherent result of the way modern societies operate. It stems from the widespread desires of people to pursue certain goals that inevitably overload existing roads and transit systems every day. But everyone hates traffic congestion, and it keeps getting worse, in spite of attempted remedies.

Commuters are often frustrated by policymakers' inability to do anything about the problem, which poses a significant public policy challenge. Although governments may never be able to eliminate road congestion, there are several ways cities and states can move to curb it.

The Real Problem

Traffic congestion is not primarily a problem, but rather the solution to our basic mobility problem, which is that too many people want to move at the same times each day. Why? Because efficient operation of both the economy and school systems requires that people work, go to school, and even run errands during about the same hours so they can interact with each other. That basic requirement cannot be altered without crippling our economy and society. The same problem exists in every major metropolitan area in the world.

In the United States, the vast majority of people seeking to move during rush hours use private automotive vehicles, for two reasons. One is that most Americans reside in low-density areas that public transit cannot efficiently serve. The second is that privately owned vehicles are more comfortable, faster, more private, more convenient in trip timing, and more flexible for doing multiple tasks on one trip than almost any form of public transit. As household incomes rise around the world, more and more people shift from slower, less expensive modes of movement to privately owned cars and trucks.

With 87.9 percent of America's daily commuters using private vehicles, and millions wanting to move at the same times of day, America's basic problem is that its road system does not have the capacity to handle peak-hour loads without forcing many people to wait in line for that limited road space. Waiting in line is the definition of congestion, and the same condition is found in all growing major metropolitan regions. In fact, traffic congestion is worse in most other countries because American roads are so much better.

Coping with the Mobility Problem

There are four ways any region can try to cope with the mobility challenge. But three of them are politically impractical or physically and financially impossible in the United States.

There are many good reasons to expand the nation's public transit systems to aid mobility, but doing so will not notably reduce either existing or future peak-hour traffic congestion.

Charging peak-hour tolls. Governments can charge people money to enter all the lanes on major commuting roads during peak hours. If tolls were set high enough and collected electronically with "smart cards," the number of vehicles on each major road during peak hours could be reduced enough so that vehicles could move at high speeds. That would allow more people to travel per lane per hour than under current, heavily congested conditions.

Transportation economists have long been proponents of this tactic, but most Americans reject this solution politically for two reasons. Tolls would favor wealthier or subsidized drivers and harm poor ones, so most Americans would resent them, partly because they believe they would be at a disadvantage.

The second drawback is that people think these tolls would be just another tax, forcing them to pay for something they have already paid for through gasoline taxes. For both these reasons, few politicians in our democracy—and so far, anywhere else in the world—advocate this tactic. Limited road-pricing schemes that have been adopted in Singapore, Norway, and London only affect congestion in crowded downtowns, which is not the kind of congestion on major arteries that most Americans experience.

Greatly expanding road capacity. The second approach would be to build enough road capacity to handle all drivers who want to travel in peak hours at the same time without delays. But this "cure" is totally impractical and prohibitively expensive. Governments would have to widen all major commuting roads by demolishing millions of buildings, cutting down trees, and turning most of every metropolitan region into a giant concrete slab. Those roads would then be grossly underutilized during non-peak hours. There are many occasions when adding more road capacity is a good idea, but no large region can afford to build enough to completely eliminate peak-hour congestion.

Greatly expanding public transit capacity. The third approach would be to expand public transit capacity enough to shift so many people from cars to transit that there would be no more excess demand for roads during peak hours. But in the United States in 2000, only 4.7 percent of all commuters traveled by public transit. (Outside of New York City, only 3.5 percent use transit and 89.3 percent use private vehicles.) A major reason is that most transit commuting is concentrated in a few large, densely settled regions with extensive fixed-rail transit systems. The nine U.S. metropolitan areas with the most daily transit commuters, when taken together, account for 61 percent of all U.S. transit commuting, though they contain only 17 percent of the total population. Within those regions, transit commuters are 17 percent of all commuters, but elsewhere, transit carries only 2.4 percent of all commuters, and less than one percent in many low-density regions.

Even if America's existing transit capacity were tripled and fully utilized, morning peak-hour transit travel would rise to 11.0 percent of all morning trips. But that would reduce all morning private vehicle trips by only 8.0 percent—certainly progress, but hardly enough to end congestion—and tripling public transit capacity would be extremely costly. There are many good reasons to expand the nation's public transit systems to aid mobility, but doing so will not notably reduce either existing or future peak-hour traffic congestion.

Living with congestion. This is the sole viable option. The only feasible way to accommodate excess demand for roads during peak periods is to have people wait in line. That means traffic congestion, which is an absolutely essential mechanism for American regions—and most other metropolitan regions throughout the world—to cope with excess demands for road space during peak hours each day.

Although congestion can seem intolerable, the alternatives would be even worse. Peak-hour congestion is the balancing mechanism that makes it possible for Americans to pursue other goals they value, including working or sending their children to school at the same time as their peers, living in low-density settlements, and having a wide choice of places to live and work.

The Principle of Triple Convergence

The least understood aspect of peak-hour traffic congestion is the principle of triple convergence, which I discussed in the original version of *Stuck in Traffic* (Brookings/Lincoln Institute of Land Policy, 1992). This phenomenon occurs because traffic flows in any region's overall transportation networks form almost automatically self-adjusting relationships among different routes, times, and modes. For example, a major commuting expressway might be so heavily congested each morning that traffic crawls for at least thirty minutes. If that expressway's capacity were doubled overnight, the next day's traffic would flow rapidly because the same number of drivers would have twice as much road space. But soon word would spread that this particular highway was no longer congested. Drivers who had once used that road before and after the peak hour to avoid congestion would shift back into the peak period. Other drivers who had been using alternative routes would shift onto this more convenient expressway. Even some commuters who had been using the subway or trains would start driving on this road during peak periods. Within a short time, this triple convergence onto the expanded road during peak hours would make the road as congested as it was before its expansion.

Experience shows that if a road is part of a larger transportation network within a region, peak-hour congestion cannot be eliminated for long on a congested road by expanding that road's capacity.

The triple convergence principle does not mean that expanding a congested road's capacity has no benefits. After expansion, the road can carry more vehicles per hour than before, no matter how congested it is, so more people can travel on it during those more desirable periods. Also, the periods of maximum congestion may be shorter, and congestion on alternative routes may be lower. Those are all benefits, but that road will still experience some period of maximum congestion daily.

If a region's population is growing rapidly, as in Southern California or Florida, any expansions of major expressway capacity may soon be swamped by more vehicles generated by the added population.

Triple Convergence and Other Proposals

Triple convergence affects the practicality of other suggested remedies to traffic congestion. An example is staggered work hours. In theory, if a certain number of workers are able to commute during less crowded parts of the day, that will free up space on formerly congested roads. But once traffic moves faster on those roads during peak hours, that will attract other drivers from other routes, other times, and other modes where conditions have not changed to shift onto the improved roads. Soon the removal of the staggered-working-hour drivers will be fully offset by convergence.

The same thing will happen if more workers become tele-commuters and work at home, or if public transit capacity is expanded on off-road routes that parallel a congested express-way. This is why building light rail systems or even new sub-ways rarely reduces peak-hour traffic congestion. In Portland, where the light rail system doubled in size in the 1990s, and in Dallas, where a new light rail system opened, congestion did not decline for long after these systems were up and running. Only road pricing or higher gasoline taxes are exempt from the principle of triple convergence.

How Population Growth Can Swamp Transportation Capacity

A ground transportation system's equilibria can also be affected by big changes in the region's population or economic activity. If a region's population is growing rapidly, as in Southern California or Florida, any expansions of major expressway capacity may soon be swamped by more vehicles generated by the added population. This result is strengthened because America's vehicle population has been increasing even faster than its human population. From 1980 to 2000, 1.2 more auto-motive vehicles were added to the vehicle population of the United States for every 1.0 person added to the human popula-tion (though this ratio declined to 1 to 1 in the 1990s). The nation's human population is expected to grow by around 60 million by 2020—possibly adding another 60 million vehi-cles to our national stock. That is why prospects for reducing peak-hour traffic congestion in the future are dim indeed.

Shifts in economic activity also affect regional congestion. During the internet and telecommunications boom of the late 1990s, congestion in the San Francisco Bay Area intensified immensely. After the economic "bubble" burst in 2000, con-gestion fell markedly without any major change in popula-tion. Thus, severe congestion can be a sign of strong regional prosperity, just as reduced congestion can signal an economic downturn.

The most obvious reason traffic congestion has increased everywhere is population growth. In a wealthy nation, more people means more vehicles. But total vehicle mileage traveled has grown much faster than population. From 1980 to 2000, the total population of the United States rose 24 percent, but total vehicle miles traveled grew 80 percent because of more inten-sive use of each vehicle. The number of vehicles per 1,000 per-sons rose 14 percent and the number of miles driven per vehicle rose 24 percent. Even without any population gain in those two decades, miles driven would have risen 47 percent.

One reason people drove their vehicles farther is that a com-bination of declining real gas prices (corrected for inflation) and more miles per gallon caused the real cost of each mile driven to fall 54 percent from 1980 to 2000. That helped raise the frac-tion of U.S. households owning cars from 86 percent in 1983 to 92 percent in 1995.

Furthermore, American road building lagged far behind increases in vehicle travel. Urban lane-miles rose by 37 percent versus an 80 percent increase in miles traveled. As a result, the amount of daily traffic that was congested in the 75 areas ana-lyzed in studies by the Texas Transportation Institute went from 16 percent in 1982 to 34 percent in 2001.

Another factor in road congestion is accidents and incidents, which some experts believe cause half of all traffic congestion. From 1980 to 2000, the absolute number of accidents each year has remained amazingly constant, and the annual number of traffic deaths in the United States fell 18 percent, in spite of the great rise in vehicle miles traveled. So accidents could only have caused more congestion because roads were more crowded, and each accident may now cause longer back-ups than before.

Incidents are non-accident causes of delay, such as stalled cars, road repairs, overturned vehicles, and bad weather. No one knows how many incidents occur, but it is a much greater num-ber than accidents. And the number of incidents probably rises along with total driving. So that could have added to greater congestion, and will in the future.

Severe congestion can be a sign of strong regional prosperity, just as reduced congestion can signal an economic downturn.

Low-Density Settlements

Another crucial factor contributing to traffic congestion is the desire of most Americans to live in low-density settlements. In 1999, the National Association of Homebuilders asked 2,000 randomly-selected households whether they would rather buy a $150,000 townhouse in an urban setting that was close to public transportation, work, and shopping or a larger, detached single-family home in an outlying suburban area, where dis-tances to work, public transportation, and shopping were longer. Eighty-three percent of respondents chose the larger, farther-out suburban home. At the same time, new workplaces have been spreading out in low-density areas in most metropolitan regions.

Past studies, including one published in 1977 by Boris S. Pushkarev and Jeffery M. Zupan, have shown that public transit works best where gross residential densities are above 4,200 persons per square mile; relatively dense housing is clustered close to transit stations or stops; and large numbers of jobs are concentrated in relatively compact business districts.

But in 2000, at least two thirds of all residents of U.S. urban-ized areas lived in settlements with densities of under 4,000 persons per square mile. Those densities are too low for public transit to be effective. Hence their residents are compelled to rely on private vehicles for almost all of their travel, including trips during peak hours.

Recognizing this situation, many opponents of "sprawl" call for strong urban growth boundaries to constrain future growth into more compact, higher-density patterns, including greater reinvestment and increased densities in existing neighborhoods. But most residents of those neighborhoods vehemently oppose raising densities, and most American regions already have densities far too low to support much public transit. So this strategy would not significantly reduce future traffic congestion.

Possible Improvements

While it's practically impossible to eliminate congestion, there are several ways to slow its future rate of increase:

Create High Occupancy Toll (HOT) lanes. Peak-hour road pricing would not be politically feasible if policymakers put tolls on all major commuter lanes, but HOT lanes can increase traveler choices by adding new toll lanes to existing expressways, or converting underused high-occupancy vehicle (HOV) lanes to HOT lanes, and leaving present conventional lanes without tolls. True, HOT lanes do not eliminate congestion. But they allow anyone who needs to move fast on any given day to do so, without forcing all low-income drivers off those same roads during peak periods. In some regions, whole networks of HOT lanes could both add to overall capacity and make high-speed choices always available to thousands of people in a hurry.

Respond more rapidly to traffic-blocking accidents and incidents. Removing accidents and incidents from major roads faster by using roving service vehicles run by government-run Traffic Management Centers equipped with television and electronic surveillance of road conditions is an excellent tactic for reducing congestion delays.

Build more roads in growing areas. Opponents of building more roads claim that we cannot build our way out of congestion because more highway capacity will simply attract more travelers. Due to triple convergence, that criticism is true for established roads that are already overcrowded. But the large projected growth of the U.S. population surely means that we will need a lot more road and lane mileage in peripheral areas.

Install ramp-metering. This means letting vehicles enter expressways only gradually. It has improved freeway speed during peak hours in both Seattle and the Twin Cities, and could be much more widely used.

Use Intelligent Transportation System devices to speed traffic flows. These devices include electronic coordination of signal lights on local streets, large variable signs informing drivers of traffic conditions ahead, one-way street patterns, Global Positioning System equipment in cars and trucks, and radio broadcasts of current road conditions. These technologies exist now and can be effective on local streets and arteries and informative on expressways.

Create more HOV (High Occupancy Vehicle) lanes. HOV lanes have proven successful in many areas such as Houston. More regions could use HOV lanes effectively if there were more lanes built for that purpose, rather than trying to convert existing ones. Merely converting existing lanes would reduce overall road capacity.

Adopt "parking cash-out" programs. Demonstration programs have shown that if firms offer to pay persons now receiving free employee parking a stipend for shifting to carpooling or transit, significant percentages will do so. That could reduce the number of cars on the road. However, this tactic does not prevent the offsetting consequences of triple convergence.

Restrict very low-density peripheral development. Urban growth boundaries that severely constrain all far-out suburban development will not reduce future congestion much, especially in fast-growing regions. And such boundaries may drive up peripheral housing prices. But requiring at least moderate residential densities—say, 3,500 persons per square mile (4.38 units per net acre)—in new growth areas could greatly reduce peripheral driving, compared to permitting very low densities there, which tend to push growth out ever farther. In 2000, thirty-six urbanized areas had fringe area densities of 3,500 or more. Those thirty-six urbanized areas contained 18.2 percent of all persons living in all 476 U.S. urbanized areas.

Transit Oriented Developments (TODs) would permit more residents to commute by walking to transit, thereby decreasing the number of private vehicles on the roads.

Cluster high-density housing around transit stops. Such Transit Oriented Developments (TODs) would permit more residents to commute by walking to transit, thereby decreasing the number of private vehicles on the roads. However, the potential of this tactic is limited. In order to shift a significant percentage of auto commuters to transit, the number of such "transit circles" within each region would have to be very large, the density within each circle would have to be much greater than the average central city density in America's fifty largest urbanized areas, and the percentage of workers living in the TODs who commuted by transit would have to greatly exceed the 10.5 percent average for central cities in 2000. Even so, developing many of these high-density clusters might make public transit service more feasible to many more parts of large regions.

Give regional transportation authorities more power and resources. Congress has created Metropolitan Planning Organizations to coordinate ground transportation planning over all modes in each region. If these were given more technical assistance and power, more rational systems could be created. Without much more regionally focused planning over land uses as well as transportation, few anti-congestion tactics will work effectively.

Raise gasoline taxes. Raising gas taxes would notably slow the rate of increase of all automotive travel, not just peak-hour commuting. But Congress has refused to consider it because it is politically unpopular and fought by industry lobbyists. Despite Americans' vocal complaints about congestion, they do not want to pay much to combat it.

Conclusion

Peak-hour traffic congestion in almost all large and growing metropolitan regions around the world is here to stay. In fact, it is almost certain to get worse during at least the next few decades, mainly because of rising populations and wealth. This will be true no matter what public and private policies are adopted to combat congestion.

But this outcome should not be regarded as a mark of social failure or misguided policies. In fact, traffic congestion often results from economic prosperity and other types of success.

Although traffic congestion is inevitable, there are ways to slow the rate at which it intensifies. Several tactics could do that effectively, especially if used in concert, but nothing can eliminate peak-hour traffic congestion from large metropolitan regions here and around the world. Only serious economic recessions—which are hardly desirable—can even forestall an increase.

For the time being, the only relief for traffic-plagued commuters is a comfortable, air-conditioned vehicle with a well-equipped stereo system, a hands-free telephone, and a daily commute with someone they like.

Congestion has become part of commuters' daily leisure time, and it promises to stay that way.

Critical Thinking

1. Why does the construction or widening of a highway seldom reduce traffic congestion for long? Why does congestion soon reemerge?

2. What is a TOD (transit-oriented development)? Explain how a TOD looks different from conventional suburban developments.

3. What policies or steps can you propose that would help to reduce automobile commuting or otherwise alleviate traffic congestion?

ANTHONY DOWNS is a senior fellow in Economic Studies at the Brookings Institution.

All data in this policy brief concerning population and travel behavior are from the Census Bureau, primarily from the 2000 Census, unless otherwise noted.

Is Congestion Pricing Ready for Prime Time?

A controversial approach comes to the fore.

MICHAEL A. REPLOGLE

For decades now, traffic congestion and transportation-related greenhouse gas pollution have been growing in most cities around the world—seemingly as much out of control as the weather. In the U.S., leaders from across the political spectrum—including the mayor of New York, the Bush administration's transportation secretary, and the top official of King County, Washington—have responded with a controversial solution: congestion pricing.

Their model is London, which in 2004 imposed a central area congestion charge. But there are other examples as well, including Singapore, which introduced a similar $3 congestion charge way back in 1975. Oslo, Bergen, and five other Norwegian cities adopted their own charges between 1986 and 2004, both to manage traffic and to finance transportation projects. Stockholm, Milan, Rome, and other cities have similar initiatives.

Meanwhile, political resistance to higher fuel taxes has led to renewed interest in tolls to finance highways. High-occupancy toll (HOT) lanes took hold in southern California in the 1990s as an alternative to public financing, then spread rapidly to Texas, Minnesota, Utah, Colorado, and Virginia. Germany in 2005 pioneered a nationwide system of emission-based truck tolls on its 7,500-mile autobahn network, collected with the help of global positioning system satellites. The tolls raised over $4.5 billion in 2006, cut greenhouse emissions from trucks by seven percent, and doubled the rate at which old trucks are replaced by newer, cleaner models.

Last year, the Dutch government announced it was phasing out charges for owning motor vehicles in favor of motorist charges based on distance driven, with higher rates for using busy roads during peak hours and for more polluting vehicles. The new, GPS-based road charges will start with trucks in 2011 and gradually extend to passenger vehicles.

Closer to home, the Puget Sound region is completing a federally funded study of a similar GPS-based traffic-management system. Preliminary findings are promising: They show that road-pricing incentives caused a sample of Seattle-area households to voluntarily cut their driving by one fourth. A similar result comes from a federally sponsored test of mileage-based fees in Oregon; it suggests that such a system could be phased in over several years to replace motor fuel taxes.

Habits Are Hard to Change

Tolls are being used to finance a growing share of new road capacity worldwide. Increasingly such tolls are higher at times and locations where demand is greatest—the core idea of congestion pricing. But applying such tolls to existing free roads is a lot tougher, even after half a century of promotion by transportation economists.

Even in the U.K., where London is a model of congestion pricing, there is resistance. Last year, 1.5 million people signed a petition opposing a central government plan for nationwide road pricing. In the U.S., proposals for congestion pricing on existing roads face political hurdles in New York, northern California, Colorado, and elsewhere. Throughout the world, the same concerns surface: Will congestion pricing harm the poor? Will it intrude on personal privacy? Is it double taxation for roads? Where will revenues go?

Research suggests that traffic, sprawl, and pollution tend to increase when tolls are used simply to expand roads. In addition, more jobs are put out of reach of the poor. In contrast, low-income households benefit and traffic and pollution are cut when tolls are used to manage congestion on existing roads.

A synthesis of public attitudes on congestion pricing prepared last year by Joanne Zmud of NuStats, an Austin-based research company, found that, while the public generally supports tolling and pricing, populist politics make it harder to implement—and to evaluate—such programs. Effective public education and leadership are needed to raise public understanding of the complex policy issues associated with congestion pricing.

Acceptance is increasing, however, prompted by the growing awareness of gridlock, local governments' well-publicized fiscal distress, and a broadening knowledge of climate change.

Leadership in London

Congestion pricing in London, as elsewhere, resulted only from decisive political leadership; after years of studies, Ken Livingstone made congestion pricing a key issue in his 2000 mayoral campaign. On taking office, he quickly put a special team into place to design and implement a system. The new charge—about $8—went live in early 2003; 26 months after the process started. The initiative initially affected about 200,000 vehicles a day operating weekdays from 7 A.M. to 6:30 P.M. in a congested 13-square-mile area of central London. Motorists may pay in retail outlets, online, via text messaging, or by phone. Scoffers face escalating penalties.

Opposition ran two to one at first, but support grew as the results came in. Congestion dropped by 30 percent in 2003 and 2004, bus speed and reliability rose 20 percent or more, and emissions fell by 15 percent. Bicycle use rose 43 percent within the congestion charging zone. To encourage participation, more than 500 buses were added during morning rush hours shortly before the charge began, and extensive improvements benefited pedestrians and cyclists.

Livingstone won reelection by a decisive margin in 2004, after promising to broaden the zone, which in February 2007 was doubled in size to include the West End. The fees (all for driving in the congestion charge zone) were boosted to $16 in July 2005. The most fuel-inefficient vehicles will pay $50 per day starting in October, even those of zone residents (who otherwise enjoy a 90 percent discount). Fees are waived for drivers of the most fuel-efficient, cleanest vehicles. Nearly half of the $520 million in annual revenues are used to administer the charging system, with the rest dedicated to public transportation.

In February of this year, a new, citywide low-emission zone went into effect. This one is based on the experience of Berlin, Germany, and Malmo, Sweden, both of which have smaller low-emission zones. In London's zone, heavy trucks that fail to meet recent European Union emission standards now pay $400 a day to drive anywhere in the city. Similar charges will extend to buses, minibuses, large vans, and ambulances this summer.

"It's an effort to save the lives of 1,000 Londoners a year who die prematurely because of the worst air quality in Western Europe," Mayor Livingstone said just before the initiative's launch. The zone is projected to cut pollution 16 percent by 2012 and save health costs of $500 million.

Transport for London, the agency that overseas the city's trains, buses, and roads, is spending $98 million to set up the new zone and $20 million a year to operate it, with annual revenue projected at $92 million. In the first month, the city counted about 50,000 trucks a week entering the zone. Eight percent failed to meet the emissions standard. Fees are refundable if the vehicle is upgraded with better pollution controls.

The new low-emission zone uses cameras to check license plate numbers against lists. If the vehicle is certified as exempt or registered as having paid the appropriate fee, the photo is discarded. If not on the list, the image is processed for billing. The city plans to adopt a toll transponder system like the U.S. EZPass to simplify toll payments. According to the *Times of London,* if Ken Livingstone wins a tough reelection campaign this May, he intends to introduce charges on congested roads outside the existing zone.

The idea is simple enough: Charge fees based on where and when motorists drive, with discounts offered during times of low demand. Used in that way, congestion pricing matches demand more closely to available road space, and boosts the efficiency, reliability, and speed of an area's transportation system. Revenues can be used to increase travel choices.

It works in Singapore. There, electronic toll charges—on the outer ring road, major arterials, and entry roads to both the central business district and a newer commercial center—are adjusted periodically for each location by hour of the week based on what is needed to keep traffic flowing freely at least 85 percent of the time.

Now try putting this idea into practice in the U.S. A major stumbling block is the common belief that inflation-eroded gas taxes have already paid for "freeways" and other roads. For many drivers, the idea of a toll conjures up images of being stuck in a long traffic jam waiting to throw your money out the window.

The Debate Continues

The HOT lanes that opened in 1995 in the median of southern California's State Road 91 broke new ground in many ways. The project demonstrated that private investment could succeed in delivering road improvements years ahead of the public sector. It significantly boosted vehicle occupancy and traffic flow along the corridor. And it showed how automated time-of-day road pricing could guarantee free-flowing traffic in a congested corridor. All that with no toll booths in sight.

During the most congested hours, SR-91's two managed lanes carry as many vehicles as four adjacent unmanaged lanes, at three times the speed. But getting to that point was not easy.

The contract for SR-91 included a non-compete agreement that barred public investment in parallel transportation improvements by state and local governments. This provision proved so unacceptable to Riverside County that the original agreement had to be renegotiated in 2002, a painful and costly process. Like many other HOT lanes, those on SR-91 were not designed to boost public transportation and actually facilitated sprawl development. After gaining temporary relief from congestion, many drivers were still stuck on clogged freeway lanes.

In contrast, the I-15 HOT lane project that opened in San Diego in 1996 offered an example of a more transit-friendly approach to managed lanes. The San Diego Association of

Governments dedicated toll revenue from the new HOT lanes (created from existing lanes) to improved public transportation. A dynamic pricing system allowed tolls to be adjusted every seven minutes, helping to keep the managed lanes flowing. With polls showing 80 percent approval of the system, San Diego is now building a regional system of managed lanes with express bus services.

Back East

Pressure to introduce congestion pricing has also been building in metropolitan New York—where more than half of all tolls in the U.S. are collected. William Vickery, a Nobel Prize-winning economist at Columbia University, first proposed the idea in 1952. In the early 1970s, he and other civic advocates actually convinced Mayor John Lindsay to try congestion pricing on the East River bridges, but the authority to do so was blocked in court.

In 2000, the political stars aligned just as the Port Authority of New York and New Jersey was set to issue a toll increase. Thanks to the efforts of a civic coalition, the Tri-State Transportation Campaign, the governors of both states supported a staff recommendation to increase peak-period Hudson River bridge and tunnel tolls, while keeping charges the same for non-peak-hour EZPass toll transponder users.

The $1.50 time-of-day toll differential was enough to shift about seven percent of the traffic from peak hour, yielding a substantial reduction in congestion. With nearly half the Port Authority's net toll revenues dedicated to improving trans-Hudson PATH passenger rail service, this initiative became a milestone on the path toward wider congestion pricing. Soon after, modest time-of-day toll differentials were introduced by the New Jersey Turnpike, the Garden State Parkway, and the New York Thruway Authority as new toll increases took effect.

Meanwhile, other states were advancing HOT lanes under the federal Congestion/Value Pricing Pilot Program, which in 1991 opened a door for states to circumvent the 35-year ban on imposing tolls on interstate highways. In the debate over the 2005 federal transportation law, opposition from U.S. trucking interests—long opposed to tolls except to build new roads—was overcome by an unusual alliance of transportation industry, state, metropolitan, and environmental interests. The states won much greater flexibility to add tolls to new or existing roads.

Fast forward to 2006, when a national congestion initiative was launched by U.S. Department of Transportation Secretary Norman Mineta and carried forward by his successor, Mary Peters. One piece of that, the Urban Partnership Agreements, promised federal funding from a dozen discretionary programs to a few cities with the most ambitious implementation plans: congestion pricing of existing roads combined with improved public transportation and traffic management. Thanks to a reduction in earmarking of transportation funds when the Democrats took over Congress, DOT was able to award $852 million to five cities under the initiative—New York, San Francisco, Seattle, Minneapolis, and Miami.

Go-Getters

Of the two dozen applications, the most ambitious was the proposal by New York Mayor Michael Bloomberg, who in 2003 submitted a budget to put congestion tolls on East River bridges but was forced to back down because he lacked needed approvals from the governor and legislature.

Last year, Bloomberg made congestion pricing a central piece of his PlaNYC vision for New York—a long-term plan to house a million more residents, enhance livability and public health, cut congestion, and trim greenhouse gas emissions by 30 percent by 2030. Bloomberg sought a green light from the state to implement his plan, which would impose a congestion charge of $8 a day on cars and $21 on trucks ($7 on low-emission trucks) entering the city's central core.

Despite opposition from key legislators, the mayor got approval to further refine the plan. The city also won a $354 million Urban Partnership grant, which it plans to use for congestion pricing, bus rapid transit initiatives, and improvements in traffic operations. But this grant is conditioned on approval by the city council and the state legislature of key planning goals—to cut Manhattan traffic by at least 6.3 percent by 2009 and to raise more than $250 million a year for transit. That condition could make the New York plan a model for future performance-based federal transportation funding.

Months of hearings led to a refined (and simpler) pricing plan that would shift the proposed zone boundaries and exemptions, produce more revenue, and lower collection costs. Polls showed that a majority of city residents supported congestion pricing so long as toll revenues would be dedicated to improving public transportation. A strong campaign by a coalition of business, civic, and environmental groups led to a 30-to-20 vote in favor of the plan by the city council, and support by the governor and state senate leader. But the plan died April 7 in the State Assembly when the deadline for action expired, a victim of election-year politics and failed deal making.

The plan's failure in Albany leaves an added $4.5 billion hole in the Metropolitan Transportation Authority's $29.5 billion, five-year capital budget, portending higher taxes and service cuts in addition to the loss of the $352 million federal grant.

With leadership from Mayor Gavin Newsom, San Francisco also won a matching $159 million DOT grant under the Urban Partnership agreement, conditioned on implementation of congestion pricing. The Bay Area Toll Authority's approval this month of a peak-period toll hike of $1 (to $6) on the bridge should be enough to guarantee the grant, which would help to cover some of the $1.1 billion cost of replacing Doyle Drive, the structurally unstable connector road south of the Golden Gate Bridge.

This is a breakthrough for a region that has for years tried to implement congestion pricing on bridges but been blocked by state legislative leaders. While suburban officials continue to resist the pricing proposal, charging that it amounts to a commuter tax, area transportation planners are making plans to implement new parking, transit, and HOT lanes under the partnership agreement. Planners in the San Francisco region

Stockholm Experiment

After a decade of studies, proposals, and other setbacks, Stockholm in January 2006 launched a seven-month congestion tax pilot project with a goal of reducing traffic and pollution. The Swedish Green Party pushed its Social Democratic coalition partners to implement the initiative, which had been held up for two years by challenges regarding legal authority and procurement.

The government invested $200 million in the revenue collection system and $300 million in related public transportation improvements. Charges were imposed between 6 A.M. and 7 P.M. weekdays at the 18 entry points surrounding the central core. Residents of a small part of the city accessible only through the charging zone were exempt; so were taxis, foreign-registered cars, the handicapped, and extremely low-emission vehicles. Others faced fees up to $3.50 for each entry or exit from the zone. The toll collection system is based primarily on automated license plate recognition.

Twelve new express bus lines, improved rail service, and 1,800 new park-and-ride spaces were designed to win over public opinion (although opponents outnumbered proponents by two to one on opening day). The results were good: Traffic fell by 15 percent, congestion delay fell by up to 50 percent, and greenhouse gases and other pollution dropped by 14 percent in the core area and by two to three percent in the region. Public transportation ridership rose by 45,000. When the charge ended, traffic quickly went back to the old, higher charge levels.

In September 2006, a non-binding referendum was held to determine whether the charge would be reinstated. The ayes had it. Although most of the parties that formed a new government following that election had campaigned against the charge, they promptly decided to restore the central area charge with minor modifications. Today, the charge generates annual revenues of over $150 million; about a fifth of the gross revenues are required to administer the system.

Last year, President Bush cited Stockholm's success in discussing his own congestion initiative. Recent Stockholm polls show nearly two-to-one public support for congestion charging.

Singapore Transformed

Pictures taken in Singapore in the mid-1970s show a city mired in congestion, with cars, trucks, buses, and motorbikes stalled for hours on hopelessly crowded roads. It's a scene reminiscent of Jakarta or Bangkok today.

No more. Singapore is a city transformed. Its roads are largely free of congestion, public transportation is outstanding, and the economy is booming. Congestion pricing is certainly part of that success story.

The world's first congestion charging system was instituted in Singapore's Central Business District in 1975. The system cut private car traffic into the core by more than half. Carpooling rose by more than a third, and bus use doubled. As Singapore's income has skyrocketed to $32,500 per capita, the number of cars has grown 2.5 times, and public transportation's share of travel has risen from four out of 10 trips to over six in 10, thanks to road pricing, a vehicle quota system that manages the number of motor vehicles, and high levels of investment in public transportation and transit-oriented development. Singapore is also a leader among the world's affluent major cities for its very low personal transportation greenhouse gas emissions.

Singapore started with a central area charge in morning peak hours, which it later extended to the evening peak and midday hours. In 1990, congestion pricing was applied to the city's ring road expressway. In 1998, Singapore implemented electronic tolling, retrofitting all vehicles with toll transponders, which work with cash cards to deduct a fee automatically when a vehicle passes a charging gantry. Different reader devices correspond to each vehicle class, with higher fees for larger vehicles. Tolls are now imposed at 55 locations, and the number will grow to 70 by the end of the year.

With electronic tolling, Singapore was able to adjust rates by hour of the week, cutting fees in some cases by half or more below what they had been with a flat $2.15 peak/$1.45 midday charge per gantry passage. Toll rates are adjusted accordingly to keep traffic generally free flowing. In July, the base toll will double to $1.45, as will the increment by which tolls are raised for particular locations and times. Road pricing now contributes over $60 million per year to Singapore's general budget, with operating costs accounting for only seven percent of that; the most efficient of any urban congestion charging system.

are also studying a central area cordon charge modeled after London, Stockholm, and Singapore.

A third winner was Seattle, where King County Executive Ron Sims and the Washington State DOT have strongly supported congestion pricing. A nearly completed federally supported study estimates that it would cost about $750 million to create a GPS satellite-based tolling system in the region and about $288 million a year to operate it, potentially generating annual revenues of $3 billion and a 6:1 benefit-to-cost ratio.

The study concludes that the technology needed for such toll collection is mature, noting that public understanding and acceptance are the keys to moving forward. In the near term, the region intends to convert State Road 167's high-occupancy vehicle lane into a HOT lane, and plans are proceeding to finance and manage the failing SR 520 Lake Washington bridge with congestion tolls.

Other initiatives for adding tolls to existing interstate highways (restriping lanes and using shoulders, for instance) are advancing in Minneapolis and Miami, which won $133 million and $63 million respectively under the Urban Partnerships program. They have agreements for HOT lane projects on I-35 and I-95, which also support new express bus services.

Other federal grants are expected this year for Congestion Reduction Demonstration pilot projects, which encourage integrated initiatives for transit, traffic operations, and congestion pricing on existing roads. More than 20 regions applied late last year for this latest round of grants. Funding levels depend on the appropriations process and the level of congressional earmarks.

U.S. federal transportation policy is at a crossroads, with widespread perception that the system is both broke and broken as the current federal transportation law expires next year and the highway trust fund runs out of money. With bridges falling down, gas prices soaring, and traffic congestion getting worse, public confidence in the current system is low. Debate is growing about how to fund and focus transportation investments, how to curb transportation-related greenhouse gas emissions, and how to boost system performance and accountability.

With dozens of new congestion pricing initiatives launched across America last year, and even more across the rest of the world, the genie conjured up by William Vickery seems finally to be out of the bottle. But just what will we ask that genie to do?

Critical Thinking

1. Explain how a system of congestion pricing would work in a city.

2. What possible criticisms can be made against the desirability of a system of congestion pricing?

MICHAEL A. REPLOGLE, a civil engineer, is transportation director for the Environmental Defense Fund and president and founder of the Institute for Transportation and Development Policy.

From *Planning*, May 2008, pp. 6–11. Copyright © 2008 by American Planning Association. Reprinted by permission via Copyright Clearance Center.

UNIT 9

The Future of Cities and Suburbs: The United States and the World

Unit Selections

Learning Outcomes

After reading this unit, you should be able to:

- Explain how global competition affects local decision-making.
- Illustrate how Japan has responded to the pressures of global competition.
- Show what is lost or ignored when countries as diverse as Japan, Brazil, and India reshape their cities for a global audience.
- Explain how LDCs use mega-events such as the Olympics and the Commonwealth Games to promote investment and to modernize their cities.
- Evaluate the slum demolition programs in cities like Delhi.
- Identify more humane and effective policies than demolition when dealing with the presence of squatter settlements and slum communities.
- Explain how the needs of women, especially low-income and working women, in a city differ from those of men.
- Document the horror of femicides in Ciudad Juárez and explain how femicides in that city are related to the growth of *maquiladoras* and a global economy.
- Explain how "hidden" urban policies in the United States act to promote suburban growth and home ownerships.
- Identify the alternative policies that European nations have enacted in an attempt to promote denser patterns of development and to reduce automobile usage and the production of single-family homes.
- Assess the various European urban-related policies, identifying just which ones should be transferred to the United States and just which ones do not represent a great "fit" in the United States.

Student Website

www.mhhe.com/cls

Internet References

Planetizen
www.planetizen.com

Planum
www.planum.net

Squatter City
http://squattercity.blogspot.com

United Nations Human Settlements Programme
www.unhabitat.org

U.S. Department of Housing and Urban Development
www.hud.gov

Will cities of the future be able to meet the needs of their people? As we have seen, cities have historically served as centers of hope and opportunity, the places to where people migrate in search of these things. Yes, cities lack the ability to cope with a great many of problems they confront. As we have already seen, forces of globalization (i.e. the decisions made by international financial institutions and major corporations; the workings of "faceless" global financial markets; an intensified intercity competition for business; and immigration) have placed cities under additional pressures. Even the leaders of Tokyo, a city clearly at the top of the global hierarchy, have had to act vigorously in the face of rising challenges from Hong Kong, Shanghai, Singapore, and other Pacific office centers (Article 43, "Japan's Cities Amid Globalization"). Tokyo has torn down low-rise neighborhoods to build new corporate and residential centers for the global elite. In Kyoto, a city of temples and shrines and the historic capital of Japan, local leaders built a soaring, glass, ultra-modern train station-hotel-shopping complex to promote new investment in the city and its downtown. Critics argue that the new construction is a scar that defaces traditional unity and the beauty of Japan's historical heart.

Cities in **lesser developed countries (LDCs)** will have a particularly difficult time in meeting the growing demands on them that will only dramatically escalate in the future. Major cities in LDCs continue to be severely overcrowded, the result of the continuing arrival of poor job seekers from the countryside. These cities lack the resources to provide housing and basic municipal services—water, electricity, adequate plumbing and sanitation—to large numbers of the poor, who wind up living in **shantytowns** or **slums** (also called **favelas** in Latin America). In many cases, residents of such areas live with the fear of eviction, as they lack legal **land tenure** or the right to occupy or own the land. In a number of cities in developing countries, the number of people who live in the **informal city** of the slums and shantytowns actually is greater than the legal or formal population.

As seen in cities in India and elsewhere in South and East Asia, public officials often face conflicting pressures when having to decide just how to deal with urban slums and other urban neighborhoods that house the poor. A municipality that provides good housing and upgraded basic services may wind up attracting thousands of new arrivals whose presence will overwhelm the city. City leaders are also under pressure to direct their attention to policies that will promote new investment and jobs. Indeed, national officials expect major cities to act as a country's **economic champions** in the global competition for major corporations. As a result, city after city has knocked down slums, squatter communities, and traditional low-rise neighborhoods, in order to build expanded business districts and modern residential spaces demanded by globally-oriented actors (Article 44, "Reinventing Rio: The Dazzling but Tarnished Brazilian City Gets a Makeover As It Prepares for the 2014 World Cup and 2016 Olympic Games" and Article 45, "Demolishing Delhi, World Class City in the Making"). The quest for rapid growth has also, too often, come at the expense of the environment. Cities and countries are only just beginning to realize that the maintenance of clean air, green space, and a livable city are important assets in the global competition for business.

© Punchstock/Japan-Tokyo vol. AI116

The central state and local governments have too frequently uprooted the poor, tearing down their homes and pushing families farther away from their jobs to even more marginalized areas on the outskirts of the city. Poor people's advocates suggest a more humane alternative path. Instead of bulldozing slums and squatter communities, which simply push the poor elsewhere and inflict even greater sufferings on the poor, cities and states can improve service provision by providing running water, sewerage, electricity, and regular trash collection to poor neighborhoods (Article 46, "No Excuses Slum Upgrading"). Government can even **regularize the status** of persons who live in squatter communities, providing the quasi-legal recognition of their tenancy that would assure residents the sense of permanency and protection that would allow them to invest their own money and labor **("sweat equity")** in making improvements to the places in which they live. Joel Kotkin (Article 47, "Urban Legends: Why Suburbs, Not Cities, Are the Answer") offers an even more thought-provoking and highly controversial alternative: instead of pursuing growth that overloads the major cities and compounds slum formation in LDCs, public policy should encourage the dispersal of businesses and residences to smaller cities and the urban periphery. Whether such a policy can succeed in the face of the pressures that drive urban growth in LDCs remains to be seen.

The discussion of service provision to squatter communities invites an important question: Just how well do cities serve their people, especially a city's more vulnerable residents? In seeking to answer this question, it is important to note that many of the residents of central cities are women and female-headed families. As much of the work in the field of gender studies has served to underscore, women in the city face problems and needs that are not always quite the same as those faced by men. Especially in LDCs, cities that are geared for growth and service to major corporations may not provide adequately for women and family in terms of affordable housing, the provision of day care, and the protection of physical safety.

Ciudad Juárez, Mexico, just across the border from El Paso, has received a lot of attention in the news as a result of deadly gang wars and skirmishes between drug lords and the government. Yet, Juárez's history of **femicides**—the murders of hundreds of women—actually pre-dates the surge in drug-related violence (Article 48, "Femicide in Ciudad Juárez: What Can Planners Do?"). In Juárez and other border communities, women make up most of the labor force in the **maquiladoras,** the factories that have sprouted up on the Mexican side of the border as a result of economic globalization. The **North American Free Trade Agreement (NAFTA)** reduced trade barriers between the U.S. and Mexico, spurring the shift of production to low-wage sites conveniently located in the Mexico border region. The factories hire women recently arrived from the impoverished countryside. Factory owners rely on the work of women, who are seen as more reliable and docile than men. Yet, these women must often travel long distances across unsafe areas in order to reach the factories. Women have been the victims of abuse, rape, and murder. The official response from the government has been far less than adequate.

Compared to the United States, metropolitan areas in Europe are more compact, with less sprawl, and with livelier central cities. Pietro Nivola (Article 49, "Are Europe's Cities Better?") points to a number of reasons for the difference: The United States provides **extensive tax subsidies** that have fueled the purchase of single-family homes. Europe has imposed heavy **automobile ownership and gasoline taxes.** Nivola also observes the toll imposed on cities by federal and judicial **mandates** that require cities to provide costly services. Nivola looks to Europe for inspiration but warns political officials in the U.S. to be cautious in adopting European-style policies that may limit the lifestyle choices that Americans so highly value.

The most pessimistic scenarios show big cities in the United States drifting toward a **Blade Runner future.** As portrayed in Ridley Scott's classic movie *Blade Runner* (starring Harrison Ford and Sean Young), the Los Angeles of the future is a hellish place that suffers the same extensive **urban dualism** that, until now, has largely been characteristic of the giant metropolises of LDCs. In *Blade Runner,* the executives of mega-corporations make the all-important decisions from the safety of their protected office towers and high-rise **gated communities.** A militarized police force monitors the activity on the street, with flying police cruisers that look down from above. The city of the future is a place of crime and routinized violence. The environment is marred by extensive air pollution and toxic rain.

In a competitive world, it remains to be seen if governments have the political will to implement policies that can ameliorate urban dualism and promote sustainable development, thereby averting the *Blade Runner* scenario.

Japan's Cities Amid Globalization

Myron A. Levine

Global pressures and influences have altered spatial planning in Japan and have reshaped the face of Japan's cities. In the years following World War II and for much of the remaining twentieth century, Japan pursued the goal of spatial deconcentration; various policies sought to preserve the population and economic stability of smaller cities across Japan by limiting the overconcentration of population and economic activity in Tokyo. In the 1960s, the public's concern over dirty air and other environmental problems strengthened the demand to limit the growth of giant Tokyo.

The various policy efforts did not fully work, and Tokyo continued to growth. Nonetheless, the central government built peripheral housing and steered R&D (research and development) activities to high-amenity regional science and technology centers in Osaka, Nagoya, and new suburban technopoles. By steering supportive economic activities to the periphery, the deconcentration policy produced an important side benefit: in the age of intensified global competition that would soon follow, the government's deconcentration policy helped to free up space in overcrowded central Tokyo, space that would be a valuable asset in the national effort to secure prime office development (Edgington 1999; Saito 2004; Sorensen 2004).

Rising competition from other office centers in the Pacific Hong Kong, Singapore, Shanghai, Bangkok, and Kuala Lumpur—eventually led Japan to abandon spatial concentration in favor of a national economic strategy that sought to build on the assets and attractiveness of Tokyo. Tokyo would be the "national champion" (Jessop and Sum 2000, 2295–2296) in the increasingly intense global battles for development. The 2001 collapse of the "bubble economy" only reinforced the sense of national urgency in transforming Tokyo for the global competition.

Both the TMG (Tokyo Metropolitan Government) and the central government sought to create new areas of the city, particularly in the southern and western sectors, that would be attractive to international firms and their high-end workforces. Traditional low-rise neighborhoods had to be cleared in order to create new spaces for global firms. The 1988 Special District Plan for Redevelopment relaxed the country's strict land-use restrictions in order to facilitate the construction of new corporate skyscrapers and condominiums. Pursuing the dense development of corporate spaces, Tokyo borrowed New York City's "bonus" system, permitting developers to build additional floors and at greater density in return for open space, plazas, and other public facilities (Sorensen 2004; Saito 2003). The City Planning Acts of 1992, 1995, and 1999 permitted a level of local initiative that was previously unseen. Tokyo and other cities were no longer merely "agents" of central planning; "planning became a local government function (*jichi jimu*) instead of a delegated function" (Sorensen 2004, 299; also see Jacobs 2003a and 2004; Muramatsu 1997).

The rise of local initiative marked an important change in a planning system that, until that point in time, had been characterized as highly central-state directed, a system of "vertical administrative control" (Muramatsu 1997, 16 and 28; also, see Gilman 1997 and Edgington 1999; Fujita 2003). Tokyo (and other cities) gained new leeway to modernize their infrastructure and to pursue economic development initiatives that would work to the nation's advantage. Local governments in Japan pushed for local economic growth projects, working within the confines of a hierarchical state-planning system.

The construction of Roppongi Hills exemplifies the upgrading of land uses and the transformation of Tokyo's cityscape. Governmental officials helped to facilitate the efforts of developers to tear down a low-rise Tokyo neighborhood to make way for a 27-acre office-residential-shopping-complex. At the time of its 2003 opening, Roppongi Hills was the largest private development in the country and included a 54-story central office tower (with Goldman Sachs, Lehman Brothers, and Yahoo! Japan as anchor tenants), over 200 shops and restaurants (including Louis Vuitton, Wolfgang Puck's, and Starbucks), a 9-screen, all-reserved-seats cinemaplex, a Hyatt Hotel, a headquarters building for Asahi Television, an outdoor concert venue, and four residential buildings with over 840 units. Roppongi Hills was meant to be exclusive. Monthly rents (2006 figures) were high: an unfurnished one-bedroom went for $5,000 (600,000 Yen); a four-bedroom apartment rented for $50,000 (5,500,000 Yen) a month.

As we shall see, the TMG pushed for the creation of other major economic megadevelopment projects, including the construction of a virtual new quarter of the city, the Rainbow Town subcenter built on an artificial island in Tokyo Bay. Other cities responded to Tokyo's success by initiating development projects of their own. In contemporary Japan, local governments "take the policy initiative and play the role of trend-setter within the state policy structure" (Fujita 2003, 265; also see Jacobs 2005). Local chambers of commerce, relatively new actors in

Japan's local arena, even joined with municipal and prefectural officials in pushing local development projects.

A Tale of Four Cities

A brief review of key development projects in Tokyo, Kyoto, Kobe, and Fukuoka will reveal the degree to which local governments have taken the initiative and are often the "drivers" of major development projects. In contemporary Japan, the pressures for development are often bottom-up and no longer just top-down and fully controlled by the central-state. Such bottom-up efforts are inconsistent with the portrayal of Japan as a central-bureaucracy-dominated developmental state. In an age of heightened global competition, the national government has welcomed the new local initiatives.

Tokyo Pushes the Creation of a Tokyo Bay Subcenter: The Development of Teleport/Rainbow Town

Over the years, the Tokyo Metropolitan Government (TMG) has rebuilt entire sections of the city to facilitate economic growth. One of the most significant TMG projects was the construction of a massive waterfront city subcenter, known over the years as Teleport Town and Rainbow Town. Located just two miles from the commercial heart of downtown Tokyo, to which it is connected by highway and train running across the Rainbow Bridge, the megadevelopment is projected to have an eventual working population of 70,000 and a residential population of 42,000 (TMG 2002, 31).

The artificial island contains striking corporate buildings (the offices of Panasonic, Suntory, and Fuji), an iconic exhibition center, hotels, teleport and business support facilities, themed multi-level shopping malls (with indoor reconstructions of the streets of "Little Hong Kong" and Renaissance Italy), concert venues, museums, and amusement complexes (including a giant Ferris wheel). The island's Odaiba shopping/entertainment area has arguably emerged as Tokyo's most important tourist destination, drawing visitors from the rest of Japan to the island's shopping malls and to the dramatic view of the Rainbow Bridge cast against the backdrop of the city's downtown.

Local officials helped initiate the Tokyo Bay project, expanded its scope, and provided political and financial support for it during the years of economic difficulty when the enthusiasm of the central government waned. In the 1980s, TMG governor Shunichi Suzuki proposed the construction of a Tokyo Bay "teleport town," a concentration of the most up-to-date satellite and telecommunications facilities that would help draw information-age businesses to Japan (Saito 2003). Amid the optimism that characterized the bubble economy, TMG officials expanded their vision to a full-fledged city subcenter with residences, shopping, and entertainment. By 1987, only two years after the initial announcement of the project, plans for the island mushroomed to 11 times the original project acreage; its budget swelled by a factor of four (Yipu 2005).

When the bubble economy burst, few observers saw the need for new office and commercial space proposed for the island. A new national government sought to cut unnecessary expenditures on an unneeded project. During that period, local officials—the TMG—kept the project alive, continuing to pour local money into roadways, rail, and infrastructure support. Even when populist national leaders criticized the project's size and extravagance, TMG careerists continued to lend their support to the project (Saito 2003; Yipu 2005). Local planners promised that the island's "lively atmosphere and broad-based appeal" (TMG 2002, 15) would help make Tokyo attractive to the managers and to workers in cutting-edge industries (Saito 2003). A new administration would eventually adopt Tokyo's perspective.

Traditional Kyoto Builds an Ultra-Modern Train Station and Gateway to the Global Economy

In Kyoto, local officials and business leaders initiated the construction of a massive rail station project from the fear that their city was being eclipsed by the construction boom in nearby Osaka and Kobe and by the opening of Osaka's new Kansai International Airport:

A task force (composed of representatives from the city, prefecture, the Chamber of Commerce and Industry, and JR West [the West Japan Railway company] organized an international competition for the design of a new station for Kyoto. The winner, the Japanese architect Hiroshi Hara, was announced in 1991. This type of competition is uncommon in Japan and shows how much was at stake in this ambitious project. (Tiry 2001)

In a city of temples and shrines, Kyoto's leaders sought an architecturally distinguished, monumental project to signal that Kyoto was no longer merely a quiet, sleepy tourist destination but a modern city that welcomed business. The striking multi-functioned megaplex (opened in 1997) contains a shopping mall, hotels, exhibition space, various support facilities, and a multi-screen theater. The "Cube" is the 16-story, two-winged heart of the project, with an open-air "Grand Staircase" that rises from below ground.

The project serves as a symbol of Kyoto's economic vitality and provides the city with an important gateway to the global economy. As Kyoto has no airport of its own (a critical impediment to the city's ability to attract international corporations), local elites sought a rail facility that would serve *de facto* as the city's airport, offering "seamless" travel to executives who can check their bags at the station without having to recheck them at Kansai Airport (Tiry 2001). The Cube abuts the high-speed Shinkansen bullet trains that connect the city to Tokyo.

Kobe Seeks Its Niche in the New Economy: From "Port City" to "International City"

Kobe's leaders followed a somewhat different development path, choosing a strategy that sought to market the city's livability, building on Kobe's environmental assets. In the wake of the Great Hanshin-Awaji Earthquake of 1995 (4,500 deaths and 120,000 damaged buildings), planners did more than just rebuild the city; they pursued a strategy for long-term economic diversification and growth. Kobe no longer promotes itself solely as the home of Japan's most active seaport. Instead, Kobe advertises itself as an "international city" with "facilities and amenities established by and for such foreign communities" (City of Kobe, 2004). Kobe residents enjoy greater green space per capita (17 square meters per person) than do the residents of any other major Japanese city (Hinrichsen, 2002).

Kobe built attractive new residential environments and promoted the city's international schools and close proximity to both the mountains and the sea. A greenbelt helps to prevent the recreational space of the Rokko Mountains, preventing new development incursions. Given its assets, municipal officials boast that "Kobe is uniquely qualified to support a comfortably refined lifestyle for just about any company or individual from any country" (City of Kobe, 2004). The striking waterfront skyline of Harborland, the large complex of office buildings, shopping malls, hotels, cinemas, restaurants, and an amusement park built on the site of the city's old freight yards, provides Kobe with the future-oriented imagery that is used to market the city to an international community.

Kobe occupies an extremely narrow strip of land between the Rokko Mountains and the Seto Inland Sea, a geographical situation that greatly restricted the supply of developable land. Before the great earthquake, Kobe had adopted an aggressive strategy of creating new sites for growth and development. Sites for Suma residential town, Kobe academic town (a university center), and the Seishin new town and high-tech park were obtained by flattening parts of the Rokko Mountain region. The removed earth was then used as fill to help create two large man-made harbor islands which were created to expand port-related activities and to create new residential opportunities.

Port Island was constructed in 1992 as a center of new facilities to alleviate bottlenecks in the old port area. But the island also became the site of residential and lifestyle activities. Port Island is envisioned to have an eventual population of 20,000, many attracted to the island's extensive sports and recreational facilities. A dozen years after its initial opening, a "second stage" expansion project was announced "to meet the needs of this new age of globalization and foreign companies" (City of Kobe, 2004). The expanded island houses the Kobe Medical Industry Development Project, a biomedical research-and-development complex and the first "Life Science super-cluster in Japan" (City of Kobe, 2004).

Kobe's effort to reposition itself as an international city with an attractive living environment—no longer just a port city—is even more clearly evident in the "new town" development at Rokko Island, the city's second large man-made island. Situated only 4 miles from downtown Kobe and 12 miles from downtown Osaka, the island is linked to the mainland by a driverless train. The new town is projected to house a residential population of 30,000. The island offers corporate offices, hotels, a convention center, a western-style cinema complex, fitness clubs, international schools, and a water amusement park.

With its tree-lined pedestrian walkways that wind along a narrow man-made "river," Rokko Island is marketed as offering a setting that is attractive to both foreign corporations and expatriate families. Procter & Gamble chose the island as the site for its offices. With its fashion center and fashion museum, the island has also become the center of Kobe's fashion industry.

Fukuoka: Building on Links to Asia, but Influenced by the United States

Faced with the decline of the regions' coal-producing and ship-building economies, Fukuoka (population 1.3 million) turned to a tourism-based strategy designed to attract visitors from nearby South Korea and mainland Asia. In terms of miles, Fukuoka actually lies closer to Seoul, South Korea, than to Tokyo! The city's Asian Art Museum, built as part of the plush Riverain shopping complex with its high-end fashion stores, is designed to appeal to visitors from South and East Asia.

A mile away, however, an American-themed shopping mall and entertainment center serves as the lure for tourism. Private developer Fukuoka Jisho acquired 9 acres of land bordering the Naka River in the city's dilapidated Hakata warehouse district. After the collapse of his initial development plans, he turned to Jon Jerde, the California designer of Horton Plaza in San Diego and the Mall of America in the Twin Cities, as the Japanese-American partnership built a fantasy/shopping theme park.

At the time of its 1996 opening, Canal City was the largest private development in Japan. A computer-orchestrated "symphony of fountains" and performing acrobats, trapeze artists, and jugglers (who perform on a small island in an artificial central canal) entice customers to the complex's shops and eateries. With bold primary colors and curved lines, Canal City was meant to stand out. In contrast to the traditional Japanese model of station-centered development (a model which still shapes the development of Tenjin, Fukuoka's rail-centered downtown), Canal City has no direct rail access; instead, customers arrive much like they do in the United States, by car as they enter the complex through a multi-decked parking structure. Canal City is Japan's version of the city as a "theme park (Sorkin 1992)".

The Refashioning of Tokyo Continues

This brief review of Tokyo's Rainbow Town, Kyoto's train station, Kobe's livability, and Fukuoka's Canal City projects all reveal that local actors have become driving forces behind major development projects in Japan. In Japan, a central-state renowned for top-down guidance and planning, gave local officials new discretion to pursue economic development, so much so that one authority on urban Japan says the word "centralized" can no longer be accurately used to describe the contemporary development system in Japan (Jacobs 2003a; also see Hein and Pelletier 2006; and Hill and Fujita 2003).

The collapse of the bubble economy heightened national government's sense of urgency in rebuilding Tokyo as a global center. Even Tokyo, clearly a top-tier city in the global hierarchy, had to be reshaped to maintain its primacy. Traditional low-rise neighborhoods were displaced to create new areas that would meet the needs of multinational corporations and their workforces.

The concern that Japanese national policy once gave to preserving regional balance in development fell by the wayside. Central authorities announced that the goal of spatial deconcentration was no longer relevant. The nation's global economic competitiveness required "compact urban structures with centripetal force" (Prime Minister of Japan and his Cabinet 2002). Faced with new competition from Shanghai, Hong Kong, Singapore and other Pacific office sites, Japan sought to strengthen Tokyo as the "global financial capital gateway to the world" (Saito 2004, 9).

With office space in Tokyo almost fully occupied (Takahashi and Sugiura 1995), planners had to create or free up new space for global-oriented development. Rainbow Town was only one of a ring of new city subcenters created for different economic functions. Shinjuku emerged as a virtual second downtown, a dense development of skyscrapers housing the government and back-office functions. Shibuya became a center of fashion and youth culture; Ikebukuro as a locus of retail activity. The new subcenters freed up space in the Marunouchi central business district for high-value corporate development. Even the fabled Tsukiji wholesale fish market, situated only a half mile from Ginza and in the shadow of the Shiodome skyscrapers, was relocated to the city's outskirts in order to make way for higher-valued land uses in the center of the city (Bestor 2004; Makino 2003) that looked increasingly toward an international corporate audience and less toward preserving tradition.

Tokyo's traditional neighborhoods were swept aside in the new global undertaking. The TMG announced Tokyo Plan 2000 to make the city a "Peerless International City" (TMG 2002, 21). The national Koizumi government sought to fast-track the "redevelopment of inner city sites into high-rise global space," allowing development authorities new leeway to sidestep "the protests of local residents and the sometimes extended processes of public consultation" (Sorensen 2003, 528). The result was a transformation of these areas and "the rapid loss of traditional townscapes" (Sorensen 2004, 334), Tokyo neighborhoods with narrow streets, small shops, and roofs slanted to the street to permit sunshine.

Roppongi Hills, in conjunction with similar mixed-use complexes that had been built nearby at ARK Hills and Izumi Garden, formed a concentration of megadevelopments that was designed to transform the Tokyo ward of Minato-ku, already a center of embassies and expatriate life, into "a magnet for the global business community" (Frederick 2003). At Roppongi Hills, English-speaking residents enjoyed a 24-hour bilingual concierge service and a Borders-type café and bookstore where half of the books are in English. Roppongi Hills, like other TMG-led entrepreneurial projects in southwestern Tokyo, resulted in new patterns of income stratification by *ku* (or ward), patterns that until recently were atypical of Japanese cities (Jacobs 2005). Japanese cities have tended to lack the degree of class stratification, and city-suburban social distance that characterizes U.S. communities. Japanese housing, land-use, and zoning policies have traditionally encouraged a mixing of social classes (Dimmer and Klinkers 2004; Fujita and Hill 1997). The new globally-oriented megadevelopments in Tokyo represent a relatively new and important exception, government-approved developments of exclusive living and work environments that violate the Japanese model of class mixing.

The transformation of Japanese cities continues. New urban forms emerge, and, in major cities, traditional urban patterns and neighborhoods are disappearing amid global influences and competitive pressures.

References

Ahlert, D., M. Blut, and H. Evanschitzky. 2006. Current status and future evolution of retail formats. In *Retailing in the 21st century: Current and future trends,* edited by M. Krafft and M. Mantrala, 289–308. Berlin: Springer.

Bestor, T. C. 2004. *Tsukiji: The fish market at the center of the world.* Berkeley: Univ. of California Press.

City of Kobe. 2004. Overview of Kobe. Retrieved January 9, 2006, from www.city.kobe.jp/cityoffice/17/020/en/outline/.

Dimmer, C., and K. Klinkers. 2004. Downtown Tokyo revisited: Restructuring and urban renaissance. University of Tokyo, Department of Urban Engineering, Urban Design Lab.

Edgington, D.W. 1999. Firms, governments and innovation in the Chukyo region of Japan. *Urban Studies* 36 (2): 305–339.

Frederick, J. 2003. TomorrowLand: Tycoon Minoru Mori wants to make Tokyo a more livable city. *Time-Asia,* August 4.

Fujita, K. 2003. Neo-industrial Tokyo: Urban development and globalization in Japan's state-centered developmental capitalism. *Urban Studies* 40 (20): 249–281.

Fujita, K., and R.C. Hill. 1993. *Japanese cities in the world economy.* Philadelphia: Temple Univ. Press.

———. 1997. Together and equal: Place stratification in Osaka. In *The Japanese city,* edited by P.P. Karan and K. Stapleton, 106–133. Lexington: Univ. Press of Kentucky.

Gilman, T. J. 1997. Urban redevelopment in Omuta, Japan, and Flint, Michigan: A comparison. In *The Japanese city,* edited by P.P. Karan and K. Stapleton, 176–220. Lexington: Univ. Press of Kentucky.

Hein, C., and P. Pelletier, eds. 2006. *Cities, Autonomy and Decentralization in Japan.* Abingdon, UK: Routledge.

Hill, R.C., and K. Fujita. 2003. The nested city: Introduction. *Urban Studies* 40 (2): 207–217.

Hill, R.C., and J.W. Kim. 2000. Global cities and developmental states: New York, Tokyo and Seoul. *Urban Studies, 37* (12): 2167–2195.

Hinrichsen, D. (2002). Kobe rises from the ashes. *PeopleandPlanet .net.* Retrieved January 9, 2006, from: www.peopleandplanet. net/doc.php?id=1799.

Jacobs, A.J. 2002. Integrated development planning, supportive public policies, and corporate commitment: A recipe for thriving major cities in Aichi, Japan. *Journal of Urban Affairs, 24* (2): 175–196.

———. 2003a. Devolving authority and expanding autonomy in Japanese prefectures and municipalities. *Governance: An International Journal of Policy, Administration, and Institutions 16* (4): 601–623.

———. 2003b. Embedded autonomy and uneven metropolitan development: A comparison of the Detroit and Nagoya auto regions, 1969–2000. *Urban Studies, 40* (2): 335–360.

———. 2004. Federations of municipalities: A practical alternative to local government consolidations in Japan? *Governance: An International Journal of Policy, Administration, and Institutions, 17* (2): 247–274.

———. 2005. Has central Tokyo experienced uneven development? An examination of Tokyo's 23 Ku relative to America's largest urban centers. *Journal of Urban Affairs, 27* (5): 521–555.

Jessop, B., and N.-L. Sum. 2000. An entrepreneurial city in action: Hong Kong's emerging strategies in and for (inter)urban competition. *Urban Studies, 37* (12): 2287–3313.

Kamo, T. 2000. An aftermath of globalisation? East Asian economic turmoil and Japanese cities adrift. *Urban Studies, 37* (12): 2245–2265.

Lathom, A. 2006. Anglophone urban studies and the European city: Some comments on interpreting Berlin. *European Urban and Regional Studies 13* (1): 88–92.

Makino, C. 2003. Eviction notice for tuna. *Christian Science Monitor.* December 10.

Muramatsu, M. 1997. *Local power in the Japanese state,* translated by B. Scheiner and J. White. Berkeley: Univ. of California Press.

Saito, A. 2003. Global city formation in a capitalist developmental state: Tokyo and the waterfront sub-centre project. *Urban Studies, 40* (2): 283–308.

———. 2004. Global city in developmental state: Urban restructuring in Tokyo.

Sorensen, A. 2003. Building world city Tokyo: Globalization and conflict over urban space. *Annals of Regional Science 37* (3): 519–531.

———. 2004. *The making of urban Japan: Cities and planning from Edo to the twenty-first century.* London: Routledge Japanese Studies Series.

Sorkin, M., ed. 1992. *Variations on a theme park: The new American city and the end of public space.* New York: Hill and Wang.

Takahashi, J., and N. Sugiura. 1995. The Japanese urban system and the growing centrality of Tokyo in the global economy. In *Emerging world cities in Pacific Asia,* edited by F-c. Lo and Y-m. Yeung, 101–143. Tokyo: United Nations Univ. Press.

Tiry, C. 2001. Stations help define urban image: Kyoto and Lille-Europe. *Japan Railway and Transport Review 28:* 18–21. Online at www.jrtr.net/jrtr28/f18_tir.html, retrieved January 2006.

Tokyo Metropolitan Government, Bureau of City Planning. 2002. *Planning of Tokyo.* Tokyo: TMG.

Yipu, Z. 2005. *Selling props, playing stars: Virtualising the self in the Japanese mediascape.* Doctoral dissertation, University of Western Sidney, Centre for Cultural Research. Available at http://library.uws.edu.au/adt-NUWS/uploads/approved/adt-NUWS20060210.104650/public/01Front.pdf, retrieved February 2006.

Critical Thinking

1. What was the goal of Japan's spatial planning policies during the half century that followed World War II? Just where did Japan seek to promote—and to limit—growth?

2. Why has Japan welcomed new mega-developments such as Tokyo's Roppongi Hills and the construction of a new Rainbow Town city subcenter? How do such projects represent Japan's response to globalization and a reversal of earlier spatial planning objectives?

3. Why did city leaders in Kyoto, the historical capital of Japan, push for the development of an ultra-modern rail station and shopping/hotel complex?

4. What is lost when Tokyo, Kyoto, and Fukuoka pursue globally-oriented developments?

An original essay written for this volume. Copyright © 2010 by Myron A. Levine.

Reinventing Rio

The Dazzling but Tarnished Brazilian City Gets a Makeover As It Prepares for the 2014 World Cup and 2016 Olympic Games

ALAN RIDING

When it comes to Rio de Janeiro there is no avoiding the obvious. The city may be as famous for its *Carnaval,* soccer, flesh and fun as it is infamous for its hillside slums and organized crime. Yet its defining feature remains its breathtaking setting. No visitor can ever forget viewing the city from on high for the first time. Even natives—the Cariocas—stand in awe of its grandeur. How could I feel different? I, too, was born there. As a writer friend, Eric Nepomuceno, put it, "only Paris comes close to matching Rio in self-love."

Mountains rise to the east and west and protrude like giant knuckles from inside the city itself. Stretching to the north is a vast bay, which Portuguese navigators evidently thought was a river when they first sighted it in January 1502. Hence the name Rio de Janeiro (River of January). For centuries, ferries carried people and cargo to and from the city of Niterói on the bay's eastern shore; today a seven-mile-long bridge crosses the bay. And standing guard at its entrance is the 1,300-foot-high granite mound known as the Pão de Açúcar—the Sugar Loaf.

To the west, two long curving beaches—Copacabana and Ipanema-Leblon—run along the city's Atlantic shoreline, only to be interrupted by twin mountains, the Dois Irmãos, or the Two Brothers. Behind the beaches lies a glistening lagoon, Lagoa Rodrigo de Freitas, and the Botanical Gardens. From there, thick tropical forest reaches up into the Tijuca National Park, "every square inch filling in with foliage," as the American poet Elizabeth Bishop put it a half-century ago. And rising 2,300 feet out of this vegetation is still another peak, the Corcovado, or the Hunchback, crowned by the 125-foot-tall—including the pedestal—statue of Christ the Redeemer.

Then there are the less sublime areas. Rio's North Zone, which begins at the city center and sprawls for miles inland, resembles many cities in developing countries, with crowded highways, run-down factories, crumbling housing projects and many of Rio's more than 1,000 shantytowns, or *favelas,* as they're known. Anyone landing at Antônio Carlos Jobim International Airport (named after the late bossa nova composer) is confronted with this unexpected, dismaying sight as they go to their likely destinations in the South Zone of the city.

Then suddenly another Rio comes into view. The bayside highway curves around the city center before dipping into the majestic Aterro do Flamengo park and sweeping past the Sugar Loaf. It then enters the tunnel leading to Copacabana and the broad Avenida Atlántica, which stretches nearly three miles along the beach. A different route south passes under the Corcovado and reappears beside the Lagoa Rodrigo de Freitas, following its shores to Ipanema-Leblon. (That was my way home when I lived in Rio in the 1980s.)

The Atlantic beaches are the city's playgrounds, with sunbathers crowding near the waves and soccer and volleyball occupying much of the rest. The beaches are also strikingly heterogeneous: people of all income levels and colors mix comfortably, while women and men of every shape feel free to wear the skimpiest of swimsuits. Actors, journalists, lawyers and the like have their favorite meeting places at beachside cafés selling beer, sodas, coconut milk and snacks. There is even a corridor for cyclists and joggers.

Away from the sea, though, the Copacabana neighborhood looks run-down and its streets are often clogged with traffic. Even the more elegant Ipanema and Leblon, one beach but two neighborhoods, coexist with those hillside favelas, highlighting the gulf between Rio's rich and poor. During violent storms in April this year it was mainly residents of the favelas who died—251 in greater Rio—as a result of landslides. Favelas are also routinely blamed for drug-related violence and all-too-frequent muggings. With the pleasures of living in the beauteous South Zone, then, comes the need for security.

Farther west, beyond Leblon and a smaller beach called São Conrado, is a third Rio, Barra da Tijuca, with 11 miles of sand and no encroaching mountains. Forty years ago, it seemed an obvious place to accommodate Rio's growing middle class. But what was intended as a model urban development has become a soulless expanse of apartment blocks, highways, supermarkets and, yes, more favelas, including the one, Cidade de Deus, that gave its name to Fernando Meirelles' award-winning 2002 movie, *City of God.*

So, for all their devotion to "the marvelous city," as they call Rio, Cariocas know full well that their hometown has been in decline. The slide began 50 years ago when Brazil's capital moved to Brasília. For two centuries before then, Rio was the capital of finance and culture as well as politics. To the rest of the world, Rio was Brazil. But once politicians, civil servants and foreign diplomats moved to the new capital in 1960, São Paulo increasingly dominated the nation's economy. Even important oil fields off the coast of Rio brought little solace. The state government received a share of royalties, but no oil boom touched the city. Rio was stripped of its political identity but found no substitute. Many Brazilians no longer took it seriously: they went there to party, not to work.

"I'd call Rio a ship adrift," says Nélida Piñón, a Brazilian novelist. "We lost the capital and got nothing in return. Rio's narcissism was once a sign of its self-sufficiency. Now it's a sign of its insecurity."

Lately, Rio has even fallen behind the rest of Brazil. For the first time in its history, Brazil has enjoyed 16 years of good government, first under President Fernando Henrique Cardoso and now under President Luiz Inácio Lula da Silva, who is to leave office on January 1, 2011. And the result has been political stability, economic growth and new international prestige. But during much of this time, Rio—both the city and the state that carries its name—has been plagued by political infighting, incompetence and corruption. And it has paid the price in poor public services and mounting crime.

Yet, for all that, when I recently returned to Rio, I found many Cariocas full of optimism. The city looked much as it did a decade ago, but the future looked different. And with good reason. Last October, Rio was chosen to host the 2016 Summer Olympics, the first to be held in South America and, after Mexico City in 1968, only the second in Latin America. As if in one fell swoop, Cariocas recovered their self-esteem. Further, Lula's strong support for Rio's Olympic bid represented a vote of confidence from Brazil as a whole. And this commitment looks secure with either of the main candidates to succeed Lula in general elections on October 3—Dilma Rousseff, Lula's hand-picked nominee, and José Serra, the opposition challenger. Now, with federal and state governments pledging $11.6 billion in extra aid to prepare the city for the Olympics, Rio has a unique chance to repair itself.

"Barcelona is my inspiring muse," Eduardo Paes, the city's energetic young mayor, told me in his downtown office, referring to how the Catalan capital used the 1992 Summer Olympics to modernize its urban structures. "For us, the Olympics are not a panacea, but they will be a turning point, a beginning of the transformation." And he listed some upcoming events that will measure the city's progress: the Earth Summit in 2012, known as Rio+20, two decades after the city hosted the first Earth Summit; the soccer World Cup in 2014, which will take place across Brazil, with the final to be held in Rio's Maracanã stadium; and the city's 450th anniversary in 2015.

For the Olympics, at least, Rio need not start from scratch. Around 60 percent of the required sports installations were built for the 2007 Pan American Games, including the João Havelange Stadium for athletics; a swimming arena; and facilities for gymnastics, cycling, shooting and equestrian events. The Lagoa Rodrigo de Freitas will again be used for the rowing competitions and Copacabana for beach volleyball, while the marathon will have numerous scenic routes to choose from. The Rio Olympics Organizing Committee will have a budget of $2.8 billion to ensure every site is in good shape.

But because many competition venues will be a dozen or more miles from the new Olympic Village in Barra da Tijuca, transportation could become an Olympic-size headache. Barra today is linked to the city only by highways, one of which goes through a tunnel, the other over the Tijuca Mountains. While about half the athletes will compete in Barra itself, the rest must be transported to three other Olympic "zones," including the João Havelange Stadium. And the public has to get to Barra and the other key areas.

To pave the way, the organizing committee is counting on a $5 billion state and municipal investment in new highways, improvements to the railroad system and an extension of the subway. The federal government has also committed to modernize the airport by 2014, a long overdue upgrade.

Yet even if the Olympics are a triumph for Rio, and Brazil does unusually well in medals, there is always the morning after. What will happen to all those splendid sports installations after the closing ceremony on August 21, 2016? The experience of numerous Olympic cities, most recently Beijing, is hardly encouraging.

"We're very worried about having a legacy of white elephants," said Carlos Roberto Osório, the secretary general of the Brazilian Olympic Committee. "With the Pan American Games, there was no plan for their use after the games. The focus was on delivering the installations on time. Now we want to use everything that is built and we're also building lots of temporary installations."

Rio already has one embarrassing white elephant. Before leaving office in late 2008, César Maia, then the mayor, inaugurated a $220 million City of Music in Barra, designed by French architect Christian de Portzamparc. It is still not finished; work on its three concert halls has been held up by allegations of corruption in construction contracts. Now the new mayor has the unhappy task of completing his predecessor's prestige project.

At the same time, Paes is looking to finance his own pet project. As part of a plan to regenerate the shabby port area on the Baía de Guanabara, he commissioned Spanish architect Santiago Calatrava, renowned for his sculptural forms, to design a Museum of Tomorrow, which would focus on the environment and, hopefully, be ready for the 2012 Earth Summit. His initial designs were unveiled this past June.

New museums with bold architecture have long been an easy way of raising a city's profile. Rio's Modern Art Museum on the Aterro do Flamengo did that in the 1960s. Since the 1990s, Oscar Niemeyer's UFO-like Contemporary Art Museum in Niterói has been the main reason for tourists to cross the bay. And construction will soon begin on a new Museum of Image and Sound, designed by the New York-based firm Diller Scofidio + Renfro, on Copacabana's Avenida Atlántica.

Culture is the one area where Rio holds its own in its decades-old rivalry with São Paulo, its larger and far richer neighbor. São Paulo boasts the country's most important universities, newspapers, publishing houses, recording companies, theaters and concert halls. But Rio remains the cradle of creativity; Brazil's dominant television network, Globo, is headquartered in the city and employs a small army of writers, directors and actors for its ever-popular soap operas. Also, Globo's nightly news is beamed across Brazil from its studios in Rio. But more importantly, as "a city that releases extravagant freedoms," in Piñón's words, Rio inspires artists and writers.

And musicians, who play not only samba, choro and now funk, but also bossa nova, the sensual jazz-influenced rhythm that gained international fame with such hits as Antônio Carlos Jobim's "Girl from Ipanema." One evening, I joined a crowd celebrating the reopening of the three cramped nightspots in Copacabana—Little Club, Bottle and Baccarat—where the bossa nova was born in the late 1950s.

"Rio remains the creative heart of Brazilian music," said Chico Buarque, who has been one of the country's most admired singer-composers for over 40 years and is now also a best-selling novelist. São Paulo may have a wealthier audience, he says, "but Rio exports its music to São Paulo. The producers, writers and performers are here. Rio also imports music from the United States, from the Northeast, then makes it its own. Funk, for instance, becomes Brazilian when it is mixed with samba."

Popular music can be heard across the city, but the downtown neighborhood of Lapa is the new hot spot. In the 19th century, it was an elegant residential district reminiscent of New Orleans and, while its terraced houses have known better days, many have been converted into bars and dance halls where bands play samba and choro and the forró rhythms of northeastern Brazil. In the weeks before the pre-Lenten Carnaval, attention turns to Rio's *escolas de samba,* or samba "schools," which are, in fact, large neighborhood organizations. During Carnaval, the groups compete for the title of champion, taking turns to parade their dancers and colorful floats through a noisy and crowded stadium known as the Sambódromo.

Rio is also a magnet for writers. As a legacy of its years as the country's capital, the city is still home to the Brazilian Academy of Letters, which was founded in 1897 and modeled on the Académie Française. Among its 40 *immortels* today are Piñón, the novelists Lygia Fagundes Telles, Rubem Fonseca and Paulo Coelho and the author of popular children's books, Ana Maria Machado. But even Fonseca's novels, which are set in Rio's underworld, rely on São Paulo for their readership.

Except for music, Cariocas are not great consumers of culture. Alcione Araújo, a playwright and lecturer, thinks he knows why. "In a city with these skies, beaches and mountains, it is a crime to lock people inside a theater," he said. And he might have added movie theaters and art galleries. Walter Moreira Salles Jr., who directed the award-winning movies *Central Station* and *The Motorcycle Diaries,* lives in Rio, but looks beyond the city for his audience. A painter friend of mine, Rubens Gerchman, who died in 2008, moved to São Paulo to be close to his market.

But Silvia Cintra, who has just opened a new gallery in Rio with her daughter Juliana, prefers to be close to her artists. "São Paulo has more money, but I think that 80 percent of Brazil's most important artists live and work in Rio," she said.

"São Paulo treats art as a commodity, while the Carioca buys art because he loves it, because he has passion. Rio has space, oxygen, energy, everything vibrates. The artist can work, then go for a swim. You know, I have never felt as happy about Rio as now."

Cariocas have long accepted the hillside favelas as part of the landscape. Writing in *Tristes Tropiques,* French anthropologist Claude Lévi-Strauss described what he saw in 1935: "The poverty-stricken lived perched on hills in favelas where a population of blacks, dressed in tired rags, invented lively melodies on the guitar which, during carnaval, came down from the heights and invaded the city with them."

Today, although many of Rio's favelas still lack running water and other basic necessities, many have improved. Brick and concrete houses have replaced wooden shacks, and most communities have shops; many have schools. Until around 20 years ago, the favelas were relatively tranquil, thanks to the power of the *bicheiros,* godfather-like figures who run an illegal gambling racket known as the "animal game." Then the drug gangs moved in.

In the late 1980s, Colombian cocaine traffickers opened new routes to Europe through Brazil. Homegrown gangsters stepped in to supply the local market, much of it found among the young and wealthy of the South Zone. Soon, protected by heavy weapons, they set up their bases inside the favelas.

The response of the state government, which is in charge of security, was largely ineffective. Police would carry out raids, engage in furious gun battles with traffickers—kill some, arrest others—then leave. With most drug gangs linked to one of three organized crime groups, Comando Vermelho (Red Command), Amigos dos Amigos (Friends of Friends) and Terceiro Comando Puro (Pure Third Command), favela residents were routinely terrorized by bloody turf wars.

The reputation of Rio's police was little better. Many were thought to be on the traffickers' payroll. A December 2009 report by the New York City-based Human Rights Watch accused police officers of routinely executing detainees they claimed had been killed resisting arrest. In some favelas, police have driven out the traffickers—only to set up their own protection rackets.

Fernando Gabeira is one politician with direct experience of urban warfare. In the late 1960s, having joined leftist guerrillas fighting Brazil's military dictatorship, he participated in kidnapping the American ambassador, Charles Burke Elbrick. Elbrick was released after he was swapped for political prisoners, while Gabeira was himself arrested and then freed in exchange for another kidnapped foreign diplomat. When Gabeira returned to Brazil after a decade in exile, he was no longer a militant revolutionary and soon won a seat in Congress representing the Green Party. Having narrowly lost in Rio's mayoral elections in 2008, he plans to challenge Sérgio Cabral's bid for re-election as state governor in October.

"The principal characteristic of the violence is not drugs, but the occupation of territory by armed gangs," Gabeira said over lunch, still dressed in beach clothes. "You have 600,000 to 1 million people living in favelas outside the control of the government. And this is the state government's responsibility." Like many experts, he rejects the automatic link between poverty and violence. "My view is that we should combine social action and technology," he said. "I suggested we use drones to keep an eye on the traffickers. I was laughed at until they shot down a police helicopter."

The downing of the helicopter last October took place just two weeks after the city was chosen to host the 2016 Olympics, following Governor Cabral's assurances to the International Olympic Committee that army and police reinforcements would guarantee the security of athletes and the public. After the helicopter was shot down, Cabral threw his weight behind a new strategy designed by the state's security secretary, José Beltrame.

Starting in the South Zone, Cabral ordered the state government to establish a permanent police presence—so-called Police Pacification Units—in some favelas. After police were met by gunfire, they began a policy of leaking to the media which favela they would next target, giving traffickers time to leave and, it soon transpired, to invade favelas farther inland.

One morning I visited Pavão, Pavãozinho and Cantagalo, a three-community favela overlooking Copacabana and Ipanema, which has been peaceful since this past December. First settled a century ago, the favela has a population estimated at 10,000 to 15,000. A cable car built in the 1980s takes residents up the slope and returns with garbage in cans. It has a primary school, running water and some drainage. For years, it was also a drug stronghold. "There were constant gun battles," recalled Kátia Loureiro, an urban planner and financial director of a community organization called Museu de Favela. "There were times when we all had to lie on the floor."

Today, heavily armed police stand at the favela's entrance, while others patrol its narrow alleys and steep steps. After visiting the local school and a boxing club, I came across the Museu de Favela, which was founded two years ago to empower favela residents to develop their community and improve living conditions. Even during the bad times, it organized courses to train cooks, waiters, seamstresses, craftsmen and artists. Now it offers tours of its "museum," which is what it calls the entire favela. Says the group's executive director, Márcia Souza: "The idea is, 'My house is in the favela, so I am part of the museum.'"

My visit began with a rooftop performance by Acme, the stage name of a local rapper and Museu founder. "We don't need more cops," he told me, "we need more culture, more rap, more graffiti, more dance." The Museu sees social exclusion, not violence, as the problem in the favelas.

I took the cable car up to the home of Antônia Ferreira Santos, who was selling local handicrafts. She showed me her rooftop garden of herbs and medicinal plants. My final stop was at a little square where 11 boys and 5 girls of the local samba school were practicing drumming. With Carnaval only two weeks away, there was no time to waste.

Just how many of the city's roughly 1,000 favelas can be "pacified" by 2016 is unclear. Of course if Rio is to fully exploit its potential as a tourist destination, it must do more. It needs an up-to-date airport, better transportation and greater overall security, as well as new hotels and easier access to popular sites like the Corcovado.

One man who believes in getting things done is the city's new cheerleader, Eike Batista, an oil and mining magnate and reputedly Brazil's wealthiest man. After working mainly abroad for years, he returned home in 2000 and, unusually for a Brazilian industrialist, chose to live in Rio rather than São Paulo. "I said at the time, 'I'm going to spend my millions to fix this city,'" he recounted when I called on him at his home overlooking the Botanical Gardens. In a city with little tradition of individual philanthropy, he started by spending $15 million to help clean the lagoon.

In 2008, Batista bought the once-elegant Hotel Glória, which is now undergoing a $100 million makeover. He then acquired the nearby Marina da Glória, a port for leisure boats, and is modernizing it at a cost of $75 million. He is putting up two-thirds of the estimated $60 million it will take to build a branch of a top-flight São Paulo hospital and has invested $20 million in movie productions in Rio. Over a dinner with Madonna last November, he committed $7 million for her children's charity. He even built his own Chinese restaurant a mile from his home. "It's difficult to fly to New York once a week to eat well," he said with a laugh.

So, yes, things are stirring in Rio. Plans and promises are in the air, objectives are being defined and, thanks to the Olympics, a deadline looms to focus the mind. True, not all Cariocas support the Rio Olympics: they fear that massive public works will bring massive corruption. But the countdown has begun and Cariocas have six years to prove they can change their city for the better. When the Olympic flame is lit in Maracanã on August 5, 2016, a verdict will be returned. Only then will they know if the entire exercise was worthwhile.

Critical Thinking

1. How does Rio illustrate the urban dualism—the side-by-side existence of the rich and the poor—that characterizes major cities in Lesser Developed Countries?

2. How do Rio's hillside *favelas* defy many of the stereotypes of squatter communities?

3. What do social activists fear will be Brazil's response to the favelas as the country prepares to host the Olympic Games?

ALAN RIDING was the Brazil bureau chief for the *New York Times*. He now lives in Paris.

Demolishing Delhi: World Class City in the Making

AMITA BAVISKAR

As London gentrifies its way toward the 2012 Olympics, social cleansing and riverine renewal proceed in parallel but more brutal form in Delhi. In preparation for the Commonwealth Games in 2010 the city's slum dwellers are being bulldozed out to make room for shopping malls and expensive real estate. Amita Baviskar reports on a tale of (more than) two cities and the slums they destroy to recreate.

Banuwal Nagar was a dense cluster of about 1,500 homes, a closely-built beehive of brick and cement dwellings on a small square of land in north-west Delhi, India. Its residents were mostly masons, bricklayers and carpenters, labourers who came to the area in the early 1980s to build apartment blocks for middle-class families and stayed on. Women found work cleaning and cooking in the more affluent homes around them. Over time, as residents invested their savings into improving their homes, Banuwal Nagar acquired the settled look of a poor yet thriving community—it had shops and businesses; people rented out the upper floors of their houses to tenants. There were taps, toilets, and a neighbourhood temple. On the street in the afternoon, music blared from a radio, mechanics taking a break from repairing cycle-rickshaws smoked bidis and drank hot sweet tea, and children walked home from school. Many of the residents were members of the Nirman Mazdoor Panchayat Sangam (NMPS), a union of construction labourers, unusual for India where construction workers are largely unorganised.

In April 2006, Banuwal Nagar was demolished. There had been occasions in the past when eviction had been imminent, but somehow the threat had always passed. Local politicians provided patronage and protection in exchange for votes. Municipal officials could be persuaded to look the other way. The NMPS union would negotiate with the local administration. Squatters could even approach the courts and secure a temporary stay against eviction. Not this time. Eight bulldozers were driven up to the colony. Trucks arrived to take people away. With urgent haste, the residents of Banuwal Nagar tore down their own homes, trying to salvage as much as they could before the bulldozers razed everything to the ground. Iron rods, bricks, doors and window frames were dismantled. TV sets and sofas, pressure cookers and ceiling fans, were all bundled up. The sound of hammers and chisels, clouds of dust, filled the air.

There was no time for despair, no time for sorrow, only a desperate rush to escape whole, to get out before the bulldozers.

But where would people go? About two-thirds of home-owners could prove that they had been in Delhi before 1998. They were taken to Bawana, a desolate wasteland on the outskirts of the city designated as a resettlement site. In June's blazing heat, people shelter beneath makeshift roofs, without electricity or water. Children wander about aimlessly. Worst, for their parents, is the absence of work. There is no employment to be had in Bawana. Their old jobs are a three-hour commute away, too costly for most people to afford. Without work, families eat into their savings as they wait to be allotted plots of 12.5 sq. m. Those who need money urgently sell their entitlement to property brokers, many of them moonlighting government officials. Once, they might have squatted somewhere else in Delhi. Now, the crackdown on squatters makes that option impossible. They will probably leave the city.

One-third of home owners in Banuwal Nagar couldn't marshal the documentary evidence of eligibility. Their homes were demolished and they got nothing at all. Those who rented rooms in the neighbourhood were also left to fend for themselves. One can visit Bawana and meet the people who were resettled, but the rest simply melted away. No one seems to know where they went. They left no trace. What was once Banuwal Nagar is now the site of a shopping mall, with construction in full swing. Middle-class people glance around approvingly as they drive past, just as they watched from their rooftops as the modest homes of workers were dismantled. The slum was a nuisance, they say. It was dirty, congested and dangerous. Now we'll have clean roads and a nice place to shop.

Banuwal Nagar, Yamuna Pushta, Vikaspuri—every day another *jhuggi basti* (shanty settlement) in Delhi is demolished. Banuwal Nagar residents had it relatively easy; their union was able to intercede with the local administration and police and ensure that evictions occurred without physical violence. In other places, the police set fire to homes, beat up residents and prevented them from taking away their belongings before the fire and the bulldozers got to work. Young children have died in stampedes; adults have committed suicide from the shock and shame of losing everything they had. In 2000, more than three million people, a quarter of Delhi's population, lived in 1160 *jhuggi bastis* scattered across town. In the last five years, about half of these have been demolished and the same fate awaits the rest. The majority of those evicted have not been resettled. Even among those entitled to resettlement, there are many who have got nothing. The government says it has no more land to give. Yet demolitions continue apace.

The question of land lies squarely at the centre of the demolition drive. For decades, much of Delhi's land was owned by the central government which parcelled out chunks for planned development. The plans were fundamentally flawed, with a total mismatch between spatial allocations and projections of population and economic growth. There was virtually no planned low-income housing, forcing poor workers and migrant labourers to squat on public lands. Ironic that it was Delhi's Master Plan that gave birth to its evil twin: the city of slums. The policy of resettling these squatter *bastis* into 'proper' colonies—proper only because they were legal and not because they had improved living conditions, was fitfully followed and, over the years, most *bastis* acquired the patina of de facto legitimacy. Only during the Emergency (1975–77) when civil rights were suppressed by Indira Gandhi's government, was there a concerted attempt to clear the *bastis*. The democratic backlash to the Emergency's repressive regime meant that evictions were not politically feasible for the next two decades. However, while squatters were not forcibly evicted, they were not given secure tenure either. Ubiquitous yet illegal, the ambiguity of squatters' status gave rise to a flourishing economy of votes, rents and bribes that exploited and maintained their vulnerability.

In 1990, economic liberalisation hit India. Centrally planned land management was replaced by the neoliberal mantra of public-private partnership. In the case of Delhi, this translated into the government selling land acquired for 'public purpose' to private developers. With huge profits to be made from commercial development, the real estate market is booming. The land that squatters occupy now commands a premium. These are the new enclosures: what were once unclaimed spaces, vacant plots of land along railway tracks and by the Yamuna river that were settled and made habitable by squatters, are now ripe for redevelopment. Liminal lands that the urban poor could live on have now been incorporated into the profit economy.

The Yamuna riverfront was the locale for some of the most vicious evictions in 2004 and again in 2006. Tens of thousands of families were forcibly removed, the bulldozers advancing at midday when most people were at work, leaving infants and young children at home. The cleared river embankment is now to be the object of London Thames-style makeover, with parks and promenades, shopping malls and sports stadiums, concert halls and corporate offices. The project finds favour with Delhi's upper classes who dream of living in a 'world-class' city modelled after Singapore and Shanghai. The river is filthy. As it flows through Delhi, all the freshwater is taken out for drinking and replaced with untreated sewage and industrial effluent. Efforts to clean up the Yamuna have mainly taken the form of removing the poor who live along its banks. The river remains filthy, a sluggish stream of sewage for most of

the year. It is an unlikely site for world-class aspirations, yet this is where the facilities for the next Commonwealth Games in 2010 are being built.

For the visionaries of the world-class city, the Commonwealth Games are just the beginning. The Asian Games and even the Olympics may follow if Delhi is redeveloped as a tourist destination, a magnet for international conventions and sports events. However wildly optimistic these ambitions and shaky their foundations, they fit perfectly with the self-image of India's newly-confident consuming classes. The chief beneficiaries of economic liberalisation, bourgeois citizens want a city that matches their aspirations for gracious living. The good life is embodied in Singapore-style round-the-clock shopping and eating, in a climate-controlled and police-surveilled environment. This city-in-the-making has no place for the poor, regarded as the prime source of urban pollution and crime. Behind this economy of appearances lie mega-transfers of land and capital and labour; workers who make the city possible are banished out of sight. New apartheid-style segregation is fast becoming the norm.

The apartheid analogy is no exaggeration. Spatial segregation is produced as much by policies that treat the poor as second-class citizens, as by the newly-instituted market in real estate which has driven housing out of their reach. The Supreme Court of India has taken the lead in the process of selective disenfranchisement. Judges have remarked that the poor have no right to housing: resettling a squatter is like rewarding a pickpocket. By ignoring the absence of low-income housing, the judiciary has criminalised the very presence of the poor in the city. Evictions are justified as being in the public interest, as if the public does not include the poor and as if issues of shelter and livelihood are not public concerns. The courts have not only brushed aside representations from *basti*-dwellers, they have also penalised government officials for failing to demolish fast enough. In early 2006, the courts widened the scope of judicial activism to target illegal commercial construction and violations of building codes in affluent residential neighbourhoods too. But such was the outcry from all political parties that the government quickly passed a law to neutralise these court orders. However, the homes of the poor continue to be demolished while the government shrugs helplessly.

Despite their numbers, Delhi's poor don't make a dent in the city's politics. The absence of a collective identity or voice is in part the outcome of state strategies of regulating the poor. Having a cut-off date that determines who is eligible for resettlement is a highly effective technique for dividing the poor. Those who stand to gain a plot of land are loath to jeopardise their chances by resisting eviction. Tiny and distant though it is, this plot offers a secure foothold in the city. Those eligible for resettlement part ways from their neighbours and fellow-residents, cleaving communities into two. Many squatters in Delhi are also disenfranchised by ethnic and religious discrimination. Migrants from the eastern states of Bihar and Bengal, Muslims in particular, are told to go back to where they came from. Racial profiling as part of the war on terror has also become popular in Delhi. In the last decade, the spectre of Muslim terrorist infiltrators from Bangladesh has become a potent weapon to harass Bengali-speaking

Muslim migrants in the city. Above all, sedentarist metaphysics are at work, such that all poor migrants are seen as forever people out of place: Delhi is being overrun by 'these people'; why don't they go back to where they belong? Apocalyptic visions of urban anarchy and collapse are ranged alongside dreams of gleaming towers, clean streets and fast-moving cars. Utopia and dystopia merge to propose a future where the poor have no place in the city.

Delhi, Mumbai, Kolkata and many other Indian cities figure prominently in what Mike Davis describes as a 'planet of slums'. Slum clearances may give India's capital the appearance of a 'clean and green Delhi' but environmental activism has simply shifted the problem elsewhere. The poor live under worse conditions, denied work and shelter, struggling against greater insecurity and uncertainty. Is Davis right? Has the late-capitalist triage of humanity already taken place? Even as demolitions go on around me, I believe that Davis might be wrong in this case. Bourgeois Delhi's dreams of urban cleansing are fragile; ultimately they will collapse under the weight of their hubris. The city still needs the poor; it needs their labour, enterprise and ingenuity. The vegetable vendor and the rickshaw puller, the cook and the carpenter cannot be banished forever. If the urban centre is deprived of their presence, the centre itself will have to shift. The outskirts of Delhi, and the National Capital Region of which it is part, continue to witness phenomenal growth in the service economy and in sectors like construction. Older resettlement colonies already house thriving home-based industry. The city has grown to encompass these outlying areas so that they are no longer on the spatial or social periphery. This longer-term prospect offers little comfort to those who sleep hungry tonight because they couldn't find work. Yet, in their minds, the promise of cities as places to find freedom and prosperity persists. In those dreams lies hope.

Critical Thinking

1. Describe the conditions of the Banuwal Nagar squatter community that was torn down in 2006. To where were they moved? Were the lives of the poor made better or worse by the relocation?

2. Why do cities like Delhi turn to programs of slum demolition instead of providing basic services to slum residents?

3. What does the author mean when he states that "New apartheid-style segregation is fast becoming the norm"?

AMITA BAVISKAR researches the cultural politics of environment and development. She is the author of *In the Belly of the River: Tribal Conflicts over Development in the Narmada Valley* and has edited *Waterlines: The Penguin Book of River Writings.*

No Excuses Slum Upgrading

**In fast-urbanizing planet, Sao Paulo develops model toolkit
to improve housing for poor, dispossessed.**

FERNANDO SERPONE BUENO AND VERIDIANA SEDEH

Seventh largest among the world's metropolises and the linchpin of Brazil's booming economy, São Paulo presents a globally relevant case study of stepped-up efforts—but continued deep challenges—if cities are to correct the deep poverty and environmental perils of massive slum settlements.

Close to a third of São Paulo's 11 million people—in a metropolitan region of almost 20 million—live in slum-like conditions. There are some 1,600 favelas (private or public lands that began as squatter settlements), 1,100 "irregular" land subdivisions (developed without legally recognized land titles), and 1,900 cortiços (tenement houses, usually overcrowded and in precarious state of repair).

Government response has progressed light years from the brutal "eradication"—bulldozing of favelas—that began with Brazil's military dictatorship of the 1960s and continued for years as millions of rural families poured into São Paulo seeking industrial jobs. Today policy makers recognize that upgrading is a far wiser course—socially, economically and politically.

But the environment complicates the task: São Paulo has a monsoon-influenced humid subtropical climate with steep hillsides that create severe drainage problems, especially when storm water flows through sewerless slums, picking up loose debris that clogs drainage channels and can imperil local drinking water supplies. Environmental laws were passed in the 1980s to protect watersheds from construction projects—but settlements sprang up there anyway.

A Toolkit for Action— but Key Questions

Official Brazilian policy shifted in the 1980s toward slum upgrading instead of its eradication—recognizing it's easier and cheaper, not to mention more humane, to improve the conditions in a slum rather than try to remove it. But the new policy lacked much weight until the federal enactment, in 2001, of a "City Statute" requiring that cities enact master plans. It also provided a set of tools that municipalities can use to control land transfer and seek to assure legal tenure for tenants—a process São Paulo formally integrated into its own master plan a year later. One of the most useful tools is letting cities create "zones of special interest" for disorganized slums, formally recognizing their existence and qualifying them for social services. Another tool authorizes joint citizen-government management councils both in new and more settled areas.

Moving to more legal tenure, experts on Brazilian slum upgrading suggest, requires three elements to be workable. First, is the location OK for human settlement—not a water pollution risk because its location is too steep or on a flood plain? Second, is the settlement legally registered, or at least in the database of city properties? And third, do its residents have legal title to the land? And if not, what can be done to assure them secure tenure?

There are clear rewards if a full process of regularization—providing clear legal tenure—can be achieved. If families can have their land title confirmed, or at least secure a certificate recognizing their occupancy rights, some taxes can be levied. Rules can be set (and enforced) to prevent building collapse. Regular streets, schools and clinics can be brought in, attracting investment. And it's easier to reduce litter by organizing residents to bring their own household waste to collection points for city pick-up.

But going the whole way continues to be difficult. While the city government works hard to give land tenure, property rights are only conceded by law once this possession is recorded in a register office. According to Nelson Saule, an Instituto Pólis lawyer, the complete process has occurred only with a few properties. In most cases dwellers received a document without clear legal value.

Allies Make a Difference

São Paulo government has clearly become more activist and attuned to long-term slum upgrading in recent years. It's also been aided since 2001 by Cities Alliance, a global alliance of national and city governments, UN-Habitat and the World Bank, focused on scaling up urban poverty solutions.

The São Paulo Municipal Housing Secretariat in 2006 created a management information system that's now able to track the status of favelas, other precarious settlements and site/flooding/water hazard areas citywide. With a priority of serving the city's most vulnerable populations, the tracking (developed in technical cooperation with Cities Alliance) provides a basis for effective targeting of upgrading efforts and environmental clean-ups. Before the system was implemented, notes Elisabete França, São Paulo's secretary of low-income housing, "data about our favelas and irregular private land subdivisions was unreliable, not reflecting the reality of these precarious settlements. The input of the new system resulted from a big field campaign, performed by our own technical staff in record time. The effort showed how people are as important as hardware and software. Now we can follow the dynamics of urban settlement. It is a new culture."

In 2008, São Paulo and Cities Alliance invited high-ranking officials from five other major cities—Cairo, Lagos, Manila, Mumbai and Ekurhuleni (South Africa)—to convene in São Paulo, examine its efforts, and discuss the broad challenges of slum upgrading. "The passion of São Paulo's technical staff in the slum upgrading process was clear for all to see," Godfrey Hiliza of the Ekurhuleni delegation noted at the end of the sessions.

Challenges

Still, São Paulo's reforms haven't come easily. Brazil's legal steps to establish clear land title are murky, unreformed nationally because of powerful rural land-holding interests fearing loss to squatters on their properties. Other pitfalls and barriers have included the high cost of land for building new housing, millions of families' lack of any credit history, and urban crime compounded by Brazil's notorious drug gangs.

And while the flow of new families from the countryside has subsided dramatically in recent years, São Paulo's deep social divisions and tenacious poverty, stemming from the late 20th century's immense in-migration of poor rural families remain. Still, the city claims that the housing issue in São Paulo can be "solved" by 2025 at current rates of city budget expenditure.

Islands of Progress

One example that inspires hope that Sao Paulo's slum upgrading works is Paraisopolis (literally Paradise City), São Paulo's second biggest slum, with 60,000 people. Residents express a strong desire to stay, not be relocated, says Violêta Kubrusly, senior technical adviser at the Municipality of São Paulo Social Housing Department. Upgrading solutions are working

and the city's long-term goals have shifted from 50 percent removal of the neighborhood's population to just 10 percent (those in risky areas like sharp slopes or drainage facilities).

One of São Paulo's goals is to bring electricity, sewage and clean water services to as many areas as it can afford. It is also seeking to enable "domicile swaps" so that the shack occupied by a family moving to a government-built apartment can be made available to a family living in a crowded, dangerous slum area.

There's a strong plus in Paraisopolis' location next to a high-income neighborhood that provides easy access to jobs (such as maid or watchman work).

Citywide, São Paulo is consciously seeking to recycle city areas left by relocated families into such common spaces as parks, playgrounds, soccer fields and skate parks—ways to help people socialize and build a sense of citizenship for remaining residents. With luck, community leadership emerges.

For example, the Jardim Iporanga neighborhood is located in a protected watershed with a stream that feeds São Paulo's main water reservoir. Before slum upgrading, the neighborhood's scattered housing without sewage treatment had been causing pollution. Then, following the environmentally-attuned upgrading, one resident constructed a house on the newly-protected space. But he quickly heard from Sandra Regina, the community's association president, that he was threatening the common good. He agreed to demolish his structure.

"Nowadays it's paradise here," Regina says. "There is clean, treated water, while before it was all sewage." The main need now, she says, is jobs—indeed across São Paulo, income generation is seen as a main challenge to a successful urbanization process. And there are some conscious job-creation efforts, with citizen groups playing a key role. In Jardim Iporanga, for instance, 30 women produce "eco-bags" made of recycled rags; they are mostly sold to the city government which uses them for booklets at seminars and congresses.

Key to Success: A Voice for the Community

There's growing agreement in São Paulo that local communities must themselves take part in the upgrading process, with a community leader acting as a mediator between the local residents and the government. Social worker Rosana Aparício says this mediation is crucial for slum upgrading to be successful.

Anaclaudia Rossbach, Cities Alliance regional advisor for Latin America and the Caribbean, reckons that to have a complete slum upgrading process, social work with the communities should continue after the construction and urbanization process is fully implemented.

There is a question: the array of housing and environmental cleanup policies in slum upgrading demand large investments. The outlays have been rising progressively over the past five years, thanks to combined efforst of federal, state and city governments, as well as contributions from international organizations.

But will they endure politically—through one or more changes of municipal administration? Rossbach believes the answer is yes. And why? Because, she insists, there's a Municipal Housing Council, created by the city in 2002, which acts as a watchdog and also has a direct role in deciding how housing fund moneys will be spent. Its members come from government agencies, unions, from socially attuned non-government organizations and from the universities. They're popularly elected in polls open to all São Paulo citizens. "The council helps to guarantee the policies' continuity," she notes.

Critical Thinking

1. What polices can a government adopt as an alternative to slum eradication and bulldozing?

2. What are the benefits of regularization, of providing squatters with a legal right to live in their housing?

3. What municipal services need to be provided and improved under a strategy of slum upgrading?

Urban Legends
Why Suburbs, Not Cities, Are the Answer

JOEL KOTKIN

The human world is fast becoming an urban world—and according to many, the faster that happens and the bigger the cities get, the better off we all will be. The old suburban model, with families enjoying their own space in detached houses, is increasingly behind us; we're heading toward heavier reliance on public transit, greater density, and far less personal space. Global cities, even colossal ones like Mumbai and Mexico City, represent our cosmopolitan future, we're now told; they will be nerve centers of international commerce and technological innovation just like the great metropolises of the past—only with the Internet and smart phones.

According to Columbia University's Saskia Sassen, mega-cities will inevitably occupy what Vladimir Lenin called the "commanding heights" of the global economy, though instead of making things they'll apparently be specializing in high-end "producer services"—advertising, law, accounting, and so forth—for worldwide clients. Other scholars, such as Harvard University's Edward Glaeser, envision universities helping to power the new "skilled city," where high wages and social amenities attract enough talent to enable even higher-cost urban meccas to compete.

The theory goes beyond established Western cities. A recent World Bank report on global megacities insists that when it comes to spurring economic growth, denser is better: "To try to spread out economic activity," the report argues, is to snuff it. Historian Peter Hall seems to be speaking for a whole generation of urbanists when he argues that we are on the cusp of a "coming golden age" of great cities.

The only problem is, these predictions may not be accurate. Yes, the percentage of people living in cities is clearly growing. In 1975, Tokyo was the largest city in the world, with over 26 million residents, and there were only two other cities worldwide with more than 10 million residents. By 2025, the U.N. projects that there may be 27 cities of that size. The proportion of the world's population living in cities, which has already shot up from 14 percent in 1900 to about 50 percent in 2008, could be 70 percent by 2050. But here's what the boosters don't tell you: It's far less clear whether the extreme centralization and concentration advocated by these new urban utopians is inevitable—and it's not at all clear that it's desirable.

Not all Global Cities are created equal. We can hope the developing-world metropolises of the future will look a lot like the developed-world cities of today, just much, much larger—but that's not likely to be the case. Today's Third World mega-cities face basic challenges in feeding their people, getting them to and from work, and maintaining a minimum level of health. In some, like Mumbai, life expectancy is now at least seven years less than the country as a whole. And many of the world's largest advanced cities are nestled in relatively declining economies—London, Los Angeles, New York, Tokyo. All suffer growing income inequality and outward migration of middle-class families. Even in the best of circumstances, the new age of the megacity might well be an era of unparalleled human congestion and gross inequality.

Perhaps we need to consider another approach. As unfashionable as it might sound, what if we thought less about the benefits of urban density and more about the many possibilities for proliferating more human-scaled urban centers; what if healthy growth turns out to be best achieved through dispersion, not concentration? Instead of overcrowded cities rimmed by hellish new slums, imagine a world filled with vibrant smaller cities, suburbs, and towns: Which do you think is likelier to produce a higher quality of life, a cleaner environment, and a lifestyle conducive to creative thinking?

So how do we get there? First, we need to dismantle some common urban legends.

Perhaps the most damaging misconception of all is the idea that concentration by its very nature creates wealth. Many writers, led by popular theorist Richard Florida, argue that centralized urban areas provide broader cultural opportunities and better access to technology, attracting more innovative, plugged-in people (Florida's "creative class") who will in the long term produce greater economic vibrancy. The hipper the city, the mantra goes, the richer and more successful it will be—and a number of declining American industrial hubs have tried to rebrand themselves as "creative class" hot spots accordingly.

But this argument, or at least many applications of it, gets things backward. Arts and culture generally do not fuel economic growth by themselves; rather, economic growth tends to create the preconditions for their development. Ancient Athens and Rome didn't start out as undiscovered artist neighborhoods. They were metropolises built on imperial wealth—largely collected by force from their colonies—that funded a new class of patrons and consumers of the arts. Renaissance Florence and Amsterdam established themselves as trade centers first and only then began to nurture great artists from their own middle classes and the surrounding regions.

Even modern Los Angeles owes its initial ascendancy as much to agriculture and oil as to Hollywood. Today, its port and related industries employ far more people than the entertainment business does. (In any case, the men who built Hollywood were hardly cultured aesthetes by middle-class American standards; they were furriers, butchers, and petty traders, mostly from hardscrabble backgrounds in the czarist *shtetls* and back streets of America's tough ethnic ghettos.) New York, now arguably the world's cultural capital, was once dismissed as a boorish, money-obsessed town, much like the contemporary urban critique of Dallas, Houston, or Phoenix.

Sadly, cities desperate to reverse their slides have been quick to buy into the simplistic idea that by merely branding themselves "creative" they can renew their dying economies; think of Cleveland's Rock and Roll Hall of Fame, Michigan's bid to market Detroit as a "cool city," and similar efforts in the washed-up industrial towns of the British north. Being told you live in a "European Capital of Culture," as Liverpool was in 2008, means little when your city has no jobs and people are leaving by the busload.

Even legitimate cultural meccas aren't insulated from economic turmoil. Berlin—beloved by writers, artists, tourists, and romantic expatriates—has cultural institutions that would put any wannabe European Capital of Culture to shame, as well as a thriving underground art and music scene. Yet for all its bohemian spirit, Berlin is also deeply in debt and suffers from unemployment far higher than Germany's national average, with rates reaching 14 percent. A full quarter of its workers, many of them living in wretched immigrant ghettos, earn less than 900 euros a month; compare that with Frankfurt, a smaller city more known for its skyscrapers and airport terminals than for any major cultural output, but which boasts one of Germany's lowest unemployment rates and by some estimates the highest per capita income of any European city. No wonder Berlin Mayor Klaus Wowereit once described his city as "poor but sexy."

Culture, media, and other "creative" industries, important as they are for a city's continued prosperity, simply do not spark an economy on their own. It turns out to be the comparatively boring, old-fashioned industries, such as trade in goods, manufacturing, energy, and agriculture, that drive the world's fastest-rising cities. In the 1960s and 1970s, the industrial capitals of Seoul and Tokyo developed their economies far faster than Cairo and Jakarta, which never created advanced industrial bases. China's great coastal urban centers, notably Guangzhou, Shanghai, and Shenzhen, are replicating this pattern with big business in steel, textiles, garments,

and electronics, and the country's vast interior is now poised to repeat it once again. Fossil fuels—not art galleries—have powered the growth of several of the world's fastest-rising urban areas, including Abu Dhabi, Houston, Moscow, and Perth.

It's only after urban centers achieve economic success that they tend to look toward the higher-end amenities the creative-classers love. When Abu Dhabi decided to import its fancy Guggenheim and Louvre satellite museums, it was already, according to *Fortune* magazine, the world's richest city. Beijing, Houston, Shanghai, and Singapore are opening or expanding schools for the arts, museums, and gallery districts. But they paid for them the old-fashioned way.

Nor is the much-vaunted "urban core" the only game in town. Innovators of all kinds seek to avoid the high property prices, overcrowding, and often harsh anti-business climates of the city center. Britain's recent strides in technology and design-led manufacturing have been concentrated not in London, but along the outer reaches of the Thames Valley and the areas around Cambridge. It's the same story in continental Europe, from the exurban Grand-Couronne outside of Paris to the "edge cities" that have sprung up around Amsterdam and Rotterdam. In India, the bulk of new tech companies cluster in campus-like developments around—but not necessarily in—Bangalore, Hyderabad, and New Delhi. And let's not forget that Silicon Valley, the granddaddy of global tech centers and still home to the world's largest concentration of high-tech workers, remains essentially a vast suburb. Apple, Google, and Intel don't seem to mind. Those relative few who choose to live in San Francisco can always take the company-provided bus.

In fact, the suburbs are not as terrible as urban boosters frequently insist.

Consider the environment. We tend to associate suburbia with carbon dioxide-producing sprawl and urban areas with sustainability and green living. But though it's true that urban residents use less gas to get to work than their suburban or rural counterparts, when it comes to overall energy use the picture gets more complicated. Studies in Australia and Spain have found that when you factor in apartment common areas, second residences, consumption, and air travel, urban residents can easily use more energy than their less densely packed neighbors. Moreover, studies around the world—from Beijing and Rome to London and Vancouver—have found that packed concentrations of concrete, asphalt, steel, and glass produce what are known as "heat islands," generating 6 to 10 degrees Celsius more heat than surrounding areas and extending as far as twice a city's political boundaries.

When it comes to inequality, cities might even be the problem. In the West, the largest cities today also tend to suffer the most extreme polarization of incomes. In 1980, Manhattan ranked 17th among U.S. counties for income disparity; by 2007 it was first, with the top fifth of wage earners earning 52 times what the bottom fifth earned. In Toronto between 1970 and 2001, according to one recent study, middle-income neighborhoods shrank by half, dropping from two-thirds of the city to one-third, while poor districts more than doubled to 40 percent. By 2020, middle-class neighborhoods could fall to about 10 percent.

Cities often offer a raw deal for the working class, which ends up squeezed by a lethal combination of chronically high housing costs and chronically low opportunity in economies dominated by finance and other elite industries. Once the cost of living is factored in, more than half the children in inner London live in poverty, the highest level in Britain, according to a Greater London Authority study. More than 1 million Londoners were on public support in 2002, in a city of roughly 8 million.

The disparities are even starker in Asia. Shenzhen and Hong Kong, for instance, have among the most skewed income distributions in the region. A relatively small number of skilled professionals and investors are doing very well, yet millions are migrating to urban slums in places like Mumbai not because they've all suddenly become "knowledge workers," but because of the changing economics of farming. And by the way, Mumbai's slums are still expanding as a proportion of the city's overall population—even as India's nationwide poverty rate has fallen from one in three Indians to one in five over the last two decades. Forty years ago, slum dwellers accounted for one in six Mumbaikars. Now they are a majority.

To their credit, talented new urbanists have had moderate success in turning smaller cities like Chattanooga and Hamburg into marginally more pleasant places to live. But grandiose theorists, with their focus on footloose elites and telecommuting technogeniuses, have no practical answers for the real problems that plague places like Mumbai, let alone Cairo, Jakarta, Manila, Nairobi, or any other 21st-century megacity: rampant crime, crushing poverty, choking pollution. It's time for a completely different approach, one that abandons the long-held assumption that scale and growth go hand in hand.

Throughout the long history of urban development, the size of a city roughly correlated with its wealth, standard of living, and political strength. The greatest and most powerful cities were almost always the largest in population: Babylon, Rome, Alexandria, Baghdad, Delhi, London, or New York.

But bigger might no longer mean better. The most advantaged city of the future could well turn out to be a much smaller one. Cities today are expanding at an unparalleled rate when it comes to size, but wealth, power, and general well-being lag behind. With the exception of Los Angeles, New York, and Tokyo, most cities of 10 million or more are relatively poor, with a low standard of living and little strategic influence. The cities that do have influence, modern infrastructure, and relatively high per capita income, by contrast, are often wealthy small cities like Abu Dhabi or hard-charging up-and-comers such as Singapore. Their efficient, agile economies can outpace lumbering megacities financially, while also maintaining a high quality of life. With almost 5 million residents, for example, Singapore isn't at the top of the list in terms of population. But its GDP is much higher than that of larger cities like Cairo, Lagos, and Manila. Singapore boasts a per capita

income of almost $50,000, one of the highest in the world, roughly the same as America's or Norway's. With one of the world's three largest ports, a zippy and safe subway system, and an impressive skyline, Singapore is easily the cleanest, most efficient big city in all of Asia. Other smaller-scaled cities like Austin, Monterrey, and Tel Aviv have enjoyed similar success.

It turns out that the rise of the megacity is by no means inevitable—and it might not even be happening. Shlomo Angel, an adjunct professor at New York University's Wagner School, has demonstrated that as the world's urban population exploded from 1960 to 2000, the percentage living in the 100 largest megacities actually declined from nearly 30 percent to closer to 25 percent. Even the widely cited 2009 World Bank report on megacities, a staunchly pro-urban document, acknowledges that as societies become wealthier, they inevitably begin to deconcentrate, with the middle classes moving to the periphery. Urban population densities have been on the decline since the 19th century, Angel notes, as people have sought out cheaper and more appealing homes beyond city limits. In fact, despite all the "back to the city" hype of the past decade, more than 80 percent of new metropolitan growth in the United States since 2000 has been in suburbs.

And that's not such a bad thing. Ultimately, dispersion— both city to suburb and megacity to small city—holds out some intriguing solutions to current urban problems. The idea took hold during the initial golden age of industrial growth—the English 19th century—when suburban "garden cities" were established around London's borders. The great early 20th-century visionary Ebenezer Howard saw this as a means to create a "new civilization" superior to the crowded, dirty, and congested cities of his day. It was an ideal that attracted a wide range of thinkers, including Friedrich Engels and H.G. Wells.

More recently, a network of smaller cities in the Netherlands has helped create a smartly distributed national economy. Amsterdam, for example, has low-density areas between its core and its corporate centers. It has kept the great Dutch city both livable and competitive. American urbanists are trying to bring the same thinking to the United States. Delore Zimmerman, of the North Dakota-based Praxis Strategy Group, has helped foster high-tech-oriented development in small towns and cities from the Red River Valley in North Dakota and Minnesota to the Wenatchee region in Washington State. The outcome has been promising: Both areas are reviving from periods of economic and demographic decline.

But the dispersion model holds out even more hope for the developing world, where an alternative to megacities is an even more urgent necessity. Ashok R. Datar, chairman of the Mumbai Environmental Social Network and a longtime advisor to the Ambani corporate group, suggests that slowing migration to urban slums represents the most practical strategy for relieving Mumbai's relentless poverty. His plan is similar to Zimmerman's: By bolstering local industries, you can stanch the flow of job seekers to major city centers, maintaining a greater balance between rural areas and cities and avoiding the severe overcrowding that plagues Mumbai right now.

Between the 19th century, when Charles Dickens described London as a "sooty spectre" that haunted and deformed its inhabitants, and the present, something has been lost from our discussion of cities: the human element. The goal of urban planners should not be to fulfill their own grandiose visions of megacities on a hill, but to meet the needs of the people living in them, particularly those people suffering from overcrowding, environmental misery, and social inequality. When it comes to exporting our notions to the rest of the globe, we must be aware of our own susceptibility to fashionable theories in urban design—because while the West may be able to live with its mistakes, the developing world doesn't enjoy that luxury.

Critical Thinking

1. What problems does Kotkin see in giant cities like Mumbai (formerly known as Bombay), Cairo, Jakarta, Manila, and Nairobi?

2. Why are these cities suffering such great growth despite their extensive problems? Why are people still moving to the slums?

3. How does Kotkin believe that a "dispersion model" will relieve some of the problems and pressures on cities such as Mumbai?

Femicide in Ciudad Juárez:
What Can Planners Do?

María Teresa Vázquez-Castillo

Femicide is a word whose definition women in Ciudad Juárez can explain very well. They learned and appropriated the word in the process of trying to make sense of the more than 400 murders of women that have taken place in this Mexican border city since 1993. In the last thirteen years, mothers, friends, activists, students, academics and other sectors inside and outside Ciudad Juárez have organized what is now an international movement of women. Their main concerns have been to find the murderers and to claim justice, to find *who* is committing these heinous crimes against women. This article, however, urges progressive planners to focus on *what* needs to be done to stop the femicide in Ciudad Juárez. In this fast-growing region characterized by uneven urbanization processes, the *maquiladora* industry, the narco-economy and corrupt police, women's lives are endangered as they move through unsafe public space that lacks protective urban infrastructure.

Many different hypotheses have emerged about the femicide. Public officials have been appointed to "investigate" the cases, only to then be removed. None of these public officials was awarded decision-making power to act or prosecute. Researchers and journalists have even denounced and publicized the names of the culprits supposedly involved in the femicide, but the Mexican government has neither taken any legal action nor initiated a serious investigation. After thirteen years the gender violence continues, and it is now spreading to other urban areas, such as Chihuahua City.

Meanwhile, some people are in jail, accused of being the murderers even though they claim they are innocent. The mothers of the victims have denounced that some of those in jail are scapegoats, there to placate the public's outrage. Yet even with these people behind bars, the murders have continued. Two lawyers of the jailed have been killed and the lives of two journalists who have written books about the femicide in Juárez—*Huesos en el Desierto* (*Bones in the Desert*) and *Harvest of Women*—have been threatened, too. One of them was even kidnapped, severely beaten and hospitalized for several months.

In order to understand this femicide, it must be put in the context—of the characteristics of the city, the urbanization that has taken place here, the profile of the women who've been murdered, and the responses that have emerged both to protest the femicide and to claim justice.

Ciudad Juárez

Ciudad Juárez is a border city of approximately 1.3 million inhabitants located across from El Paso, Texas. About 60 percent of the population is immigrants who are unable to cross the border into the United States and therefore stay in Ciudad Juárez. The city has become one of the fastest growing in Mexico, not only because of the immigration, but also because of the investment made here. In the 1960s the Border Industrialization Program started promoting assembly plants, or *maquiladoras*. In 1992, with the passage of the North American Free Trade Agreement (NAFTA), favorable conditions for foreign capital permitted the siting of further *maquiladoras*. According to the *Instituto de Estadística, Geografía e Informática* (INEGI), by 2000, about 308 *maquiladoras* employing 250,000 workers existed in Ciudad Juárez. Many of those employed are single young women migrating from others states. Sexist men in border states who resent the increasing presence of working females in public spaces call these women *maquilocas*, meaning flirtatious women who work in *maquiladoras*.

Race and Class of the Femicide

It is not difficult to infer the class and racial implications of the atrocious murders of the more than 400 women who have been reported kidnapped, raped, tortured, mutilated and killed. The murderers have been killing only young working-class women of a certain profile: short and thin with long, dark hair and brown skin. The victims have been between fifteen to thirty-nine years old, and many were originally from other Mexican states.

While the murderers enjoy impunity, public officials and the local police have accused the victims of being prostitutes, of leading double lives and of being the provokers of the assaults. The records, however, show that many of the victims were *maquiladora* workers, while others were students, housewives or workers in another economic sector.

Roles of the Urbanization, Maquiladoras, and the Narco-Economy

Many explanations for the femicide have been advanced. From a planning perspective, it is important to understand the urbanization of Ciudad Juárez and the roles of the *maquiladora* industry and the criminal economy. First, as new waves of immigrants, attracted by the possibility of crossing the border and by the jobs available in the maquiladora industry, have arrived in Ciudad Juárez, the pressures on housing and urban services have increased. As has been the case in other Mexican and Latin American cities, the new arrivals tended to relocate to the edge of city, where land was cheaper but infrastructure and urban services were lacking. The layout of Ciudad Juárez is sprawling, and many of the women kidnapped and murdered either lived in the "new" settlements on the edges of the city or their bodies were found in these newly urbanized areas.

The murderers have attacked women who are most vulnerable in the urban space of Ciudad Juárez—those who use public transportation, who do not have a car and who, in many cases, walk long distances in order to take a bus or a collective taxi. Thus, the rapid urbanization process prompted by the relocation of global capital to the border area has created an unsafe city that lacks urban infrastructure, some of the most important of which are affordable housing, appropriate transportation and public lighting.

Impunity in the city is rampant in this border area that is now known as one of the most dangerous cities for women. The criminal narco-economy has free rein and has taken the lives of both men and women in the region. Some of the names denounced as possible culprits have been identified as men belonging to the high society of Ciudad Juárez and to the business and economic elites in the region. In addition, some local journalists affirm that those potential murderers might be linked to the criminal economy in the area.

A Planning Point of View

From a gendered planning perspective, the built environment of this city contributes to the violation of human rights. You might ask: How can a city reproduce human rights violations of young low-income women? I recently saw the answer in one of the latest European documentaries about the murders in Ciudad Juárez. In this film, the filmmaker follows the routine of a young woman from the time she leaves home to the time she comes back home from work. The woman leaves home late at night to go to her job in the maquiladora. Maquiladoras have different shifts and her shift starts at midnight. In order to catch the bus, she needs to walk in the dark, with no sidewalks or streetlights to guide her way. She carries a flashlight to see where she is walking. Like many other people who go to Ciudad Juárez either looking for a job in the maquiladoras or trying to cross the border, this young woman lives in the informal settlements of Ciudad Juárez, many of which lack access to urban services. This lack of urban services has a gender component, that of not providing safety to women in Ciudad Juárez.

The work of the mothers, relatives, activists, academics, students and other men and women in the region and around the world has created a growing global movement of women protesting the femicide in Juárez. At the local level, the light posts in Ciudad Juárez, painted in pink with a black cross in the middle, serve as memorials for the murdered women. In some cases, those post have the legend: *¡Ni Una Más!* Not one more!

Big crosses have been planted around the city as if the city itself had become a huge cemetery as well as a huge memorial site for the murdered women. In addition to crosses, the residents of Juárez witness the visits of women from around the globe who travel to take back the streets and participate in international demonstrations in Ciudad Juárez. In 2004, the US portion of a demonstration gathered in El Paso, Texas, the twin city of Ciudad Juárez, and marched, crossing the border to meet the women in Ciudad Juárez.

Different local and bi-national organizations have emerged to respond to the femicide. Some have survived the threats, intimidation and lack of resources for many years, while others have not. These organizations include: Justicia para Nuestras Hijas (Justice for Our Daughters); Nuestras Hijas de Regreso a Casa (Our Daughter Come Back Home); Comité Independiente de Derechos Humanos de Chihuahua (Independent Committee for Human Rights in Chihuahua); Casa Amiga (Friendly House); Amigos de las Mujeres de Juárez (Friends of the Women of Juárez); El Paso Coalition Against Violence on Women and Children at the Border; and other human rights organizations and NGOs.

These groups have organized conferences and meetings and presented two films about the femicide: *Señorita Extraviada* or *Missing Young Woman* (Lourdes Portillo) and *La Batalla de las Cruces* (Patricia Ravelo). The Mexico Solidarity Network organizes groups in the United States to periodically visit the mothers of the victims and learn about Juárez so as to serve as constant witness to the violence.

What Remains to Be Done?

The question always remains for progressive planners and planning academics as to what needs to be done by different social actors in the city and in the world to stop this femicide and to make both private and public spaces safer for the women of Juárez. The response needs to be informed by the twelfth demand of the Resolutions of the International Conference on the Killings of Women of Juárez hosted by the Chicano Studies Department at UCLA on November 1, 2003. The mothers and activists who attended the conference wrote these resolutions, the twelfth demand of which reads:

> 12. We demand that the government of Ciudad Juárez, its planning entities and major employers in the region work jointly to provide the necessary infrastructure that will make Ciudad Juárez a safer place for everybody, in which women can have the freedom of movement, as any other human being, without fearing for their lives and their safety.

After the failure of the political and legal entities to bring justice to the murders of the women of Juárez, women participating in this transnational and international women's movement have started pointing out some solutions, very basic in appearance: adequate street lighting, transportation provided for the *maquiladora* workers and affordable housing close to jobs. These solutions target the provision of safer urban infrastructure. This war against women is affecting all residents of the city as the impact of the tragedy has resulted in the disintegration of families, the departure of families from Juárez and, in some cases, the suicide of men close to the victims.

The call then is for progressive planners to get involved and support the women of Juárez. Through a participatory approach, and in conjunction with different community organizations inside and outside Juárez, progressive planners could help develop a city plan from the grassroots, a plan that includes elements to be implemented at both the individual and group levels in order to end the violence. This is a call for Planners Network to establish a relationship with the groups supporting the movement of the Women of Juárez in order to jointly organize a bilateral/international meeting to work out a grassroots plan for Ciudad Juárez. This plan, the purpose of which would be to make Juárez a safer city and to stop the femicide and the terror, could effectively be carried out by grassroots organizations and civil society actors in Juárez.

Conclusion

Roads, housing and other urban services are not in place to support the labor force that has emerged as a result of the infusion of global capital in the form of the *maquiladoras*. Therefore, men and women working in the *maquiladoras* look for shelter in areas that were previously undeveloped, but these areas lack services. Globalization, which has manifested itself in the movement of firms to other countries, has prompted an unplanned urbanization in Mexico for which the planning offices have not made the *maquiladoras* accountable. I am not saying that we need to take away our eyes from the murderers, but I am saying that, in addition to finding *who* is responsible, we need to think about *what* can be done to create an infrastructure that makes Ciudad Juárez a safer city for all women and men. Although new infrastructure, an improved urban form and community development will not stop the femicide, these are powerful tools for creating safer urban spaces. In addition, women and men in Ciudad Juárez deserve a democratic, grassroots planning process led by their voices and their demands.

For socially responsible planners, to ignore the femicide in Ciudad Juárez is to ignore justice in cities, especially now that the femicide has spread to other countries like Guatemala, El Salvador and Honduras. These countries have also opened their doors to the *maquiladoras,* and the women murdered have been mostly indigenous women.

Critical Thinking

1. What is a *maquiladora?* What factors led to the growth of maquiladoras?

2. Why do you think that women make up the vast majority of the workforce in the *maquiladoras?*

3. How has the physical layout of work sites and housing in Ciudad Juárez and the operations of the maquiladoras added to the physical jeopardy faced by young women?

4. What can cities do to meet the needs of women, especially poor women? Why has the response of Juárez been far, far less than adequate?

María Teresa Vázquez-Castillo is an assistant professor in the Department of Urban Studies and Planning at California State University-Northridge.

Are Europe's Cities Better?

PIETRO S. NIVOLA

Cities grow in three directions: *in* by crowding, *up* into multi-story buildings, or *out* toward the periphery. Although cities everywhere have developed in each of these ways at various times, nowhere in Europe do urban settlements sprawl as much as in the United States. Less than a quarter of the U.S. population lived in suburbia in 1950. Now well over half does. Why have most European cities remained compact compared to the hyperextended American metropolis?

At first glance, the answer seems elementary. The urban centers of Europe are older, and the populations of their countries did not increase as rapidly in the postwar period. In addition, stringent national land-use laws slowed exurban development, whereas the disjointed jurisdictions in U.S. metropolitan regions encouraged it.

But on closer inspection, this conventional wisdom does not suffice. It is true that the contours of most major urban areas in the United States were formed to a great extent by economic and demographic expansion after the Second World War. But the same was true in much of Europe, where entire cities were reduced to rubble by the war and had to be rebuilt from ground zero.

Consider Germany, whose cities were carpet bombed. Many German cities today are old in name only, and though the country's population as a whole grew less quickly than America's after 1950, West German cities experienced formidable economic growth and in-migrations. Yet the metropolitan population density of the United States is still about one-fourth that of Germany. New York, our densest city, has approximately one-third the number of inhabitants per square mile as Frankfurt.

Sprawl has continued apace even in places where the American population has grown little or not at all in recent decades. From 1970 to 1990, the Chicago area's population rose by only 4 percent, but the region's built-up land increased 46 percent. Metropolitan Cleveland's population actually declined by 8 percent, yet 33 percent more of the area's territory was developed.

The fragmented jurisdictional structure in U.S. metropolitan areas, wherein every suburban town or county has control over the use of land, does not adequately explain sprawl either. Since 1950, about half of America's central cities at least doubled their territory by annexing new suburbs. Houston covered 160 square miles in 1950. By 1980, exercising broad powers to annex its environs, it incorporated 556 square miles. In the same 30-year period, Jacksonville went from being a town of 30 square miles to a regional government enveloping 841 square miles—two-thirds the size of Rhode Island. True, the tri-state region of New York contains some 780 separate localities, some with zoning ordinances that permit only low-density subdivisions. But the urban region of Paris—Ile de France—comprises 1,300 municipalities, all of which have considerable discretion in the consignment of land for development.

To be sure, European central governments presumably oversee these local decisions through nationwide land-use statutes. But is this a telling distinction? The relationship of U.S. state governments to their local communities is roughly analogous to that of Europe's unitary regimes to their respective local entities. Not only are the governments of some of our states behemoths (New York State's annual expenditures, for example, approximate Sweden's entire national budget) but a significant number have enacted territorial planning legislation reminiscent of European guidelines. Indeed, from a legal standpoint, local governments in this country are mere "creatures" of the states, which can direct, modify, or even abolish their localities at will. Many European municipalities, with their ancient independent charters, are less subordinated.

The enforcement of land-use plans varies considerably in Europe. In Germany, as in America, some *Länder* (or states) are more restrictive than others. The Scandinavians, Dutch, and British take planning more seriously than, say, the Italians. The late Antonio Cederna, an astute journalist, wrote volumes about the egregious violations of building and development codes in and around Italy's historic centers. Critics who assume that land regulators in the United States are chronically permissive, whereas Europe's growth managers are always scrupulous and "smart," ought to contemplate, say, the unsightly new suburbs stretching across the northwestern plain of Florence toward Prato, and then visit Long Island's East End, where it is practically impossible to obtain a building permit along many miles of pristine coastline.

Big, Fast, and Violent

The more important contrasts in urban development between America and Europe lie elsewhere. With three and half million square miles of territory, the United States has had much more space over which to spread its settlements. And on this vast expanse, decentralizing technologies took root and spread decades earlier than in other industrial countries. In 1928, for example, 78 percent of all the motor vehicles in the world were located in the United States. With incomes rising rapidly, and the costs of producing vehicles declining, 56 percent of American families owned an automobile by that time. No European country reached a comparable level of automobile ownership until well after the Second World War. America's motorized multitudes were able to begin commuting between suburban residences and workplaces decades before such an arrangement was imaginable in any other advanced nation.

A more perverse but also distinctive cause of urban sprawl in the United States has been the country's comparatively high level of violent crime. Why a person is ten times more likely to be murdered in America than in Japan, seven times more likely to be raped than in France, or almost four times more likely to be robbed at gun point than in the United Kingdom, is a complex question. But three things are known.

First, although criminal violence has declined markedly here in the past few years, America's cities have remained dangerous by international standards. New York's murder rate dropped by two-thirds between 1991 and 1997, yet there were still 767 homicides committed that year. London, a mega-city of about the same size, had less than 130. Second, the rates of personal victimization, including murder, rape, assault, robbery, and personal theft, tend to be much higher within U.S. central cities than in their surroundings. In 1997, incidents of violent crime inside Washington, D.C., for instance, were six times more frequent than in the city's suburbs. Third, there is a strong correlation between city crime rates and the flight of households and businesses to safer jurisdictions. According to economists Julie Berry Cullen of the University of Michigan and Steven D. Levitt of the University of Chicago, between 1976 and 1993, a city typically lost one resident for every additional crime committed within it.

Opinion surveys regularly rank public safety as a leading consideration in the selection of residential locations. In 1992, when New Yorkers were asked to name "the most important reason" for moving out of town, the most common answer was "crime, lack of safety" (47.2 percent). All other reasons—including "high cost of living" (9.3 percent) and "not enough affordable housing" (5.3 percent)—lagged far behind. Two years ago, when the American Assembly weighed the main obstacles to business investments in the inner cities, it learned that businessmen identified lack of security as *the* principal impediment. In short, crime in America has further depopulated the cores of metropolitan areas, scattering their inhabitants and businesses.

The Not-So-Invisible Hand

In addition to these fundamental differences, the public agendas here and in major European countries have been miles apart. The important distinctions, moreover, have less to do with differing "urban" programs than with other national policies, the consequences of which are less understood.

For example, lavish agricultural subsidies in Europe have kept more farmers in business and dissuaded them from selling their land to developers. Per hectare of farmland, agricultural subventions are 12 times more generous in France than in the United States, a divergence that surely helps explain why small farms still surround Paris but not New York City.

Thanks to scant taxation of gasoline, the price of automotive fuel in the United States is almost a quarter of what it is in Italy. Is it any surprise that Italians would live closer to their urban centers, where they can more easily walk to work or rely on public transportation? On a per capita basis, residents of Milan make an average of 350 trips a year on public transportation; people in San Diego make an average of 17.

Gasoline is not the only form of energy that is much cheaper in the United States than in Europe. Rates for electric power and furnace fuels are too. The expense of heating the equivalent of an average detached U.S. suburban home, and of operating the gigantic home appliances (such as refrigerators and freezers) that substitute for neighborhood stores in many American residential communities, would be daunting to most households in large parts of Europe.

Systems of taxation make a profound difference. European tax structures penalize consumption. Why don't most of the Dutch and Danes vacate their compact towns and cities where many commuters ride bicycles, rather than drive sport-utility vehicles, to work? The sales tax on a new, medium-sized car in the Netherlands is approximately nine times higher than in the United States; in Denmark, 37 times higher. The U.S. tax code favors spending over saving (the latter is effectively taxed twice) and provides inducements to purchase particular goods—most notably houses, since the mortgage interest is deductible. The effect of such provisions is to lead most American families into the suburbs, where spacious dwellings are available and absorb much of the nation's personal savings pool.

Tax policy is not the only factor promoting home ownership in the United States. Federal Housing Administration and Veterans Administration mortgage guarantees financed more than a quarter of the suburban single-family homes built in the immediate postwar period. In Europe, the housing stocks of many countries were decimated by the war. Governments responded to the emergency by erecting apartment buildings and extending rental subsidies to large segments of the population. America also built a good deal of publicly subsidized rental housing in the postwar years, but chiefly to accommodate the most impoverished city-dwellers. Unlike the mixed-income housing complexes scattered around London or Paris, U.S. public housing projects further concentrated the urban poor in the inner cities, turning the likes of Chicago's South Side into breeding grounds of social degradation and violence. Middle-class city-dwellers fled from these places to less perilous locations in the metropolitan fringe.

Few decisions are more consequential for the shape of cities than a society's investments in transportation infrastructure. Government at all levels in the United States has committed hundreds of billions to the construction and maintenance of highways, passenger railroads, and transit systems. What counts, however, is not just the magnitude of the commitment but the *distribution* of the public expenditures among modes of transportation. In the United States, where the share claimed by roads has dwarfed that of alternatives by about six to one, an unrelenting increase in automobile travel and a steady decline in transit usage—however heavily subsidized—was inevitable.

Dense cities dissipate without relatively intensive use of mass transit. In 1945, transit accounted for approximately 35 percent of urban passenger miles traveled in the United States. By 1994, the figure had dwindled to less than 3 percent—or roughly one-fifth the average in Western Europe. If early on, American transportation planners had followed the British or French budgetary practice of allocating between 40 and 60 percent of their transport outlays to passenger railroads and mass transit systems, instead of nearly 85 percent for highways, there is little question that many U.S. cities would be more compressed today.

Dense cities also require a vibrant economy of neighborhood shops and services. (Why live in town if performing life's simplest everyday functions, like picking up fresh groceries for supper, requires driving to distant vendors?) But local shopkeepers cannot compete with the regional megastores that are proliferating in America's metropolitan shopping centers and strip malls. Multiple restrictions on the penetration and predatory pricing practices of large retailers in various European countries protect small urban businesses. The costs to consumers are high, but the convenience and intimacy of London's "high streets" or of the corner markets in virtually every Parisian *arrondissement* are preserved.

"Shift and Shaft" Federalism

Europe's cities retain their merchants and inhabitants for yet another reason: European municipalities typically do not face the same fiscal liabilities as U.S. cities. Local governments in Germany derive less than one-third of their income from local revenues; higher levels of government transfer the rest. For a wide range of basic functions—including educational institutions, hospitals, prisons, courts, utilities, and so on—the national treasury funds as much as 80 percent of the expense incurred by England's local councils. Localities in Italy and the Netherlands raise only about 10 percent of their budgets locally. In contrast, U.S. urban governments must largely support themselves: They collect two-thirds of their revenues from local sources.

In principle, self-sufficiency is a virtue; municipal taxpayers ought to pay directly for the essential services they use. But in practice, these taxpayers are also being asked to finance plenty of other costly projects, many of which are mandated, but underfunded, by the federal government. Affluent jurisdictions may be able to absorb this added burden, but communities strapped for revenues often cannot. To satisfy the federal government's paternalistic commands, many old cities have been forced to raise taxes and cut the services that local residents need or value most. In response, businesses and middle-class households flee to the suburbs.

America's public schools are perhaps the clearest example of a crucial local service that is tottering under the weight of unfunded federal directives. Few nations, if any, devote as large a share of their total public education expenditures to *nonteaching* personnel. There may be several excuses for this lopsided administrative overhead, but one explanation is almost certainly the growth of government regulation and the armies of academic administrators needed to handle the red tape.

Schools are required, among other things, to test drinking water, remove asbestos, perform recycling, insure "gender equity," and provide something called "special education." The latter program alone forces local authorities to set aside upwards of $30 billion a year to meet the needs of students with disabilities. Meanwhile, according to a 1996 report by the U.S. Advisory Commission on Intergovernmental Relations, the federal government reimburses a paltry 8 percent of the expense. Compliance costs for urban school districts, where the concentrations of learning-disabled pupils are high and the means to support them low, can be particularly onerous. Out of a total $850 million of local funds budgeted for 77,000 students in the District of Columbia, for instance, $170 million has been earmarked for approximately 8,000 students receiving "special education."

Wretched schools are among the reasons why most American families have fled the cities for greener pastures. It is hard enough for distressed school systems like the District's, which struggle to impart even rudimentary literacy, to compete with their wealthier suburban counterparts. The difficulty is compounded by federal laws that, without adequate recompense, divert scarce educational resources from serving the overwhelming majority of students.

Schools are but one of many municipal services straining to defray centrally dictated expenses. Consider the plight of urban mass transit in the United States. Its empty seats and colossal operating deficits are no secret. Less acknowledged are the significant financial obligations imposed by Section 504 of the Rehabilitation Act and subsequent legislation. To comply with the Department of Transportation's rules for retrofitting public buses and subways, New York City estimated in 1980 that it would need to spend more than $1 billion in capital improvements on top of $50 million in recurring annual operating costs. As the city's mayor, Edward I. Koch, said at the time, "It would be cheaper for us to provide every severely disabled person with taxi service than make 255 of our subway stations accessible."

Although the Reagan administration later lowered these costs, passage of the Americans with Disabilities Act in 1990 led to a new round of pricey special accommodations in New York and other cities with established transit systems. Never mind that the Washington Metro is the nation's most modern and well-designed subway system. It has been ordered to tear up 45 stations and install bumpy tiles along platform edges to accommodate the sight impaired, a multi-million dollar effort. At issue here, as in the Individuals with Disabilities Education Act, is not whether provisions for the handicapped are desirable and just. Rather, the puzzle is how Congress can sincerely claim to champion these causes if it scarcely appropriates the money to advance them.

Nearly two decades ago, Mayor Koch detailed in *The Public Interest* what he called the "millstone" of some 47 unfunded mandates.[1] The tally of national statutes encumbering U.S. local governments since then has surpassed at least one hundred. And this does not count the hundreds of federal court orders and agency rulings that micromanage, and often drain, local resources. By 1994, Los Angeles estimated that federally mandated programs were costing the city approximately $840 million a year. Erasing that debit from the city's revenue requirements, either by meeting it with federal and state aid or by substantial recisions, would be tantamount to reducing city taxes as much as 20 percent. A windfall that large could do more to reclaim the city's slums, and halt the hollowing out of core communities, than would all of the region's planned "empowerment zones," "smart growth" initiatives, and "livability" bond issues.

Follow Europe?

To conclude that greater fiscal burden sharing and a wide range of other public policies help sustain Europe's concentrated cities is not to say, of course, that all those policies have enhanced the welfare of Europeans—and hence, that the United States ought to emulate them. The central governments of Western Europe may assume more financial responsibilities instead of bucking them down to the local level, but these top-heavy regimes also levy much higher taxes. Fully funding all of Washington's many social mandates with national tax dollars would mean, as in much of Europe, a more centralized and bloated welfare state.

Most households are not better off when farmers are heavily subsidized, or when anticompetitive practices protect micro-businesses at the expense of larger, more efficient firms. Nor would most consumers gain greater satisfaction from housing strategies that encourage renter occupancy but not homeownership, or from gas taxes and transportation

policies that force people out of their cars and onto buses, trains, or bicycles.

In fact, these sorts of public biases have exacted an economic toll in various Western European countries, and certainly in Japan, while the United States has prospered in part because its economy is less regulated, and its metropolitan areas have been allowed to decompress. So suffocating is the extreme concentration of people and functions in the Tokyo area that government planners now view decentralization as a top economic priority. Parts of the British economy, too, seem squeezed by development controls. A recent report by McKinsey and Company attributes lagging productivity in key sectors to Britain's land-use restrictions that hinder entry and expansion of the most productive firms.

The densely settled cities of Europe teem with small shops. But the magnetic small-business presence reflects, at least in part, a heavily regulated labor market that stifles entrepreneurs who wish to expand and thus employ more workers. As the *Economist* noted in a review of the Italian economy, "Italy's plethora of small firms is as much an indictment of its economy as a triumph: many seem to lack either the will or the capital to keep growing." The lack of will is not surprising; moving from small to midsize or large means taking on employees who are nearly impossible to lay off when times turn bad, and it means saddling a company with costly mandated payroll benefits. Italy may have succeeded in conserving clusters of small businesses in its old cities and towns, but perhaps at the price of abetting double-digit unemployment in its economy as a whole.

Striking a Balance

America's strewn-out cities are not without their own inefficiencies. The sprawling conurbations demand, for one thing, virtually complete reliance on automotive travel, thereby raising per capita consumption of motor fuel to four times the average of cities in Europe. That extraordinary level of fossil-fuel combustion complicates U.S. efforts to lower this country's considerable contribution to the buildup of greenhouse gases. Our seemingly unbounded suburbanization has also blighted central cities that possess irreplaceable architectural and historic assets. A form of metropolitan growth that displaces only bleak and obsolescent urban relics, increasingly discarded by almost everyone, may actually be welfare-enhancing. A growth process that also blights and abandons a nation's important civic and cultural centers, however, is rightfully grounds for concern.

Still, proposals to reconfigure urban development in the United States need to shed several misconceptions. As research by Helen Ladd of Duke University has shown, the costs of delivering services in high-density settlements frequently increase, not decrease. Traffic congestion at central nodes also tends to worsen with density, and more people may be exposed to hazardous levels of soot and smog. (The inhabitants of Manhattan drive fewer vehicle miles per capita than persons who inhabit New York's low-density suburbs. Nevertheless, Manhattan's air is often less healthy because the borough's traffic is unremittingly thick and seldom free-flowing, and more people live amid the fumes.) Growth boundaries, such as those circumscribing Portland, Oregon, raise real estate values, so housing inside the boundaries becomes less, not more, "affordable." Even the preservation of farmland, a high priority of managed growth plans, should be placed in proper perspective. The United States is the world's most productive agricultural producer, with ample capacity to spare. Propping up marginal farms in urbanizing areas may not put this acreage to uses most valued by society.

In sum, the diffuse pattern of urban growth in the United States is partly a consequence of particular geographic conditions, cultural characteristics, and raw market forces, but also an accidental outcome of certain government policies. Several of these formative influences differ fundamentally from those that have shaped European cities. Critics of the low-density American cityscape may admire the European model, but they would do well to recognize the full breadth of hard policy choices, and tough tradeoffs, that would have to be made before the constraints on sprawl in this country could even faintly begin to resemble Europe's.

Note

1. Edward I. Koch, "The Mandate Millstone," *The Public Interest*, Number 61, Fall 1980.

Critical Thinking

1. What policies have European countries adopted that have served to limit urban sprawl, preserve farmland, and promote the revitalization of core communities?

2. In contrast, how has the United States promoted automobile usage, the purchase of single-family homes, and urban sprawl?

3. What explains the general unwillingness of Americans to turn to European-style urban policies?

4. What are "unfunded mandates"? Give two or three examples of unfunded mandates and the burdens they impose on cities.

From *The Public Interest*, Fall 1999, pp. 73–84.

Test-Your-Knowledge Form

We encourage you to photocopy and use this page as a tool to assess how the articles in *Annual Editions* expand on the information in your textbook. By reflecting on the articles you will gain enhanced text information. You can also access this useful form on a product's book support website at www.mhhe.com/cls.

NAME:

DATE:

_____

TITLE AND NUMBER OF ARTICLE:

_____

BRIEFLY STATE THE MAIN IDEA OF THIS ARTICLE:

_____

LIST THREE IMPORTANT FACTS THAT THE AUTHOR USES TO SUPPORT THE MAIN IDEA:

_____

WHAT INFORMATION OR IDEAS DISCUSSED IN THIS ARTICLE ARE ALSO DISCUSSED IN YOUR TEXTBOOK OR OTHER READINGS THAT YOU HAVE DONE? LIST THE TEXTBOOK CHAPTERS AND PAGE NUMBERS:

_____

LIST ANY EXAMPLES OF BIAS OR FAULTY REASONING THAT YOU FOUND IN THE ARTICLE:

_____

LIST ANY NEW TERMS/CONCEPTS THAT WERE DISCUSSED IN THE ARTICLE, AND WRITE A SHORT DEFINITION:

We Want Your Advice

ANNUAL EDITIONS revisions depend on two major opinion sources: one is our Advisory Board, listed in the front of this volume, which works with us in scanning the thousands of articles published in the public press each year; the other is you—the person actually using the book. Please help us and the users of the next edition by completing the prepaid article rating form on this page and returning it to us. Thank you for your help!

ANNUAL EDITIONS: Urban Society 15/e

ARTICLE RATING FORM

Here is an opportunity for you to have direct input into the next revision of this volume.
We would like you to rate each of the articles listed below, using the following scale:

1. **Excellent: should definitely be retained**
2. **Above average: should probably be retained**
3. **Below average: should probably be deleted**
4. **Poor: should definitely be deleted**

Your ratings will play a vital part in the next revision.
Please mail this prepaid form to us as soon as possible.
Thanks for your help!

RATING	ARTICLE
	1. Why Cities Matter
	2. Eds, Meds and Urban Revival
	3. Can They Save Youngstown?
	4. Return to Center
	5. Predatory Lending: Redlining in Reverse
	6. Bridge Blockade after Katrina Remains Divisive Issue
	7. Movers and Shakers: How Immigrants Are Reviving Neighborhoods Given up for Dead
	8. Swoons over Miami
	9. Outsourcing: Beyond Bangalore
	10. The Rise of the Creative Class
	11. Too Much Froth
	12. Studies: Gentrification a Boost for Everyone
	13. Throwaway Stadium
	14. Skybox Skeptics
	15. "A Lot of Hooey": Heywood Sanders on Convention Center Economics
	16. Eminent Domain Revisited
	17. Jane Jacobs' Radical Legacy
	18. Neighbor Power: Building Community the Seattle Way
	19. New Life in Newark
	20. The Performance of Charter Schools in Wisconsin
	21. Charter Schools
	22. D.C. School Reform in Question after Mayor Fenty's Loss
	23. With More Choice Has Come Resegregation
	24. Here Comes the Neighborhood
	25. Schools Seek New Diversity Answers after Court Rejects Race as Tiebreaker
	26. The UCLA Civil Rights Project State of Segregation: Fact Sheet, 2007
	27. Joint Statement of Nine University-Based Civil Rights Centers on Today's Supreme Court Rulings on Voluntary School Desegregation: McFarland v. Jefferson County Public Schools & Parents Involved in Community Schools v. Seattle School District No. 1

RATING	ARTICLE
	28. Broken Windows
	29. How an Idea Drew People Back to Urban Life
	30. 200 Cops to be Reassigned from Community Policing
	31. The Six Suburban Eras of the United States
	32. Patio Man and the Sprawl People: America's Newest Suburbs
	33. Affluent, but Needy (First Suburbs)
	34. Principles of New Urbanism
	35. The New Urbanism: A Limited Revolution
	36. HOPE VI and the New Urbanism: Eliminating Low-Income Housing to Make Mixed-Income Communities
	37. Regional Coalition-Building and the Inner Suburbs
	38. Is Regional Government the Answer?
	39. Firebugs: Build It in California's Foothills, and It Will Burn
	40. New German Community Models Car-Free Living
	41. Traffic: Why It's Getting Worse, What Government Can Do
	42. Is Congestion Pricing Ready for Prime Time?
	43. Japan's Cities Amid Globalization
	44. Reinventing Rio: The Dazzling but Tarnished Brazilian City Gets a Makeover As It Prepares for the 2014 World Cup and 2016 Olympic Games
	45. Demolishing Delhi: World Class City in the Making
	46. No Excuses Slum Upgrading
	47. Urban Legends: Why Suburbs, Not Cities, Are the Answer
	48. Femicide in Ciudad Juárez: What Can Planners Do?
	49. Are Europe's Cities Better?

BUSINESS REPLY MAIL
FIRST CLASS MAIL PERMIT NO. 551 DUBUQUE IA

POSTAGE WILL BE PAID BY ADDRESSEE

McGraw-Hill Contemporary Learning Series
501 BELL STREET
DUBUQUE, IA 52001

ABOUT YOU

Name   Date

Are you a teacher? ❑ A student? ❑
Your school's name

Department

Address   City   State   Zip

School telephone #

YOUR COMMENTS ARE IMPORTANT TO US!

Please fill in the following information:
For which course did you use this book?

Did you use a text with this ANNUAL EDITION? ❑ yes ❑ no
What was the title of the text?

What are your general reactions to the Annual Editions concept?

Have you read any pertinent articles recently that you think should be included in the next edition? Explain.

Are there any articles that you feel should be replaced in the next edition? Why?

Are there any World Wide Websites that you feel should be included in the next edition? Please annotate.

May we contact you for editorial input? ❑ yes ❑ no
May we quote your comments? ❑ yes ❑ no